Russian Poetry

RUSSIAN POETRY
Meter,
Rhythm, and
Rhyme

BARRY P. SCHERR

University of California Press

BERKELEY · LOS ANGELES · LONDON

University of California Press
Berkeley and Los Angeles, California

University of California Press, Ltd.
London, England

© 1986 by
The Regents of the University of California

Library of Congress Cataloging in Publication Data

Scherr, Barry P.
  Russian poetry.

  Bibliography: p.
  Includes indexes.
  1. Russian language—Versification. I. Title.
PG2511.S33   1986   891.71′009   84-28045
ISBN 0-520-05299-4

Printed in the United States of America

1 2 3 4 5 6 7 8 9

Portions of this book originally appeared in the articles "Syllabotonic Versification," "Tonic Versification," "Rhyme," "Blank Verse," "Free Verse," and "The Onegin Strophe," in the *Handbook of Russian Literature*, edited by Victor Terras, and are reprinted by permission of Yale University Press.

The publisher gratefully acknowledges the support of the Andrew W. Mellon Foundation in the publication of this book.

For my mother and father

Contents

Tables

Preface

SINCE THE MIDDLE of the eighteenth century most Russian poems have been composed in the so-called syllabo-tonic system. Some people have given it other names (syllabo-accentual, accentual-syllabic), but whatever the terminology, the definition has remained largely the same: verse in which the lines display a regular alternation of "strong" (always or often stressed) and "weak" (usually unstressed) syllables. Such a brief formula, however, tells us relatively little and leaves numerous questions unanswered: What kinds of alternations are found? Why is this system and not some other more suited to the language? What other formal characteristics distinguish Russian verse?

These and many other issues have been the subject of research, discussion, and polemics ever since two eighteenth-century poets, Lomonosov and Trediakovsky (who themselves argued over a number of points), first proposed the new principles that led to the establishment of the syllabo-tonic system in Russia. Today, even though the best essays by poets and scholars from the eighteenth and nineteenth centuries retain a degree of usefulness, they are somewhat dated. The field of Russian verse theory came into its own only during the first quarter of the twentieth century, when, interestingly enough, some of the leading poets of the day were active in the research. Valery Briusov composed a number of experimental poems, wrote essays, and proposed a classification of his own to describe Russian meters and rhythms.[1] Most of his ideas ultimately received little support, but his younger colleague in the symbolist movement, Andrei Bely, mixed equally idiosyncratic theories with an approach to gathering and compiling data that foreshadowed subsequent developments.[2] Working independently, Boris Tomashevsky formulated the methodology that gave rise to the modern study of Russian poetry. His work was soon complemented by the work of fellow scholars, most notably Viktor Zhirmunsky and Roman Jakobson—the latter doing most of his work in the field after having left the Soviet Union.[3]

This triumvirate—along with Kiril Taranovsky, author of a seminal study of eighteenth- and nineteenth-century metrics, *The Russian Binary Meters*—continued to be at the forefront of Russian verse studies for the next several decades. Then during the late 1950s and early 1960s there was a large influx of younger scholars into the field as well. As a result, during the past two decades or so Russian versification has been studied in greater detail than ever before. Several articles of the past few years have examined and classified the complete works of individual poets; others have cast new light on various periods of Russian poetry. The techniques of applying statistical analysis to poetic rhythm—an idea suggested by Bely but developed in a logical manner by Tomashevsky— have been further refined and extended. A number of studies discuss rhyme and stanzaic patterns, two aspects of Russian poetry that earlier received relatively little attention. Also, a great deal of progress has been made toward analyzing and defining the meters that first gained popularity among Russian poets around the beginning of the twentieth century.

Why study versification at all? Admittedly, few people are primarily interested in scansion or in examining rhyme schemes when they read a poem for pleasure. However, a knowledge of verse traditions can provide some worthwhile insights to a specific poem. It becomes possible to tell whether the poem is typical for a particular poet or age, or whether certain features are unusual and worthy of special mention. Also, a careful examination of the poem's formal elements can often point to crucial lines or words that hold the key to the poem's meaning. On a broader scale, studying meters, rhythms, and rhymes is one way of tracing developments in poetry and determining how one period differs from another. In other words, familiarity with versification provides the knowledge for objectively describing verse structure and also enables factually based comments on a poem's relationship to other works and on its meaning.

The aim of this book is to present a general account of Russian versification in light of current research. I assume no previous study of the field and define on first mention all but the most basic terms. I have tried to provide explanations of Russian prosodic features that are not only clear and detailed but also up-to-date.

While the present study is primarily intended for those without any background in Russian versification, I have included some material that should prove interesting to the more advanced student as well. Tomashevsky said that he was drawn to verse study because almost everything in it is open to dispute.[4] Although recent work in this field has perhaps settled a few of the long-standing questions, it has created others. There are still disagreements regarding definitions, methodology, and even about the essential principles that govern Russian poetry. I have not ignored these problems, but have attempted to discuss the issues and indicate which explanations now seem most reasonable. Those interested in pursuing specific topics further will find suggested readings in the annotated bibliography at the end of the book.

The introduction and first chapter are meant to provide a general background and overview for the narrower topics that follow. Since most readers will be somewhat familiar with English prosody, which like Russian employs the syllabo-tonic system, I begin with a brief comparison of the two languages and the two poetic traditions. Chapter 1 contains definitions of many of the terms and concepts that are referred to throughout the study, as well as a brief historical survey of Russian verse up to the reforms of Trediakovsky and Lomonosov in the mid-eighteenth century. The syllabo-tonic meters that have predominated ever since are analyzed in detail in chapter 2. Chapter 3 treats other types of verse forms, most of which have become widely used only during the twentieth century. The fourth chapter examines the related topics of rhyme and stanzaic forms, while chapter 5 lists several of the less salient rhythmic features of Russian verse as well as some of the ways in which a poem's phonological and metrical features may contribute to its meaning. The influence of verse form on meaning is a relatively new area of research and some of the findings in it are still tentative, but they do point the way for much worthwhile, if challenging, work in the future.

Much of the research for this book was carried out at the libraries of Dartmouth College and Harvard University as well as at the Lenin State Library in Moscow; I would like to thank the staffs of those institutions for their help. Warmest appreciation goes to Patricia Carter of Dartmouth's Interlibrary Loan Office, who tracked down innumerable items for me. I am much indebted to Nellie Plummer, who deciphered my handwriting in order to type the manuscript. Many people have offered advice and information. I am particularly grateful to James Bailey and G. S. Smith, both of whom read an earlier version of this study and provided me with abundant suggestions for improvements and corrections. Ian Lilly, who somewhat inadvertently introduced me to Russian verse theory, has been a valuable colleague over the years. And I especially treasure the support of Sylvia and Sonia and David, who have given the most.

Editorial Note

FOR THE SAKE OF READABILITY, the transliteration system used for proper names in the text differs slightly from that in the footnotes and in the bibliography. The notes employ the Library of Congress system without diacritics. Within the text, proper names that would normally end in *-ii* or *-yi* become simply *-y* (Tomashevskii becomes Tomashevsky), and soft signs are omitted entirely. While quotations from poems are given in Cyrillic, titles and individual words are transliterated, except in the sections dealing with rhyme (chapter 4), where the many references to rhyme words and endings are in Cyrillic.

One area of dispute that deserves special mention is terminology. Researchers have argued about the meaning of certain terms and have occasionally used different words to describe the same phenomenon. At times people have simply invented their own terms to replace those in general use. Since much of the current terminology *is* objectionable for one reason or another (even the hallowed iamb and trochee are not above reproach), one solution might be to propose another set of terms. But the situation is complicated enough without adding to the muddle. Therefore I generally use only those terms that have found broad acceptance among scholars of Russian verse, and where controversy exists I indicate which term or definition seems preferable. I introduce English terms of my own only in those two or three cases where none of the usual translations from Russian seem satisfactory.

As with terminology, I have used a standard system of signs for presenting various metrical and rhythmic forms.

(1) A metrical scheme (in this case, that of the iambic tetrameter) is designated as follows: ∪–∪–∪–∪–́(∪). The breve [∪] indicates a normally unstressed ("weak") syllable; the macron [–] stands for an ictus ("strong" syllable); [–́] represents an obligatory stress; and the breve in parentheses signifies optional syllables (zero, one, or more).

Ictuses are the syllables that can bear the metrical stresses. In Russian poetry the final ictus of a line carries an obligatory stress, while stress may be omitted on one or more of the other ictuses.

(2) The representation of an actual line of poetry, then, might have this appearance; ⌣́⌣́⌣‿⌣́⌣. The acute accent [´] indicates the stresses; the other syllables are unstressed. In this line there is hyper-metrical stressing—a stress not predicted by the meter—on the first syllable, the third ictus is unstressed, and there is one syllable after the final ictus, features that are all common in Russian poetry.

(3) To represent the stress of a given word outside the context of a poem, just the acute accent and the breve are used; thus ⌣⌣´⌣ represents a four-syllable word with stress on the third syllable.

(4) When it is necessary to indicate caesuras or word boundaries, I use a double vertical line to stand for the caesura and a single vertical line to represent word boundaries. An iambic pentameter line with a caesura after the fourth syllable would appear as follows: ⌣́⌣́ ‖ ⌣́⌣́⌣́. A trochaic tetrameter line with words of three, two, and two syllables would be represented as follows to show the word breaks: ‿⌣́ | ⌣́ | ⌣́.

The quotations from poems in the text purposefully represent a wide range of poets and works. I have tried to strike a balance among the various chronological periods while not slighting the work of contemporary poets. Except for selections from Old Russian literature or folk poetry, all quotations are dated. Brackets are used to indicate an approximate date; the sign < means no later than. Thus [<1961] indicates the poem was written in 1961 or earlier.

Introduction

VERSE AND LANGUAGE

Two opposing tendencies operate in the creation of poetry. On the one hand poetry, to paraphrase Roman Jakobson, is a form of violence done to language. (Вне насилия нет поэзии. Without violence there is no poetry.) Words are not allowed to flow unregulated but are forced into lines of a particular length, are made to correspond to the requirements of a meter, are placed so as to form rhyme. One factor distinguishing prose and poetry is the poet's greater care in the use of words. A good prose writer will certainly pay close attention to the choice of words and to their combination; better writers often develop an individual manner that sensitive readers can recognize at once. Still, the poet is trying to do more things in less space. A lyric poem often consists of just a few lines within which the poet establishes a rhythm while simultaneously developing the message imparted to the reader. Sound and meaning complement each other; for the poem to achieve its fullest potential, each word, each phoneme within the word, must play a role. There is no room for anything extraneous to the overall scheme. Thus the selection of words and their placement within the line and the poem as a whole require extreme care and yet boldness. The craft of poetry is not for the impatient or the timid.

On the other hand, language and the literary tradition it articulates impose certain restraints on the poet. *Poetic license* is the term generally used to imply the poet's right to bend certain rules or to employ words or forms of words that are not part of everyday speech. But if a poet were to abuse that license by using too many obscure words or taking too many liberties with syntax, readers could well be faced with unnecessary or unintended difficulties. Similarly, the history of Russian, and for that matter of English prosody, reveals a growing tendency for poets to select rhythms that do not depart too greatly from the natural

I

rhythm of the language. Strict metrical rules that would impose an ar-
tificial regularity are eventually modified or even abandoned. Tradition
has proved to be less of a constraint than language, but even today, in an
age when there are seemingly no rules that cannot be broken, the poet
must be aware of the risks being taken. Free verse is still quite rare in
Russian, and the poet who would use it must carefully weigh its effect
on the reader. English rhyme is to a great degree monosyllabic, or mas-
culine. Thus if a poet attempts to employ a series of feminine rhymes,
the result will often appear strained or comic. Tradition may also im-
pose more subtle restraints. English, with shorter words than Russian,
nevertheless came to prefer a longer line: the iambic pentameter, instead
of the iambic tetrameter, which was favored by Russian throughout the
nineteenth century. In English the longer lines became established owing
to the influence of Italian and French models dating back to the thirteenth
century. In early Russian syllabo-tonic poetry, that of the eighteenth
century, the long iambic hexameter appeared most frequently. However,
possibly because of a reaction against previous norms, shorter lines
quickly became predominant and Russian poetry has continued to use
the tetrameter ever since.

The critical factor is language, for language is the very material out
of which a poem is made. Consequently, the rhythm and sound of po-
etry written in one language are necessarily different from those written
in any other, though the degree of difference varies. If two languages
share certain prosodic features, then their verse systems will likely be
similar. For instance, word stress plays an important role in English,
German, and Russian; and poets in all three languages have employed
the syllabo-tonic system. Thus it is easier for a native speaker of one of
these languages to appreciate the sound of poetry in the other two than
in a language such as French, in which word stress does not play a sig-
nificant role.

ENGLISH AND RUSSIAN

A comparison between two of these similar languages, English and
Russian, not only illustrates why the two poetic systems developed as
they did but also introduces some of the prosodic features to be dis-
cussed in detail later on. Both Russian and English have a long history
of syllabo-tonic poetry; it has dominated Russian poetry for more than
two hundred years and has existed in English ever since the time of
Chaucer. In both languages, unlike French, for example, word stress is

not confined to a specific position within words; also both make rela-
tively clear distinctions between stressed and unstressed syllables—
though Russian has far fewer ambiguous cases in this regard than does
English. The importance of stress in both languages made them recep-
tive to the syllabo-tonic system, and since adopting it they have favored
iambic meters over all others. Yet even a cursory juxtaposition of an En-
glish and a Russian poem written in the same meter is likely to reveal
noticeably different rhythms. Other contrasts between Russian and En-
glish poetry—in the types of meters used over the years, in the nature of
rhyme—are also evident to those who pursue the comparison.[1]

Given the apparent similarities between Russian and English, why
does their poetry differ so sharply? Since stress is the most important
prosodic feature in both, an obvious way to begin answering this ques-
tion is to examine the words and types of stress that are found in English
and in Russian. A mere survey of words in the dictionary is not ade-
quate; it is necessary to look at the literary lexicon that poets draw
upon. Boris Tomashevsky has pointed out that a writer will use some-
what different words in poetry than in prose works owing to the exigen-
cies of meter.[2] Therefore surveys of prose provide a more general in-
dication of the vocabulary that makes up the literary language.

Table 1 is based on two-thousand-word excerpts taken from represen-
tative works by four American authors. The roman numerals indicate
the number of syllables in each word. Within the monosyllabic category
(I), strongly stressed words—including nouns, verbs, adjectives, and
some pronouns—are indicated by the letter a. Less strongly stressed
monosyllables—most possessive pronouns, prepositions, articles, and
conjunctions—are indicated by the letter b. Arabic numbers show
which syllable within the word is stressed; the plus sign ($+$) indicates
the presence of secondary stress.

Table 2 is based on calculations done by Georgy Shengeli, who ex-
amined five thousand word-units (that is, counting enclitics and pro-
clitics as part of the main word) by each of ten Russian authors active
during the nineteenth or beginning of the twentieth century. Roman and
arabic numbers are used as in table 1. Because Shengeli does not con-
sider enclitics and proclitics separately, his figures are not reliable in-
dicators of word length in Russian. Gustav Herdan, however, has pub-
lished data that indicate that 33 percent* of the words used in Russian

---

*Here and elsewhere in the text, as opposed to the tables, percentages are approximate,
unless a decimal point is supplied. Thus 80 percent means about 80 percent; 80.0 percent
means exactly 80 percent.

TABLE I
Syllable and Stress Patterns in English Words (N = 8,000)

Word Type	Author/Work				Total	Percentage
	Melville, *Moby Dick*	Twain, *Huckle- berry Finn*	Faulkner, *The Sound and the Fury*	Hemingway, *A Farewell to Arms*		
I a	942	972	909	1,025	3,848	48.1
b	618	647	600	543	2,408	30.1
	1,560	1,619	1,509	1,568	6,256	78.2
II 1	277	243	342	255	1,117	13.96
2	57	56	71	66	250	3.13
1+2	0	1	1	3	5	0.06
	334	300	414	324	1,372	17.15
III 1	42	38	24	43	147	1.84
1+	11	11	15	1	38	0.47
2	22	13	17	27	79	0.99
2+	0	1	2	0	3	0.04
3	0	0	0	0	0	—
3+	2	0	0	5	7	0.09
	77	63	58	76	274	3.43
IV 1	5	2	0	6	13	0.16
1+	6	12	5	0	23	0.29
2	8	1	8	5	22	0.28
2+	0	0	0	0	0	—
3	0	0	0	9	9	0.11
3+	3	0	3	7	13	0.16
4	0	0	0	0	0	—
4+	0	0	0	0	0	—
	22	15	16	27	80	1.00
V	6	2	2	4	14	0.17
VI	1	0	1	1	3	0.04
VII	0	1	0	0	1	0.01
Total	2,000	2,000	2,000	2,000	8,000	100.00

prose have one syllable, 33 percent have two syllables, 22 percent have three, 10 percent have four, and 3 percent have more than four syllables.[3] While neither table employs samples large or broad enough to be authoritative, the contrasts between Russian and English are sufficiently clear so that possible errors of a percentage point or two are not significant for our purposes.

Taken by itself, table 1 contains some surprises. Few people would guess that 75 to 80 percent of all words in an English literary text are likely to contain just one syllable. Because each of the passages sampled included at least some dialogue, which tends to contain shorter words than the written language, the figures for monosyllabic words are probably a bit higher than they would be for samplings that contained only descriptive prose. Still, words of one syllable clearly dominate in English. Words with just three syllables are quite scarce; in none of the four samples did they quite reach 4 percent. Words of five or more syllables appear very infrequently and hardly cause a ripple in the statistics. The only seven-syllable word, in fact, is not a word at all, but a neologism, *preforeordestination*, used by one of Mark Twain's characters. Differences between writers are less than might be supposed. Hemingway uses more short words than Faulkner, as a casual reader of the two authors' works might suspect, but, in this sample at least, Hemingway also employs more words of three or more syllables. On the

TABLE 2
Syllable and Stress Patterns in Russian Word-Units

Word Types	Subtotal	Total	Percentage
I	7,747	7,747	15.49
II 1	7,953	16,137	32.28
2	8,184		
III 1	3,386	14,222	28.44
2	6,767		
3	4,069		
IV 1	474	7,980	15.96
2	3,081		
3	3,860		
3	565		
V 1	36	2,968	5.94
2	527		
3	1,625		
4	737		
5	43		
VI		796	1.59
VII		150	0.30
Total		50,000	100.00

Source: Georgii Shengeli, *Traktat o russkom stikhe*, pp. 20–21.

average, Melville's words are a little longer than Mark Twain's, but here the contrast is less than might be predicted. The similarity among all the authors is partly accounted for by the large number of prepositions and articles found in all English writing. (Russian, in contrast, lacks articles.) The effect is to increase the number of monosyllables in each sample and to leave relatively little room for variations in the use of longer words. Still, nearly half the words used by every author (48 percent of the entire eight-thousand-word survey) are monosyllables that bear a fairly strong stress. In other words, many nouns, verbs, and adjectives in English contain only one syllable, and writers necessarily must use such words quite often.

Table 1 shows that stress occurs quite frequently in English, with approximately 5,700 stressed syllables among the more than 10,000 syllables in the total sample. Although the question of precisely which monosyllabic words have a stronger and which a weaker stress has been controversial, and there is potential disagreement about categorization of these words, the questionable cases would not alter the results significantly. English stresses about one syllable out of every 1.8, or a little more than half.

Although table 2 does not reproduce Shengeli's breakdown of his figures by author, individual samples fluctuate within a relatively narrow range. For example, eight of the ten authors use between 14 and 17 percent one-syllable word-units; all ten fall between 26 and 31 percent for word-units of three syllables. That is, like their American counterparts, Russian authors of even widely divergent styles use words of similar length and position of stress. Again, the language itself inhibits their choices. And Russian words are clearly longer. Whereas in English only about 5 percent of the words contain three or more syllables, according to Herdan more than 33 percent of the words used in Russian attain that length. Since Russian words do not, as a rule, have more than one stress apiece, the frequency of stress is quite a bit less than in English. There is some disagreement as to whether certain Russian monosyllabic words (primarily pronouns) should be considered stressed or unstressed, but the problems are less severe than in English. For the most part, Russian maintains a clear distinction between full stressed vowels and "reduced" unstressed vowels. Thus Russian stresses one out of every 2.7 or 2.8 syllables—a little more than one in three.

The location of stress within words differs for Russian and English. Russian words favor stress in the middle of the word and perhaps slightly toward the end as well. Thus, as table 2 shows, in three-syllable words the middle syllable is stressed far more often than either of the extremes, while the last syllable is stressed slightly more often than the first. In four-syllable words the middle two syllables are stressed more frequently than the extremes.[4] English words overwhelmingly prefer stress at the beginning. More than 80 percent of the words with two syllables and more than 66 percent of those with three syllables have initial stress. None of the four-syllable words and very few of those with three syllables have a stressed final syllable.

Poets must, of course, select words that will fit the given meter. Interestingly, figures produced by both Tomashevsky and Shengeli indicate that the iambic tetrameter, the most popular lyric meter in Russian, causes poets to accentuate the tendencies already inherent in the language. The two researchers have shown that Pushkin's *Eugene Onegin*, written in iambic tetrameter, contains even more words of two and three syllables than do samples of his prose. Moreover, these two- and three-syllable words favor end and middle stress, respectively, to a greater extent than do words of these lengths in Pushkin's prose writings.[5] The iambic tetrameter causes the poet to select more words of certain types than he would if he were writing prose, but at the same time the kinds of words he favors reflect the inherent features of the language. In other words, both the tendencies in the creation of poetry are at work here.

The lengths of Russian words put still another restraint on the poet. A line of iambic tetrameter will usually be eight or nine syllables long, depending on whether the rhyme is masculine or feminine (although longer rhymes and hence longer lines are possible). In any case, the meter calls for up to four metrical stresses in the eight or nine syllables, but the frequency of stress in the language predicts that on the average only about three stresses would be found in lines of this length. And indeed, rather than try to stress every ictus, poets often leave one, or possibly even two, unstressed within a given iambic tetrameter line. Most often, it is the third ictus that lacks stress. In his autobiography, *Speak, Memory*, Vladimir Nabokov has remarked upon the prevalence of such lines in Russian poetry and how easily a beginning poet could use a long adjective in the middle of the line to form correct, if not necessarily inspired, verse.[6]

The situation in English is quite different. Whereas in Russian fully stressed lines are less common than those that omit at least one stress, in English the opposite is true.[7] Since words are short and stress frequent, English has no difficulty in providing enough stresses to fill iambic and trochaic meters. If anything, there tend to be too many potential stresses

in an English line, and one of the vexing problems for English met-
rists has long been that of deciding which syllables are more strongly
stressed than others.[8]

Tables 1 and 2 also help explain some other features of English verse.
Ternary meters, in which every third syllable is an ictus, occur more
frequently in Russian than English, where the presence of a stress on
more than half the syllables makes it difficult to maintain a ternary
scheme. Similarly, rhymes of more than one syllable are much more
common in Russian, which not only has longer words than English but
which also is an inflected language.[9] As a result, Russian contains many
endings with two or more syllables that make it easy for poets to find
polysyllabic rhymes. In English rhymes of more than one syllable are
rare and often connote satirical or light poetry. Today such rhymes are
likely to recall Ogden Nash or the lyrics of a musical comedy. In Rus-
sian, on the other hand, bisyllabic or feminine rhymes are just as com-
mon as masculine rhymes.

A look at a poem in each language will help illustrate the differences
between English and Russian meters. The following sonnet by Shake-
speare was composed in iambic pentameter, the most common meter in
English poetry. Below it is the opening stanza of a poem written by
Pushkin in the same meter.

That tíme of yéar thou máyst in mé behóld	∪´∪´∪´∪´∪´
When yéllow léaves, or nóne, or féw, do háng	∪´∪´∪´∪´∪´
Upón those bóughs which sháke agáinst the cóld,	∪´∪´∪´∪´∪´
Báre rúined chóirs, where láte the swéet bírds sáng.	´∪´∪´∪´∪´∪´
In mé thou sée'st the twílight of such dáy	∪´∪´∪´∪—∪´
As áfter súnset fádeth in the wést,	∪´∪´∪´∪—∪´
Which bý and bý bláck níght doth táke awáy,	∪´∪´∪´∪´∪´
Déath's sécond sélf, that stéals up áll in rést.	´∪´∪´∪´∪´
In mé thou sée'st the glówing of such fíre	∪´∪´∪´∪—∪´
That on the áshes of his yóuth doth líe,	∪—∪´∪´∪´∪´
As the death-béd whereón it múst expíre,	∪—∪´∪´∪´∪´
Consúmed with thát which ít was nóurished bý.	∪´∪´∪´∪´∪´
This thóu percéiv'st, which mákes thy lóve more stróng,	´∪´∪´∪´∪´
To lóve that wéll which thóu must léave ere lóng.	∪´∪´∪´∪´∪´
Была́ пора́: наш пра́здник молодо́й	∪´∪´∪´∪—∪´
Сия́л, шуме́л и ро́зами венча́лся,	∪´∪´∪´∪—∪´∪
И с пе́снями бока́лов зво́н меша́лся,	∪´∪—∪´∪´∪´∪
И те́сною сиде́ли мы́ толпо́й.	∪´∪—∪´∪´∪´
Тогда́, душо́й беспе́чные неве́жды,	∪´∪´∪´∪—∪´∪
Мы жи́ли все́ и ле́гче и смеле́й,	∪´∪´∪´∪—∪´
Мы пи́ли все́ за здра́вие наде́жды	∪´∪´∪´∪—∪´∪
И ю́ности и все́х её зате́й.	∪´∪—∪´∪´∪´

1836

The poems support several of the points made above:

(1) English is more difficult to scan than Russian. Is it death-béd that best fits the meter, or deáth-bed, or perhaps deáth-béd? Should *thou* in lines 1 and 5 be stressed? Most readers would probably stress either *that* or *on* at the beginning of line 10, though here I have left both unstressed. The Russian excerpt presents few such difficulties. The only ambiguous cases are the monosyllabic pronouns, which I mark as stressed only when they correspond with an ictus or seem to receive an especially strong phrase stress.

(2) Since stress occurs more frequently in English, lines of English poetry contain more stresses than Russian lines of the same length. Shakespeare does omit stress on a few ictuses in this sonnet, but he employs enough hypermetrical stressing so that the average is close to five stresses per line. The Russian passage happens to omit precisely one stress in each line (a larger excerpt would reveal lines with three or five stresses as well) and thus averages four stresses.

(3) English words are shorter than Russian. The English lines contain from seven up to the maximum of ten words, and no single word is longer than two syllables. The Russian lines have only four to seven words, and there are many words of three or more syllables. The frequency of monosyllabic words in English is, of course, responsible for much of the difficulty in scanning English poetry.

(4) English poetry prefers masculine rhyme. In Shakespeare's sonnet there are no feminine rhymes, while Pushkin's stanza is equally divided between feminine and masculine rhymes.

Of all the differences, the most important is the generally clear-cut distinction between stressed and unstressed syllables in Russian as opposed to the confusion that frequently arises in English. Scansion in English can depend on the syntactic use of a word, its position within the line, and the degree to which surrounding words are stressed. In fact, many English poems exhibit far more irregular stressing patterns than does this sonnet, and the very problem of defining the distinguishing characteristics of English meters is still the subject of much inquiry.[10] Conversely, the ease of determining Russian stress has made it easier for researchers to compile much statistical data regarding the distribution of stress in Russian poetry. Since stress is the chief determinant of rhythm, the data can be utilized to determine the rhythmic patterns preferred by individual poets, to find the most common rhythmic forms of various meters, and to trace the manner in which given meters have been used throughout the history of Russian poetry. With the exception

of some individuals familiar with the "Russian approach" to verse, few
scholars have attempted to use concrete statistical data for the study of
English poetry.[11]

The relative ease of determining which syllables are stressed in Rus-
sian as well as the ability to find rhyme more readily is at least partly
responsible for the resistance that Russian has shown both to free and
blank verse. Free verse has become prominent in English, and un-
rhymed poetry has always been fairly common; even in so-called
rhymed verse, a very common quatrain has rhyme only in the even
lines, while the odd are unrhymed. Although free verse has gained a
foothold in the Russian tradition, it still accounts for only a handful of
poems, perhaps 1 or 2 percent of all verse. Blank verse has existed in
Russian for a long time—particularly in the nineteenth-century iambic
pentameter line used in drama, largely owing to the influence of Shake-
speare and other foreign authors. Still, blank verse too has remained
less significant, and the main question for modern Russian poets is not
so much whether a poem should have rhyme than what types (exact
rhymes, various kinds of approximate rhymes) to employ. In other
words, Russian poetry today shows much greater structural regularity
than English, and therefore a knowledge of the forms used by Russian
poets is a prerequisite for the study of the verse.

1

Definitions and Background

SOME BASIC TERMS

TYPES OF METERS

There are two groups of so-called classical meters in Russian. One group consists of the binary meters, in which, according to the metrical scheme, stressed and unstressed syllables alternate. Binaries may be either iambic, in which the odd syllables are weak and the ictuses fall on the even syllables (∪−∪−∪−), or trochaic, in which the even syllables are weak and the ictuses fall on the odd-numbered syllables (−∪−∪−∪). The other group consists of the ternary meters, which contain two weak syllables alternating with an ictus. The three kinds of ternary meters are dactyls (−∪∪−∪∪), amphibrachs (∪−∪∪−∪), and anapests (∪∪−∪∪−). All other Russian verse forms (the various types of accentual meters, free verse) are called nonclassical; each of these forms will be discussed and analyzed in chapter 3.

The terms *iamb*, *anapest*, and so forth were originally used to describe Greek and Latin meters; the meters they refer to in Russian poetry are not precisely the same as their ancient counterparts. For instance, the macrons and breves used to represent ictuses and unstressed syllables in Russian verse do not imply anything about length. Classical Greek and Latin based their lines on alternations of long and short syllables; in modern Russian (and for that matter in English and German as well) stress is the basic prosodic feature in the verse system, while length plays no significant role. In other words, even though the Greek and Latin systems provide the terminology for modern syllabo-tonic poetry, the linguistic differences between these ancient and modern languages mean that their prosodic systems do not share the same features. Adopting a complete new set of terms to describe modern syllabo-tonic systems would save a lot of confusion, but by now words like *dactyl* and *trochee* are too well established to be easily replaced. The best solution seems to be to continue using the classical terms, but to remember precisely what they mean when applied to a language like Russian and to avoid searching for ancient metrical units, such as antispast and bacchius, which do not have analogues in modern stressed languages.

FEET

The very term *foot* has been the source of much confusion, again largely through the failure to distinguish between Russian and classical meters. In Greek and Latin poetry it was often possible to "substitute" one kind of foot for another, usually in accord with fairly strict and well-defined rules. Since the basic unit was length and two short syllables were considered equal to one long, a spondee (two long syllables) could replace a dactyl (one long and two short). Also, some line types mixed different feet: thus the elegiambus was a line with a dactylic colon (i.e., line segment) followed by a colon in iambs; the reverse combination, when the iambic colon came first, was called an iambelegus. Again, the combinations of different kinds of feet followed certain traditional patterns.

However, except for one or two types of line that were specific imitations of classical meters, Russian poetry during the second half of the eighteenth and all of the nineteenth century normally maintained the same alternation of ictuses and weak syllables throughout the line. Thus an iambic poem contains ictuses on all the even syllables; a dactylic poem has ictuses on every third syllable in the line, beginning with the first. More irregular schemes are common in twentieth-century poetry, but these belong to quite different meters (the *dol'nik* and accentual verse). A line that presents a pattern of stressing such as ∪ ´ ∪ ´ ∪ ∪ ´ ∪ ∪ ´ is probably written in some kind of accentual meter; in any case, it should not be considered to consist of two iambs followed by two anapests.

Thus to speak of mixing different kinds of feet on the same line when discussing Russian poetry is misleading. For in Russian prosody, feet are not independent units that can be mixed on the line at will; instead, saying that a poem is written using a particular foot describes the placement of ictuses on the line—for instance, a trochaic poem has ictuses on the odd syllables. The number of feet is equal to the number of ictuses. The "third foot" of a line in trochees, for example, refers to the third occurrence of the combination $-\cup$, where the macron signifies an ictus, which may or may not be stressed, and the breve a syllable that will normally be unstressed.

In many textbooks it is customary to refer to unfulfilled ictuses as pyrrhic feet (after the pyrrhic foot of Latin and Greek poetry, $\cup\cup$). A line in trochaic pentameter such as И звезда́ с звездо́ю говори́т ($-\cup\acute{\cup}-\cup\acute{\cup}-\cup-\cup\acute{\cup}$) would be said to have pyrrhics in the first and fourth feet. My own preference is to talk of unstressed ictuses rather than pyrrhics and thereby avoid at least one unneeded term.[1]

LINES

Simply put, the basic unit of meter in Russian poetry is the line, not the foot. A given meter is described by the *type* of alternation it contains (iambic, anapestic, etc.) and by the *number* of ictuses in each line (trimeter, tetrameter, etc.). Thus the trochaic pentameter is a line written in trochees with a total of five ictuses; an abstract representation of the meter would be as follows: $-\cup-\cup-\cup-\cup\acute{-}(\cup)$. The final ictus in Russian contains the rhyme (if any) and must be stressed.[2] Each of the other ictuses may or may not be fulfilled; in practice, a trochaic or iambic line with five ictuses is likely to have anywhere from three to five stresses (and occasionally as few as two). Some scholars prefer to divide the line into three parts: the *anacrusis*, which contains the syllables preceding the first ictus; the *stem*, which consists of the syllables from the first through last ictus; and the *clausula*, or the syllables that follow the final ictus. Thus the trochaic pentameter has a zero anacrusis, a stem of nine syllables, and a clausula that may normally range from zero to two syllables, depending on whether the rhyme is masculine, feminine, or dactylic. The anapest trimeter, $\cup\cup\acute{-}\cup\cup\acute{-}\cup\cup\acute{-}(\cup)$, has a two-syllable anacrusis, a stem of seven syllables, and a clausula that usually has from zero to two syllables. Note that the clausula tends to vary within a poem and that the length of the clausula has little effect on the rhythm. The anacrusis varies only rarely in the classical meters, primarily in the ternaries, though it frequently varies in the accentual meters. Differences in the anacrusis often have a noticeable effect on the rhythm.

To establish the meter of a poem, it may be necessary to analyze more than a single line. For example, a poem written in one of the accentual meters may include two or three lines that seem to be perfect iambs. At times poems written in ternaries will alternate meters between lines. The shifting may involve a fairly simple pattern, as in the opening stanza of this poem by Konstantin Sluchevsky,

И они́ в зву́ках пе́сни, как ры́бы в воде́,　　　∪∪́∪́∪∪́∪∪́∪∪́
　　Пла́вали, пла́вали!　　　　　　　　　　　　́∪∪́∪∪
И трево́жили но́чь, благово́нную но́чь,　　　∪∪́∪∪́∪∪́∪∪́
　　Зву́ками, зву́ками!　　　　　　　　　　　　́∪∪́∪∪

[< 1883]

where anapest tetrameters in the odd lines alternate with dactylic dimeters in the even lines. Somewhat more interesting is the following example, in which Lermontov's first stanza has amphibrach tetrameters in odd lines and anapest trimeters in the even, and the second stanza inverts the pattern—anapest tetrameter in odd lines and amphibrach trimeter in even:

Как зе́млю нам бо́льше небе́с не люби́ть?　　∪́∪∪́∪∪́∪∪́∪∪́
　　Нам небе́сное сча́стье темно́;　　　　　　∪∪́∪∪́∪∪́∪∪́
Хоть сча́стье земно́е и ме́ньше в сто́ ра́з,　∪́∪∪́∪∪́∪∪́∪∪́
　　Но мы зна́ем, како́е оно́.　　　　　　　　∪∪́∪∪́∪∪́∪∪́

О наде́ждах и му́ках былы́х вспомина́ть　　∪∪́∪∪́∪∪́∪∪∪́
　　В нас та́йная скло́нность кипи́т;　　　　　∪́∪∪́∪∪́∪∪́
Нас трево́жит неве́рность наде́жды земно́й,　∪∪́∪∪́∪∪́∪∪́∪∪́
　　А кра́ткость печа́ли смеши́т.　　　　　　∪́∪∪́∪∪́∪∪́

1830–31

Finally, the pattern may be complex, as in the next poem by Aleksandr Blok, where the odd lines are anapests, the even amphibrachs, and the number of ictuses varies from one to three.

Во́т он – ве́тер,　　　　　　　　　　　∪́∪∪́∪
Звеня́щий тоско́ю остро́жной,　　　　　∪∪́∪∪́∪∪́∪
Над бескра́йною то́пью　　　　　　　　∪∪́∪∪́∪
Ого́нь невозмо́жный,　　　　　　　　　∪∪́∪∪́∪
Распростёршийся при́зрак　　　　　　　∪∪́∪∪́∪
Ветлы́ придоро́жной...　　　　　　　　　∪∪́∪∪́∪

Во́т – что ты́ мне сули́ла:　　　　　　∪́∪∪́∪∪́∪
Моги́ла.　　　　　　　　　　　　　　　∪∪́∪

1908

Such poems are written in *mixed ternary meters*, which may still be thought of as a variant of the classical meters. Other circumstances, far more complicated, occasionally arise within a given poem. Thus P. A. Rudnev has used the term *polymetrical composition* to describe the mixture of meters in certain works by Blok and other poets.[3] In short, it is always advisable to look at the whole poem, or at least a substantial portion of it, before deciding what meter it is written in.

METER AND RHYTHM

The terms *meter* and *rhythm* will be used often in the text. What is the precise difference between them? Meter is an abstract pattern, such as that given above for the trochaic pentameter. The pattern in turn represents a set of norms, established by the practice of poets writing within the tradition, that will be followed by lines written in a given meter. Remember that norms are not necessarily absolutes; for the most part metrists speak of dominants and tendencies.[4] For example, the trochaic pentameter schema implies only two constants—the obligatory stress on the final ictus and the existence of nine syllables in the stem. It further indicates that the even-numbered syllables are normally not stressed (these are metrical dominants), and that the first through fourth ictuses may carry stress (these are metrical tendencies). Rhythm, on the other hand, is the actual pattern of stressing that occurs within the poem.[5] Rhythm is not "opposed" to meter; the norms for a meter allow for the variations that make up the rhythmic forms of that meter.[6] Rather, rhythm and meter interact; after just a couple of lines, for instance, a poem written in the trochaic pentameter creates the expectation of stress on the odd syllables; when stress is omitted at an ictus (or, less commonly, when hypermetrical stressing occurs on one of the even syllables) the expectation is frustrated. If stresses were to appear on every ictus in a trochaic or iambic poem, the rhythm would be monotonous.

THE CAESURA

Lines of Russian poetry having five or more ictuses are frequently divided by a *caesura*. The meaning of this term, as is the case with many of the other words that describe verse structure, has frequently varied. In Greek and Latin metrics, for instance, the caesura referred to a word that ended within a foot; in English verse it is often defined as a pause within the line, which may shift its position more or less freely from one line to the next.[7] The caesura in Russian poetry is a word break that occurs at the same position in the line throughout an entire poem.[8] For example, in iambic hexameter poems a constant word boun-

dary almost always occurs immediately after the third foot. The regu-
larity of this feature may cause the poet to create syntactic breaks at that
spot as well. Examples of the caesura in various meters will be given
later; for now it is sufficient to keep three points in mind. First, the cae-
sura is normally employed only in fairly long lines. Binary meters with
six or more ictuses only rarely fail to exhibit a caesura, and the caesura
is also frequent in ternary meters with four or more ictuses. It is unusual
in binary meters with four ictuses and almost nonexistent in still shorter
lines. The iambic pentameter is a transitional case; it is found both with
a caesura after the fourth syllable (primarily in works through the first
third of the nineteenth century) and without a caesura.[9] Second, since
the line is broken into two hemistichs, the end of the first hemistich can
behave somewhat like the end of the line. That is, the ends of the first
hemistichs may rhyme, and they may be truncated or add a syllable
(though none of these features occurs very frequently). Third, the pres-
ence of a caesura noticeably affects the rhythm. Compare the following
two excerpts from poems written by Pushkin; the first contains a caesura
and the second does not.

Кто́ ви́дел кра́й, где ро́скошью приро́ды	◡◡◡ ‖ ◡◡◡◡
Оживлены́ дубра́вы и луга́,	◡◡◡ ‖ ◡◡◡◡
Где ве́село шумя́т и бле́щут во́ды	◡◡ ‖ ◡◡◡◡◡
И ми́рные ласка́ют берега́,	◡◡ ‖ ◡◡◡◡
Где на холмы́, под ла́вровые сво́ды,	◡◡ ‖ ◡◡◡◡◡
Не сме́ют ле́чь угрю́мые снега́?	◡◡◡ ‖ ◡◡◡◡
Скажи́те мне́: кто́ ви́дел кра́й преле́стный,	◡◡◡ ‖ ◡◡◡◡◡
Где я́ люби́л, изгна́нник неизве́стный?	◡◡◡ ‖ ◡◡◡◡◡

1821

Немно́го отдохнём на э́той то́чке.	◡◡◡◡◡◡◡◡
Что́? переста́ть или *пусти́ть на пе́?*	◡◡◡◡◡◡◡
Призна́ться ва́м, я́ в пятисто́пной стро́чке	◡◡◡◡◡◡◡◡
Люблю́ цезу́ру на второ́й стопе́.	◡◡◡◡◡◡◡
Ина́че, сти́х то́ в я́ме, то́ на ко́чке,	◡◡◡◡◡◡◡◡
И хоть лежу́ тепе́рь на канапе́,	◡◡◡◡◡◡◡
Всё ка́жется мне, бу́дто в тря́ском бе́ге	◡◡◡◡◡◡◡◡
По ме́рзлой па́шне мчу́сь я на теле́ге.	◡◡◡◡◡◡◡◡

1830

In the first example the caesura causes the lines to split into two hemi-
stichs. More often than not a slight syntactic break occurs after the
fourth syllable, and this pause becomes a part of the rhythmic inertia for
the lines written with a caesura. The second example lacks both the cae-
sura and any regular syntactic break within the lines. The patterns of

stressing underscore the difference. In the first example the third ictus (that is, the first ictus after the caesura) is stressed in every line. Since the final ictus in Russian poetry carries an obligatory stress and since there are on the average only about two stresses for every six syllables in Russian, it is no surprise to see that the fourth ictus in these lines carries a stress only two out of eight times. In the second example the absence of a caesura means that it is unnecessary to reestablish the rhythm consistently by stressing the third ictus in the line. Hence, stress on that ictus is less frequent than in the first example, and the fourth ictus receives stress correspondingly more often.[10] Thus the presence or absence of a caesura has a significant effect on the rhythm of a poem.

GENERAL FEATURES OF RUSSIAN VERSE

Some basic principles of Russian verse are now evident:

(1) The main prosodic element in Russian poetry is the distinction between stressed and unstressed syllables; all other considerations are of secondary importance.

(2) The one virtually absolute requirement that applies to Russian poetry is the presence of a constant stress on the final ictus; exceptions to this rule are extraordinarily rare.

(3) While the precise way in which strong (potentially stressed) and weak (normally unstressed) syllables occur on the line is important, and noticeable rhythmic differences occur between, for instance, iambic and trochaic lines, feet as such exist within the context of the line; therefore it is not correct to speak of mixing various feet on the same line.

(4) Since the meters in modern Russian are based on stress, the dominant feature for each meter can be expressed in terms of stressed or unstressed syllables.[11]

> (i) In binary meters the metrical dominants are the weak syllables, those that are generally unstressed. The ictuses, other than the final ictus, only tend to be stressed, for omitted stresses are quite common. On the other hand, hypermetrical stressing on the weak syllables is relatively infrequent, occurring most often in the anacrusis syllables and *only* on monosyllabic words. Therefore the lack of stress on these syllables is the most consistent feature of binary lines.

> (ii) Ternary meters have two weak positions between the ictuses.

As a result, the ictuses normally are fulfilled, and they become the metrical dominants.

(iii) In accentual meters the number of syllables between ictuses fluctuates (though generally within certain limits). In the *dol' nik*, where there are only one or two syllables between ictuses, omitted stress on an ictus is more common than hypermetrical stressing on the weak syllables; therefore, the latter are the dominants. In other kinds of accentual meters the ictuses are normally fulfilled, thus serving as the dominants.

TARANOVSKY'S LAWS

The discussion of stressing in lines with caesura implies the existence of still another set of rules. The obligatory stress on the final ictus, along with the presence of stress in Russian on barely more than a third of the syllables, gives rise to certain tendencies in the rhythms of the binary meters. The same was not true of ternary meters in the nineteenth century, which rarely omitted stress on the ictus. However, in the twentieth century ternaries omit stress more often and have begun to reveal patterns of stressing that follow the same norms as those for binaries. The *dol' nik*, the most common of the accentual meters, also tends to omit stress in the same manner as in the binary meters. Kiril Taranovsky has suggested two laws that govern these tendencies:

(1) the law of the stabilization of the first ictus after the first weak position; and

(2) the law of regressive accentual dissimilation.[12]

The first law simply means that the first ictus in a particular type of line carries a stress relatively often if that ictus occurs after a weak syllable. If, on the other hand, the first ictus coincides with the first syllable in a line, then that ictus tends to be stressed relatively less often. Therefore the first ictus in iambic ($\cup$ –) and amphibrach ($\cup$ – $\cup$) lines has a propensity to bear stress, because it follows a weak position. On the other hand, the first ictus in trochaic (– $\cup$) and dactylic (– $\cup$ $\cup$) lines often does not receive a stress, since it is not preceded by a weak position; instead, the second ictus in these lines is stressed relatively often.

The second law follows from the obligatory stress on the final ictus. If the next-to-last ictus is also stressed, two stresses must appear within the space of three syllables. Since stress occurs only slightly more often than once every three syllables, binary meters will be most strongly inclined to avoid stress on that ictus. The same pattern continues backward throughout the line. As a result of the frequent omission of stress on the next-to-last ictus, the third ictus from the end *will* tend to bear a stress. However, stress here is not obligatory and therefore not as strong as on the final ictus. The fourth ictus from the end will again be weak (that is, likely to omit a stress), but the tendency will be less pronounced than for the next-to-last ictus since the fourth ictus from the end is not followed by an ictus with an obligatory stress. In other words, strong and weak ictuses alternate backward from the end of the line in a wavelike fashion. The distinction between strong and weak ictuses is most pronounced at the end of the line, becoming progressively weaker as one moves toward the beginning (hence the dissimilation is regressive).

Taranovsky's figures for the frequency of stressing in the iambic pentameter without caesura during the twentieth century reflect his laws. The first ictus is stressed in 82.8 percent of the lines, the second 69.1 percent, the third 83.1 percent, the fourth 41.3 percent, and the fifth 100 percent.[13] That is, the next-to-last ictus is the weakest, the third from the last is again strong, the fourth weak (but not as weak as the next to last), and so forth. The first ictus is relatively strong owing to the combined effects of the first and second laws. In an iambic tetrameter line, however, the two laws conflict. (The same is true of all iambic lines with an even number of feet and of all trochaic lines with an odd number of feet.)[14] The fourth ictus is a constant, but both the second ictus (as a result of the second law) and the first ictus (the first law) are relatively strong. Further consequences of these laws will be discussed in chapters 2 and 3.

MONOSYLLABLES

Finally, monosyllabic words in Russian poetry deserve some special attention. Many one-syllable words such as prepositions and conjunctions are unstressed; others such as pronouns occupy a gray area; while verbs and nouns carry stress. But stress in all monosyllabic words differs from stress in words of two or more syllables because it cannot serve the important function of distinguishing between two words that differ only in the location of stress (e.g., пра́ва, genitive singular of "law," and права́, short-form adjective of "right"; ве́шу, first-person singular of "weigh," and вешу́, first-person singular of "to mark out").[15] In other words, stress in monosyllabic nouns and verbs is not phonemic. Thus a *hypermetrical stress* (a stress occurring on a weak syllable) is less disruptive when it occurs in a monosyllabic rather than in a polysyllabic word. As a result Russian poetic practice limits hypermetrical stressing in the binary meters (that is, iambic and trochaic lines) to monosyllabic words. For example, it is not rare for a stressed monosyllabic word to appear at the start of an iambic line, as in this example from Evgeny Baratynsky: Снóв золоты́х судьбá благáя ($\smile - \smile \acute{} \smile \acute{} \smile \acute{} \smile$), or this from Fedor Tiutchev: Мы́сль изречённая éсть лóжь ($\smile - \smile \acute{} \smile - \smile \acute{}$). Yet polysyllabic words, stressed on the first syllable and placed at the start of iambic lines, are not used by Russian poets.[16] Also, one-syllable words, lacking word-distinguishing stresses, tend to appear more often on the weaker ictuses. In the trochaic tetrameter, for instance, the fourth, or last, ictus is the strongest; the second will be strong as well; and the first and third will be weak (as predicted by Taranovsky's two laws). Theoretically, then, the monosyllables should favor the first and third ictuses, and figures for Pushkin's "Tale of Tsar Saltan" ("Skazka o tsare Saltane") support the hypothesis: 33 percent and 20 percent of the stresses on the first and third ictuses are monosyllables, but only 8 percent of the stresses on the second ictus consist of one-syllable words as well as 6 percent of the stresses on the fourth (and strongest) ictus.[17]

FOLK POETRY

Before turning to the analysis of modern Russian meters, it is useful to survey the poetry that preceded the establishment of the syllabo-tonic tradition. While literary poetry prior to the seventeenth century constitutes only a minor tradition, the corpus of Russian folklore (most of it admittedly recorded in more recent times) more than makes up for the lack. Epic songs (*byliny*), laments (*prichitaniia*), lyric songs, and even riddles and proverbs all show evidence of a highly developed verse tradition dating back to ancient times. Of these the first two are recited or narrative verse (*retsitativnyi stikh*), the lyrics are sung (*pesennyi stikh*), while the small poetic genres such as riddles and proverbs are spoken (*skazovyi stikh*). To give an adequate description of the metrical systems in folklore would require a separate book; the following pages are meant to provide a skeletal introduction to a very complex topic. Only one genre, the *bylina*, is discussed here in any detail, though several others are described briefly. Still, even a brief overview may prove useful, since sooner or later a reader of Russian poetry will come across literary imitations of folk verse and will find it useful to be aware of the models.

The *bylina* is perhaps the most widely studied of all the folk verse forms.[18] As expected, no direct records exist of the *byliny* as they were sung six or eight hundred years ago, though some epic songs were written down as early as the sixteenth century. However, the first recordings lack the accuracy needed for metrical analysis. Singers often resort to nonliterary stressing and dialect words; for the sake of rhythm they add or truncate syllables in endings and interject many particles. All these features make precise transcription of a performance extremely difficult. Fortunately, in the second half of the nineteenth century, when the scholarly study of folklore was already well under way, the tradition of the *bylina* was discovered to be alive, and indeed flourishing, in northern Russia. The most painstaking and accurate of the early collectors was A. F. Gilferding; the songs that he gathered during an intensive summer's work in 1871 have been reprinted several times.

Gilferding found the predominant meter of the *bylina* to consist of five- and six-foot trochees with a dactylic clausula, although he noted that the singers appeared to use other meters as well.[19] In several respects his analysis remains valid; some songs are indeed composed largely of five- and six-foot trochees and, while references to a single epic meter are common, other research has supported the hypothesis that more than one meter exists. Also, Gilferding recognized the importance of the musical accompaniment for the performer's ability to maintain a poetic rhythm.[20] (Note that melody is also significant for several other types of folk poetry, such as the laments and, of course, lyric songs.) However, it is necessary to account for the large number of nontrochaic lines in a more systematic fashion than that attempted by Gilferding. Scholars still do not agree on a solution to the problem, but recent analyses of Gilferding's original collection have made great progress toward defining what appear to be two main types of epic meters.[21]

The first of the meters—employed by T. G. Riabinin, one of the most skilled *bylina* singers, in fifteen out of the eighteen songs he recorded for Gilferding—employs *variable trochees* (*vol'nye xorei*), that is, trochaic lines with a varying number of feet. (See chapter 2 for a discussion of this meter in literary verse.) In Riabinin's use of this meter, nearly all the lines have dactylic endings, and although 87 percent of all the lines consist of either five- or six-foot trochees, at the extreme lines vary from three to ten feet in length.[22] Each work generally contains a handful of iambic lines as well as a very few that are metrically irregular. However, folk meters traditionally put fewer restraints on nonmetrical stressing than their literary equivalents, and the mixture of iambic lines with trochaic—extremely rare in literary verse—occurs regularly in trochaic folk poetry.[23] In accordance with Taranovsky's laws, both the first and next-to-last ictuses are stressed less often than the others in all lengths of the trochaic lines. And the stresses that do appear on the less frequently stressed ictuses in each type of line are generally from dependent function words; these stresses are weaker than those on, for instance, nouns and verbs. As a result both the five- and six-foot lines generally contain about three strong stresses.

The following example of Riabinin's trochaic meter is taken from "Ilia Muromets and Tsar Kalin" ("Ilia Muromets i Kalin-tsar'") and illustrates the typical use of trochees in the *bylina*.

```
"Ка́к пое́дешь ты́ во сто́льний Ки́ев-гра́д,        ´∪´∪´∪´∪´∪∪
Бу́дешь ты́, посла́нник, в стольне́ём во Ки́еве      ´∪´∪´∪—∪´∪´∪∪
Да у сла́вного у кня́зя у Влади́мира,              —∪´∪—∪´∪—∪´∪∪
Бу́дешь на него́ на широ́ком дворе́,               ´∪—∪´∪—∪´∪∪
И сойдёшь как ту́т ты со добра́ коня́,             —∪´∪´∪—∪´∪∪
Да й спуща́й коня́ ты на посы́льный дво́р,          —∪´∪´∪—∪´∪∪
Са́м поди́-тко во пала́ту белока́менну;             ´∪´∪—∪´∪—∪´∪∪
Да пройдёшь пала́той белока́менной,               —∪´∪´∪—∪´∪∪
Да й войдёшь в его́ столо́вую во го́ренку,          —∪´∪´∪´∪—∪´∪∪
На пяту́ ты две́рь да поразма́хивай,               —∪´∪´∪—∪´∪∪
Не снима́й-ко кивера́ с голо́вушки,                —∪´∪—∪´∪´∪∪
Походи́-ко ты́ ко сто́лику к дубо́вому,             —∪´∪´∪´∪—∪´∪∪
```

In this small excerpt all the lines consist of five- or six-foot trochees. The first ictus (in trochaic lines, the first syllable) lacks a strong stress in all but the second and fourth lines, as does the next-to-last ictus (the fifth syllable from the end) in all but the first, second, and eleventh lines. The word *ty* appears to be weakly stressed, when it is stressed at all. When all the weak stresses and unstressed ictuses are taken into account, most lines indeed have three strong stresses. Thus the first line, which seems to have five stresses, has one stress on the word *ty* and another on the word *grad*, which is subordinate to *Kiev*. The main stresses in the line fall on *poédesh'*, *stól'nii*, and *Kíev*. Only the second appears to have as many as four strong stresses. Two remarks are in order. First, even though the basic ending is dactylic (´∪∪), the final syllable may carry a hypermetrical stress. However, this apparently extra stress is often very weak, since in folk verse often only one main stress occurs in a phrase. In line four, for example, the main stress in *na shirokóm dvore* falls on the word *shirokóm*; the word *dvore* is only weakly stressed and is subordinate to the preceding adjective. Second, stressing in the *bylina* is frequently nonliterary, as is the case with *shirokóm*. Stress may be different within the word, or it may shift to a preposition or a verbal prefix.[24]

The other common meter is a three-stress accentual line in which the intervals between stresses may vary widely. However, most intervals are either two or three syllables, and generally more than 90 percent of the intervals in a song fall in the range of one to three syllables. To an extent, then, the accentual verse in the *bylina* is, as Gasparov notes, similar to the *taktovik* (or "strict accentual verse") of literary poetry. (See chapter 3 for remarks on this meter.) But since the folk meter allows a broader range in the intervals between stresses than its literary counterpart, it seems best to refer to this meter simply as *accentual verse*. This form is used by Riabinin in his remaining songs and also by many other singers. There are three notable tendencies in the accentual meter of the *bylina*: the line usually has three strong stresses, the intervals between stresses vary between one and three syllables (but may occasionally be longer), and the ending is most often dactylic (though both longer and shorter endings occur).

In order to characterize accentual verse further, it is necessary to consider the types of lines it may include. Note that in binary meters the intervals between stresses are normally one or, in the case of an unfulfilled ictus, three syllables. The intervals between stresses in ternary meters are two syllables, and in the *dol'nik* (discussed in chapter 3) one or two syllables. Therefore if all the intervals on a line are either one or three syllables, then the line is equivalent to one of the trochaic or iambic meters; if all the intervals are two syllables, then the line is equivalent to one of the ternary meters. Only when there is a mixture of two- and three-syllable intervals or some other combination not equivalent to a binary or ternary meter are the individual lines specifically accentual.

As it turns out, a *bylina* written in accentual verse normally includes a fair number of binary lines, ranging from about 15 to 33 percent or more, which often is as many as the number of accentual lines in the work. Most singers favor trochaic lines (Riabinin used them almost exclusively in his three songs containing this meter), but some use many iambic lines as well. Ternary lines are generally in third place, followed by *dol'niki*. Lines with long intervals that do not appear to result from an omitted stress are considered to be nonmetrical. Occasionally, songs performed in an accentual meter will contain as much as 15 to 20 percent of such lines.

Riabinin's "Volga and Mikula" ("Volga i Mikula") is sung in this meter:

Пе́рвыим го́родом – Гу́рчовцем,	´∪∪ ´∪∪ ´∪∪
Дру́гим го́родом – Оре́ховцем,	´∪ ´∪∪∪ ´∪∪
Тре́тьим го́родом – Крестья́новцем.	´∪ ´∪∪∪ ´∪∪
Мо́лодой Вольга́ Святосла́вгович,	´∪∪∪ ´∪∪ ´∪∪
Он пое́хал к города́м и за полу́чкою	´∪ ´∪∪∪ ´∪∪∪ ´∪∪
Со свое́й дружи́нушкой хоро́брою.	∪∪ ´∪ ´∪∪∪ ´∪∪
Вы́ехал Вольга́ во чисто́ по́ле,	´∪∪∪ ´∪∪ ´∪ ´
Он услы́шал во чи́стом по́ле ра́тая.	´∪ ´∪∪ ´∪ ´∪ ´∪∪
А орёт в по́ле ра́тай, пону́кивает,	∪∪ ´´∪ ´∪∪ ´∪∪∪
А у ра́тая-то со́шка поскри́пывает,	∪∪ ´∪∪∪ ´∪∪ ´∪∪∪
Да по ка́мешкам оме́шики прочи́ркивают.	∪∪ ´∪∪∪ ´∪∪∪ ´∪∪∪

Note that each of the first four lines, for instance, contains three stresses, and in each case the first stress falls on the first syllable (Riabinin stressed both *molodoi* and *drugoi* on the first syllable). In fact, since the stress on *pole* in lines 7 through 9 appears to be subordinated to the neighboring stresses, each of the lines has precisely three strong stresses. But the rhythm is varied; within the first four lines, the first follows a ternary schema, the second and third a trochaic, and the fourth an accentual (intervals of three and then two syllables). Since many trochaic lines are employed, a listener may still perceive a vaguely trochaic impetus behind the rhythm, but the large number of lines in different meters clearly indicates that the meter of the work as a whole is not trochaic but accentual.

In some cases it is difficult to discern any regular pattern for a song as a whole, even though individual lines may appear to resemble one of the recognized meters. Such works are for all practical purposes nonmetrical. Most lines will still contain from two to four stresses, and rarely will more than four syllables occur between stresses, but these are simply constraints of the language itself. Although occasional lines will still be quite regular, the intervals between stresses for the poem as a whole vary widely and do not seem to result from any particular plan. Still, even here the dactylic clausula predominates. Also, epics of this type often make heavy use of anaphora, which helps give the lines a bit

more structure. An example of a work sung in this fashion is A. So-
rokin's version of "Sadko":

А опя́ть как прошла́ топе́рь тёмна но́чь,
А-й опя́ть как на дру́гой де́нь
Не зову́т Садка́ да на поче́стен пи́р,
А дру́гой-то да не зову́т его на поче́стен пи́р,
А-й как тре́тий-то де́нь не зову́т на поче́стен пи́р.
А-й как опя́ть Садку́ топе́рь да соску́чилось,
А пошёл Садке́ ко Ильмень да о́н ко о́зеру,
А-й сади́лся он опя́ть на си́нь да на горю́ч камень
У Ильмень да он у озе́ра,
А-й как на́чал игра́ть он опя́ть во гу́сли во яро́вчаты,
А игра́л уж как с утра́ день до ве́чера.
А-й как по ве́черу опя́ть как по по́зднему,
А-й волна́ уж как в о́зере сходи́лася,
А-й как вода́ с песко́м топе́рь смути́лася,
А-й устраши́лся опя́ть Садке́ да новгоро́дскии,
Одоле́л Садка́ уж как стра́х топе́рь вели́кии.

It is hard to be sure how many of the function words in this excerpt
would have carried a stress when the song was performed, but at least
two of the lines (the second and the ninth) have only two prominent
stresses apiece, while several other lines have at least four stresses.
Some of the lines form regular binary or ternary meters, but many
others are not consistent with any particular scheme.

James Bailey has described two types of narrative folk verse that oc-
cur less frequently. One he calls the short epic line, which has only two
stresses instead of the more common three main stresses. The anacrusis
and the clausula are both variable, though in each case two syllables is
the most common length (that is, this type of line also favors a dactylic
clausula). The interval between the two main stresses is usually two or
three syllables, and the historical prototype for this line was most likely
an eight-syllable line with ictuses on the third and sixth syllables ($\cup\cup\acute{-}$
$\cup\cup\acute{-}\cup\cup$). The other type of line derives from the *trochaic 5 + 5 line*,
which is common in folk songs. Again, there are two main stresses. The
two-syllable anacrusis and clausula are more regular features than in the
short epic line (the dactylic clausula, in fact, is almost a constant), but
the interval between the two main stresses is noticeably greater—gener-
ally four or five syllables.

To summarize: In most epics the three-stress line and the dactylic
clausula predominate. The most metrically regular songs are usually
trochaic; although the number of syllables per line will vary, the major-
ity of lines in such songs will have eleven or thirteen syllables and are

thus five- or six-foot trochees with dactylic clausula. Some singers fa-
vored one meter but would employ a second occasionally. Since the
epics were sung, the choice of meter and the ability to maintain a meter
more or less consistently for hundreds of lines were dependent, in all
likelihood, on the use of a particular melody. Nothing has been said
about rhyme, for it is not a regular feature of the *bylina*. However, asso-
nance, consonance, and grammatical rhyme all occur upon occasion
(cf. lines 1–3, 5–6, and 9–11 in the above quotation from "Volga and
Mikula").[25]

Among the other genres, laments are particularly interesting because
of their many similarities to epics. Thus Roman Jakobson has shown
that two types of line occur in the lament, one with eight or nine syl-
lables and the other with twelve or thirteen (depending on the type of
clausula).[26] The rhythm is often trochaic; indeed, the longer of these
lines exhibits a pattern of stressing the same as that of the trochaic
epics. Consider, for example, the following excerpt from a lament by
Irina Fedosova, a well-known nineteenth-century mourner:[27]

Я гляжу́-смотрю́, печа́льная голо́вушка,	´∪ ´∪ ´∪ ´∪∪∪ ´∪∪
Мно́го-мно́жество попо́в стои́т духо́вных,	´∪ ´∪∪∪ ´∪ ´∪ ´∪
Еще бо́льше е причётен-то церко́вных;	∪∪ ´∪∪∪ ´∪∪∪ ´∪
Всё сокру́чены во ри́зах во опа́льныих,	´∪ ´∪∪∪ ´∪∪∪ ´∪∪
Погребе́ньице пою́т да уныльне́шенько.	∪∪ ´∪∪∪ ´∪∪∪ ´∪∪
На гробу́ да э́та ри́за золочёная,	∪∪ ´∪ ´∪ ´∪∪∪ ´∪∪
На бе́лых гру́дях кни́га э́та бо́жья,	∪ ´∪ ´∪ ´∪ ´∪ ´∪
Кругом-на́окол подсве́чники злачёные,	∪∪ ´∪∪∪ ´∪∪∪ ´∪∪
Всё зажга́ны све́чи да там наме́стные,	´∪ ´∪ ´∪∪∪ ´∪∪
Мно́го-мно́жество наро́ду лю́дей до́брыих	´∪ ´∪∪∪ ´∪ ´∪ ´∪∪
Сожали́ют-то попа́-отца́ духо́вного;	∪∪ ´∪∪∪ ´∪ ´∪ ´∪∪

Line 9 is not completely regular, and line 7 is actually iambic instead of
trochaic. (Since line 7 is also a syllable shorter than any of the others
here, Fedosova probably omitted a syllable at the beginning of the line.)
The dactylic clausula predominates, and the three lines with a feminine
clausula in this example may well reflect errors in the recording. Essen-
tially, this passage is very close to the trochaic meter of the *bylina*. If
phrases like *mnogo-mnozhestvo* and *popa-ottsa* are considered to have
only one strong stress, then the majority of lines here, as in the *bylina*,
have just three strong stresses.

As for lyric songs, they too exhibit trochaic rhythms, though by no
means exclusively. The oldest songs were unrhymed and generally con-
tained a varying number of syllables per line, though each line would

have the same number of stresses. The more recent songs, from the
eighteenth century on, also tend toward isosyllabism, or an equal num-
ber of syllables in each line.[28] As the discussion of the *bylina* has al-
ready illustrated, folk poetry allows more deviations from its metrical
norms than does literary verse. Thus iambic lines are not rare in trochaic
folk verse, whereas they are virtually unheard of in trochaic poems be-
longing to the literary tradition. Similarly, stress in folk works can shift
from the ictus to a neighboring syllable, and in this way the entire tro-
chaic rhythm is interrupted.[29] As might be expected, original folk songs
display considerably more irregularities than literary imitations of this
genre, and for that matter the imitations of folk verse are themselves
often less regular than other literary poetry.[30] Folk songs are written in a
wide variety of lines, ranging from six to fourteen syllables. Perhaps the
most common is a trochaic tetrameter line with a dactylic or feminine
ending.

Special mention should be made of the ten-syllable line, the so-
called trochaic 5+5 meter, which was popularized in literary verse by
Aleksei Koltsov in the nineteenth century.[31] Both before and after his
time many poets have used the meter for literary imitations of folk
songs. The line consists of two five-syllable hemistichs; a word break
(i.e., a caesura) almost always occurs after the fifth syllable; and the
third and eighth syllables of the line are always stressed. The traditional
Russian folk song lacked rhyme, though some literary imitations of the
meter may employ a rhyme scheme. Almost all the poets who have used
the 5+5 meter tended to stress the tenth, or final, syllable least of all;
thus the constant stress on the eighth syllable created a dactylic clau-
sula—much like that in the *bylina*. Koltsov and other poets who have
used the meter emphasized the break after the fifth syllable by writing
out each hemistich on a separate line; the following example from
Koltsov will illustrate the meter.

Áх, зачéм меня́
Си́лой вы́дали
За неми́лова –
Му́жа ста́рова.

Небо́сь вéсело
Тепéрь ма́тушке
Утира́ть мой
Слёзы го́рькие;
      1838

These eight lines are in effect four, with a rhythmic pattern as follows:

```
´ ∪ ´ ∪ ´ || ´ ∪ ´ ∪∪
∪∪ ´ ∪∪ || ´ ∪ ´ ∪∪
∪∪ ´ ∪∪ || ∪∪ ´ ∪∪
∪∪ ´ ∪ ´ || ´ ∪ ´ ∪∪
```

Both *nebos'* and *teper'* in line 3 take a very weak stress on the second syllable, but given the rhythm for the song as a whole, they can reasonably be considered unstressed. Note the complete lack of stress on the tenth syllable in this sample, the constant stress on the third and eighth syllables, and the lack of rhyme.

Spoken verse (*skazovyi stikh*) is found in proverbs, sayings, riddles, magic spells, and toasts. Unlike the epics and early lyric songs, which lack rhyme, all these short forms depend heavily on sound repetitions to achieve their effect. In fact, one type of spoken verse, the *raeshnik*, is distinguished only by rhyme; it contains neither an equal number of syllables nor, necessarily, an equal number of stresses per line. Often humorous or satirical in intent, the *raeshnik* came to be used during the late eighteenth century in several types of traditional entertainment and also appeared in the inscriptions of the *lubok*, a type of popular woodcut depicting folk motifs.

Often various types of spoken verse occur in lines of four stresses; the first and third stresses tend to be omitted at times and, when they appear, are often on the less strongly stressed function words. The line generally contains two distinct halves, with the break signaled both by an intonational pause and by rhyme or some other kind of sound repetition between the two parts of the line. If the proverb or riddle extends beyond one line, rhyme may occur at the end of paired lines.[32] Let us look at a few proverbs taken from a single page of Vladimir Dahl's well-known collection:[33]

От во́лка бежа́л, да на медве́дя попа́л   ∪ ´∪∪ ´ |∪∪∪ ´∪∪ ´
(напа́л).

Сча́стье пыта́ть – де́ньги теря́ть.   ´∪∪ ´ | ´∪∪ ´

Сча́стье без ума́ – дыря́вая сума́.   ´∪∪∪ ´ |∪ ´∪∪∪ ´

Although each of the three lines contains a distinct pattern of stressed and unstressed syllables, the intervals between stresses are fairly regular between the two parts of each line. At times, as in the second example here, the two halves of a line will be perfectly symmetrical.[34] Obviously, not all proverbs adhere strictly to any one formula. But, interestingly enough, older variants of a proverb often show a greater tendency toward sound repetitions (including rhyme) and rhythmical regularity than do the more recent versions.[35] Thus the evidence indicates that both features were probably important traits of proverbs in the older folk tradition.[36]

A word needs to be said here about the most recent form of Russian folklore, the *chastushka*.[37] *Chastushki* are short (most often, four lines), humorous verses that may be recited but are more often sung—frequently to the accompaniment of a musical instrument—or danced to. Although they arose sometime during the second half of the nineteenth century and are thus a relatively new phenomenon, both their origin and their precise form have not yet been satisfactorily explained. Unlike most folk genres, the *chastushka* is found in urban as well as rural environments, and it may contain literary as well as folk elements. Two *chastushki*, expressing opposing sentiments, will give an idea of their general form:[38]

Говорят, что в ба́бах ху́до,   ◡◡ ´◡ ´◡ ´◡
В де́вках ху́же и того́:   ´◡ ´◡◡◡ ´
Повернёшься с бо́ку на́ бок – ◡◡ ´◡ ´◡ ´◡
Ря́дом не́ту никого́.   ´◡ ´◡◡◡ ´

По́й-ка, ми́лка, как поётся, ´◡ ´◡◡◡ ´◡
Вы́йдешь за́муж, как ведётся, ´◡ ´◡◡◡ ´◡
Не придётся тебе́ пе́ть,   ◡◡ ´◡◡ ´ ´
Бу́дешь го́рюшко терпе́ть. ´◡ ´◡◡◡ ´

An important feature of the *chastushka* is rhyme, which is often either paired or alternating.[39] The meter varies; the two above are trochaic, but some correspond to one of the other classical meters and many are composed in accentual verse. Still, a large number of *chastushki* consist of regular trochees, and it seems that trochaic meters (usually trochaic tetrameter or trochaic tetrameter lines alternating with trochaic trimeter) are the most commonly employed in these works.

Thus no single "folk meter" accounts for all the forms found in the various oral genres. And yet a few general statements are possible. Epics and the oldest lyric songs, as well as the laments, lacked rhyme and favored a dactylic clausula. On the other hand, the short genres—proverbs, riddles, *chastushki*—all make some use of rhyme as well as consonance, assonance, and word play. The meters in folk verse are most often trochaic or accentual, and the number of strong stresses in both the *bylina* and the lament is most often three per line. While the number of syllables in each line of a work may vary widely, the great majority of lines will generally fall within fairly narrow limits. Rhythmically, some noticeable differences occur between folk meters and their literary counterparts; the former tend to allow greater freedom in the use of nonmetrical or hypermetrical stressing and also make a sharper distinction between the strong and weak ictuses. As a result, literary works written in imitation of folklore favor trochaic and accentual meters and may feature a dactylic clausula; furthermore, they can differ noticeably from other literary verse both rhythmically and in their use (or lack) of rhyme.[40]

THE EARLY LITERARY TRADITION

The main question to be addressed in connection with Russian literature prior to the seventeenth century is the extent to which verse existed as a distinct phenomenon. Texts from the beginning period of Russian literature—the eleventh through the start of the thirteenth centuries— show that the Orthodox liturgy included Russian recensions of Church Slavonic poetry, which in turn was generally translated from Greek. Since the translations not only maintained but at times strengthened the syllabic symmetry of the originals, the Russian authors must have been aware that they were writing poetry.[41] One cannot always be sure which elements were regarded as poetic by the Slavs; in the case of at least one Church Slavonic translation, syllabo-accentual regularity is less than in the original Greek, while the occurrences of sound repetitions and grammatical figures are greater.[42] Although some poetic tradition did exist at the dawn of Russian literature, it is difficult to determine whether any of the major works in Old Russian literature should be regarded as poems.[43] For instance, the *Igor Tale* (*Slovo o polku Igoreve*), Hilarion's *Sermon on Law and Grace* (*Slovo o zakone i blagodati*), and the *Supplication of Daniil Zatochnik* (*Molenie Daniila Zatochnika*) all contain readily noticeable rhythmic elements. Yet the difficulties in finding a developed poetic system behind any of these works are enormous. For one thing, the surviving texts are not always accurate copies of the originals; for another, any "method" that may have been known at the time was probably not based on the easily observed features of syllabo-tonic poetry, but might have involved a looser and less clearly defined set of principles.

Efforts to determine the rhythmic structure of the *Igor Tale* illustrate some of the obstacles and pitfalls that have awaited researchers. Perhaps least convincing among the more recent theories is L. I. Timofeev's belief that the tale's rhythmic structure is borrowed from folk verse.[44] He bases his statement on the claim that the *Igor Tale* contains many lines with a dactylic clausula, as in the Russian epic. However, Timofeev begins by asserting that the surviving version of the *Igor Tale* contains numerous errors and that it is necessary to "reconstruct" the original form. Perhaps not accidentally, his emendations consist largely of transposing words to increase the number of dactylic endings, and thus his findings are open to question.

Others have offered stronger arguments. For example, Riccardo Picchio has attempted to apply his "isocolic principle" to the *Igor Tale*. Essentially, his idea is that certain texts can be broken down into syntactic-intonational units called cola; series of cola with equal numbers of stresses are called isocola.[45] Groups of cola tend to contain regular numbers of stresses according to some pattern; thus four-stressed may alternate with three-stressed cola, or several four-stressed cola may be followed by a series with three stresses and then a return to four-stressed cola. Still another scholar, V. I. Stelletsky, likewise breaks the text into units, the boundaries of which are determined by meaning as well as by syntax.[46] He considers various rhetorical devices such as syntactic parallelism and anaphora and concludes that the *Igor Tale* contains three types of writing: prose with a weakly developed rhythm, prose with a strongly developed rhythm, and a kind of highly organized writing that approaches verse. The style varies from one section of the tale to the next; thus the dream of Sviatoslav and the lament of Iaroslavna are dominated by long lines implying solemnity or majesty.

Unfortunately, however, whatever the other merits of their analyses, neither Picchio nor Stelletsky is particularly concerned with verse. All that Picchio says could apply equally well to prose or poetry, while Stelletsky views the *Igor Tale* as rhythmic prose containing a few passages that are closer to poetry. A. N. Pozdneev, on the other hand, has claimed that a system of versification did exist in Old Russian literature; he calls it *kondakarnyi stikh*—verses that lack rhyme and have varying numbers both of syllables and stresses in each line.[47] The rhythmic basis of *kondakarnyi stikh*, which he finds in the *Igor Tale* and other works, is apparently the phrase or semantic unit, but Pozdneev does not say precisely how this type of verse differs from rhythmic prose.[48] He does

point to a tendency (though only a tendency) toward a certain regularity
in the number of stresses per line, and he links this feature to the devel-
opment of accentual verse in the folk tradition. However, the evidence
he offers for this connection is skimpy at best, and in any case his defi-
nition appears too vague to serve as the description of a literary poetic
tradition.

The most convincing effort to discover a system of verse in Old Rus-
sian literature has been made by Kiril Taranovsky. According to his find-
ings, a system of *molitvoslovnyi stikh* (religious verse) existed, distin-
guished by a tendency to mark the start of each line by frequent use of
vocative and imperative forms as well as by syntactic inversion. The
importance placed on line beginnings also leads to the use of anaphora
(beginning successive lines with the same word or words) and acros-
tics.[49] As an example of *molitvoslovnyi stikh*, Taranovsky divides the
concluding section of Hilarion's *Sermon on Law and Grace* into lines:[50]

1. *Въстани,* о честнаа главо, от гроба твоего,
2. *Въстани,* отряси сонъ,
3. *Нѣси* бо умерлъ, нъ спиши до обьщааго всем въстаніа.
4. *Въстани, нѣси* умерлъ,
5. *Нѣстъ* бо ти лѣпо умрѣти,
6. Вѣровавъшу въ Христа, живота всему миру.
7. *Отряси* сонъ, възведи очи, да видиши,
8. *Какоя* тя чьсти господь тамо съподобивъ,
9. И на земли не беспамятна оставилъ сыномъ твоимъ.

Note that the lines do not contradict Pozdneev's definition of *kondakar-
nyi stikh*. They are of varying lengths, they contain different numbers of
stressed syllables, and they lack rhyme. The strong markings of line be-
ginnings (in seven out of nine instances) are the sole rhythmic element,
but at least Taranovsky suggests positive criteria for assigning works to
the category of religious verse.

However, even Taranovsky's suggestions have been met by other re-
searchers with skepticism. L. I. Sazonova, after examining Hilarion's
sermon itself, has concluded that the work is "not verse, but prose, al-
though rhythmically organized."[51] She admits that the last section of the
sermon reveals a definite rhythmic structure, but she suggests that even
this part of the work does not constantly adhere to the principles de-
scribed by Taranovsky. A. M. Panchenko, surveying the sources of Rus-
sian literary verse, notes that the vocative and imperative forms appear
frequently in solemn oratory and, like Sazonova, believes that *molitvo-
slovnyi stikh* is not so much verse as a type of rhythmic prose.[52]

Part of the problem involves definitions. While translated poetic works can be found in the liturgy, and at times the oral poetry of folk-lore was reflected in written works, for the most part the significant literary documents from the earliest times appear to consist of what we would now call prose.[53] Still, the elements discerned by Taranovsky point at the very least to an embryonic tradition that required the impetus of a strong foreign influence before a clearly recognizable type of verse could emerge. The works of Old Russian literature, no matter how rhythmical they may have been, did not have a direct influence on the development of Russian poetry in the seventeenth and eighteenth centuries.[54]

SYLLABIC VERSE

An active tradition of literary poetry in Russia dates back only to the beginning of the seventeenth century. Two explanations have been given for the relatively sudden appearance of written poetry at this time. According to some, the first *presyllabic* poetry was closely related to the rhymed prose that was popular in the late sixteenth and seventeenth centuries. Others hold that versification came to Russia from Poland and the Ukraine. By the end of the sixteenth century Poland already had a highly developed poetry. The influence of Polish culture began to filter into Russia both after the Time of Troubles at the beginning of the seventeenth century and again toward the middle of the century when the Ukraine, previously part of the Polish state, came under Russian control. This second explanation appears to be the more likely. Had rhymed prose and presyllabic poetry been part of the same phenomenon, both should have undergone a similar development. But in fact presyllabic verse soon gave way to syllabic poetry—again, apparently as the result of Ukrainian and Polish influences—while rhymed prose continued to exist as an independent tradition.[55] Thus the first literary poetry in Russian appeared largely as a result of foreign influences, even though the prior existence of rhymed prose may well have helped prepare the way for the acceptance of a poetic tradition.

The term *presyllabic verse* (*dosillabicheskii stikh*) is applied to the system of versification that came into being during the first three decades of the seventeenth century, a time when only a handful of poems were actually written in Russian. Works in both presyllabic and the later syllabic verse are sometimes referred to as *virshi*. During the presyllabic period, rhyme is the one constant feature of the poetry (much as is the case with the *raeshnik*); both the number of syllables and the number of stresses in each line may vary. The following example is taken from Prince Ivan Andreevich Khvorostinin, one of the first to use this form.

Каин со Авелем две церкви знаменуют,
Но из Адама два естества именуют,
Яже богу всесожженную жертву принесли,
За нь же молитвы свои к тому вознесли.
Яко Каин грешный богу не угоди
И лукавым сердцем к нему приходи,
Веселый Авель от бога милость принял,
А его же господь дары и всесожжение внял.
Но внегда молитвы Авель богу воздал,
А Каин его тщательно убити помышлял.

1623-25

The rhyme is paired, but unlike the subsequent syllabic verse, presyllabic poetry allowed not only feminine, but also masculine, dactylic, and even hyperdactylic rhyme. Nor is the rhyme always exact as it is here; at times assonance or consonance will be used instead. However, perhaps as a result of the relatively loose rules for creating this type of poetry, the authors frequently resorted to acrostics as a way of further distinguishing their work from ordinary prose.[56] Thus in the above example the first letter of each line spells out the first part of the author's name.

The two main developments in Russian poetry during the seventeenth and eighteenth centuries came about quite suddenly and can be traced to the influence of specific individuals. The second change, the introduction of syllabo-tonic poetry, had the more lasting influence, but the first was itself important, for it marked the origin of a significant Russian poetic tradition. This earlier development was the shift from presyllabic to syllabic poetry and is associated with the name of Simeon Polotsky. A monk who had written poems in Ukrainian, Polish, and Latin, Polotsky came to Moscow in 1664, after his home town of Polotsk had been captured by the Poles. Here he became a favorite of Tsar Aleksei and among other things began to serve as a kind of court poet. But Simeon Polotsky was more than just a versifier; he had a deep interest in literature and soon came to write a new kind of *virshi* in Russian. Although there was a fairly extensive body of work in presyllabic poetry by the midseventeenth century,[57] the number of poets was still small. The new method quickly won favor throughout this limited group, and within a few years the presyllabic system had virtually disappeared.

Polotsky's verse was based on Polish syllabic poetry, which he himself had written before coming to Moscow. The Polish versification principles then in vogue had been popularized by Jan Kochanowski, a sixteenth-century writer. All the lines within a given poem were of equal length (this, of course, is the basic feature of all syllabic verse); the most common line lengths for Polish poetry were thirteen or eleven syllables. Furthermore, the line was divided into two parts (7+6 or 5+6) by a caesura. Both the clausula and the caesura were generally feminine (´˘). However, the tendency to use feminine endings was less of a restriction on Polish writers than was isosyllabism.[58] Given the nature of Polish stress, which normally falls on the next-to-last syllable of a word, feminine endings were to be expected in the majority of cases; for that matter, masculine and dactylic endings were not absolutely forbidden and occasionally occurred when monosyllabic words or enclitics appeared at the caesura or the end of the line.

Russian employed three of the four main features in Polish syllabic verse. It too (1) used lines of the same length throughout the poem (and, as in Polish, preferred poems with lines of thirteen or eleven syllables), (2) contained a caesura that divided the line into two halves or hemistichs (again, 7+6 or 5+6), and (3) used a feminine clausula, which formed rhymed couplets. However, the caesura in Russian was not necessarily feminine but could be masculine or dactylic as well, as is illustrated in these excerpts from Polotsky's "Painting" ("Zhivopisanie") and Feofan Prokopovich's "On Compiling Lexicons" ("K slozheniiu leksikov"):

Бе живопи́сец до́бре изучённый   ˘˘˘´˘ ‖ ´˘˘˘´˘
   в Ро́де, и́менем Протоге́н речённый.   ´˘˘˘ ‖ ˘˘´˘´˘
Сей ря́бку та́ко жи́во написа́ше,   ˘´˘´˘ ‖ ´˘˘˘´˘
   да́же к не́й живы́х мно́жество лета́ше.   ´˘´˘´ ‖ ´˘˘˘´˘
И́нде зми́й та́ко живопи́сан бя́ше,   ´˘´´˘ ‖ ˘˘´˘´˘
   я́ко же в птенце́х пе́ние держа́ше,   ´˘˘˘´ ‖ ´˘˘˘´˘
И́же Ле́пиду не дая́ху спа́ти;   ´˘˘´˘ ‖ ˘˘´˘´˘
   зми́й за то стра́хом не́ дал им писка́ти.   ´˘˘´˘ ‖ ´˘˘˘´˘
              [<1680]

Е́сли в мучи́тельские осужде́н кто ру́ки,   ´˘˘´˘˘˘‖ ˘˘´˘´˘
   ждёт бе́дная голова́ печа́ли и му́ки,   ´´˘˘˘˘´‖ ˘´˘˘´˘
Не вели́ томи́ть его́ де́лом ку́зниц тру́дных,   ˘˘´˘´´˘‖ ´˘´˘´˘
   ни посыла́ть в тя́жкия рабо́ты ме́ст ру́дных.   ˘˘˘´´˘˘˘‖ ˘´´˘´˘
Пусть ле́ксики де́лает: то одно́ довле́ет,   ˘´˘˘´˘˘‖ ˘˘´˘´˘
   всех му́к роды́ сей оди́н труд в себе́ име́ет.   ´´˘´˘˘´ ‖ ´˘´˘´˘
              [early 18th c.]

The poem by Polotsky is in the eleven-syllable meter, which he favored; that by Prokopovich has thirteen-syllable lines, which overall were the most common in Russian syllabic poetry. Both poets used feminine endings and a caesura throughout, while, except for the penultimate syllable, stress appears more or less at random on each line. In Polish all or nearly all the caesuras would be feminine, but here Polotsky used masculine and dactylic breaks as well, while Prokopovich avoided the feminine caesura entirely. In practice, not all the poems were as regular as the two quoted above; sometimes rhymes were not adjoining but alternating, and lines within a single poem could even vary slightly in length.[59] Still more rarely, poets would use an occasional nonfeminine rhyme.[60] One peculiarity of syllabic verse is the relative frequency with which strong stresses appear on contiguous syllables; there are several instances in the Prokopovich example, such as at the beginning of line 2 and twice in line 4. The same phenomenon is found in syllabo-tonic poetry, but there its usage is much more circumscribed. During the period when syllabic poetry was predominant, from about 1670 through 1730, the first part of the line exhibited strong stressing on adjoining syllables on about one line in five; the second part of the line contained such stressing approximately once every ten lines.[61]

The seemingly casual employment of adjoining strong stresses calls into question the extent to which syllabic verse served as a direct precursor of the syllabo-tonic system. For some seventy years syllabic poetry reigned supreme; its major practitioners, besides Polotsky and Prokopovich, included Silvestr Medvedev, Karion Istomin, Antiokh Kantemir, and the young Vasily Trediakovsky. Yet within two decades after Trediakovsky had written "New and Brief Method for Composing Russian Verse" in 1735, the syllabo-tonic system had almost entirely replaced syllabic poetry. Did the new method evolve from the old, or did one system abruptly replace the other? Presumably, had syllabic poetry led directly into the syllabo-tonic system, poets writing syllabic verse would have gradually (1) decreased the amount of contiguous stressing and (2) favored trochaic rhythms, since Trediakovsky, who was the first to formulate a theory of syllabo-tonic poetry and who had originally written syllabic poetry himself, believed that trochaic meters were the most suitable for Russian. However, as M. L. Gasparov has shown, contiguous stressing, if anything, was used slightly more often until Trediakovsky's reform. After the reform it declined dramatically in the late poetry of Kantemir and in Trediakovsky's subsequent syllabic poetry.[62] As for trochaic rhythms, a tendency for lines to sound more trochaic should be accompanied first of all by a decrease in the frequency of a feminine caesura (´˘). Since the first hemistich usually had either five or seven syllables, a feminine caesura places a stress on an even syllable (either the fourth or the sixth), while in trochaic meters the ictuses are only on the odd syllables. In fact, until the time of Kantemir and Trediakovsky about half of all the lines contained a feminine caesura and therefore necessarily lacked a strongly trochaic rhythm. Only after 1735 did Kantemir and (especially) Trediakovsky consistently use masculine or, to a lesser extent, dactylic caesuras instead.[63] Second, if purely syllabic poetry had been gradually developing into syllabo-tonic, the second hemistich of syllabic lines should have begun to use trochaic rhythms more and more consistently. Since the second hemistich of both the eleven- and thirteen-syllable lines contains six syllables and has a required stress on the penultimate syllable, its schema is as follows (where x stands for a syllable that may either be stressed or unstressed): $xxxx´˘$. Therefore, in lines without contiguous stressing, only five types of second hemistich are possible:

(1) ´˘´˘´˘
(2) ˘˘´˘´˘
(3) ´˘˘˘´˘
(4) ˘´˘˘´˘
(5) ˘˘˘˘´˘

The first three resemble trochees and the fourth amphibrachs. The "theoretical expectation," which Gasparov has calculated using examples of prose, is that about 55 percent of the second hemistichs should be trochaic, assuming that poets were not striving to favor any one type of rhythm over the others. Indeed, poets stayed close to this theoretical figure until the 1730s, after which Trediakovsky abruptly began to use trochaic rhythms almost exclusively. Since the presence of feminine rhyme means that 55 percent of the lines would show a trochaic rhythm in the second hemistich even if poets were not attempting to use such a rhythm consciously, it is easy to see why some have felt that syllabic verse exhibited a "trochaic cadence."[64] But the failure of poets to exceed the 55 percent "norm" before Trediakovsky's time shows that they were not aware of, or at least not trying to emphasize, a trochaic cadence. Furthermore, in the first hemistich, where the placing of stress was much more varied, there was no tendency to favor trochaic rhythms at all until after Trediakovsky wrote his essay. Every change that took place occurred suddenly; just after Trediakovsky wrote "Method," the feminine caesura virtually disappeared, the second hemistich became much more trochaic, and contiguous stressing dropped dramatically. Gasparov, and S. M. Bondi before him, therefore believed that the change to a new system was a "revolutionary" rather than an evolutionary process.[65]

Why did the syllabic system lose favor so suddenly and so completely? Scholars are of two minds on this issue. Some hold that the reasons are largely linguistic: languages like Polish, with fixed stress, tend to favor syllabic systems in which stress plays little or no role as a distinguishing feature; on the other hand, languages like English, German, and Russian—in which stress appears at various positions in words and has therefore come to be quite prominent—prefer *tonic* systems in which stress is the main prosodic feature of the language. Therefore the switch to a syllabo-tonic system in Russian is seen as a natural development, and the only question might be why the syllabic system reigned as long as it did.[66] Others have cast doubt on some of these premises. For instance, Ukrainian, which phonologically is very close to Russian, retains a syllabic tradition; conversely, Polish, with its fixed stress, later came to use some syllabo-tonic poetry. Also, syllabic poetry is not necessarily "unnatural" to Russian; if anything, it puts fewer restraints on the language than the strict laws of syllabo-tonic poetry. If linguistic features are not the answer, then changes in the cultural background and outside influences must be considered paramount.[67]

The answer seems to lie somewhere between the two positions. The cultural environment probably played some role, since early in the eighteenth century a strong German influence existed in the Court and at the Academy of Sciences. German poetry was syllabo-tonic, and Mikhail Lomonosov based his important revisions of Trediakovsky's "Method" on German models. Lomonosov had picked up most of his ideas in Germany itself, but German poetry was also well known in Russia and some Germans in St. Petersburg even wrote early examples of Russian syllabo-tonic poetry. However, linguistic influences cannot be ignored. Russian folk verse, in which stress has always played a major role, shows that from the earliest times stress has been recognized as an important prosodic element in Russian. And according to some critics, syllabic verse, by putting few restraints on the language, was still perceived as close to prose. Therefore, syllabic poetry could be used to create successful satires and the like, but it appeared to be less suitable for the more "formal" genres, such as the ode and the narrative poem.[68]

All this may help account for the rapid ascension of syllabo-tonic poetry, but the failure of syllabic verse to continue as at least a minor tradition is more difficult to explain. Perhaps the answer lies in the relatively small and self-contained circle of poets active during the first half of the eighteenth century. The influence of the new system would be quickly felt by every poet of any significance then active, and since the prevailing feeling seemed to be that syllabo-tonic verse was more suitable for serious poetry, the desire of every young poet to master the new method is not surprising. Furthermore, once syllabo-tonic poetry had been around for even a short while, changes took place in Russian poetic practice that made it difficult to reestablish a syllabic system. Almost from the start (or at least from the time of Lomonosov) Russian syllabo-tonic poetry mixed different kinds of rhyme in the same poem; thus a poem written in iambic tetrameter could have eight syllables (masculine rhyme), nine syllables (feminine rhyme), or even ten (dactylic rhyme). Further, mixed meters (e.g., tetrameter lines alternating with iambic trimeter) came into existence. Hence isosyllabism, the basic feature of syllabic poetry, was no longer an absolute principle for poems written in Russian. Second, a regular interval between stresses became the norm, and this feature soon assumed a greater importance than the caesura for determining the structure of the line. Third, long lines, predominant in Russian syllabic meters, gradually gave way to shorter lines of eight or nine syllables; this too lessened the need for the pause created by a caesura. Thus, of the three main features of Russian syllabic poetry, two—isosyllabism and exclusively feminine endings—became rarities, while the third, the caesura, became less prominent as Russian poetry moved into the nineteenth century. Interestingly, two attempts during the 1920s to imitate syllabic poetry show just how far removed Russians were from the syllabic tradition, for both attempts broke the cardinal rule of that system—they failed to maintain an equal number of syllables on each line.[69]

2

The Classical Meters

THE ESTABLISHMENT of the syllabo-tonic system for Russian verse was an extremely rapid process.[1] In some ways Trediakovsky's "New and Brief Method for Composing Russian Verse," published in April 1735 by the Russian Academy of Sciences, was hardly a radical departure from the syllabic system. He advocated lines of thirteen or eleven syllables, with a caesura after the seventh or fifth syllable, respectively, and he favored the exclusive use of feminine rhymes.[2] However, Trediakovsky introduced one crucial difference: instead of just specifying a constant stress on the penultimate syllable of the line (for the sake of the feminine rhyme), he talked in terms of feet, which implied a regular alternation of stressed and unstressed syllables. Trediakovsky did not include in his schema all the features of what was to become the syllabo-tonic system—for instance, he did not use ternary feet, and he favored trochees over iambs—but he did take the crucial first step.

The second step came just four years later, when Mikhail Lomonosov, then studying in Germany, composed "Letter on the Rules of Russian Versification." Lomonosov had taken to Germany a copy of Trediakovsky's "Method," but while abroad he was influenced by German verse practice, which already employed the syllabo-tonic system.[3] His theory went beyond Trediakovsky's proposals in at least seven ways. First, unlike Trediakovsky (who considered all monosyllables stressed), Lomonosov distinguished between those that carry stress (*khram, sviat*) and others (*zhe, da*) that do not.[4] Second, Lomonosov abandoned reliance on the old syllabic lines and admitted lines varying in length from trimeters to hexameters. Next, his system included ternary meters (anapests and dactyls—he said nothing about the amphibrach) in addition to the binary meters allowed by Trediakovsky. Fourth, he did not favor trochees; on the contrary, he noted that iambs are especially effective in solemn odes. Again contrary to Trediakovsky's practice, Lomonosov employed masculine and dactylic as well as feminine rhyme; furthermore, he advocated using alternating as well as adjacent rhyme. Sixth, Lomonosov made the caesura an optional feature even in long lines. Finally, he remarked that iambs and trochees are opposed to each other and did not recommend using both in the same line.

While Lomonosov's theory marked the end of the syllabic system in Russian poetry,[5] it still differs from modern verse theory in two important details. First, according to Lomonosov, an unfulfilled ictus (what he termed a "pyrrhic foot") was a defect, and he suggested avoiding it except in songs, which he regarded as a less serious type of poetry. However, attempting to fulfill all ictuses is unnatural in Russian, where stress occurs only once in every 2.7 or 2.8 syllables. Neither German poetry, which apparently inspired Lomonosov's statement, nor his own early syllabo-tonic poetry followed this rule absolutely, but at the start Lomonosov attempted to stress as many ictuses as possible. Soon, possibly in part because of the influence of Aleksandr Sumarokov's poetry of the mid-1740s, Lomonosov's own practice became freer, and by the end of the decade he was ignoring his own stricture against so-called pyrrhic feet.[6] Second, Lomonosov originally believed that iambs and anapests could be mixed on the same line to create another meter, as could trochees and dactyls. In fact, both trochees and dactyls appear in the Greek and Latin hexameter line, which has been used on occasion in Russian poetry (see the beginning of chapter 3),[7] but the concept of combining different "feet" on the same line was essentially foreign to Russian syllabo-tonic poetry.

After Lomonosov's theory the tide in favor of syllabo-tonic poetry met little resistance. One of the few defenders of syllabic verse, Antiokh Kantemir, wrote "Letter of Khariton Makentin to a Friend on Composing Russian Verse" in 1743. Since the name in the title is an anagram of Kantemir's, he was clearly replying to Trediakovsky's "Method." Kantemir clung to the basic principle of syllabic poetry, believing that it was superfluous to consider feet in composing verse.[8] He suggested several reforms in the syllabic system that would have increased the likelihood of a trochaic cadence in the first half of the line, as in Trediakovsky's "Method,"[9] but his effort to maintain the tenets of syllabic poetry had little effect on his younger colleagues. In 1752 Trediakovsky published a new version of his "Method" in which he accepted most of the changes advocated by Lomonosov and moved much closer to modern verse theory.[10] By the 1770s when Sumarokov composed the essay "On Versification," the general understanding of syllabo-tonic poetry differed little from our own. Sumarokov was the first to mention the amphibrach and thus the first to list the five types of meter that make up classical Russian verse: iambs, trochees, anapests, dactyls, and amphibrachs. He also recognized that the spondee and the pyrrhic were not independent feet but result from permissible rhythmic variations in trochaic and iambic lines.[11] In just forty years syllabo-tonic prosody had become fully established.

Although the dominance of classical meters has been challenged in the twentieth century, it is used by nearly all Russian poets in most of their poetry. Classical Russian syllabo-tonic poetry requires fixed intervals between the ictuses, or positions that take stress. If the number of syllables between stresses varies throughout the line, then the poem is written in one of the nonclassical meters or in free verse. Classical poetry consists of the binary and ternary meters—such as iambic trimeter, trochaic hexameter, and dactylic tetrameter. However, the lengths of lines may vary within a poem. When the different lengths form a regular pattern, the poem is said to be *raznostopnyi* (in unequal feet) or written in a mixed (*smeshannyi*) meter. Thus a poem may contain iambic tetrameter lines alternating with others in iambic dimeter, or amphibrachic tetrameter lines alternating with amphibrachic trimeter. As long as the same pattern is repeated, the alternation may be quite complex. For example, in the following poem by Blok the first and third lines of each stanza are written in iambic tetrameter, the second in iambic dimeter, and the fourth in iambic trimeter:

Испу́гом схва́чена, влеко́ма   ◡∸◡∸◡_◡∸◡
    В водоворо́т...   ◡_◡∸
Как э́та ко́мната знако́ма!   ◡∸◡∸◡_◡∸◡
    И всё наве́к пройдёт?   ◡∸◡∸◡∸

И, в у́жасе, несвя́зно ше́пчет...   ◡∸◡_◡∸◡∸◡
    И скры́в лицо́,   ◡∸◡∸
Пугли́вых ру́к свива́ет кре́пче   ◡∸◡∸◡∸◡∸◡
    Певу́чее кольцо́...   ◡∸◡_◡∸

...И у́тра пе́рвый лу́ч звеня́щий   ◡∸◡∸◡∸◡∸◡
    Сквозь жёлтых што́р...   ◡∸◡∸
И че́ртит бо́г на те́ле спя́щей   ◡∸◡∸◡∸◡∸◡
    Свой светово́й узо́р.   ◡_◡∸◡∸

                    1914

When line lengths alternate irregularly, the meter is called variable (*vol' nyi*); such verse will be discussed later in the chapter.

I follow Russian scholars by including imitations of certain verse forms in classical (Greek and Latin) poetry—such as the hexameter line—among the types of nonclassical Russian verse.[12] On the other hand, I depart from their practice by identifying two other types of poetry as classical. Thus the 5 + 5 trochaic line from folk verse (*piatislozhnik*) is best thought of as a type of binary meter with strong caesura and will be discussed along with other types of strong caesura at the end of the section dealing with binary meters.[13] Poems mixing various ternary meters, such as amphibrachs and anapests, are often called ternary meters with a variable anacrusis; these too will be considered classical.[14] Such poems meet the main criterion for Russian classical verse, since they have fixed intervals between stresses. Furthermore, poets have combined the various ternary meters regularly since the nineteenth century and have apparently treated this construction as an accepted variant within the syllabo-tonic tradition.[15] And since ternary meters, at least throughout the nineteenth century, only rarely omit stress on an ictus, all three types of ternary meters (dactyls, amphibrachs, and anapests) exhibit a similar inner structure. Therefore varying the anacrusis and thus mixing the types of meters does not greatly interrupt the rhythm of the poetry. In this regard ternary meters do not resemble iambs and trochees. The interaction of Taranovsky's two laws causes iambic and trochaic lines of the same length to favor different stress patterns; hence the rhythms of, for instance, iambic tetrameter and trochaic tetrameter lines are usually quite distinct from each other. Poets, therefore, have rarely mixed iambic and trochaic meters in a poem, although this feature is occasionally found in folk verse.[16]

BINARY METERS

Binary meters may vary in length from one to more than eight feet, though in the vast majority of poems the range is from three to six. In iambic meters the odd syllables form the weak positions and do not normally carry stress. The even syllables form the strong positions, or ictuses; these tend to be stressed, though stress may be omitted on any ictus except for the final one in the line. In trochaic meters the odd syllables are strong and the even weak. The weak positions in binary meters may occasionally contain a stress (hypermetrical stressing), though in these cases stressing is limited to monosyllabic words. In iambic meters hypermetrical stressing occurs most often on the first syllable of the line. At times the hypermetrical stress will be followed by an unstressed second syllable; therefore the first metrical stress does not occur until the fourth syllable of the line. Tiutchev showed a particular fondness for this rhythmic feature; in the following example, it occurs in the even lines, along with another hypermetrical stress in the first.

День – сей блистательный покров –
День, земнородных оживленье,
Души болящей исцеленье,
Друг человеков и богов!

1831-39

The first two lines of this passage from Vladislav Khodasevich likewise exhibit hypermetrical stressing:

Глаз отдыхает, слух не слышит,
Жизнь потаённо хороша,
И небом невозбранно дышит
Почти свободная душа.

1921

The following discussion proceeds through the iambic meters in order of their approximate popularity over the years. The trochaic meters are then covered in a similar fashion, though with somewhat less detail—partly because some of what is said about the iambic meters applies here as well, partly because historically the trochaic meters have been less important in Russian poetry than their iambic counterparts.

IAMBIC TETRAMETER

The iambic tetrameter has been employed in so many genres and has been the favorite meter of so many poets that it is difficult to discern particular trends. It was used early on by Lomonosov in "Ode on the Taking of Khotin," the poem many consider the first written according to the rules of modern Russian prosody. Since then, Pushkin, Tiutchev, Lermontov, Afanasy Fet, Nikolai Nekrasov, Blok, Bely, Valery Briusov, and a host of other poets have favored this meter above all others. It has been popular in odes, elegies, lyric poetry, and narrative poems, and is the meter Pushkin chose for his "novel in verse," *Eugene*

TABLE 3
Rhythmic Variations of the Iambic Tetrameter

Number of Omitted Stresses	Number of Variation	Form	Example
0	I	∪́∪́∪́∪́ (∪)	Жени́х бледнёл и бро́ви сдви́нул
1	II	∪–∪́∪́∪́ (∪)	Воспомина́ния пре́жних ле́т
	III	∪́∪–∪́∪́ (∪)	Нера́достным веща́ют зво́ном
	IV	∪́∪́∪–∪́ (∪)	Её свята́я красота́
2	V	∪́∪–∪–∪́ (∪)	Над ру́хнувшею баррика́дой
	VI	∪–∪́∪–∪́ (∪)	Благоуха́нную сига́ру
	VII	∪–∪–∪́∪́ (∪)	Мы материали́сты с ва́ми
3	VIII	∪–∪–∪–∪́ (∪)	Хоть и не без предубежде́нья

Onegin. While the iambic tetrameter was used in fewer works during the eighteenth century than either variable iambs or the iambic hexameter, it moved into first place by the 1820s; in every decade since it has been either first or second in popularity among Russian poets.

The schema for the iambic tetrameter is as follows: ∪–∪–∪–∪́ (∪). Two ways to describe the usage of this or any other meter in a poem are as follows: "horizontally," that is, to consider all the possible rhythmic variations of lines written in the meter and then to see how often each of these variations is employed; and "vertically," to count how often each ictus carries a stress in all the lines of a poem.

The first method becomes awkward when used with some of the longer meters, since so many rhythmic variations can occur.[17] However, the method is practical when employing the iambic tetrameter, which has just eight possible variations. The numbering on table 3 and for the other binary meters described in this chapter follows that of Taranovsky;[18] variations V through VII of the iambic tetrameter are ordered differently by some scholars. All the examples of iambic tetrameter lines, except for the seventh, are taken from three poems in Andrei Bely's collection *Ashes* (*Pepel*, 1909). Only variants I through IV and VI are common; the fifth is generally rare since most Russian poets tend to avoid two unstressed ictuses in a row. Numbers VII and VIII exist more in theory than in practice. Variant VII is taken from Andrei Voznesensky's poem "Table Manners" ("Pravila povedeniia za stolom," 1971); most other occurrences of the seventh variant in actual poems turn out,

TABLE 4
Stressing and Rhythmic Variations in the Iambic Tetrameter

	Stressing (by ictus)				Rhythmic Variations						Average Stressing (for all ictuses)
	I	II	III	IV	I	II	III	IV	V	VI	
1. 18th century	93.2%	79.7%	53.2%	100%	31.1%	3.4%	18.7%	41.9%	1.5%	3.4%	81.5%
2. 1814–20	87.7	87.7	43.2	100	27.2	5.2	10.9	48.3	1.4	7.1	79.7
3. Pushkin (1814–20)	90.5	90.5	40.8	100	27.3	4.3	9.2	53.7	0.3	5.2	80.5
4. Pushkin (Onegin)	84.4	89.9	43.1	100	26.8	6.6	9.7	47.5	0.4	9.0	79.4
5. 19th century (younger poets)	82.1	96.8	34.6	100	24.9	6.7	3.0	54.0	0.2	11.2	78.4
6. Early 20th century	83.5	87.4	49.1	100	30.0	7.9	11.2	40.9	1.4	8.6	80.0
7. Soviet poets (older)	81.4	87.5	45.2	100			—				78.5
8. Soviet poets (younger)	82.3	84.2	47.3	100			—				78.4
9. Evtushenko (1963–64)	74.5	99.5	40.0	99.5			—				78.4
10. Evtushenko ("Na smert' sobaki"—40 lines)	60.0	97.5	45.0	100	17.5	27.5	0.0	40.0	2.5	12.5	75.6
11. Akhmadulina (1962–68)	83.5	68.0	51.0	100			—				75.6
12. Akhmadulina ("Son"—44 lines)	84.1	65.9	70.5	100	27.3	9.1	34.1	22.7	0.0	6.8	80.1

Sources: Figures for lines 1–5 come from tables 2 and 3 appended to Taranovsky, *Ruski dvodelni ritmovi*; line 6 is from idem, "O ritmicheskoi strukture russkikh dvuslozhnykh razmerov," p. 428; lines 7–9 and 11 are from Gasparov, "Iamb i khorei sovetskikh poetov," p. 91; lines 10 and 12 are based on my own calculations.

upon closer inspection, to have a possible weak stress on the first ictus (cf. the line как бы погружено́ в весне́ in Tiutchev, where the бы may carry a weak stress).[19] Variant VIII is also extremely rare; Bely himself called his use of this example in "The Wedding" ("Svad'ba," 1906) "unsuccessful."[20]

The second method involves finding the percentage of times that a given ictus is stressed in all the lines of a poem and comparing that percentage against the figures for other poems—perhaps with the poet's other works in that meter or with a particular period in Russian poetry. While stress on the fourth ictus in the iambic tetrameter is a constant, stress on the other three may vary considerably. The relative frequency of stressing among the ictuses indicates the rhythmic structure of the poem as a whole. In theory the figures showing the usage of each rhythmic variation (the horizontal analysis) can also provide information about the percentage of stressing on each ictus. For instance, only variations IV, V, and VI (the eighth is virtually never met in practice) omit stress on the third ictus. By adding the percentage of times that each form appears and then subtracting that figure from 100, it is possible to obtain the percentage of stressing for the third ictus. However, carrying out this operation mentally for three or four ictuses at once is difficult; therefore, even when percentages for rhythmic variations are given, a separate set of figures for the vertical picture, or stressing on each ictus, is normally provided as well.

Both methods of analysis require accurate marking of stressed and unstressed syllables. As mentioned in the introduction, Russian stress offers far fewer ambiguities than English. A number of monosyllabic and a few bisyllabic words in Russian are normally considered to be unstressed; these include conjunctions, prepositions, and particles. Nouns, verbs, and adjectives almost always have a single stress. The main problems occur with pronouns and some adverbs. These can be considered as stressed, but stress on them is clearly weaker than on nouns or verbs.[21] Most poets treat them as either stressed or unstressed, depending on the needs of the meter. In my own scansion I count these words as stressed if they coincide with an ictus and as unstressed if they do not. However, if the syntax indicates that they receive a strong phrase stress, then I mark them as stressed even when they appear at a weak position.

The figures in table 4 point to the existence of two main variants in the use of the iambic tetrameter. As noted above, when Lomonosov first introduced the meter, he attempted to stress virtually every ictus. After he recognized the need to omit stress at least occasionally, he and other eighteenth-century poets still tried to mark the iambic cadence at the beginning of the line by stressing the first ictus. During the early nineteenth century stress on the first and third ictuses began to weaken and that on the second to strengthen.[22] By the 1820s a whole new type of rhythm had come to the fore. In the eighteenth century stress was strongest at the beginning and at the end of the line. During the Pushkin era the line developed a wavelike structure, with strong stresses on the second and fourth ictuses alternating with weaker stresses on the first and third. Around the beginning of the twentieth century poets once again began to experiment with the rhythm of the iambic tetrameter. Many poets, in at least some of their work, began to use a form that was closer to the eighteenth-century model. Today both types of iambic tetrameter coexist, though individual poets generally show a clear preference for one type over the other.[23]

Why these types of rhythm? The two tendencies, or laws, discovered by Taranovsky conflict in the iambic tetrameter. The "stabilization of the first ictus after the first weak position" implies a strong first ictus. The law of regressive accentual dissimilation, on the other hand, implies a strong second ictus and weak third and first ictuses. During the eighteenth century, the first tendency predominated among poets, as the first stanza of this ode by Sumarokov reveals:

Взойди́, багря́ная Авро́ра,	⏑́⏑́⏑́⏑_⏑́⏑
Споко́йно в ти́хи небеса́!	⏑́⏑́⏑́⏑_⏑́
В луга́х цветы́ рассы́пли, Фло́ра,	⏑́⏑́⏑́⏑́⏑
Цвета́ми украси́ леса́!	⏑́⏑_⏑́⏑́
Победоно́сных во́йск успе́хом	⏑_⏑́⏑́⏑́⏑
Разда́йся по доли́нам э́хом,	⏑́⏑_⏑́⏑́⏑
Прия́тный, вожделе́нный гла́с:	⏑́⏑_⏑́⏑́
"Войну́ судьби́на оконча́ла	⏑́⏑́⏑_⏑́⏑
И но́вым ла́вром увенча́ла	⏑́⏑́⏑_⏑́⏑
Мона́рхиню и с не́ю на́с!"	⏑́⏑_⏑́⏑́

1771

Unlike Lomonosov in his early poetry, Sumarokov readily omitted stress—only one of the ten lines contains stress on all four ictuses. In this short excerpt Sumarokov omitted stress on the second ictus more often than was usual in the eighteenth century, but otherwise the stanza adheres closely to the predominant rhythmic pattern of the time. Stress is omitted on the first ictus just once, but four times on the third. The fourth and the third rhythmic variations are, as expected, quite common—between them they account for eight of the ten lines. The law of regressive accentual dissimilation has little effect on either the first or the second ictus, but the law favoring stress on the ictus after the first weak position helps bring about the strong stressing on the first ictus.

The dominant rhythmic patterns began to change during the second decade of the nineteenth century, and here Pushkin's work closely reflects the tendencies of all Russian poetry of the time (table 4, lines 2–3). Poets began to stress the second ictus more often and to weaken the third noticeably. The fourth rhythmic variation, which omits stress on the third ictus, became still more common; fully stressed lines (the first rhythmic variation) appeared less often.

И днесь учи́тесь, о цари́:	∪⌣∪⌣∪—∪⌣
Ни наказа́нья, ни награ́ды,	∪—∪⌣∪⌣∪⌣∪
Ни кро́в темни́ц, ни алтари́	∪⌣∪⌣∪—∪⌣
Не ве́рные для ва́с огра́ды.	∪⌣∪—∪⌣∪⌣∪
Склони́тесь пе́рвые главо́й	∪⌣∪⌣∪—∪⌣
Под се́нь надёжную зако́на,	∪⌣∪⌣∪—∪⌣∪
И ста́нут ве́чной стра́жей тро́на	∪⌣∪⌣∪⌣∪⌣∪
Наро́дов во́льность и поко́й.	∪⌣∪⌣∪—∪⌣

Pushkin, in a stanza from his poem "Liberty" ("Vol'nost'," 1817), continued to stress the first ictus regularly, but then made a much clearer distinction between the next two ictuses: the second is quite strong, while the third is by far the weakest in the line.

Thus the effect of regressive accentual dissimilation spread to the second ictus in the line; within a few years Pushkin and his contemporaries were writing poetry in which this tendency affected the first ictus as well, weakening it and thereby causing a distinct alternation of strong and weak ictuses throughout the entire line. Typical is the following stanza from *Eugene Onegin*:

Им овладе́ло беспоко́йство,	∪—∪⌣∪—∪⌣∪
Охо́та к переме́не ме́ст	∪⌣∪—∪⌣∪⌣
(Весьма́ мучи́тельное сво́йство,	∪⌣∪⌣∪⌣∪⌣∪
Немно́гих доброво́льный кре́ст).	∪⌣∪—∪⌣∪⌣
Оста́вил он своё селе́нье,	∪⌣∪⌣∪⌣∪⌣∪
Лесо́в и ни́в уедине́нье,	∪⌣∪⌣∪—∪⌣∪
Где окрова́вленная те́нь	∪—∪⌣∪—∪⌣
Ему́ явля́лась ка́ждый де́нь,	∪⌣∪⌣∪⌣∪⌣
И на́чал стра́нствия без це́ли,	∪⌣∪⌣∪—∪⌣∪
Досту́пный чу́вству одному́;	∪⌣∪⌣∪—∪⌣
И путеше́ствия ему́,	∪—∪⌣∪—∪⌣
Как всё на све́те, надое́ли;	∪⌣∪⌣∪—∪⌣∪
Он возврати́лся и попа́л,	∪—∪⌣∪—∪⌣
Как Ча́цкий, с корабля́ на ба́л.	∪⌣∪—∪⌣∪⌣

1829-30

The rhythmic tendencies of Pushkin's work from the 1820s on became even more pronounced in the poems of younger writers (table 4, lines 4–5). As the first ictus weakened and the second became stronger; the sixth rhythmic variation, which omits stress on both the first and third ictuses, became more widely used. The third rhythmic variation, which lacks stress on the second ictus, became more rare. Eventually the iambic tetrameter lines occasionally inclined toward splitting into two halves, since the weak first and strong second ictuses at the beginning of the line came to mirror the weak third and strong fourth ictuses at the end. As a result, parallels in syntax and intonation sometimes occurred between the two halves of the line.[24]

At the beginning of the twentieth century several important poets such as Briusov and Bely began to cultivate the eighteenth-century rhythm in some of their poetry. Bely in turn developed a new form of the iambic tetrameter in which the second ictus—rather than the third—became the weakest in the line. He used this rhythm in various poems written between 1904 and 1909: Stressing on the first ictus is high (86.9 percent), that on the second is very low (43.3 percent), and the third is relatively high (67.7 percent). The frequency of the third rhythmic variation jumps to 50.8 percent while that of the first (10.1 percent) and fourth (20.1 percent) drop sharply. The normally rare fifth variation, which omits stress on the second and third ictuses, shows up with unaccustomed regularity (5.9 percent). Overall stressing becomes less frequent, as on the average fewer than 75 percent of all the ictuses are fulfilled.[25]

The rhythm introduced by Bely did not become well established. According to Gasparov's figures, no single contemporary poet appeared to follow it in the majority of his poetry,[26] although several poets adopted the rhythm from time to time. Some poets now follow the rhythmic pattern of the eighteenth century by stressing the first ictus more often than the second, while others have continued to work in the nineteenth-century tradition. Thus the percentages for the twentieth century (table 4, lines 7–8) are less meaningful than those for earlier periods, when nearly all poets were adhering to the same general patterns. Now the composite figures only mask the opposing manners of Evgeny Evtushenko, who alternates strong and weak ictuses even more noticeably than most nineteenth-century poets, and of Bella Akhmadulina, whose poems often have approximately the same rhythmic structure as works of two centuries ago.

An excerpt from Evtushenko's "On the Death of a Dog" ("Na smert' sobaki") illustrates one type of rhythm prevalent among contemporary poets:

Подсти́лку в ко́рчах распоро́в,	∪∪́∪∪́∪∪∪∪́
он навсегда́ проща́лся с на́ми	∪∪∪∪́∪∪́∪∪́∪
под сто́н подо́пытных коро́в	∪∪́∪∪́∪∪∪∪́
в ветерина́рном гря́зном хра́ме.	∪∪∪∪́∪∪́∪∪́∪
Во фра́зах не витиева́т,	∪∪́∪∪∪∪∪∪́
сосредото́ченно рассе́ян,	∪∪∪∪́∪∪∪∪́∪
напо́лнил шприц ветерина́р	∪∪́∪∪∪∪∪∪́
его́ уби́йственным спасе́ньем.	∪∪́∪∪́∪∪∪∪́∪
Уткну́лась Га́ля мне́ в плечо́.	∪∪́∪∪́∪∪́∪∪́
Невыноси́мо милосе́рдье,	∪∪∪∪́∪∪∪∪́∪
когда́ еди́нственное – что́	∪∪́∪∪́∪∪∪∪́
мы мо́жем сде́лать – по́мощь сме́ртью.	∪∪́∪∪́∪∪́∪∪́∪

1969

The percentages for stressing and rhythmic variations throughout the poem are provided in line 10 of table 4. While even forty lines do not provide a large enough sample from which to draw broad statistical conclusions, the analysis of a single poem can still show the rough outline of a particular rhythmic pattern. Here the comparison with Evtushenko's use of this meter over a two-year period (line 9) as well as the contrast with Akhmadulina's iambic tetrameter poems (lines 11 and 12) is instructive. Except for the lighter than usual stressing on the first ictus, the poem is close to the typical rhythm of Evtushenko's work. He makes the second ictus a virtual constant (in this poem only one line of forty lacks stress on that ictus) and prefers to keep the first ictus relatively weak. Had the statistics for this poem been placed directly below line 5 in the table, they would represent a culmination of the tendencies that began in the 1810s, became prominent in the 1820s, and were further strengthened throughout the rest of the nineteenth century.

Akhmadulina, on the other hand, strengthens the first ictus and weakens the second. As a whole, her iambic tetrameter poetry resembles that of the eighteenth century (lines 1 and 11), although she tends to omit stress more often throughout the line. Occasionally, however, she deviates from this format:

Но незнако́мый садово́д	∪∪∪∪́∪∪∪∪́
возде́лывает са́д знако́мый	∪∪́∪∪∪∪́∪∪́∪
и говори́т, что о́н зако́нный	∪∪∪∪́∪∪́∪∪́∪
владе́лец. И войти́ зове́т.	∪∪́∪∪∪∪́∪∪́

Войти? Как можно? Столько раз   ∪́∪́∪́∪́
я знала здесь печаль и гордость,   ∪́∪́∪́∪́∪
и нежную шагов нетвёрдость,   ∪́∪∪∪́∪́∪
и нежную незрячесть глаз.   ∪́∪∪∪́∪́

Уж минуло так много дней,   ∪́∪∪́∪́∪́
а нежность – облаком вчерашним,   ∪́∪́∪∪∪́∪
а нежность – обмороком влажным   ∪́∪́∪∪∪́∪
меня омыла у дверей.   ∪́∪́∪∪∪́

[1960's]

Here the third ictus is actually stressed more often than the second, which now becomes the weakest in the poem (line 12). In other words, the rhythm is similar to that used by Bely in some of the poetry he wrote between 1904 and 1909. Akhmadulina does not make the second ictus as weak as Bely did, nor does she use as few fully stressed lines, but in this poem she too favors the third rhythmic variant (omission of stress on the second ictus) over the fourth.

This last example warns us specifically about the use of statistics and secondarily about the study of metrics. Even though a composite picture of metric practice for an entire period or for all of a poet's work may contain much information, looking more closely at individual works or poets is often necessary. Thus the overall statistics on Soviet poetry of the past several decades do not reveal the great variety in different poets' usage of the iambic tetrameter. Furthermore, as Taranovsky has shown in his study of Bely's iambic tetrameter, a poet may use different rhythmic patterns from one period to the next or may write poems with quite different rhythms during the same period. In addition, thematic connections may exist among poems using a particular rhythmic pattern.[27] Other studies of the iambic tetrameter in poets ranging from Nekrasov to Voznesensky have borne out Taranovsky's findings.[28] Vast statistical surveys are adequate for indicating the background and the dominant tendencies of a given era or poet, but the analysis of specific poems or groups of poems against that background is often necessary to elucidate more subtle qualities.

IAMBIC PENTAMETER

Throughout much of the twentieth century the iambic pentameter has rivaled the iambic tetrameter as the most popular of Russian meters, but it did not become widely used until the nineteenth century. K. D. Vishnevsky, in his extensive survey of eighteenth-century poetry, examined over six thousand works; of these only fourteen were written in iambic pentameter.[29] Lomonosov was the first to use the meter in a translation of Horace's *Exegi monumentum* made especially for *Short Guide to Rhetoric*.[30]

Я знак бессмертия себе воздвигнул	⏑⎯⏑⎯⏑⎯‖⏑⎯⏑⎯⏑
Превыше пирамид и крепче меди,	⏑⎯⏑⎯⏑⎯‖⏑⎯⏑⎯⏑
Что бурный аквилон сотреть не может,	⏑⎯⏑⎯⏑⎯‖⏑⎯⏑⎯⏑
Ни множество веков, ни едка древность.	⏑⎯⏑⎯⏑⎯‖⏑⎯⏑⎯⏑
Не вовсе я умру; но смерть оставит	⏑⎯⏑⎯⏑⎯‖⏑⎯⏑⎯⏑
Велику часть мою, как жизнь скончаю.	⏑⎯⏑⎯⏑⎯‖⏑⎯⏑⎯⏑
Я буду возрастать повсюду славой,	⏑⎯⏑⎯⏑⎯‖⏑⎯⏑⎯⏑
Пока великий Рим владеет светом.	⏑⎯⏑⎯⏑⎯‖⏑⎯⏑⎯⏑

[1744]

Superficially, the form is close to that of the iambic pentameter as popularized by Pushkin in *Boris Godunov* and other works, for the verse here is unrhymed and contains a caesura. However, in the nineteenth century the caesura appeared after the second foot instead of the third, and the line endings were not exclusively feminine, as they are here. Lomonosov's poem seems to have had little influence on subsequent poetry, including his own. He wrote virtually nothing in this meter afterward, and examples of the iambic pentameter among other eighteenth-century poets are similarly isolated. However, shortly after Vasily Zhukovsky, along with Pushkin, began to use the meter in the second decade of the nineteenth century, it began to play an important role in Russian poetry. By the 1820s the meter appeared frequently in lyric poetry, and Pushkin, thanks largely to the example of *Boris Godunov*, made the unrhymed iambic pentameter a fixture of drama, especially historical drama.[31] The meter appears in Pushkin's *Little Tragedies*, as well as in plays by Aleksandr Ostrovsky and in Aleksei K. Tolstoi's trilogy devoted to Ivan the Terrible and Boris Godunov. Perhaps because of its association with the English unrhymed version of the same meter, the iambic pentameter is the only verse form in Russian to have an extensive tradition of unrhymed poetry. For example, Blok's "Free Thoughts" (*"Vol'nye mysli,"* 1907) as well as numerous original and translated plays from the end of the nineteenth and the beginning of the twentieth century used unrhymed iambic pentameter.[32] Throughout the nineteenth century the iambic pentameter, usually with rhyme, was found in lyric poetry as well. But the meter remained a relatively minor form until the period from 1890 to 1920, when it grew steadily in usage to the position it has maintained until the present.[33]

TABLE 5
Rhythmic Variations of the Iambic Pentameter

Number of Omitted Stresses	Number of Variation	Form	Example
0	I	⏑´⏑´⏑´⏑´⏑´(⏑)	Трещáл морóз, дерéвья взя́ли в крýжке
1	II	⏑´⏑´⏑´⏑—´⏑´(⏑)	И озари́ли чáсть егó на ди́во
	III	⏑´⏑´⏑´⏑—´⏑´(⏑)	Врывáются ищá губáми гýб
	IV	⏑´⏑´⏑—´—´⏑´(⏑)	Желéзных кры́ш авторитéтный тéзис
	V	⏑´⏑´⏑´⏑—´⏑´(⏑)	Прострáнство спи́т, влюблённое в прострáнство
2	VI	⏑—´⏑´—´⏑´⏑´(⏑)	Как позапрóшлый и как прóшлый гóд
	VII	⏑—´⏑´—´⏑´⏑´(⏑)	И полубóгом сдéлался поэ́т
	VIII	⏑—´⏑´—´⏑—´⏑´(⏑)	Нарéзавшись до положéнья ри́з
	IX	⏑—´⏑´—´⏑—´⏑´(⏑)	И фы́ркали, салáт пересоли́в
	X	⏑´⏑´—´⏑—´⏑´(⏑)	Готóв к прищéствно сверхчеловéка
3	XI	⏑—´⏑´—´—´⏑´(⏑)	По вдохновéнью, а не по устáву
	XII	⏑´⏑´—´—´—´(⏑)	Им вы́несено и совершенó
2	XIII	⏑—´⏑´—´⏑´⏑´(⏑)	Лишь удесятери́л слепýю си́лу
3	XIV	⏑—´⏑´—´—´⏑´(⏑)	И одухотворя́лся и теря́л
	XV	⏑—´⏑´—´—´⏑´(⏑)	—
4	XVI	⏑—´⏑´—´—´—´(⏑)	—

The schema for the iambic pentameter is as follows: ∪‒∪‒∪‒∪‒
∪‒(∪). While the tetrameter has only eight possible variations, there
are theoretically sixteen different variations for the iambic pentameter
without caesura (actually, numbers XV and XVI are virtually unknown
in practice). Table 5 gives examples for the remaining fourteen; all but
one are from Boris Pasternak's narrative poem *Spektorskii* (1925–31).
The example of the rare variation XII is from his lyric "The Victor"
("Pobeditel'," 1944). Variations XIII through XVI are set off from the
first twelve by a line because of the impossibility of their usage in works
with a caesura after the second foot; the obligatory word break would
require at least one stress among the first four syllables. Since Russian
poetry tends to avoid consecutive unstressed ictuses, numbers VIII, X,
and XI are all among the less-used variations. However, numbers XII
through XIV are the rarest of the lines that are used at all; they are prac-
tically absent from nineteenth-century poetry, and each occurs only
about three or four times per ten thousand lines of poetry in James
Bailey's extensive survey of this meter for the period 1890–1922.[34] In
the case of variation XII, not two but three unstressed ictuses occur in a
row. As for variants XIII and XIV, Taranovsky has pointed out that Rus-
sian poetry tends to stress the first ictus following a weak position in the
line. If that ictus is not stressed, then the likelihood of stressing the fol-
lowing ictus becomes all the greater. Therefore consecutive unstressed
ictuses at the beginning of a line, as in variants XIII and XIV, will be
extremely uncommon. By comparison, note that the seventh variation
of the iambic tetrameter (∪‒∪‒∪‒∪‒) almost never occurs in practice.
The fully stressed variation is more difficult to maintain here than in the
iambic tetrameter and therefore is used less often (generally about one
line in five instead of one in three or four). Once again, forms that omit
stress on the next-to-last ictus are particularly common; variants V, VII,
and IX all share both this feature and another—they do not contain any
consecutive unstressed ictuses; therefore they are among the most
widely used variations of this meter.

The history of the iambic pentameter is complicated by the appear-
ance of the caesura after the fourth syllable. When the meter was first
introduced, the caesura was virtually obligatory, but as early as 1830
Pushkin himself switched to writing poetry without it. Throughout the
rest of the nineteenth century and into the twentieth a number of poets
resorted to a movable caesura that may shift to a neighboring syllable in
a certain percentage of lines.[35] Meanwhile, the constant caesura had vir-

tually gone out of use by the end of the nineteenth century, and since the
time of Pushkin a growing number of poets have preferred to use no
caesura at all.[36]

The effect of the caesura on the rhythm has been discussed briefly in
the introduction, but now it will be helpful to consider the matter more
closely. Below is an excerpt from *Boris Godunov*, which has a constant
caesura, and another from Pushkin's *Mozart and Salieri*, which lacks it:

Смиряй себя молитвой и постом,
И сны твои видений лёгких будут
Исполнены. Доныне – если я,
Невольною дремотой обессилен,
Не сотворю молитвы долгой к ночи –
Мой старый сон не тих и не безгрешен;
Мне чудятся то шумные пиры,
То ратный стан, то схватки боевые,
Безумные потехи юных лет!

1825

Не бросил ли я всё, что прежде знал,
Что так любил, чему так жарко верил,
И не пошёл ли бодро вслед за ним
Безропотно, как тот, кто заблуждался
И встречным послан в сторону иную?
Усильным, напряжённым постоянством
Я наконец в искусстве безграничном
Достигнул степени высокой. Слава
Мне улыбнулась; я в сердцах людей
Нашёл созвучия своим созданьям.

1830

As these examples and table 6 indicate, the caesura affects the third
ictus most directly. In poems with a caesura, the third ictus is stressed
almost constantly in order to reestablish the rhythm after the break.
Stressing on the fourth ictus, which is surrounded by one constantly
stressed ictus (the fifth) and one on which stressing is almost a constant,
falls to a relatively low level. When the caesura is not used, stressing on
the third ictus remains high, as is predicted by the law of regressive ac-
centual dissimilation, but there is no need for it to be a near constant. As
a result, stressing throughout the line becomes more even. (In the ex-
ample from *Mozart and Salieri* I have indicated hypermetrical stressing
on certain monosyllabic pronouns that usually are considered un-
stressed. Given the nature of Salieri's monologue, there is reason to as-
sume that the personal pronoun *I* should be stressed throughout. In any
case, these stresses do not alter the main rhythmic impulse of the pas-

TABLE 7
Rhythmic Variations in the Iambic Pentameter

	I	II	III	IV	V	VI	VII	VIII	IX	X	XI	XII	XIII	XIV
1.	20.0%	7.0%	10.0%	3.4%	29.8%	1.1%	8.6%	1.2%	18.7%	0.1%	0.0%	0.1%	—	—
2.	22.1	5.1	7.5	3.0	36.1	0.7	8.1	0.9	16.4	0.1	0.01	0.01	—	—
3.	15.3	7.0	17.5	11.4	21.8	2.6	10.0	1.3	10.9	2.2	0.0	0.0	0.0	0.0
4.	20.9	7.0	11.6	10.4	24.2	2.6	7.4	1.3	13.5	0.9	0.2	0.0	0.0	0.0
5.	22.4	4.8	7.2	7.4	33.6	1.7	7.3	0.9	14.0	0.5	0.13	0.03	0.01	0.03
6.	22.7	6.8	12.5	8.9	24.2	2.3	6.7	1.3	13.6	0.8	0.2	0.01	0.03	0.02
7.	—	—	—	—	—	—	—	—	—	—	—	—	—	—
8.	14.3	0.0	10.7	7.1	25.0	7.1	14.3	0.0	21.4	0.0	0.0	0.0	0.0	0.0
9.	4.2	0.0	8.3	12.5	33.3	0.0	25.0	4.2	12.5	0.0	0.0	0.0	0.0	0.0
10.	16.7	0.0	8.3	16.7	25.0	0.0	8.3	0.0	16.7	8.3	0.0	0.0	0.0	0.0

Sources: See table 6.

sage.) In the excerpt from *Boris Godunov* (nine lines), the five ictuses are stressed eight, five, nine, four, and nine times. Thus a sharp distinction exists between the strong and weak ictuses. The second quotation has ten lines, and the ictuses are stressed seven, seven, eight, six, and ten times—lessening the distinction between strong and weak ictuses. A similar phenomenon is observed when the works as a whole are compared (table 6, lines 1 and 3) or when poems written throughout the nineteenth century with a caesura are contrasted against those without (lines 2 and 4).[37]

However, whether or not the caesura is present, the approximate contours of the line remain similar. The iambic pentameter has generally used relatively strong first, third, and fifth ictuses, thereby displaying a distinct wavelike progression of strong and weak ictuses, as in these stanzas by Ivan Elagin:

А ра́з уж самолёт пришёлся к сло́ву,	∪∪́—∪∪́∪∪́∪∪́∪
То е́сли к самолёту присмотре́ться,	∪∪́∪—∪∪́∪∪́—∪∪́∪
Легко́ пове́рить Ильфу и Петро́ву,	∪∪́∪∪́∪∪́∪—∪∪́∪
Что э́то то́лько тра́нспортное сре́дство.	∪∪́∪∪́∪∪́∪—∪∪́∪
Пора́ поко́нчить с болтовнёй мисти́чной	∪∪́∪∪́∪—∪∪́∪∪́∪
И позабы́ть про ве́чные зага́дки,	∪—∪∪́∪∪́∪—∪∪́∪
А е́сли ду́мать, то́ о методи́чной,	∪∪́∪∪́∪∪́∪—∪∪́∪
Споко́йной, своевре́менной поса́дке.	∪∪́∪—∪∪́∪—∪∪́∪

[<1982]

As expected, the third, fifth, and ninth rhythmic variations all occur frequently in the poem as a whole (table 7, line 8).

A second type of iambic pentameter rhythm, used in some early poems, loosely follows the structure of the French decasyllable and therefore is sometimes called the "French" form.[38] This pattern occurred in the poetry of Petr Viazemsky by 1820 and has remained a minor tradition in the Russian usage of the iambic pentameter.[39] James Bailey's figures for the alternating and French pattern in lyric poetry from 1890 to 1922 illustrate the differences between the two patterns.[40] In the alternating pattern stress declines from 87.4 percent on the first ictus to 74.6 percent on the second; in the French pattern it *rises* from 81.4 percent to 85.8 percent (stress on the remaining ictuses is about the same in the two patterns). Thus in the French pattern the second ictus becomes at least as strong as the first. Either the second or the third ictus is stressed most often (after the constantly stressed final ictus). Osip Mandelshtam used this form in a number of poems, such as "The Lutheran" ("Liuteranin"):[41]

Я на прогу́лке по́хороны встре́тил   ∪–∪́–∪́–∪–∪́∪
Близ протеста́нтской ки́рки, в воскресе́нье.   ∪–∪́–∪́–∪–∪́∪
Рассе́янный прохо́жий, я заме́тил   ∪́∪–∪–∪́∪–∪́∪
Тех прихожа́н суро́вое волне́нье.   ∪–∪́–∪́∪–∪–∪́∪

Чужа́я речь не достига́ла слу́ха,   ∪́∪∪–∪–∪́∪–∪́∪
И то́лько у́пряжь то́нкая сия́ла,   ∪́∪–∪́∪–∪–∪–∪́∪
Да мостова́я пра́здничная глу́хо   ∪–∪́–∪́∪–∪–∪́∪
Лени́вые подко́вы отража́ла.   ∪́∪–∪–∪́∪–∪–∪́∪

1912

Stressing is light throughout the poem (cf. table 6, line 9), as is usual
for Mandelshtam; in all of the binary meters he generally resorted to
fully stressed lines as little as possible.[42] More than 40 percent of the
lines in "The Lutheran" omit two stresses—for most poets the norm is
25 to 30 percent—and only one line in the entire poem is fully stressed.
Mandelshtam achieved the French rhythm not so much by strengthening
the second ictus as by weakening the first (as well as the fourth), so by
comparison the second and third ictuses are strong.

Taranovsky describes two other types of rhythm for iambic pen-
tameter, both of which arose during the nineteenth century. They were
particularly employed in translations from English (and to a lesser de-
gree, German) dramatic verse.[43] In one, stress falls steadily from the
first through the fourth ictuses; in the other, stressing remains fairly
level for the first three ictuses before falling on the fourth. Both types
were at first limited to translated dramatic works, until Briusov's interest
in rhythmic experimentation led him to introduce the "falling" rhythm
in his original poetry.[44] The level type has remained fairly rare, but since
Briusov's time the falling rhythm has continued to be used in Russian
poetry. An example is Evgeny Vinokurov's brief poem "Adam":

Лени́вым взгля́дом обозре́в окру́гу,   ∪́∪–∪́∪–∪–∪́∪–∪́∪
Он в са́мый пе́рвый де́нь траву́ примя́л   ∪́∪–∪́∪–∪́∪–∪́∪–∪́
И лёг в тени́ смоко́вницы,   ∪–∪́–∪́∪–∪–∪́
                                  и, ру́ку
Заве́дши за́ голову,   ∪́∪–∪–∪́∪–∪–∪́
                                  задрема́л.

Он сла́дко спа́л. Он спа́л невозмути́мо   ∪–∪́∪–∪́∪–∪–∪́∪
Под тишино́й эде́мской синевы́.   ∪–∪–∪́∪–∪–∪́
...Во сне́ он ви́дел пе́чи Освенци́ма   ∪–∪́–∪́∪–∪–∪́∪
И тру́пами напо́лненные рвы́.   ∪́∪–∪–∪́∪–∪–∪́

Свои́х дете́й он ви́дел!..   ∪–∪́∪–∪–∪–∪́∪
                                  В не́ге ра́я
Была́ улы́бка на лице́ светла́.   ∪–∪́–∪–∪́∪–∪́

Дрема́л он, ничего́ не понима́я,   ∪́—∪—∪́—∪—∪́—∪

Не зна́ющий ещё добра́ и зла́.   ∪́—∪—∪—∪́—∪—

1961

Here the first ictus is very strong and the third unusually weak—the two features that distinguish this rhythmic pattern from the other two common patterns of the iambic pentameter. (See tables 6 and 7, line 10 for an analysis of the poem.)

IAMBIC HEXAMETER

The Russian iambic hexameter was derived from the French Alexandrine, a twelve-syllable line with an obligatory phrase stress on the sixth and twelfth syllables as well as a caesura after the sixth syllable. The term *Alexandrine* (*Aleksandriiskii stikh*) is sometimes applied specifically to iambic hexameter poems written in couplets, where paired masculine rhymes alternate with paired feminine. This type of poem remained common well into the nineteenth century and is exemplified by the opening lines of this work by Vladimir Benediktov:

Есть чу́вство а́дское: оно́ вскипи́т в крови́   ∪—∪—∪—‖∪—∪—∪—

И, вы́звав де́монов, всели́т их в ра́й любви́,   ∪—∪—∪—‖∪—∪—∪—

Лобза́нья отрави́т, оледени́т объя́тья,   ∪—∪—∪—‖∪—∪—∪—∪

Вздо́х неги преврати́т в хрипя́щий во́пль

    проклятья,   ∪́—∪—∪—‖∪—∪—∪—∪

Отни́мет всё – и све́т, и слёзы у оче́й,   ∪—∪—∪—‖∪—∪—∪—

В прельсти́тельных власа́х ука́жет сви́тых

    змей,   ∪—∪—∪—‖∪—∪—∪—

В улы́бке а́лых уст – гее́нны оскалбле́нье   ∪—∪—∪—‖∪—∪—∪—∪

И в лёгком шёпоте – ехи́днино шипе́нье.   ∪—∪—∪—‖∪—∪—∪—∪

                          [1845]

The meter did not enter Russian literature directly from the French but through the intermediary of German poetry, from which it was borrowed by Lomonosov. Throughout the eighteenth century the longer and more serious genres—including dramatic works, narrative poems, and long epistles—tended to be written in the iambic hexameter; as a result, more lines of verse were written in this meter than in any other.[45] During the early nineteenth century it quickly lost ground to other meters, especially the iambic tetrameter and pentameter. It was again employed widely in lyric poetry during the 1840s and then revived another time in the 1880s, when Semen Nadson and some of his contemporaries turned to it often. The symbolists likewise continued to use the meter with some frequency, but since the 1920s the iambic hexameter has once more fallen into disfavor.[46]

The iambic hexameter in its main form, with a caesura after the third ictus, has twenty-eight possible variations. In practice, about half of these variations are extremely rare; during the nineteenth century, for instance, thirteen variations each appear in fewer than 0.01 percent of all the lines. Just six of the variations account for over 80 percent of all the lines, and of these the three most widely used all omit stress on the next-to-last ictus: ◡∸◡∸◡∸◡∸◡−◡∸(◡), ◡∸◡−◡∸◡∸◡−◡∸(◡), and ◡∸◡∸◡−◡∸ ◡−◡∸(◡). The other important variations include the fully stressed lines and lines with stress omitted on just the second or third ictus.[47]

The caesura has remained more of a fixture in the iambic hexameter than in the pentameter and consequently has had a greater effect on the rhythmic structure of the line throughout the meter's history. Two basic rhythmic types are found in the rhythmic hexameter. In the first, the caesura strongly interferes with the effect of regressive accentual dissimilation. As a result the line breaks into two symmetrical halves, with strong first and third ictuses in the first part of the line mirroring the strong fourth and sixth ictuses in the second part. In the other "asymmetrical" form, the effect of regressive accentual dissimilation (according to which the fifth, third, and first ictuses should all be relatively weak) partially crosses back into the first hemistich and weakens the third ictus. The strong ictuses are then the first, fourth, and sixth (see table 8, lines 8 and 9 for profiles of asymmetrical verse). During the eighteenth century the symmetrical form predominated; around the second decade of the nineteenth century, when regressive accentual dissimilation began to be felt more strongly in all the binary meters, the asymmetrical form became more common (contrast lines 1 and 2 in table 8).[48] However, after about 1840 the symmetrical form once again came to the fore and has remained the preferred rhythmic pattern to the present. If anything, poets during the Soviet era have preferred the symmetrical form even more strongly than poets of the mid-nineteenth century. Symptomatic of the growing partiality was Nikolai Zabolotsky's switch to the symmetrical line during the final decade of his career; in his early poetry he had used the asymmetrical form. As a result stressing on the third ictus of his line more than doubled in frequency (from 37.9 percent to 76.3 percent), while that on the second markedly decreased (from 84.8 percent to 69.9 percent).[49] Contemporary poets, when using the symmetrical form, have been inclined to stress the third

TABLE 8
Stressing in the Iambic Hexameter

	Stressing (by ictus)						Average Stressing
	I	II	III	IV	V	VI	
1. 18th century	91.8%	64.4%	73.1%	95.1%	44.1%	100%	78.1%
2. 1820–40	88.6	69.5	67.1	94.4	38.8	100	76.4
3. 1840–90	90.3	66.9	69.2	93.9	39.5	100	76.6
4. 1890–1920	88.5	72.9	64.7	82.2	42.3	100	75.1
5. Soviet	82.7	61.5	81.7	89.2	45.8	100	76.8
Symmetrical Verse							
6. 19th century	90.7	64.7	75.5	94.1	39.8	100	77.5
7. Soviet	84.5	53.5	93.5	90.5	44.0	100	77.7
Asymmetrical Verse							
8. 19th century	89.6	70.3	64.1	95.0	38.1	100	76.2
9. Soviet	80.0	73.0	63.5	87.5	49.0	100	75.5
10. V. Pereleshin ("Na tetushke tvoei"— 14 lines)	92.3	35.7	100	78.6	35.7	100	73.8
11. M. Voloshin ("Starinnym zolotom"— 14 lines)	100	71	50	100	50	100	78.5
12. V. Sosnora ("Muzykant"— 54 lines)	74.1	98.1	33.3	94.4	16.7	100	69.4

Sources: Lines 1–3 are based on Taranovsky, *Ruski dvodelni ritmovi*, table 6 in appendix; lines 4–9 are from Gasparov, "Iamb i khorei," pp. 116–17; lines 10–12 are my own calculations.

ictus even more regularly than did poets in the eighteenth century (table 8, compare lines 1 and 7). Some poets have come close to making the third ictus a constant, thereby emphasizing even more the tendency of the caesura to break the line down into two separate halves.[50]

Typical in this regard are the following lines by Valery Pereleshin:

На тётушке твоей я должен был жениться,	◡́◡◡–◡́ ‖ ◡́◡◡́◡◡◡
Чтоб и тебе теперь не числиться чужим,	◡–◡́◡́ ‖ ◡́◡◡–◡́
Увы, от брачных уз мы смолоду бежим:	◡́◡◡–◡́ ‖ ◡́◡◡–◡́
Нам Геба дорога, нам Афродита снится!	◡́◡◡–◡́ ‖ ◡–◡́◡́◡◡

Прости же мой просчёт. Бастилия-больница	◡́◡◡́◡–◡́ ‖ ◡́◡◡–◡́◡
Незыблемо блюдёт болезненный режим.	◡́◡◡–◡́ ‖ ◡́◡◡–◡́
Ты бледен, измождён и головокружим,	◡́◡◡–◡́ ‖ ◡–◡–◡́
И близкая толпа вокруг тебя теснится.	◡́◡◡–◡́ ‖ ◡́◡́◡◡́◡◡

1973

For the poem as a whole (cf. table 8, line 10) both the third and the sixth ictuses are constants, while each hemistich adheres to the norms of Russian rhythm for the iambic trimeter. Therefore only the rhyme scheme, which marks the ends of the lines, prevents the listener from perceiving each hemistich as a separate line in its own right.

As an example of the asymmetrical meter, let us consider this sonnet by Maksimilian Voloshin:

Старинным золотом и жёлчью напитал   ∪ –́ ∪ –́ ∪ – ‖ ∪ –́ ∪ – ∪ –́
Вечерний свет холмы. Зардели, красны,
                                   буры,   ∪ –́ ∪ –́ ∪ –́ ‖ ∪ –́ ∪ – ∪ –́ ∪
Клоки косматых трав, как пряди рыжей
                                 шкуры.   ∪ –́ ∪ –́ ∪ –́ ‖ ∪ –́ ∪ – ∪ –́ ∪
В огне кустарники, и воды как металл.   ∪ –́ ∪ –́ ∪ – ‖ ∪ –́ ∪ – ∪ –́

А груды валунов и глыбы голых скал   ∪ –́ ∪ – ∪ –́ ‖ ∪ –́ ∪ – ∪ –́
В размытых впадинах загадочны и хмуры.   ∪ –́ ∪ –́ ∪ – ‖ ∪ –́ ∪ – ∪ –́ ∪
В крылатых сумерках – намёки
                            и фигуры...   ∪ –́ ∪ –́ ∪ – ‖ ∪ –́ ∪ – ∪ –́ ∪
Вот лапа тяжкая, вот челюсти оскал,   ∪ –́ ∪ –́ ∪ – ‖ ∪ –́ ∪ – ∪ –́

Вот холм сомнительный, подобный
                           вздутым рёбрам.   ∪ –́ ∪ –́ ∪ –́ ‖ ∪ –́ ∪ – ∪ –́ ∪
Чей согнутый хребет порос, как шерстью,
                            чобром?   ∪ –́ ∪ – ∪ – ‖ ∪ –́ ∪ – ∪ –́ ∪
Кто этих мест жилец: чудовище? титан?   ∪́ –́ ∪ –́ ∪ –́ ‖ ∪ – ∪ – ∪ –́

Здесь душно в тесноте... А там – простор,
                             свобода,   ∪ –́ ∪ – ∪ –́ ‖ ∪ –́ ∪ – ∪ –́ ∪
Там дышит тяжело усталый Океан,   ∪ –́ ∪ – ∪ –́ ‖ ∪ –́ ∪ – ∪ –́ ∪
И веет запахом гниющих трав и йода.   ∪ –́ ∪ –́ ∪ – ‖ ∪ –́ ∪ – ∪ –́ ∪

                        1907

The asymmetrical rhythm appears in stark outline; usually the first and fourth ictuses are occasionally left unstressed. Still, the weak third ictus, here stressed only half the time, remains the main feature of this rhythmic pattern. Contrast this piece with the excerpt from the poem by Pereleshin, where stress on the third ictus is a constant. The caesura causes the lines in both works to break into two halves syntactically, but rhythmically the poems create quite different impressions.

Mandelshtam is credited with being one of the first to employ a third form of this meter in which regressive accentual dissimilation is fully effective across the entire line.[51] In other words, the second, fourth, and sixth ictuses are all strongly stressed, while stress is noticeably less frequent on the first, third, and fifth ictuses. This wavelike structure has

remained fairly rare, but it occurs in "The Musician" ("Muzykant"), a
poem by the Leningrad poet Viktor Sosnora.

Мы́ – Му́ки тво́рчества. Нас ждёт вели́кий
                                                      су́д.
У на́с, у Му́ков, у́ши дли́нные расту́т.
Но на́ши у́ши постепе́нно отцвели́,
спаса́ет ду́ши повседне́вный оптими́зм.

Я презира́ю мо́й му-чи́тельный тала́нт...
А по моста́м ходи́ли бе́лые тела́.
Как све́чи бе́лые, мая́чили в ночи́
тела́ оде́тые у же́нщин и мужчи́н.

                                                1965

For the poem as a whole, Sosnora (see table 8, line 12) follows a pattern
that is very close to Mandelshtam's, who also used moderate stressing
on the first ictus (69.2 percent), very light on the third (26.7 percent),
and still lighter on the fifth (20.8 percent), along with very heavy stress-
ing on the second and fourth ictuses.[52] In his use of rhythmic variations,
Sosnora is also close to Mandelshtam; both rely heavily on variation
XV, ∪́∪́∪–∪́∪–∪́(∪), which appears in 48 percent of Sosnora's
lines and in 42.5 percent of Mandelshtam's, while neither is inclined to
use fully stressed lines (5.5 percent in Sosnora, none at all in Man-
delshtam). The caesura, the feature that normally prevents regressive
accentual dissimilation from acting across the entire line, is absent. The
development of this new rhythmic pattern, albeit in a limited number of
poems, is further evidence of the continuing search for ways to revise
and bring variety to the long-established classical meters.

IAMBIC TRIMETER

Unlike the meters discussed previously, the iambic trimeter has never
been among the most popular meters used by Russian poets. However,
throughout the history of syllabo-tonic poetry nearly every author has
used it in a scattering of poems. In the eighteenth century its use was
confined largely to the lighter genres such as songs, romances, love
poems, and other short lyrics.[53] It has appeared only rarely in longer
works, most notably in Nekrasov's narrative poem *Who Can Live Well
in Russia?* (*Komu na Rusi zhit' khorosho*):

Неда́ром на́ши стра́нники
Пору́гивали мо́крую,

Холо́дную весну́. $\cup\acute{\cup}\cup\_\cup\acute{\_}$
Весна́ нужна́ крестья́нину $\cup\acute{\_}\cup\acute{\_}\cup\acute{\_}\cup\cup$
И ра́нняя и дру́жная, $\cup\acute{\_}\cup\_\cup\acute{\_}\cup\cup$
А ту́т – хоть во́лком во́й! $\cup\acute{\_}\cup\acute{\_}\cup\acute{\_}$
Не гре́ет зе́млю со́лнышко, $\cup\acute{\_}\cup\acute{\_}\cup\acute{\_}\cup\cup$
И облака́ дождли́вые, $\cup\_\cup\acute{\_}\cup\acute{\_}\cup\cup$
Как до́йные коро́вушки, $\cup\acute{\_}\cup\_\cup\acute{\_}\cup\cup$
Иду́т по небеса́м. $\cup\acute{\_}\cup\_\cup\acute{\_}$

                    1863-77

Nekrasov's poem contains numerous folk motifs. Usually when imitating folk genres he used trochaic, dactylic, or nonclassical meters;[54] here the most notable formal folk element is the unrhymed dactylic endings—though Nekrasov used masculine endings as well, particularly at the ends of sentences. For the most part, though, other poets employed the iambic trimeter in lyric poetry. From the end of the 1820s, when the iambic hexameter was falling sharply in popularity, the iambic trimeter began to be used more often. Since the iambic hexameter with caesura is often similar to two iambic trimeters linked together, this reciprocal development is not surprising. Today the iambic trimeter is still not among the more popular meters, occurring in 3 percent of all works.[55]

There are only four possible rhythmic variants for this meter, as shown in table 9. In practice, the last of these variants is extremely rare; Taranovsky found it only three times while analyzing about six thousand lines of eighteenth- and nineteenth-century poetry.[56] For most poets the third variant is the most common, followed by the first. The second—omission of stress on the first syllable—occurs in a relatively small number of lines, generally fewer than 10 percent.

TABLE 9
Rhythmic Variations of the Iambic Trimeter

Number of Omitted Stresses	Number of Variation	Form	Example
0	I	$\cup\acute{\_}\cup\acute{\_}\cup\acute{\_}\,(\cup)$	Сквозь то́лщих на́ших щёк
1	II	$\cup\_\cup\acute{\_}\cup\acute{\_}\,(\cup)$	Не просочи́тся све́т
	III	$\cup\acute{\_}\cup\_\cup\acute{\_}\,(\cup)$	Напи́санных сами́м
2	IV	$\cup\_\cup\_\cup\acute{\_}\,(\cup)$	Авиазаказно́й

Source: Voznesensky's poem, "Nam, kak appenditsit" (1967).

In other words, this meter tends to show the strong effect of Taranov-sky's two laws, which here—as in the iambic pentameter—act in harmony. Stress is constant on the third ictus, is omitted often on the second, and is generally present on the first (owing both to regressive accentual dissimilation and to the stabilization of the first ictus after the first weak position in the line). In this quotation from Tiutchev, the structure is followed closely:

В часы́, когда́ быва́ет	◡ ◡́ ◡ ◡́ ◡ ◡́ ◡
Так тя́жко на груди́,	◡ ◡́ ◡ ◡ ◡́
И се́рдце изныва́ет,	◡ ◡́ ◡ ◡́ ◡ ◡́ ◡
И тьма́ лишь впереди́;	◡ ◡́ ◡ ◡ ◡́
Без си́л и без движе́нья,	◡ ◡́ ◡ ◡ ◡́ ◡
Мы та́к удручены́,	◡ ◡́ ◡ ◡ ◡́
Что да́же утеше́нья	◡ ◡́ ◡ ◡́ ◡ ◡́ ◡
Друзе́й нам не смешны́, –	◡ ◡́ ◡ ◡ ◡́

[1858]

The poem as a whole is rhythmically close to Pushkin's use of this meter; compare lines 1 and 2 in table 10.

In the twentieth century a few poets have tended to level out the stressing pattern. Whereas in the eighteenth and nineteenth centuries stressing rarely fell below 90 percent on the first ictus, some twentieth-century poets have brought that figure into the 85 percent range. At the same time stressing on the second ictus approaches the upper values for the earlier periods. The second rhythmic variant consequently becomes more common, the third less so. Evtushenko uses this rhythmic structure often (table 10, line 3); it is also found in Rimma Kazakova's poem "Tania" (cf. table 10, line 4):

К приме́ру, жениха́ется	◡ ◡́ ◡ ◡ ◡́ ◡ ◡
смазли́венький оди́н.	◡ ◡́ ◡ ◡ ◡́
Из на́ших же, монта́жник.	◡ ◡́ ◡ ◡ ◡́ ◡
Сам из себя́ блонди́н.	◡ ◡ ◡́ ◡ ◡́
Ко мне́ подхо́дит ро́стом.	◡ ◡́ ◡ ◡́ ◡ ◡́ ◡
Име́ет мотоши́кл.	◡ ◡́ ◡ ◡ ◡́
Ну и хожу́ с ним про́сто...	◡ ◡ ◡́ ◡ ◡́ ◡
В кино́. А ка́к-то – в ци́рк.	◡ ◡́ ◡ ◡́ ◡ ◡́

[<1974]

Thus the iambic trimeter presents little rhythmic variety. The main form features a strong first and a very weak second ictus; the secondary

TABLE 10
Stressing and Rhythmic Variations in the Iambic Trimeter

	Stressing (by ictus)			Rhythmic Variations				Average Stressing
	I	II	III	I	II	III	IV	
1. Pushkin (1814)	98.0%	41.4%	100%	39.4%	2.0%	58.6%	0%	79.8%
2. Tiutchev ("V chasy"—28 lines)	96.4	32.1	100	28.6	3.6	67.9	0	76.2
3. Evtushenko (1963–69)	86.5	57	100					81.2
4. Kazakova ("Tania"—56 lines)	85.7	55.4	100	41.1	14.3	44.6	0	80.4

Sources: Line 1 is from Taranovsky, *Ruski dvodelni ritmovi*, table 5; line 3 is from Gasparov, "Iamb i khorei," p. 123; lines 2 and 4 are based on my own calculations.

form's line has the same basic contour, but the amount of stressing from one ictus to the next is leveled out somewhat.

TROCHAIC TETRAMETER

Until recently, the trochaic tetrameter has been by far the most widely used of all the trochaic meters. Lomonosov was the first to use this meter in his "Ode of Fénelon" ("Oda Fenelona," 1738), and for the rest of the century this one meter accounted for 10 percent of all Russian poetry—thus becoming the fourth most popular meter after free iambs, iambic hexameter, and iambic tetrameter. Most Russian poets of the time wrote some verse in trochaic tetrameter; typical are these lines from a song by Sumarokov:

Кто́ мне ми́л, в тебе́, дубро́ва,	—◡—◡—◡—◡
То́т быва́ет завсегда́:	—◡—◡—◡—
Мо́лвил ли хотя́ три́ сло́ва	—◡—◡—◡—◡
О́н, в тебе́ о мне́ когда́?	—◡—◡—◡—
И́ль притво́рно он вздыха́ет,	—◡—◡—◡—◡
И меня́ пересмеха́ет,	◡—◡—◡—◡—◡
Ви́дя сла́бости мои́,	—◡—◡—◡—
И успе́хи в ни́х свои́?	◡—◡—◡—◡—

[<1770]

At any given time since the establishment of the syllabo-tonic system in Russian poetry, at least two or three different iambic meters have been in fashion among the poets of the day. However, during the eighteenth century over 80 percent of the works and more than 90 percent of the lines written in trochaic verse were tetrameters. Indeed, no other trochaic meter accounted for as much as 1 percent of the total number of verses written during the eighteenth century.[57] Well into the 1800s the tetrameter remained by far the most popular of all the trochaic lines. Of the 101 works in which Pushkin used a single type of trochaic line, 94 are trochaic tetrameter; for Lermontov the corresponding figures are 21 out of 26.[58] By midcentury, as trochaic verse began to be used more widely, other types of trochee—most notably the pentameter, the hexameter, and mixed forms—started to appear in a significant number of poems. Thus the trochaic tetrameter, while it continued to account for about 10 percent of all poetry, was no longer as dominant among the other trochaic meters as earlier. Fet and Nekrasov, for example, used the trochaic tetrameter for only 66 percent of their trochaic works.[59] During the twentieth century—more specifically, since the late 1920s—

the trochaic tetrameter has lost still more ground. Throughout the nineteenth century it was often the second or third most popular meter; during the last few decades it has slipped to fifth place, behind even the trochaic pentameter, and now accounts for only about 5 percent of all poetry.[60]

Like its popular counterpart, the iambic tetrameter, the trochaic tetrameter appears in virtually every genre and in the work of virtually every poet. However, over the years poets have believed (as we have seen, with some justification) that the trochaic meters are particularly suitable for imitations of folklore. Similarly, the trochee has also seemed appropriate for songs and romances. Thus, in the eighteenth century, while the trochaic tetrameter appeared in a handful of narratives and solemn odes, poets employed it most frequently for light poetry and especially for works meant to be sung.[61] In the nineteenth century Pushkin used this meter for some of his fairy-tale imitations—such as "Tale of Tsar Saltan" ("Skazka o tsare Saltane") and "Tale of the Golden Cockerel" ("Skazka o zolotom petushke")—and for other works containing folk motifs. The trochaic tetrameter with unrhymed dactylic endings appeared as a folk element in verse from the late eighteenth century right into the twentieth, as in Sergei Esenin's "Song of Evpaty Kolovrat" ("Pesnia o Evpatii Kolovrate").[62]

The form of the trochaic tetrameter is as follows: $-\cup-\cup-\cup\acute{-}(\cup)$. As with the iambic tetrameter, eight rhythmic variations are possible, seven of which normally occur in poetry (see table 11). Only the first, second, fourth, and sixth are encountered regularly; the third and fifth are fairly rare (especially in work from the nineteenth century); and the seventh occurs in only a scattering of lines. The distribution of rhythmic variations means that stress is often omitted on the first ictus (the second and sixth variations) and on the third (fourth and sixth). The low frequency of variations that omit stress on the second ictus implies strong stressing at this position in the line. Line 3 of table 12 shows a typical stress profile for the trochaic tetrameter, with a sharp distinction between the very strong second and fourth ictuses and the much weaker first and third. Taranovsky's two laws operate in harmony here. Since the first ictus appears on the first syllable of the line, it is not preceded by a weak position and therefore is not so likely to be stressed; the first strong ictus is the second. Similarly, the law of regressive accentual dissimilation also predicts a strong second ictus. In the work of many poets from the early nineteenth century on, stress on the second ictus has become a virtual constant.

TABLE 11

Rhythmic Variations of the Trochaic Tetrameter

Number of Omitted Stresses	Number of Variation	Form	Example
0	I	́∪ ́∪ ́∪ ́ (∪)	Ша́пки, шу́бы, ды́м из тру́б
1	II	∪ ́∪ ́∪ ́ (∪)	На столе́ стака́н не до́пит
	III	́∪ ∪ ́∪ ́ (∪)	Кры́ши городо́в доро́гой
	IV	́∪ ́∪ ∪ ́ (∪)	В чёрном ко́тике коке́тства
2	V	́∪ ∪ ∪ ́ (∪)	Э́того хоть захлебни́сь
	VI	∪ ́∪ ∪ ́ (∪)	Лихора́дило в гриппу́
	VII	∪ ∪ ́∪ ́ (∪)	И на чердаке́ черто́г
3	VIII	∪ ∪ ∪ ́ (∪)	—

Source: Pasternak's cycle of poems, "Khudozhnik" (1936).

Contrasting the trochaic with the iambic tetrameter shows clearly the differences between iambic and trochaic lines. In the iambic tetrameter Taranovsky's first law predicts a strong first ictus, while the second law points to a strong second but weak first and third ictuses. Since the two laws conflict at the beginning of the line, the iambic tetrameter has exhibited a variety of rhythmic patterns throughout its history (cf. table 4, lines 1, 2, 9, 12). On the whole, the first ictus has remained fairly strong and at times has been even stronger than the second. In the trochaic tetrameter, on the other hand, the first ictus has generally been much weaker than the second. Furthermore, a single structure has predominated throughout the history of the meter (table 12, lines 1, 3, 5–7). Since the two laws operate in harmony, and in the great majority of poems no complicating factors such as a caesura exist, there has been little impetus to develop other rhythmic patterns for the trochaic tetrameter. What is true for the tetrameter is true for the other line lengths as well; trochaic and iambic lines of the same length tend to have different internal structures since the rhythmic laws do not affect them in the same way.

Even though the general contours of the trochaic tetrameter have remained stable over the past two hundred years, a few developments are worthy of note. During the eighteenth century stress was not yet a near constant on the second ictus, and thus the third rhythmic variant accounted for nearly 10 percent of the lines. By the nineteenth century stressing on the first ictus had declined and that on the second increased;

TABLE 12

Stressing and Rhythmic Variations in the Trochaic Tetrameter

	Stressing (by ictus)				Rhythmic Variations							Average Stressing
	I	II	III	IV	I	II	III	IV	V	VI	VII	
1. 18th century	63.3%	89.5%	54.8%	100%	24.8%	20.2%	9.7%	28.1%	0.7%	16.4%	0.1%	76.9%
2. Sumarokov	61.2	88.6	53.2	100	21.5	20.6	11.0	28.4	0.3	18.1	0.1	75.8
3. 19th century	54.3	98.8	46.4	100	22.6	22.8	1.1	30.6	0.1	22.9	0.05	74.9
4. Pushkin (1824–28)	56.4	99.3	40.6	100	21.6	18.3	0.7	34.1	—	25.3	—	74.1
5. Early 20th century	58.3	99.1	50.0	100								76.9
6. Soviet poets (older)	58.2	96.9	49.8	100								76.2
7. Soviet poets (younger)	50.9	94.4	47.6	99.9								73.2
8. Esenin ("Dorogaia, siadem")—32 lines	71.9	96.9	71.9	100								85.2
9. Pasternak (3 poems in cycle "Khudozhnik")—108 lines	56.5	91.7	57.4	100	43.8	25.0	3.1	25.0	—	3.1	—	76.4
10. Tsvetaeva (1922–23)	85.3	49.5	53.9	100	29.6	20.4	6.5	19.4	0.9	22.2	0.9	72.2
11. Tsvetaeva ("Bich zhandarmov")—72 lines	81.9	79.2	37.5	100	19.4	9.7	8.3	41.7	12.5	8.3	—	76.4

Sources: Lines 1–4 are from table 1, appended to Taranovsky, *Ruski dvodelni ritmovi*; lines 5–7 are from Gasparov, "Iamb i khorei," p. 96; line 10 is from G. S. Smith, "The Versification of Marina Tsvetayeva's Lyric Poetry, 1922–23," p. 31; and lines 8, 9, and 11 are based on my own calculations.

the latter approached, and for individual poets and poems sometimes reached, 100 percent. Typical for the nineteenth century are the opening lines of this poem by Pushkin:

Во́рон к во́рону лети́т,	´∪´∪_∪´
Во́рон во́рону кричи́т:	´∪´∪_∪´
"Во́рон, где́ б нам отобе́дать?	´∪´∪_∪´∪
Ка́к бы на́м о то́м прове́дать?"	´∪´∪´∪´∪
Во́рон во́рону в отве́т:	´∪´∪_∪´
"Зна́ю, бу́дет на́м обе́д;	´∪´∪´∪´
В чи́стом по́ле под раки́той	´∪´∪_∪´∪
Богаты́рь лежи́т уби́тый.	_∪´∪´∪´∪

1828

As the figures on lines 3 and 4 of table 12 show, usually the second ictus is strongly stressed, the third the most weakly stressed, and the first noticeably weaker than the second. The fourth variation (omission of stress on the third ictus) is the most common, but it does not approach the 50 percent level—as it often does in the iambic tetrameter. Also, the second and sixth rhythmic variations, neither of which normally appear regularly in iambic tetrameter poetry, account for 20 percent or more of the trochaic tetrameter lines.

The same rhythmic pattern continues into the twentieth century. Esenin, who was one of the few poets to prefer trochees to iambs,[63] made the stress on the second ictus a near constant in his poetry:

Дорога́я, ся́дем ря́дом,	_∪´∪´∪´∪
Погляди́м в глаза́ друг дру́гу.	_∪´∪´∪´∪
Я хочу́ под кро́тким взгля́дом	´∪´∪´∪´∪
Слу́шать чу́вственную вью́гу.	´∪´∪_∪´∪
Э́то зо́лото осе́ннее,	´∪´∪_∪´∪∪
Э́та пря́дь воло́с беле́сых –	´∪´∪´∪´∪
Всё яви́лось, как спасе́нье	´∪´∪_∪´∪
Беспоко́йного пове́сы.	_∪´∪_∪´∪

[1923]

For this poem as a whole (table 12, line 8), Esenin used many fully stressed lines: fourteen out of thirty-two. The sixth rhythmic variation, which omits stress on the first and third ictuses, would normally appear about six or eight times in a poem of this length; here it occurs only once. As a result, stressing on the first and third ictuses is higher than usual, but the rhythmic structure of the poem as a whole still resembles the pattern found in trochaic poetry of the previous century.

However, as lines 6 and 7 of table 12 reveal, some minor changes have occurred in modern times. The table shows a slight decrease in stressing on the second ictus; moreover, examining the practice of individual poets brings to light two opposing trends. On the one hand, many poets, like Esenin, continue the nineteenth-century practice of treating stress on the second ictus as a near constant. Others, like Pasternak, have begun to stress the second ictus a little less regularly (though still about 90 percent of the time), thereby bringing more variety to the rhythm of the line:

Ра́зве въе́зд в эпо́ху за́перт?   ⌣́ ∪ ⌣́ ∪ ⌣́ ∪ ⌣́ ∪
Пу́сть он кре́пость, пу́сть и хра́м, ⌣́ ∪ ⌣́ ∪ ⌣́ ∪ ⌣́
Въе́ду на коне́ на па́перть.   ⌣́ ∪ _ ∪ ⌣́ ∪ ⌣́ ∪
Ло́шадь осажу́ к дверя́м.   ⌣́ ∪ _ ∪ ⌣́ ∪ ⌣́

Не гусля́р и не бала́кирь,   _ ∪ ⌣́ ∪ _ ∪ ⌣́ ∪
Ло́шадь взви́л я на дыбы́,   ⌣́ ∪ ⌣́ ∪ _ ∪ ⌣́
Что́б тебя́, вое́нный ла́герь,   _ ∪ ⌣́ ∪ ⌣́ ∪ ⌣́ ∪
Увида́ть с высо́т судьбы́.   _ ∪ ⌣́ ∪ _ ∪ ⌣́

И, едва́ пово́дья тро́нув,   _ ∪ ⌣́ ∪ ⌣́ ∪ ⌣́ ∪
Порыва́юсь науга́д   _ ∪ ⌣́ ∪ _ ∪ ⌣́
В широту́ твои́х прого́нов,   _ ∪ ⌣́ ∪ ⌣́ ∪ ⌣́ ∪
Что ещё во тьме́ лежа́т.   _ ∪ ⌣́ ∪ _ ∪ ⌣́

       1936

These lines, from the fourth poem grouped under the general title "The Artist" ("Khudozhnik") in Pasternak's collection *On Early Trains* (*Na rannikh poezdakh*), are typical of the second rhythmic type. Three of the four poems in this small cycle are written in trochaic tetrameter and contain a total of 108 lines (table 12, line 9). The chief difference between Pasternak's use of this meter and that favored in the nineteenth century is his tendency to employ the fourth rhythmic variation less frequently, while turning more often to fully stressed lines and to the omission of stress on the second ictus. Average stressing for the poem as a whole is higher than that favored in the nineteenth century. Still, the poem's stress and rhythmic patterns show Pasternak's work to be close to eighteenth-century practice, thus typifying what Gasparov calls the "archaizing trend" evident in some developments during the twentieth century.[64]

Only one poet has managed to develop a radically different rhythmic form for the trochaic tetrameter, but the failure of this form to achieve any popularity among contemporary poets illustrates the extent to which the two laws formulated by Taranovsky have affected the actual

usage of this meter. Marina Tsvetaeva, who often strove for rhythmic
innovation in her poetry, created the form in the early 1920s;[65] it fea-
tures greatly reduced stressing on the second ictus and relatively strong
stressing on the first (cf. table 12, line 10). Tsvetaeva often placed great
emphasis on the beginning of the line,[66] and thus her motivation for in-
venting a new type of rhythm probably stemmed from her preference for
stressing the first ictus as often as possible. The reduced stressing on the
second ictus followed as a natural result. A variant of this rhythm is
evident in the first of "Poems to Pushkin" ("Stikhi k Pushkinu"):

Две́ ноги́ свои́ – погре́ться –	´υ´υ´υ´υ
Вы́тянувший, и на сто́л	´υ–υ–υ´
Вспры́гнувший при самоде́ржце	´υ–υ–υ´υ
Африка́нский самово́л –	–υ´υ–υ´
На́ших пра́дедов умо́ра –	´υ´υ–υ´υ
Пу́шкин – в ро́ли гуверне́ра?	´υ´υ–υ´υ
Чёрного не перекра́сить	´υ–υ–υ´υ
В бе́лого – неисправи́м!	´υ–υ–υ´
Недурён росси́йский кла́ссик,	–υ´υ´υ´υ
Не́бо Африки – свои́м	´υ´υ–υ´
Зва́вший, не́вское – прокля́тым.	´υ´υ–υ´υ
– Пу́шкин – в ро́ли русопя́та?	´υ´υ–υ´υ

                                     1931

In the poem as a whole (table 12, line 11) Tsvetaeva stresses the second
ictus much more often than she did in the early 1920s, but stressing for
that ictus is still below the norm for other poets. Her tendency to avoid
fully stressed lines and her regular use of the extremely rare line that
omits stress on both the second and third ictuses (the fifth variation)
combine to make her rhythm unique. For most other poets, though, the
trochaic tetrameter has exhibited much less variety in its rhythmic
forms than has its iambic counterpart.

TROCHAIC PENTAMETER

No other meter has had a more unusual history than the trochaic pen-
tameter. Today it is the most popular of all trochaic meters, having
clearly surpassed the long-dominant trochaic tetrameter. However, dur-
ing the first century of syllabo-tonic poetry in Russia trochaic pen-
tameter was quite rare, accounting for only a minute fraction of the po-
etry written before 1840. Lomonosov included a two-line example in

his *Short Guide to Rhetoric*, Trediakovsky used the meter for a translation from Horace, and Sumarokov employed the line in a handful of songs—nearly the only examples of the meter from this period. In a few poems trochaic pentameter lines alternated with trochaic lines of other lengths, but on the whole the trochaic pentameter played no significant role in eighteenth-century Russian poetry.[67] Nor did the situation change much during the first third of the nineteenth century: Baratynsky and Pushkin, among others, did not use the line at all. Lermontov, however, wrote four poems in trochaic pentameter. While the number itself is not impressive, one of those works, "I walk out onto the road alone" ("Vykhozhu odin ia na dorogu"), became extremely popular and to this day remains one of Lermontov's best known poems:

Выхожу́ оди́н я на доро́гу;
Сквозь тума́н кремни́стый пу́ть блести́т;
Но́чь тиха̀. Пусты́ня вне́млет бо́гу,
И звезда́ с звездо́ю говори́т.

В небеса́х торже́ственно и чу́дно!
Спи́т земля̀ в сия́нье голубо́м...
Что́ же мне́ так бо́льно и так тру́дно?
Жду́ ль чего́? жале́ю ли о чём?

Уж не жду́ от жи́зни ничего́ я,
И не жа́ль мне про́шлого ничу́ть;
Я́ ищу́ свобо́ды и поко́я!
Я́ б хоте́л забы́ться и засну́ть!

Но не те́м холо́дным сно́м моги́лы...
Я́ б жела́л наве́ки так засну́ть,
Чтоб в груди́ дрема́ли жи́зни си́лы,
Чтоб, дыша̀, вздыма́лась ти́хо гру́дь;

Чтоб всю ́ночь, ве́сь де́нь мой слу́х леле́я,
Про любо́вь мне сла́дкий го́лос пе́л,
Надо мно́й чтоб, ве́чно зелене́я,
Тёмный ду́б склоня́лся и шуме́л.

1841

Partly because of its popularity, this poem greatly influenced subsequent writers of trochaic pentameter; many works employing the meter have contained thematic and stylistic echoes of Lermontov's work.[68] Still, for the rest of the nineteenth century the trochaic pentameter remained far less common than the tetrameter; only around 1900 did poets begin to use it widely. Since the 1920s the trochaic pentameter has steadily become more common than the tetrameter; in more recent years, the pentameter has accounted for about 50 percent of all the verse written in trochees.[69]

Over the years the usage of the trochaic pentameter has paralleled that of the iambic in many ways. Both meters were extremely rare during the eighteenth century, coming into general usage during the nineteenth but remaining less common than the corresponding tetrameter lines. Around the beginning of the twentieth century the pentameter line in each case began to overtake the tetrameter, though for the iambic meters tetrameter works remain about as common as those written in pentameter.[70] Thus the long-standing preference for tetrameter lines in binary verse has given way in the course of the twentieth century. Fragmentary evidence indicates that in the past decade this trend may have been reversed; at the very least, it has certainly slowed. Thus the iambic and trochaic tetrameters remain very important meters.

The schema for the trochaic pentameter is as follows: $-\cup-\cup-\cup-\cup$ $\angle(\cup)$. As with the iambic pentameter, there are sixteen possible variations for this meter (see table 13). Only the first twelve may occur if a caesura is placed after the third or fourth syllable. Variations XV and XVI, which would begin the line with three and four unstressed ictuses respectively, are virtually unknown in practice. Variation XII, with three consecutive unstressed ictuses, is almost as rare. Throughout the nineteenth century, variations VIII and X through XIV (all those with two or more consecutive unstressed ictuses) occurred only in a handful of lines. In fact, just four of the variations predominated in the works of most nineteenth-century poets: the fully stressed line (I), the lines omitting stress on the first and fourth ictuses respectively (II and V), and the line omitting stress on both the first and fourth ictuses (VII). As lines 1 through 7 of table 14 show, the poems written in this meter have most often stressed the first and fourth ictuses relatively lightly and showed strong stressing on the second, third, and fifth ictuses.

The stress pattern that has been predominant in trochaic pentameter poetry results from a clash of the two basic laws. According to regressive accentual dissimilation, the first and third ictuses should be strong, the second and fourth weak. The other law predicts a weak first and strong second ictus. Here, the latter takes precedence. Thus, in the example by Lermontov quoted above and in most of the nineteenth-century poetry written in this meter, the second ictus is stressed much more often than the first.

The caesura, which had a marked effect on the rhythm of iambic

TABLE 13
Rhythmic Variations of the Trochaic Pentameter

Number of Omitted Stresses	Number of Variation	Form	Example
0	I	´˘´˘´˘´˘´(˘)	Жизнь и смерть давно беру в кавычки
1	II	˘˘´˘´˘´˘´(˘)	Человек вошёл—любой—(любимый—
	III	´˘—˘´˘´˘´(˘)	Первое письмо тебе с вчерашней—
	IV	´˘´˘—˘´˘´(˘)	Стих! Как пишется в хорошей жисти
	V	´˘´˘´˘—˘´(˘)	Целый ряд значений и созвучий
2	VI	—˘´˘—˘´˘´(˘)	С доказуемости мысом крайним
	VII	˘˘´˘´˘—˘´(˘)	От орлов, сказал, не отстающих
	VIII	´˘—˘´˘—˘´(˘)	Загородом! И кому же машет
	IX	˘˘´˘—˘—˘´(˘)	Первое виденье вселенной
	X	´˘´˘—˘—˘´(˘)	Зрел. Напряженная перебёжка
3	XI	—˘—˘—˘´˘´(˘)	И не начатого соловьями
	XII	´˘´˘—˘—˘—(˘)	Выстуженный Северовостóк
2	XIII	—˘—˘´˘´˘´(˘)	Приоблокотясь на алый обод
3	XIV	—˘—˘´˘—˘´(˘)	Не землетрясенье, не лавина
	XV	—˘—˘—˘—˘´(˘)	—
4	XVI	—˘—˘—˘—˘—(˘)	—

Sources: Example XII is from Voloshin's poem "Severovostok" (1920) (cited in Taranovsky, *Ruski dvodelni ritmovi*, p. 294). All other examples are taken from Tsvetaeva's long poem, "Novogodnee" (1927).

TABLE 14
Stressing in the Trochaic Pentameter

	Stressing (by ictus)					Average Stressing
	I	II	III	IV	V	
1. Lermontov (1831–41)	58.8%	97.5%	95.0%	51.3%	100%	80.5%
2. Early 19th century	62.8	83.3	84.6	55.7	100	77.3
3. Nekrasov (1851–77)	54.5	94.9	92.2	32.0	100	74.7
4. Late 19th century	50.0	91.0	87.9	48.3	100	75.4
5. 1890–1920	52.1	87.5	87.6	44.9	100	74.4
6. Soviet era (younger poets)	58.7	76.4	86.3	37.3	100	71.7
7. Vinokurov ("Vernite"—28 lines)	53.6	82.1	85.7	39.3	100	72.1
8. Evtushenko ("Tolstoi"—100 lines)	69	65	98	23	100	71.0
9. Odoevtseva ("On skazal"—36 lines)	77.8	66.7	88.9	50.0	100	76.7
10. Tsvetaeva ("Novogodnee"—186 lines)	56.5	77	52	71	100	71.3
11. Tsvetaeva ("Rel'sy"—24 lines)	79.2	20.8	83.3	25.0	100	61.7

Sources: Lines 1 and 3 are from table 14 appended to Taranovsky, *Ruski dvodelni ritmovi*. Line 2 contains composite figures based on lines 2–6 in Taranovsky's table; line 4 is based on lines 8–9 and 12–14 in the same table. Lines 5–6 and 10 are from Gasparov, "Iamb i khorei," pp. 110–11. Lines 7–8 and 11 are from my own calculations.

TABLE 15

Rhythmic Variations in the Trochaic Pentameter

	I	II	III	IV	V	VI	VII	VIII	IX	X	XI	XII	XIII	XIV
1.	27.5%	17.5%	1.2%	3.8%	25.0%	1.2%	22.5%	0.0%	1.2%	—	—	—	—	—
2.	18.9	14.9	6.9	8.9	18.1	4.7	17.2	1.3	8.3	0.4%	0.1%	—	0.1%	0.2%
3.	12.9	10.3	1.0	3.7	32.8	3.9	31.3	0.2	3.9	—	—	—	—	—
4.	15.1	19.8	1.8	5.6	23.1	5.8	23.6	0.2	4.2	0.05	0.5	—	—	0.25
5.														
6.														
7.	3.6	17.8	3.6	7.1	25.0	3.6	25.0	3.6	10.7	—	—	—	—	—
8.	5	9	7	1	29	1	20	—	27	—	—	—	—	1
9.	13.9	13.9	13.9	5.6	22.2	2.8	5.6	—	19.4	2.8	—	—	—	—
10.														
11.	—	—	8.3	8.3	4.2	—	8.3	8.3	50.0	—	—	—	—	12.5

Sources: See table 14.

pentameter poetry, seems to have played a lesser role in the history of
the trochaic pentameter. The trochaic pentameter entered the repertoire
of Russian poets relatively late, at a time when the caesura was already
less of a fixture in the iambic pentameter than it had been in the first
decades of the nineteenth century. Perhaps for this reason the trochaic
pentameter never developed a tradition of a regular caesura, although
Taranovsky has detected a so-called movable caesura in which the word
break occurs after either the third or fourth syllable in nearly every
line.[71] Often the movable caesura resulted in particularly heavy stressing
on the second ictus (cf. lines 1 and 3, table 14), but this was not always
the case. In fact, perhaps because it is movable, this kind of caesura
does not appear to have had any consistent effect on the rhythmic struc-
ture of the line.

Throughout its early history the trochaic pentameter showed remark-
ably little variety. The differences between individual poets are often
slight; thus Lermontov and Nekrasov create similar rhythmic patterns
in their use of the meter. Likewise, not much difference occurs from
one period to the next (cf. lines 2, 4, 5, table 14). The main change has
been a gradual decrease in stressing for the line as a whole; between the
early nineteenth and the early twentieth centuries the weak first and
fourth ictuses became still weaker. This type of rhythm has remained
the most common to the present day; the basic structure is evident in the
final lines of Evgeny Vinokurov's "Return the Manuscript" ("Vernite
rukopis'"):

Возврати́те ру́копись. Верни́те!	$-\cup\acute{-}\cup\acute{-}\cup-\cup\acute{-}\cup$
Óн стара́лся всё-таки! Писа́л!	$\acute{-}\cup\acute{-}\cup\acute{-}\cup-\cup\acute{-}$
Не чета́ како́му-то лома́ке,	$-\cup\acute{-}\cup\acute{-}\cup-\cup\acute{-}\cup$
Óн всё ждёт. Так бу́дьте же добре́й!	$\acute{-}\acute{-}\cup\acute{-}\cup\acute{-}\cup-\cup\acute{-}$
Возврати́те! Та́м одно́й бума́ги	$-\cup\acute{-}\cup\acute{-}\cup\acute{-}\cup\acute{-}\cup$
На деся́тки, мо́жет быть, рубле́й.	$-\cup\acute{-}\cup\acute{-}\cup\acute{-}\cup\acute{-}$
Ва́с рассу́дят в бу́дущем пото́мки.	$\acute{-}\cup\acute{-}\cup\acute{-}\cup-\cup\acute{-}\cup$
А пока́ верни́те-ка наза́д!..	$-\cup\acute{-}\cup\acute{-}\cup-\cup\acute{-}$
...Па́пка. И кальсо́нные тесёмки	$\acute{-}\cup-\cup\acute{-}\cup-\cup\acute{-}\cup$
Из неё зага́дочно вися́т.	$-\cup\acute{-}\cup\acute{-}\cup-\cup\acute{-}$

1965

In this excerpt only two stresses occur on the fourth ictus, and three of
the four stresses on the first ictus are on relatively weakly stressed mono-
syllabic pronouns. For the entire poem (table 14, line 7) Vinokurov
stressed both the second and third ictuses more than 80 percent of the
time. Here the stressing profile resembles the nineteenth-century prac-
tice, the major difference being that Vinokurov, like many twentieth-

century poets, largely avoids fully stressed lines and has a relatively low average stressing for the line as a whole.

Around the turn of the century a second type of rhythm appeared and has since recurred continually as a minor form of this meter. In this second type regressive dissimilation becomes the more dominant of the two laws and overcomes the usual tendency of trochaic lines to avoid strong stressing on the first ictus. Thus the strong ictuses are the fifth, the third, and generally the first. The second ictus, which in the predominant rhythmic form of this meter is strongly stressed, now becomes much weaker. The figures in line 6 of table 14, which indicate that modern poets stress the first ictus more and the second less frequently, result from a second rhythmic structure for this meter in twentieth-century poetry. Evtushenko employs the newer form in a number of poems; one example is "Tolstoy," which comprises the fourth section of the narrative poem "Kazan University" ("Kazanskii universitet"):

Ю́ными надме́нными глаза́ми
гля́дя на биле́т, как на пусто́й,
де́ржит по исто́рии экза́мен
граф Ле́в Никола́евич Толсто́й.

Знамени́т он – е́док и зади́рист –
то́лько те́м, что гра́ф и вертопра́х,
те́м, что у него́ орло́вский вы́езд,
те́м, что у него́ шине́ль в бобра́х.

                                                1970

For the entire poem Evtushenko makes the stress on the third ictus a virtual constant (tables 14 and 15, line 8), employs relatively strong stressing on the first ictus, and keeps stressing on the fourth ictus quite low. He particularly favors the ninth rhythmic variation, which omits stress on both the second and fourth ictuses, and he uses fully stressed lines only five times in the one-hundred-line poem. A similar rhythm is employed by Irina Odoevtseva:

Гу́бы шевели́ться переста́ли
И в груди́ не слы́шу тёплый сту́к.
Я́ стою́ на бе́лом пьедеста́ле,
Щи́т в рука́х и за плеча́ми лу́к.

У́тро... С молоко́м прохо́дят ба́бы;
Де́ти и чино́вники спеша́т;
Зво́н трамва́ев, до́ждь и ве́тер сла́бый
И тако́й обы́чный Петрогра́д.

                                                [1922]

For a trochaic poem this work has heavy stressing on the first ictus (table 14, line 9), and overall the effect of regressive accentual dissimilation creates a pattern more reminiscent of the iambic pentameter.

Marina Tsvetaeva, whose unique rhythmic variant of the trochaic tetrameter has been discussed already, was equally original in her use of the trochaic pentameter. She used the newer rhythmic form with its alternating strong odd and weak even ictuses, but in her works the distinction between strong and weak ictuses could be much sharper than that of most poets. A case in point is the short lyric, "Rails" ("Rel'sy"). Of the twenty-four lines, twelve use the ninth rhythmic variation. Stressing on the second and fourth ictuses is very light throughout the poem, while that on the first ictus is abnormally high for a work written in trochees (table 14, line 11). Not a single line is fully stressed, only five lines omit a single stress, and three lines employ the rare fourteenth variation, which contains only two of the five possible stresses. Even more unusual is the stressing pattern of "New Year's" ("Novogodnee"), the narrative poem that provides the examples for table 13. Here the strong ictuses are the second, fourth, and fifth, while the third is far weaker than in the vast majority of trochaic pentameter poems (table 14, line 10). Still another example of Tsvetaeva's rhythmic inventiveness is the following work, quoted in its entirety:

Прорица́ниями рокоча́,	_∪́_∪_∪_∪́
Нераска́яннного скрипача́	_∪́_∪_∪_∪́
Piccicáta'ми... Разры́вом бу́с!	_∪́_∪_∪́_∪́
Паган́иниевскими "добью́сь!"	_∪́_∪_∪_∪́
Опроки́нутыми...	
Но́т, плане́т –	_∪́_∪_∪́_∪́
Ли́внем!	
– Вы́везет!!!	
– Коне́ц... На-не́т...	́_∪́_∪_∪́_∪́
Недоска́занностями тиши́зн	_∪́_∪_∪_∪́
Загова́ривающие жи́знь:	_∪́_∪_∪_∪́
Стради́ва́риусами в ночи́	_∪́_∪_∪_∪́
Пролива́ющиеся ручьи́.	_∪́_∪_∪_∪́

1923

Seven of the ten lines contain the uncommon eleventh rhythmic variation; partly for this reason both the second and fifth ictuses are stressed constantly. There are no stresses at all on the third ictus, and average stressing is a minimal 48 percent. Of course, the poem, with its plethora of very long words, is a tour de force, but it serves to illustrate the range of possibilities allowed by the meter.

Only in the twentieth century have poets begun to explore other rhythms in the trochaic pentameter. During the nineteenth century the basic form, with strong second, third, and fifth ictuses, was used almost exclusively, and it remains the most common today. Still, as Tsvetaeva's poetry shows, the trochaic pentameter has the potential for much rhythmic variety.

TROCHAIC HEXAMETER

The trochaic hexameter has never been particularly common in Russian poetry. During the second half of the nineteenth century usage of this meter, especially the variant with caesura, reached a peak, but even then it accounted only for a small percentage of the poems being written.[72] In the eighteenth century the trochaic hexameter was used only a few more times than the pentameter: a couple of examples in Lomonosov's *Short Guide to Rhetoric*, a lament by Trediakovsky on the death of Peter the Great, a few songs by Sumarokov, and a scattering of other poems.[73] From the beginnings of syllabo-tonic poetry two distinct forms of the meter have existed, one with a caesura and the other without. The type with caesura remained extremely rare during the first half of the nineteenth century, but over the next several decades was used in the works of poets such as Nekrasov, Lev Mei, Dmitry Minaev, Iakov Polonsky, and Nadson. The trochaic hexameter without caesura owes its origins to folk poetry and appears off and on into the twentieth century in literary imitations of folk verse.[74] In the twentieth century a number of poems not connected with the folk tradition also employ this variant. The trochaic hexameter without caesura was the more popular of the two in the second half of the nineteenth century; today both forms are equally uncommon, together accounting for less than 1 percent of all Russian verse.

The trochaic hexameter may be represented without caesura: $-\cup-\cup$ $-\cup-\cup-\cup\acute-(\cup)$; with caesura: $-\cup-\cup\acute-\cup \| -\cup-\cup\acute-(\cup)$. Since the type without caesura has five ictuses that may or may not be stressed, there are thirty-two possible rhythmic variations for that form. The trochaic hexameter with caesura has a constant stress on the third ictus, and as a result all the rhythmic variations that omit stress on that ictus are eliminated. Therefore the number of possible variations is reduced from twenty-eight—if the line had a caesura but not a constant stress on the third ictus—to just sixteen.

In practice, poets have tended to use only a narrow range of these variations. Thus in the trochaic hexameter with caesura, since all the lines with consecutive unstressed ictuses are quite rare, only nine of the sixteen variations are employed for more than 95 percent of the lines in the work of most poets. Two main rhythmic patterns can be discerned in the trochaic hexameter with caesura. One roughly corresponds to the "symmetrical" form of the iambic hexameter: the line breaks down into two symmetrical halves, in which the relatively weak second and fifth ictuses are both surrounded by strong ictuses. Ivan Bunin used the pattern in a poem that opens with the following lines:

Ми́л мне же́мчуг не́жный, чи́стый да́р море́й!   ‒∪‒∪‒∪ ‖ ‒∪‒∪‒
В ло́не океа́на, в ра́ковине те́сной,   ‒∪‒∪‒∪ ‖ ‒∪‒∪‒∪
Ро́с он одино́ко, как цвето́к безве́стный.   ‒∪‒∪‒∪ ‖ ‒∪‒∪‒∪
На обло́мках мши́стых мёртвых корабле́й.   ‒∪‒∪‒∪ ‖ ‒∪‒∪‒

Бу́рею весе́нней вы́брошен со дна́,   ‒∪‒∪‒∪ ‖ ‒∪‒∪‒
Он лежа́л в прибо́е на прибре́жье ди́ком,   ‒∪‒∪‒∪ ‖ ‒∪‒∪‒∪
Где носи́лись ча́йки над водо́ю с кри́ком,   ‒∪‒∪‒∪ ‖ ‒∪‒∪‒∪
Где его́ кача́ла шу́мная волна́...   ‒∪‒∪‒∪ ‖ ‒∪‒∪‒

1901

The poem's rhythmic pattern resembles the practice of Vasily Kurochkin as well as the rhythm of Zhukovsky's 1851 work "The Swan of Tsarskoe Selo" ("Tsarskosel'skii lebed'"), in which the distinction between strong and weak ictuses is more clear-cut (table 16, lines 1–3).

The other rhythmic pattern for the trochaic hexameter with caesura is asymmetrical: the second ictus in the line is stronger than the first, and as a result the two halves of the line no longer follow precisely the same pattern. This form was the most common in the late nineteenth century, and it remains popular among the relatively few poems written in this meter during the twentieth century. The illustration is from a poem by Nikolai Kliuev:[75]

На пого́сте све́чкой те́плятся гнилу́шки,   ∪‒∪‒∪ ‖ ‒∪‒∪‒∪
Доплета́ет ле́ший ла́поть на опу́шке,   ∪‒∪‒∪ ‖ ‒∪‒∪‒∪
Верезжи́т в осо́ке про́клятый младе́нчик...   ∪‒∪‒∪ ‖ ‒∪‒∪‒∪
Пе́тел ждёт, чтоб зо́рька наряди́лась в ве́нчик.   ‒∪‒∪‒∪ ‖ ∪‒∪‒∪

У зари́ наря́дов три́девять укла́док...   ∪‒∪‒∪ ‖ ‒∪‒∪‒∪
На уще́рбе но́чи со́н кури́ный сла́док: ∪‒∪‒∪ ‖ ‒∪‒∪‒∪
Спя́т мона́шка-га́лка, воробе́й-горо́шник...   ‒∪‒∪‒∪ ‖ ∪‒∪‒∪
Но едва́ забре́зжит зарево́й коко́шник –   ∪‒∪‒∪ ‖ ∪‒∪‒∪

1914 or 1915

TABLE 16
Stressing in the Trochaic Hexameter

	Stressing (by ictus)						Average Stressing
	I	II	III	IV	V	VI	
1. Kurochkin	71.4%	60.4%	100%	69.2%	59.3%	100%	76.8%
2. Zhukovsky	77.1	45.7	100	81.4	31.4	100	72.6
3. Bunin ("Mil mne"— 16 lines)	81.2	68.7	100	62.5	56.2	100	78.1
4. Pleshcheev	57.7	74.9	100	72.6	54.9	100	76.7
5. Kliuev ("Galka-staroverka"— 22 lines)	50.0	72.7	100	68.2	54.5	100	74.2
6. Polonsky	43.7	99.7	42.1	99.3	30.1	100	69.2
7. Voznesensky ("Ialtinskaia"— 31 lines)	41.9	100	22.6	100	3.2	100	61.3

Sources: Lines 1, 2, 4, and 6 are from table 15 in the appendix of Taranovsky, *Ruski dvodelni ritmovi*. Lines 3, 5, and 7 are based on my calculations.

The poem is notable for its rhythmic variety; within just twenty-two lines Kliuev manages to include each of the nine rhythmic variations commonly found in the trochaic hexameter with caesura. The rhythmic pattern for the poem as a whole differs little from that which predominated in the work of such nineteenth-century poets as Aleksei Pleshcheev (table 16, lines 4–5). In this pattern the law affecting the beginning of the line takes precedence over the tendency to alternate strong and weak ictuses within a given hemistich.

For the trochaic hexameter without caesura, the two basic laws of Russian verse work in harmony. They predict strong even and weak odd ictuses. Indeed, in the work of most poets all the even ictuses have become constants, or at least near constants, leaving only eight rhythmic variations likely to be used with any frequency at all. (Since the third ictus is not one of the constants, as it is in the trochaic hexameter with caesura, these eight rhythmic variations for the most part do not correspond to the nine used most commonly in the line with caesura.) Voznesensky employs the meter without caesura in his "Yalta Criminal Laboratory" ("Ialtinskaia kriminalisticheskaia laboratoriia"). Individual lines in Voznesensky's works are occasionally shorter than the others in the poem;[76] here, one of the lines is written in trochaic pentameter.[77]

In the other thirty-one lines Voznesensky employs only five different variations, and one of these—the twentieth rhythmic variation, which omits stress on all the odd syllables—appears in 50 percent of the poem's lines. The concluding section of the poem is typical in this regard:

И, глядя́ в меня́ глаза́ми потепле́вшими, $\_\cup\acute{-}\cup\acute{-}\cup\acute{-}\cup\_\cup\acute{-}\cup\cup$
инстинкти́вно проклина́емое мно́й, $\_\cup\acute{-}\cup\_\cup\acute{-}\cup\_\cup\acute{-}$
обвиня́емое и́ли потерпе́вшее, $\_\cup\acute{-}\cup\_\cup\acute{-}\cup\_\cup\acute{-}\cup\cup$
во́ет Вре́мя над мое́ю голово́й! $\acute{-}\cup\acute{-}\cup\_\cup\acute{-}\cup\_\cup\acute{-}$

Победи́тели, прико́ванные к пле́нным. $\_\cup\acute{-}\cup\_\cup\acute{-}\cup\_\cup\acute{-}\cup$
Невменя́емой эпо́хи лабири́нт. $\_\cup\acute{-}\cup\_\cup\acute{-}\cup\_\cup\acute{-}$
Просветле́ние на гра́ни преступле́ния. $\_\cup\acute{-}\cup\_\cup\acute{-}\cup\_\cup\acute{-}\cup$
Бо́же пра́вый, Са́шка Ма́рков, разбери́сь! $\acute{-}\cup\acute{-}\cup\acute{-}\cup\acute{-}\cup\_\cup\acute{-}$

1968

Stressing for the entire poem is quite light; despite the use of constant stresses on the three even ictuses, only 61.3 percent of all the ictuses are actually stressed. Voznesensky completely avoids fully stressed lines and omits at least two stresses on all but five of the lines, creating a rhythm different from that of nineteenth-century poets like Polonsky (table 16, lines 6–7). The line begins similarly in the work of the two poets, but Voznesensky goes on to create a significantly sharper distinction between the strong and weak ictuses.

On the whole the use of constant stresses in the trochaic hexameter has reduced the rhythmic variety of this meter throughout its history. Except for a gradual decrease in the average number of stresses per line, the meter has shown relatively little development over the years.

TROCHAIC TRIMETER

Like the trochaic hexameter, the trimeter has never enjoyed wide popularity. However, during the middle decades of the nineteenth century—a time when the only often-used trochaic meter was the tetrameter—the trimeter was the second most common trochaic meter.[78] The trimeter was extremely rare during the first decades of Russian syllabo-tonic poetry; it was employed only in a few short pieces by Sumarokov and several other poems.[79] The meter remained in the shadows during the early nineteenth century until Aleksei Koltsov used it frequently in his widely popular songs. Koltsov was greatly influenced by folklore, and his songs contain various folk elements, most notably the appearance of nonmetrical stressing on polysyllabic words and the absence of rhyme:

С ра́дости-весе́лья	´⌣‒⌣´⌣
Хме́лем ку́дри вью́тся;	´⌣‒⌣´⌣
Ни с како́й забо́ты	‒⌣‒⌣´⌣
Они́ не секу́тся.	‒⌣́‒⌣´⌣
И́х не гре́бень че́шет:	´⌣‒⌣´⌣
Золота́я до́ля.	‒⌣‒⌣´⌣
Завива́ет в ко́льцы	‒⌣‒⌣´⌣
Молоде́цка у́даль.	‒⌣‒⌣´⌣
Не роди́сь бога́тым,	‒⌣‒⌣´⌣
А роди́сь кудря́вым:	‒⌣‒⌣´⌣
По щу́чью веле́нью	‒⌣́‒⌣´⌣
Всё тебе́ гото́во.	´⌣‒⌣´⌣

1837

In the example lines 4 and 11 have nonmetrical stressing on the second syllable. In Russian binary meters hypermetrical stressing, it will be recalled, is normally limited to monosyllabic words; however, trochaic meters composed in imitation of folk verse allow for exceptions to this rule.[80] After Koltsov, the trochaic trimeter was used regularly by several nineteenth-century poets, but the meter soon receded into the background again. It has remained there ever since, though many poets turn to it on occasion, and, in recent years at least, it has been used more often than the trochaic hexameter.

The structure of the trochaic trimeter is as follows: $‒\cup‒\cup‒(\cup)$. As with the iambic trimeter, there are only four possible rhythmic variations (see table 17). Variation IV is uncommon, though it occurs a bit more often than its equivalent in the iambic trimeter, perhaps because the trochaic variation IV has only four instead of five unstressed syllables at the beginning of the line.

The two basic rhythmic laws clash in this meter; therefore, unlike the iambic trimeter in which a single pattern occurs almost exclusively, the trochaic trimeter has two main rhythmic forms. In one, the alternation of strong and weak ictuses predominates, making the second ictus relatively weak and the first a bit stronger. The following poem by Fedor Sologub illustrates this rhythm:

Вы́вески цветны́е,	´⌣‒⌣´⌣
Бу́квы золоты́е;	´⌣‒⌣´⌣
Со́лнцем залиты́е,	´⌣‒⌣´⌣
Магази́нов ря́д	‒⌣‒⌣‒

TABLE 17
Rhythmic Variations of the Trochaic Trimeter

Number of Omitted Stresses	Number of Variation	Form	Example
0	I	∠∪∠∪∠(∪)	Ко́нчить но́вый кру́г
1	II	_∪∠∪∠(∪)	Переда́м перу́
	III	∠∪_∪∠(∪)	Ме́сяцы по стро́чке
2	IV	_∪_∪∠(∪)	И преображе́нья

Note: Voznesensky's poem "Vremia na remonte" contains a four-line stanza in which all four of the rhythmic variations are used:

Реставрацио́нщик
потроши́т Да Ви́нчи.
«Ле́рмонтов» в ремо́нте.
Что́-то та́м дови́нчивают.
                          1969

Source: Tarkovsky's poem, "Novogodniaia noch'" [<1966].

С бо́йкою прода́жей,   ∠∪_∪∠∪
Гро́хот экипа́жей, –   ∠∪_∪∠∪
Го́род со́лнцу ра́д.   ∠∪∠∪∠
                          1896

For the entire poem the first ictus is stressed twelve out of fourteen times, the second only four times. In larger samples the differences tend to be less extreme (cf. lines 1 and 2 of table 18, which are based on 229 and 196 lines respectively).

In the other type of rhythm the clash of the two laws leaves both the first and second ictuses about equal: the law of regressive accentual dissimilation weakens the second ictus, while the law affecting the beginning of the line weakens the first. The effect can be seen in this poem by Iury Kublanovsky:

На тропе́ петля́ющей   _∪∠∪∠∪∪
ши́шки да песо́к.   ∠∪_∪∠
Парохо́да ла́ющий   _∪∠∪∠∪∪
та́ющий свисто́к.   ∠∪_∪∠

С мо́ром на юро́дивых,   ∠∪_∪∠∪∪
стра́нников, зайк –   _∪_∪∠
ка́к уви́дишь Ро́дины   ∠∪∠∪∠∪∪
потаённый ли́к?   _∪∠∪∠
                          1978

TABLE 18
Stressing and Rhythmic Variations in the Trochaic Trimeter

	Stressing (by ictus)			Rhythmic Variations				Average Stressing
	I	II	III	I	II	III	IV	
1. Mei	68.1%	58.5%	100%	27.5%	31.0%	40.6%	0.9%	75.5%
2. Pleshcheev	74.0	60.7	100	35.2	25.5	38.8	0.5	78.4
3. Sologub ("Vyveski"— 14 lines)	85.7	28.6	100	14.3	14.3	71.4	0	71.4
4. Nikitin	63.3	63.9	100	27.2	36.7	36.1	0	75.7
5. Fet	65.0	67.5	100	33.3	34.2	31.7	0.8	77.5
6. Pasternak ("Skazka"— 100 lines)	60	66	100	26	40	34	0	75.3
7. Kublanovsky ("Molochko"— 24 lines)	62.5	62.5	100	25	37.5	37.5	0	75.0

Sources: Lines 1–2 and 4–5 are from Taranovsky, *Ruski dvodelni ritmovi*, pp. 302, 304; lines 3, 6, and 7 are based on my calculations.

This poem as a whole has precisely equal stressing on the first and second ictuses, though in most cases there usually is a small difference (table 18, lines 4–7).

Thus the trochaic trimeter has shown a little more rhythmic variety than the iambic. In recent years both the trimeters have maintained their minor roles in the repertoire of Russian poets at the same time that the iambic and trochaic hexameters have declined sharply in popularity.

TERNARY METERS

The Russian ternary meters (dactyls, anapests, and amphibrachs) generally do not display the wide variety of rhythms found in most of the binary meters, and therefore they will be discussed in much less detail. Their uniformity is caused mainly by the infrequency with which they omit stress on an ictus. Since stress in Russian speech occurs about once every 2.7 or 2.8 syllables and the ternary meters have ictuses only once every three syllables, it is natural for them to have a stress at virtually every ictus. Another factor inhibiting the omission of stress within ternary lines is the interval of five unstressed syllables that arises when an ictus lacks stress (´∪∪–∪∪´∪). Such intervals occasionally occur in Russian speech, but they are far less common than the span of three unstressed syllables caused by the omission of stress in a binary meter (´∪–∪´∪).

The only place where ternary meters have always omitted stresses with some frequency is at the beginning of dactylic lines. Here the absence of stress means that only three unstressed syllables occur in a row (–∪∪´∪∪´). Other ictuses in dactylic lines and all ictuses in the other two types of ternary meters have been (at least until the twentieth century) stressed consistently.[81] The special behavior of dactylic meters indicates that Taranovsky's law regarding the stabilization of the first ictus *after* the first weak position in the line holds for ternary as well as for binary meters.

While the differences in the anacrusis (zero, one, or two syllables) make for differences in the opening of the lines, the infrequency with which stress is omitted creates similar internal structures for all three types of ternary meters.[82] Consequently, various kinds of ternary meters are sometimes combined within the same poem to create *mixed ternary meters*. Often such poems contain a regular alternation, as in the following poem by Fet, where the odd lines are in dactylic trimeter and the even in amphibrachic trimeter:

В пе́не несётся пото́к,   ́∪∪́∪∪́

Ладью́ обгоня́ют буру́ны,   ∪́∪∪́∪∪́∪

  Ко́рмчий гляди́т на восто́к   ́∪∪́∪∪́

И бу́дит дрожа́щие стру́ны.   ∪́∪∪́∪∪́∪

В бу́рю челно́к полете́л,   ́∪∪́∪∪́

Пусть ко́рмчий поги́бнет в ней шу́мно,   ∪́∪∪́∪∪́∪

Се́рдце, могу́чий, он пе́л –   ́∪∪́∪∪́

То се́рдце, что лю́бит безу́мно.   ∪́∪∪́∪∪́∪

[1866]

Several other examples of this phenomenon are given in chapter 1 (in the section dealing with lines). As those quotations illustrate, the combination is not always as orderly as it is here, but may include a mix of lines in different lengths and meters. Iambic and trochaic meters, as has been noted, are normally not combined within the same work, though some exceptions can be found in folklore and in the work of a few twentieth-century poets.

Until now a certain monotony among the ternary meters has been implied. If the three types differ little except in the anacrusis, and if stresses are rarely omitted within the line, then much opportunity for variety would not seem to exist. However, were that the complete picture it would be hard to account for their sudden growth during the mid-nineteenth century and for their continued popularity since. While they have never quite challenged the overall supremacy of the binary meters, they occupy an important niche in the work of many twentieth-century poets.

Other factors need to be considered as well. First, while the ternary meters in themselves may not afford much variation or contrast, they offer an alternative to the long-predominant binary meters. Many twentieth-century poets have preferred to use a wide range of verse forms, and, while hardly shunning iambs and trochees, they have included a significant number of ternaries in their varied repertoire. Second, even without omitting stresses or changing line lengths, a certain amount of rhythmic diversity can be achieved by changing the combinations of word types from one line to the next. The differences in word lengths and, in words of the same length, in the position of stress create rhythmic distinctions between lines that have identical stress patterns.[83] (The problem of "word boundaries" and their effects on rhythm are discussed in chapter 5.) Third, a large percentage of ternaries are written in one form or another of mixed meter besides that in which the anacrusis varies (as described in the previous paragraph). Thus amphibrachic tetrameter lines may alternate with amphibrachic trimeter, dactylic pentameter with dactylic trimeter, and so forth. Such combinations are by no means rare in binary meters, but they occur relatively more frequently in ternary meters and serve to vary the rhythm from line to line.

A fourth element is hypermetrical stressing. Since the interval between stresses is two syllables, both monosyllabic and disyllabic words may carry hypermetrical stress without disrupting the meter. In binary meters, it will be recalled, hypermetrical stressing is limited to monosyllables. Even in ternaries, though, hypermetrical stressing is most likely to occur on words that are less heavily stressed—for instance, on pronouns and adverbs rather than on verbs and nouns. Conversely, the stresses on the ictuses tend to involve verbs, nouns, and other strongly stressed words.[84] The most common place for hypermetrical stressing is on the initial syllable in amphibrachic and (especially) anapestic lines, just as in binary meters hypermetrical stressing appears most often on the first syllable of iambic lines. Thus in Nekrasov's poetry about 30 percent of all his anapests have hypermetrical stressing on the first syllable.[85] In an extensive survey M. L. Gasparov has determined that the majority of hypermetrical stressing—and the great majority of all such stressing involving strongly stressed words—occurs at the beginning of the line and decreases steadily toward the end in both anapests and amphibrachs. In amphibrachic poems, stressing on the first syllable generally takes place in 10 to 20 percent of all lines; in anapests the figure often exceeds 40 percent.[86] Consider the following poem by Anna Akhmatova, written in alternating anapestic tetrameter and trimeter:

Ста́ли но́чи тепле́е, подта́ивал сне́г,
Вы́шла я́ погляде́ть на луну́,
И спроси́л меня́ ти́хо чужо́й челове́к,
Ме́жду со́сенок встре́тив одну́:

1916

Only once, in the third line, does hypermetrical stressing occur within the line. However, three of the four lines have hypermetrical stressing on the anacrusis, and in the first two cases it occurs on verbs—words that are normally strongly stressed. Poets may well concentrate hypermetrical stressing at the start of the line because an extra stress, especially if it occurs on a noun or a verb, is less likely to have a disruptive effect at the beginning than within the line, where it could cause a break in the rhythmic flow.[87] Also, without hypermetrical stressing, amphi-

brachic lines could not start with words containing initial stress, and
anapestic lines could not open with words stressed on either of the first
two syllables; consequently, by employing hypermetrical stressing on
the first syllable or two of the line the poet achieves greater freedom in
choosing words.

Fifth, ternary meters occasionally contain a significant number of
unstressed ictuses. While omitted stresses played a minimal part in de-
termining the rhythm of ternary meters during the nineteenth century,[88]
they have begun to play a larger role in the twentieth. Many poets occa-
sionally leave ictuses within the line unfulfilled, though only a few au-
thors such as Pasternak have done so often enough to have had a dis-
cernible effect on the rhythm.[89] Pasternak, in at least one case, even
omitted stresses on two consecutive ictuses, thereby creating an interval
of eight consecutive unstressed syllables:

Расска́льзывающаяся артилле́рия   ⌣⌣́⌣⌣–⌣⌣–⌣⌣́⌣⌣
Таре́лями ла́стится к о́тзывам ве́тра   ⌣⌣́⌣⌣⌣́⌣⌣⌣́⌣⌣⌣́⌣
                    1914

More commonly, Pasternak would omit only one stress per line, but he
by no means limited himself to the initial syllable of dactylic lines. Five
of the seven stresses that he omits in the fifty-two-line poem "Space"
("Prostranstvo"), written in amphibrachic trimeter, are on the second
ictus:

Черне́ют серёжки берёз.   ⌣⌣́⌣⌣⌣́⌣⌣⌣́
Лозня́к отлива́ет изна́нкой.   ⌣⌣́⌣⌣⌣́⌣⌣⌣́⌣
Нена́стье, дымя́сь, как обо́з,   ⌣⌣́⌣⌣⌣́⌣⌣⌣́⌣
Заде́рживается по зна́ку,   ⌣⌣́⌣⌣–⌣⌣⌣́⌣
....
Недо́лго прихо́дится жда́ть.   ⌣⌣́⌣⌣⌣́⌣⌣⌣́
Движе́нье нахму́ренной вы́си, –   ⌣⌣́⌣⌣⌣́⌣⌣⌣́⌣
И до́ждь, затяжно́й, как нужда́,   ⌣⌣́⌣⌣⌣́⌣⌣⌣́
Выве́шивает свой би́сер.   ⌣⌣́⌣⌣–⌣⌣́⌣
                    1927

In the second of the quoted stanzas Pasternak shortens the last line by a
syllable; in twentieth-century Russian practice there is nothing unusual
about dropping a syllable when stress is omitted in a ternary line. The
rhythmic pattern for the poem is as follows: I, 96.2 percent; II, 90.4
percent; III, 100 percent. Here the rhythm tends toward the alternation
of strong and weak ictuses found in the iambic trimeter; thus in at least
some instances the omission of stress follows the tendencies predicted

by Taranovsky's laws for binary meters.[90] In Pavel Antokolsky's "On the Debate about Realism" ("K diskussii o realizme"), written in anapestic tetrameter, the second ictus lacks stress four times and the third three times in the course of twenty-eight lines:

Воробьи́ – э́то при́сказка, при́тча, причу́да,   ⌣⌣⌣̲⌣⌣⌣̲⌣⌣⌣̲⌣⌣⌣̲⌣
Лжесвиде́тели предгрозово́го безмо́лвия.   ⌣⌣⌣̲⌣⌣–⌣⌣⌣̲⌣⌣⌣̲⌣⌣
Да́йте сро́к, реали́ст, – ещё бры́знут отту́да   ⌣̲⌣⌣̲⌣⌣⌣̲⌣⌣̲⌣⌣⌣̲⌣
Сногсшиба́тельные, многово́льтные мо́лнии!   ⌣⌣⌣̲⌣⌣–⌣⌣⌣̲⌣⌣⌣̲⌣⌣

Да́йте сро́к!.. Но внеза́пно оно́ и разве́рзлось!   ⌣̲⌣⌣⌣̲⌣⌣⌣̲⌣⌣⌣̲⌣⌣
Но отсю́да мора́ль не дерзка́, не задири́ста.   ⌣⌣⌣̲⌣⌣⌣̲⌣⌣⌣̲⌣⌣⌣̲⌣⌣
Потому́ что в поэ́зии де́рзость не в де́рзость,   ⌣⌣⌣̲⌣⌣⌣̲⌣⌣⌣̲⌣⌣⌣̲⌣
Два́жды два́ не четы́ре, да и не четы́реста.   ⌣̲⌣⌣̲⌣⌣⌣̲⌣⌣–⌣⌣⌣̲⌣⌣

[1964, 1969]

Stressing per ictus for the twenty-eight lines is as follows: I, 100 percent; II, 89.3 percent; III, 85.7 percent; IV, 100 percent. In fact, the stressing is close to the early form of the iambic tetrameter. In 1743, when Lomonosov was still using relatively few unfulfilled ictuses in his syllabo-tonic poetry, his stressing for the iambic tetrameter was as follows: I, 98.4 percent; II, 89.5 percent; III, 82.7 percent; IV, 100 percent.[91] By no means all or even most of the ternary poems written today omit as many stresses as the two examples discussed here, and in general too little material exists to make broad generalizations about patterns of stressing in ternaries. Still, it appears that when stress is omitted with any frequency in a given poem, the resulting pattern often adheres closely to the laws that govern the behavior of binary meters.

Ternaries appeared in Russian poetry almost from the beginning, but throughout the eighteenth century they remained rare. Only a handful of poets—Sumarokov, Mikhail Kheraskov, Gavrila Derzhavin—used them with any frequency. For the most part they appeared in works meant to be accompanied by music—songs, romances, and arias. Poets generally avoided using them in longer poems. Ternary lines tended to be shorter than in the nineteenth or twentieth centuries; the most common length was the dimeter, or two-foot line. While the most widely used single meter was the amphibrachic dimeter, overall there were more dactyls than amphibrachs, with anapests a distant third.[92] During the early nineteenth century the use of ternaries began to grow. While they comprised only about 2 percent of all verse written in the eighteenth century, they comprised about 7 percent of the verse written in the first quarter of the nineteenth century, 18 percent written during the second quarter, and more than 25 percent written throughout the last half.[93] The figures for the leading poets of each era were generally in close agreement with the figures for the period as a whole. Thus Sumarokov wrote ternaries only about 2 percent of the time, Pushkin 3 percent, Lermontov 6 percent, Fet 20 percent, and Nekrasov 27 percent. Throughout the years the favorite types of meters changed frequently. Amphibrachs replaced dactyls as the most common type of ternary meter in the first half of the nineteenth century; all three types were used widely in the second half of that century. As the period drew to a close, anapests emerged as the most popular ternary meter. During the early twentieth century the use of dactyls dropped sharply to where they now occur in only about 10 percent of the ternary meters (or about 2 percent of all Russian poetry), while anapests and amphibrachs make up the rest, with the former a little more widespread.[94] Ternaries are used slightly less often than they were during the latter part of the nineteenth century, though they are still found in about 20 percent of all poems. An extensive survey of Soviet Russian poetry that covered the period 1957–69 offers a good overview of current practice. Out of over 2,700 poems examined, more than 500 were written in ternaries—just under twenty percent. Of these, less than 10 percent were dactyls, about 47 percent anapests, and the remaining 43 percent amphibrachs. The two most widely used meters—the anapestic trimeter and the amphibrachic trimeter—together accounted for almost 50 percent of all ternaries. Other common lines include the anapestic dimeter and tetrameter, the amphibrachic tetrameter, and the dactylic tetrameter.[95]

DACTYLS

Like the other ternary meters, dactyls ordinarily occur in line lengths ranging from the dimeter through the pentameter. Also like the other ternary meters, they frequently combine lines of different lengths within the same poem, most often using a regular pattern such as dactylic tetrameter alternating with dactylic dimeter. Iambs and trochees most often occur in lengths from the trimeter through the hexameter. It is only natural for the binary meters to have, on the average, lines with more ictuses, since an ictus occurs every two syllables in the binaries but only every three in the ternaries. As a result ternary meters with three ictuses—the trimeters—have about as many syllables as iambic and trochaic tetrameters.

Until the second third of the nineteenth century the dactylic dimeter was a widely used verse form, but since then the tetrameter has been by far the most common type of line—a tendency that has, if anything, become even stronger in recent years.[96] Among the binary meters, the most popular lines (the tetrameters and the pentameters) have between seven and eleven syllables when the rhymes are masculine and feminine, and ternary meters seem to favor similar lengths. The dactylic tetrameter generally has ten or eleven syllables (–⏑⏑–⏑⏑–⏑⏑–́(⏑)) and thus falls within these limits. Below are examples of the two dactylic lines most popular in modern times; the trimeter is from Nekrasov and the tetrameter from Zhukovsky:

```
"Мне́ бы хоть де́сять копе́ечек          –́⏑⏑–́⏑⏑–́⏑⏑
С пренумера́нта извле́чь:                 –⏑⏑–́⏑⏑–́
Ведь дарово́ых-то стате́ечек              –⏑⏑–́⏑⏑–́⏑⏑
Мно́го... куда́ их бере́чь?                –́⏑⏑–́⏑⏑–́
Ну́жно во всём беспристра́стие:           –́⏑⏑–́⏑⏑–́⏑⏑
Вы́ их смеша́йте, друзья́,                 –́⏑⏑–́⏑⏑–́
Да и бери́те на сча́стие...               –⏑⏑–́⏑⏑–́⏑⏑
                        1863
```

```
Бы́ли и ле́то и о́сень дожддли́вы;        –́⏑⏑–́⏑⏑–́⏑⏑–́⏑
Бы́ли пото́плены па́жити, ни́вы;           –́⏑⏑–́⏑⏑–́⏑⏑–́⏑
Хле́б на поля́х не созре́л и пропа́л;      –́⏑⏑–́⏑⏑–́⏑⏑–́
Сде́лался го́лод; наро́д умира́л.          –́⏑⏑–́⏑⏑–́⏑⏑–́

Но́ у епи́скопа ми́лостью не́ба            (–́)⏑⏑–́⏑⏑–́⏑⏑–́⏑
По́лны амба́ры огро́мные хле́ба;           –́⏑⏑–́⏑⏑–́⏑⏑–́⏑
Жи́то сберёг прошлого́днее о́н:            –́⏑⏑–́⏑⏑–́⏑⏑–́
Бы́л осторо́жен епи́скоп Га́ттон.          –́⏑⏑–́⏑⏑–́⏑⏑–́
                        1831
```

The Nekrasov excerpt shows the frequency with which poets sometimes omitted stress on the first ictus in dactylic lines even during the nineteenth century. Here the stress is omitted no fewer than three times in seven lines. Zhukovsky, on the other hand, clearly preferred fully stressed lines; he probably intended the conjunction *no* at the beginning of line 5 to be treated as a stressed syllable, since no ictus in the entire poem is definitely unstressed. The Nekrasov lines further point to one reason why dactyls may have fallen out of favor. It is only natural to begin a certain number of lines in a poem with unstressed particles or prepositions or with polysyllabic words stressed on some syllable other than the first. Thus some trochaic and dactylic lines are likely to omit stress on the first syllable—as is predicted by Taranovsky's law regarding the stabilization of the first ictus after the first weak position in the line. In trochaic lines this leads to an interval of two unstressed syllables at the beginning of the line; in a dactylic poem the interval becomes three unstressed syllables, and far fewer words or word combinations fit into the necessary pattern. Amphibrachs and anapests, which normally do not omit stress on the first ictus but do allow some hypermetrical stressing on the syllables preceding that ictus, offer poets a more flexible choice for beginning the line.[97]

AMPHIBRACHS

The most common line length for the amphibrach is the trimeter, which in recent years has appeared in over twice as many poems as all the dactylic meters combined.[98] The tetrameter also occurs with some frequency, and a few poems are written in both the dimeter and pentameter. The trimeter (especially) and the tetrameter are close to the preferred line lengths for binary meters: eight or nine syllables ($\cup-\cup\cup-\cup\cup\pm(\cup)$) and eleven or twelve ($\cup-\cup\cup-\cup\cup-\cup\cup\pm(\cup)$). As with the dactyl, the dimeter was popular in the eighteenth and early nineteenth centuries. While the amphibrachic dimeter is still more common than the binary dimeters, it is now one of the lesser-used forms. Throughout the years amphibrachs have remained consistently in the repertoire of Russian poets. Among the ternary meters they were second to dactyls in the eighteenth century, the most widely used of all the ternaries during the first half of the nineteenth century, more or less on an equal footing with the other two types during the second half of that century, and in recent years seem to have been employed a bit less often than the anapests. In the early days, though, poets were slow to take note of them. As mentioned earlier, the first writer to treat them at all was Sumarokov. By comparison, in English prosody some question exists as to whether the amphibrach should even be considered an independent type of meter.[99] The experience of the past two hundred years, however, leaves no doubt about the viability of the amphibrach for Russian verse.

Below is a poem by Georgy Ivanov written in amphibrachic trimeter and the beginning of a well-known World War II poem by Konstantin Simonov written in amphibrachic tetrameter:

История. Время. Пространство.	$\cup\pm\cup\cup\pm\cup\cup\pm\cup$
Людские слова и дела.	$\cup\pm\cup\cup\pm\cup\cup\pm$
Полвека войны. Христианства	$\cup\pm\cup\cup\pm\cup\cup\pm\cup$
Двухтысячелетняя мгла.	$\cup-\cup\cup\pm\cup\cup\pm$

Пора́ бы и угомони́ться...   ⌣⏜⌣⌣–⌣⌣⏜⌣
Но ду́мает ка́ждый – посто́й,   ⌣⏜⌣⌣⏜⌣⌣⏜
А, мо́жет быть, мне́ и присни́тся   ⌣⏜⌣⌣⏜⌣⌣⏜⌣
Бессме́ртия со́н золото́й!   ⌣⏜⌣⌣⏜⌣⌣⏜

    1954

Ты по́мнишь, Алёша, доро́ги Смоле́нщины,   ⌣⏜⌣⌣⏜⌣⌣⏜⌣⌣⏜⌣⌣
Как шли́ бесконе́чные, злы́е дожди́,   ⌣⏜⌣⌣⏜⌣⌣⏜⌣⌣⏜
Как кри́нки несли́ нам уста́лые же́нщины,   ⌣⏜⌣⌣⏜⌣⌣⏜⌣⌣⏜⌣⌣
Прижа́в, как дете́й, от дождя́ их к груди́,   ⌣⏜⌣⌣⏜⌣⌣⏜⌣⌣⏜

Как слёзы они́ вытира́ли укра́дкою,   ⌣⏜⌣⌣⏜⌣⌣⏜⌣⌣⏜⌣⌣
Как всле́д нам шепта́ли: – Госпо́дь вас   ⌣⏜⌣⌣⏜⌣⌣⏜⌣⌣⏜
 спаси́! –
И сно́ва себя́ называ́ли солда́тками,   ⌣⏜⌣⌣⏜⌣⌣⏜⌣⌣⏜⌣⌣
Как вста́рь повело́сь на вели́кой Руси́.   ⌣⏜⌣⌣⏜⌣⌣⏜⌣⌣⏜

    1941

In the Ivanov poem a stress is omitted in each of the fourth and fifth
lines, which would have been unthinkable in the nineteenth century.
Many poets, though, as in the Simonov excerpt, continue to stress every
(or nearly every) ictus in works employing amphibrachs or anapests.

ANAPESTS

The anapests were the last of the ternary meters to become well es-
tablished. During the eighteenth and the first quarter of the nineteenth
centuries they were used far more rarely than either dactyls or amphi-
brachs.[100] But around the middle of the nineteenth century, when the ter-
nary meters were first used widely, the anapests suddenly became the
most frequently employed of all the ternary meters. Their popularity
has since fluctuated, but they have remained first or a close second.
While the trimeter is easily the most common of all the anapest meters,
significant numbers of both the dimeter and tetrameter have been used
as well. Over the years anapests have been written in dimeters more
often than in any of the other ternary meters; this is probably because
the minimal length for this line is six syllables, in the case of masculine
rhyme, while for other types of ternary meters these already short lines
are shorter by a syllable (in the case of amphibrachs) or two (with dac-
tyls). The distinguishing trait of many anapestic poems is the frequent
use of hypermetrical stressing, especially on the first syllable of the
line. Following are examples of the anapestic trimeter by Boris Poplav-
sky and the anapestic tetrameter by Nikolai Gumilev:

"Кто там хо́дит?" – "Поги́бшая па́мять".
– "Где любо́вь?" – "Возврати́лась к царю́".
Сне́г покры́л, то́чно а́лое зна́мя,
Мертвецо́в, отоше́дших в зарю́.

Им не на́до ни сча́стья, ни ве́ры,
Им миле́й абсолю́тная но́чь,
Кто дости́г ледяно́го барье́ра
Хо́чет то́лько года́ превозмо́чь.

1925

Це́лый де́нь над водо́й, сло́вно ста́я стреко́з,
Золоты́е летучие ры́бы видны́,
У песча́ных, серпа́ми изо́гнутых ко́с,
Ме́ли, то́чно цветы́, зелены́ и красны́.

Бле́щет во́здух, нали́тый прозра́чным огнём,
Со́лнце ска́зочной пти́цей гляди́т с высоты́:
– Мо́ре, Кра́сное мо́ре, ты ца́рственно днём,
Но нoча́ми вдвойне́ ослепи́тельно ты́!

1918

For Poplavsky's "Vspomnit'—Voskresnut'" ("To Remember Is to Resurrect") as a whole, 25 percent of the lines begin with a definite hypermetrical stress, and several others begin with interrogative words that bear at least a weak stress. The excerpt from Gumilev's "Red Sea" ("Krasnoe more") contains particularly frequent hypermetrical stressing that falls on nouns, verbs, and an adjective. Five of the eight lines have a prominent hypermetrical stress on the opening syllable. Interestingly, in the first twelve lines of the poem Gumilev only once places a hypermetrical stress on the first syllable; possibly he felt freer to use this device once the metrical pattern of the poem was already well established.

MIXED AND UNUSUAL CLASSICAL METERS

MIXED METERS

The term *mixed meters* is applied to poems written in a particular type of line (iambic, trochaic, dactylic), but with line lengths that vary according to some regular pattern. In the case of ternary meters the mixture may also involve a varying anacrusis; that is, as discussed in the previous section, the same poem may contain, for instance, both dactyls and amphibrachs. There is nothing particularly unusual about mixed meters; almost all poets have used them upon occasion, and they occur in a wide variety of patterns. The most common are those involving a regular alternation of just two line lengths. Thus in iambic poetry the tetrameter sometimes alternates with the trimeter or dimeter, the hexameter with the tetrameter, and the pentameter with the trimeter, or, as in the following poem by Khodasevich, the tetrameter:

Слепая сердца мудрость! Что ты значишь?	∪́∪́∪́∪́∪́∪
На что ты можешь дать ответ?	∪́∪́∪́∪́
Сама томишься, пленница, и плачешь:	∪́∪́∪́∪‒∪́∪
Тебе самой исхода нет.	∪́∪́∪́∪́
Рождённая от опыта земного,	∪́∪‒∪́∪‒∪́∪
Бессильная пред злобой дня,	∪́∪‒∪́∪́
Сама себя ты уязвить готова,	∪́∪́∪‒∪‒∪́∪
Как скорпион в кольце огня.	∪‒∪́∪́∪́

1921

In trochaic poetry, at least in the nineteenth century, the tetrameter was by far the most common line, and most of the mixed meters consequently included it as one element. Typical combinations were the trochaic tetrameter and trimeter as well as the tetrameter and dimeter, as in these lines by Sologub:

За рекой я вижу крышу,	‒∪́∪́∪́∪
Мамин дом.	́∪́
Песню сестрину я слышу	́∪́∪‒∪́∪
За холмом.	‒∪́
Мост на речке там пониже,	́∪́∪́∪́∪
Где завод,	́∪́
Только есть дорога ближе,	́∪́∪́∪́∪
Этот брод.	́∪́

1900

Generally, the lines involved differ in length by only one or two feet; thus a combination such as iambic pentameter and dimeter occurs less often than iambic tetrameter with either trimeter or dimeter. Trochaic and iambic dimeters, which are both rarely used as the sole meter throughout a poem, appear regularly as a component in mixed meters. Even single-foot lines (monometers), which are virtually never employed as a poem's only meter, occasionally alternate with some longer line throughout a poem.

Mixed meters are by no means limited to every-other-line alternations. The opening two stanzas of this Polonsky poem illustrate the fairly common practice of using a short line to end a stanza. Though the

difference between these lines is an unusually large three feet, the hex-
ameter and trimeter go well together since the trimeter is the equivalent
of one hemistich in the iambic hexameter with caesura:

Я, двух корабликов хозяин с юных дней,
Стал снаряжать их в путь; один кораблик
    мой
Ушёл в прошедшее, на поиски людей,
    Прославленных молвой,

Другой – заветные мечты мои помчал
В загадочную даль – в туман грядущих
    дней.
Туда, где братства и свободы идеал,
    Но – нет ещё людей.

                                                        1870

While the pattern is normally the same from stanza to stanza, the actual
pattern within each stanza may be quite complex.[101] As mentioned
above, ternaries, possibly because they omit stress less often than the
binaries and thus need other ways to create rhythmic variety, mix lines
of different length relatively more often than do iambic and trochaic
verse. The following amphibrachic poem by Minsky uses lines of three
different lengths (as do some iambic and trochaic poems); here, the first
and third lines of each stanza are in tetrameter, the second in pen-
tameter, and the fourth in dimeter:

На том берегу наше солнце зайдёт,
Устав по лазури чертить огневую дугу.
И крыльев бесследных смирится полёт
    На том берегу.

На том берегу отдыхают равно
Цветок нерасцветший и тот, что завял на лугу.
Всему, что вне жизни, бессмертье дано
    На том берегу.

                                                        1896

    Whenever any of the less regular forms appear, even within the Rus-
sian classical meters, problems of nomenclature and classification arise.
One such difficulty concerns nonstanzaic poems in which two lines of
different lengths alternate irregularly. In the following work Evgeny
Baratynsky uses both iambic hexameter and iambic tetrameter lines:

Узнал ли друга ты? – Болезни и печали
Его состарили во цвете юных лет;
Уж много слабостей тебе знакомых нет,
Уж многие мечты ему чужими стали!

Рассу́док тве́рже и верне́й,
Посту́пки, разгово́р скромне́е;
Он осторо́жней ста́л, быть мо́жет ста́л умне́е,
Но, ве́рно, сча́стием тепе́рь стокра́т бедне́й.

∪́∪́∪́—∪́
∪́∪—∪́∪́
∪—∪∪́∪́ ‖ ∪́∪́∪́∪
∪́∪́∪— ‖ ∪́∪́∪́

[1819]

The entire poem contains thirty-six lines, of which twenty-eight are in iambic hexameter and the remainder in iambic tetrameter. Russian metrists call such poems *transitional forms* (*perekhodnye formy*), by which is meant a poem written primarily in one meter but containing a few lines (up to about 25 percent) of another meter (or meters).[102] The Baratynsky poem has been described as a transitional form between iambic hexameter and variable (or "free") iambs.[103] Iambic hexameter lines clearly predominate in the poem, but if it contained a few more lines in tetrameter it would belong to a different category.

One further point regarding mixed meters deserves mention. Russian classical meters normally have the same number of ictuses per line throughout the poem as well as the same type of alternation of strong and weak positions (that is, ictuses and syllables that are normally left unstressed). In the mixed meters the first of these two features no longer applies. While the mixed meters have been around since the beginning of Russian syllabo-tonic poetry, they appeared comparatively more often in the ternary meters, which became widely used only in the second half of the nineteenth century. The next step, introducing entirely new meters into Russian poetry, occurred around the turn of the next century. Perhaps the wider use of different line lengths within the same poem helped pave the way for poets to take certain liberties within the line as well.

VARIABLE (FREE) METERS

The word *vol'nyi* when it occurs in the context of Russian metrics is generally translated as "free," but this rendering creates confusion between *vol'nyi stikh* and *svobodnyi stikh*, both of which translate as "free verse." Only the latter refers to what is traditionally known as free verse; *vol'nyi stikh* maintains a given type of line throughout, but the lines are of varying length (thus *vol'nye iamby*, *vol'nye khorei*). To avoid confusion about what is and is not free verse, I propose to use the term *variable* when discussing the various kinds of *vol'nyi stikh*.

The variable meters in some ways resemble the mixed meters, which could be classified as a special case of variable verse.[104] However, the term *variable verse* is primarily applied to poems in which line lengths are mixed according to no particular pattern. During the eighteenth and nineteenth centuries variable verse was, for the most part, limited to iambs. In the eighteenth century Sumarokov wrote a few fables in other variable meters: trochaic, amphibrachic, and anapestic. However, most of his own variable verse as well as that of nearly all his successors was iambic.[105] Only around the beginning of the twentieth century did other variable meters begin to appear in noticeable numbers, though none have been used remotely as often as were the variable iambs in the eighteenth and the first half of the nineteenth centuries. The spurt of interest in new forms of variable meters at the beginning of the twentieth century has since receded; nowadays variable meters continue to occur, but they have become something of a rarity.[106]

In the eighteenth century variable iambs were one of the predominant verse forms, appearing in more than 25 percent of all works and 12 percent of all lines. The occurrence of this meter in a higher percentage of works than of lines suggests that many of the works were short, and such is the case. The variable iamb came to be associated most clearly with the fable, beginning with Sumarokov and continuing with Vasily Maikov, Mikhail Kheraskov, Ivan Khemnitser, and Ippolit Bogdanovich. In the nineteenth century the connection continued in the fables of Zhukovsky, Ivan Dmitriev, and, most importantly of all, Ivan Krylov. However, many longer works were also written in variable iambs throughout the eighteenth century: plays by Iakov Kniazhnin and Gavrila Derzhavin; epistles by Sumarokov, Kheraskov, and others; odes by such poets as Sumarokov and Derzhavin; and long narrative poems, most notably Bogdanovich's *Dushen'ka*.[107] In the nineteenth century, besides the three poets already mentioned, Batiushkov, Baratynsky, Pushkin, Griboedov, and Lermontov all wrote much verse in variable iambs. Two of the better-known plays from that era—Lermontov's *The Masquerade* (*Maskarad*) and Griboedov's *Woe from Wit* (*Gore ot uma*)— both used this meter, as did many elegies and a wide variety of lyric poetry.[108] After about 1830 the number of variable iambs dropped markedly, mostly as a result of the decline in popularity of both the fable and the elegy.[109]

Perhaps the most famous works in variable iambs are Krylov's fables and Griboedov's *Woe from Wit*. Following are Krylov's "The Kite" ("Bumazhnyi zmei") and an excerpt from a monologue by Chatsky in Griboedov's play:

Запущенный под облака,
Бумажный Змей, приметя свысока
В долине мотылька,
"Поверишь ли! – кричит, – чуть-чуть тебя
            мне видно:
Признайся, что тебе завидно
Смотреть на мой высокий столь полёт". –
"Завидно? Право, нет!
Напрасно о себе ты много так мечтаешь!
Хоть высоко, но ты на привязи летаешь.
      Такая жизнь, мой свет,
      От счастия весьма далёко;
      А я, хоть, правда, невысоко,
            Зато. лечу
            Куда хочу;
Да я же так, как ты, в забаву для другого,
            Пустого
      Век целый не трещу".

                              1814

Что это? слышал ли моими я ушами!
Не смех, а явно злость. Какими чудесами?
      Через какое колдовство
Нелепость обо мне всё в голос повторяют!
      И для иных как словно торжество,
      Другие будто сострадают...
      О! если б кто в людей проник:
      Что хуже в них? душа или язык?
            Чьё это сочиненье?
Поверили глупцы, другим передают,
      Старухи вмиг тревогу бьют –
      И вот общественное мненье!

                              1822-24

The Krylov fable is notable in that it contains the full range of line lengths employed by Krylov: from one foot through six. The passage from Griboedov consists only of lines ranging from three to six feet, though he too has some one- and two-foot lines. In fact, both Krylov and Griboedov favored similar line lengths. Each used iambic hexameter in more than 40 percent of the lines, pentameter in 15 percent, tetrameter in 33 percent. A smattering of shorter lines occurred as well—though in Krylov the shorter lines amount to a significant 13 percent, whereas in Griboedov they total only 4 percent. Throughout the eighteenth and nineteenth centuries lines longer than six feet were extremely rare; Krylov did not use any lines with seven feet, and no other nineteenth-century poet used them more than once.[110]

While Griboedov and Krylov present the typical usage of the variable iamb during the early nineteenth century, the distribution of line lengths has tended to reflect their popularity in other types of verse. Originally, poets turned to this meter at least partly to avoid the regularity of iambic verse written in a single meter; by varying line lengths they were able to impart to their poetry some of the rhythm of ordinary speech. Initially, variable iambs substituted for the relatively monotonous and heavy Alexandrine (iambic hexameter)—a very common meter in the eighteenth century.[111] At least 40 percent and often more than 50 percent of the lines in the variable iambs of all eighteenth-century poets were hexameters. For a while the second most common line was the trimeter (i.e., simply half the hexameter line), so the early examples of this meter showed a 6-3 profile. In the latter part of the eighteenth century the iambic tetrameter began to win wide favor for use in all verse, including variable iambs, and thus a 6-4-3 pattern predominated. At the beginning of the next century the trimeter rapidly fell out of favor, while the previously uncommon iambic pentameter became an important line for the variable iamb. The preferred lengths were then 6-4-5, as in both Krylov and Griboedov. Subsequently, the pentameter became still more popular: already in Lermontov's work the most widely used lines for the variable iamb were 6-5-4; in Nekrasov, and still later in Esenin, the predominant pattern evolved into 5-4-6.[112]

The actual types of lines used came to depend somewhat on the genre. According to Boris Tomashevsky, during the height of their popularity variable iambs appeared in three main kinds of works: lyrics (primarily elegies in the early nineteenth century), didactic narratives (fables), and dramatic verse.[113] Krylov's fables, which attempt to capture a light conversational tone, use more short lines than do the more formal epistles and elegies. Also, some genres were quicker to adapt to the iambic pentameter line than were others; narrative poetry and drama showed the most marked change between the eighteenth and nineteenth centuries, while the short lyrical forms adapted to the newly popular lengths more slowly.[114]

Despite the changes in line lengths, several features of the variable iamb remained constant throughout the eighteenth and nineteenth centuries. First, the line length stayed within the limits of one to six feet, though one-foot lines were relatively uncommon, accounting for from 0 to 3 percent in the work of individual poets. Seven-foot lines were rare in the eighteenth century and rarer still in the nineteenth. Since line lengths may vary, the end of the line was determined less by metrical

necessity than by the demands of intonation and syntax. This in turn
created a more "conversational" tone, for the lines were lengthened or
shortened according to the natural flow of the phrases. Enjambment was
virtually unnecessary and was called upon only rarely to create special
emphasis. Finally, rhyme, as a result of the changing line lengths, be-
came the main means for signaling arrival at the end of the line and so
was especially noticeable.[115] In the Krylov fable quoted above, as is
often the case in variable iambs, many of the rhymes are adjacent; alter-
nating rhyme occurs in the variable iamb, but adjacent rhymes make it
easier to signal the ends of lines. As in the first three lines of this fable,
poets often employed triple adjacent rhymes and sometimes even qua-
druple rhyme.[116]

Variable verse changed in the early twentieth century. Most notable
was its appearance in line types other than iambic. The variable trochee
occurred in a handful of poems, though the first, and quite possibly the
only, poet to use variable trochees extensively was Vladimir Maiakov-
sky. A few of his lyrics were composed entirely in this meter, as were
major portions of several longer works.[117] Among the poems written en-
tirely in variable trochees is "To Sergei Esenin" ("Sergeiu Eseninu"),
from which the following excerpt is taken:

Не откро́ют
     нам
          причи́н поте́ри   — ∪ ∸ ∪ ∸ ∪ ∸ ∪ ∸ ∪
ни петля́
     ни но́жик перочи́нный.   — ∪ ∸ ∪ ∸ ∪ — ∪ ∸ ∪
Мо́жет,
     окажи́сь
          черни́ла в "Англете́ре",   ∸ ∪ — ∪ ∸ ∪ ∸ ∪ — ∪ ∸ ∪
ве́ны
     ре́зать
          не́ было б причи́ны.   ∸ ∪ ∸ ∪ ∸ ∪ — ∪ ∸ ∪
Подража́тели обра́довались:
              би́с!   — ∪ ∸ ∪ — ∪ ∸ ∪ — ∪ ∸
Над собо́ю
     чу́ть не взво́д
          распра́ву учини́л.   — ∪ ∸ ∪ ∸ ∪ ∸ ∪ ∸ ∪ — ∪ ∸
Почему́ же
     увели́чивать
          число́ самоуби́йств?   — ∪ ∸ ∪ — ∪ ∸ ∪ — ∪ ∸ ∪ — ∪ ∸
Лу́чше
     увели́чь
          изготовле́ние черни́л!   ∸ ∪ — ∪ ∸ ∪ — ∪ ∸ ∪ — ∪ ∸

                              1926

Owing to Maiakovsky's "stepladder" (*lesenka*) technique of breaking the line into smaller units for emphasis, the twenty-two lines that appear graphically represent only eight lines of actual verse, ranging from five to eight feet (5-5-6-5-6-7-8-7). Over the entire poem Maiakovsky uses primarily six- and five-foot lines, with seven-foot lines a distant third. The work has two lines in octameter, one each in monometer and dimeter, and not a single line in trimeter or tetrameter. What distinguishes Maiakovsky's variable verse from nineteenth-century practice is, first, his very use of trochees, and second, his propensity toward long lines. If the typical nineteenth-century poem in variable iambs favored a 6-4-5 or 6-5-4 frequency of line lengths, then in Maiakovsky's work the preferred lines are 6-5-7, with tetrameter lines a very weak fourth. Octameter lines appear every so often, and he even has a few lines in nine and ten feet.[118] Nor was Maiakovsky the only poet to experiment with long lines. Ehrenburg used long lines in both variable iambic and variable trochaic poetry, while Pasternak wrote variable iambs with line lengths similar to those of Maiakovsky.[119] Below is the opening of Ilia Ehrenburg's "Russia" ("Rossija"), written in variable iambs; none of the poem's twenty lines contains fewer than five feet:

> Смердишь, распухла с голоду, сочатся   ∪́∠∪∠∪∠−∪∠∪∠∪∠∪∠∪∠
>   кровь и гной из ран отверстых.
> Вопя и корчась, к матери-земле   ∪∠∪∠∪∠∪−∪∠∪∠∪∠
>   припала ты.
> Россия, твой родильный бред они   ∪∠∪∠∪∠∪∠∪∠∪∠∪∠∪
>   сочли за смертный,
> Гнушаются тобой, разумны и чисты.   ∪∠∪−∪∠∪∠∪∠∪∠∪−∪∠
> Бесплодно чрево их, пустые груди   ∪∠∪∠∪∠∪∠∪∠−∪∠∪
>   каменеют.
> Кто древнее наследие возьмёт?   ∪́∠∪−∪∠∪∠−∪∠
> Кто разожжёт и дальше понесёт   ∪́−∪∠∪∠∪−∪∠
> Полупогасший факел Прометея?   ∪−∪∠∪∠∪−∪∠∪

1920

While variable verse still occurs in Russian poetry, few attempts have been made to continue the 1890–1930 experiments. Most poems in the variable binary meters stay within the six-foot limit that prevailed during the nineteenth century. However, one effect of the innovations remains: variable trochees and even variable ternary meters can be found alongside variable iambs. Ternary poems with varying line lengths have always been rare; Bunin was one of the first to use such meters, but neither he nor anyone else worked with them to any great extent. A more

recent example can be seen in this excerpt from a poem by Boris Sluts-
ky, written in variable anapests ranging from one to four feet:

У хоро́ших писа́телей ме́тод просто́й: ∪∪⊥∪∪⊥∪∪⊥∪∪⊥
Повою́й, как Толсто́й.   ∪∪⊥∪∪⊥
Походи́ по Руси́, сло́вно Го́рький, пешко́м, ∪∪⊥∪∪⊥∪∪⊥∪∪⊥
С посошко́м   ∪∪⊥
И запле́чным мешко́м.   ∪∪⊥∪∪⊥

Е́сли е́сть в тебе́ да́р, так стреля́й, как Гайда́р, ∪∪⊥∪∪⊥∪∪⊥
И, как Ба́йрон, плыви́ по волна́м.   ∪∪⊥∪∪⊥∪∪⊥
Во́т кому́ не зави́довать сле́дует на́м,   ∪∪⊥∪∪⊥∪∪⊥∪∪⊥
Про́сто сле́довать сле́дует на́м.   ∪∪⊥∪∪⊥∪∪⊥

                  [< 1963]

SHORT AND LONG LINES

Iambic or trochaic lines with fewer than three feet generally appear
only as part of a mixed or variable meter, while poems consisting en-
tirely of lines written with more than six feet are fairly rare. Ternaries,
especially anapests, are more likely than binary meters to appear in
lines with as few as two feet. Conversely, ternary lines longer than five
feet must contain a minimum of sixteen syllables (in the case of dactylic
hexameter with masculine rhyme) and are thus generally avoided. Theo-
retically and in practice, lines longer or shorter than the standard lengths
are possible, and often they are used quite successfully. Lines as short as
the monometers, with a single foot and about two to four syllables in
length, are obviously difficult to sustain for an entire poem. But dimeter
lines are at least possible for trochees (three or four syllables, assuming
masculine or feminine rhyme) and iambs (four or five syllables), and
they are not difficult to write in the ternary meters (four to seven syl-
lables). Longer lines too appear in the Russian poetic tradition. In the
eighteenth and first half of the nineteenth century many poets employed
an imitation of the Greek and Latin hexameter. The Russian line was
based on the dactylic hexameter with unrhymed feminine ending. It
could drop one or two (and occasionally more) unstressed syllables but
it still usually contained from fifteen to seventeen syllables on each
line—quite a few more than the typical Russian line length of about
eight to eleven syllables.

Thus, even though long lines virtually require a caesura for structural
purposes, no strictures seem to exist against employing lines with up to

sixteen or eighteen syllables. At that point the line begins to become unwieldy, and some of the poems written in extremely long lines are more notable for their experimental than their poetic value. Some long lines may seem to consist of two shorter lines written together on one line. Thus the iambic or trochaic octameter at times appears to comprise pairs of tetrameter lines. However, the same could be said about many poems in iambic or trochaic hexameter with caesura, especially those in which the two halves of the line show symmetrical patterns of stressing. In such cases accepting the author's intention seems best; indeed, upon close examination the long lines often reveal a rhythmic unity that distinguishes them from a combination of two shorter lines.[120]

The iambic dimeter, while hardly a popular meter, has consistently remained within the repertoire of Russian poets. The following two examples are from Nikolai Iazykov and Viacheslav Ivanov:

Очарова́нье
Мои́х оче́й!
В стекле́ зыбе́й
Зари́ сия́нье,
Как в небеса́х;
Струи́ дрожа́ли,
Они́ игра́ли
В её луча́х...
1824

И го́рлиц ро́кот
Мне воркова́л:
Но прерыва́л
Их о́рлий клёкот.

И не́ги ле́пет
Меня́ ласка́л:
Но звёзд сверка́л
Ревни́вый тре́пет.
[1904]

As is evident, the iambic dimeter has only two rhythmic types: the fully stressed line and the line lacking stress on the first ictus. Not only is rhythmic variety limited, but the extremely short lines limit the words that can be used. Thus the tendency for poets to avoid this line is understandable.

Even more limited is the trochaic dimeter, which, because the ictuses fall on the odd syllables, is a syllable shorter than the already short iambic dimeter. Again, only two possible rhythmic variants exist, but unlike iambic dimeter, where the fully stressed line is more common, the trochaic is affected by the tendency in Russian poetry to avoid heavy stressing of the first ictus when it coincides with the first syllable of the line. The line therefore often begins with two unstressed syllables, making it difficult, if not impossible, to distinguish the trochaic dimeter from the anapestic monometer. Both have constant stress on the third syllable of the line and occasional stress on the first. In the first of the following examples taken from Fet, the use of both masculine and feminine rhymes makes some of the lines as long as two full feet; also, more than 33 percent of the lines have stress on the first syllable, and thus some grounds exist for regarding the poem as trochaic dimeter. The second poem, by Ivan Miatlev, has less stressing on the first syllable and, because of its constant masculine rhymes, contains precisely three syllables per line. Thus it might better be considered an example of anapestic monometer:

Неизбе́жно,	– ∪ ´∪
Стра́стно, не́жно	´∪ ´∪
Упова́ть,	– ∪ ´
Без уси́лий	– ∪ ´∪
С пле́ском кры́лий	´∪ ´∪
Залета́ть	– ∪ ´
В ми́р стремле́ний,	´∪ ´∪
Преклоне́ний	– ∪ ´∪
И моли́тв;	– ∪ ´
Ра́дость чу́я,	´∪ ´∪
Не хочу́ я	– ∪ ´∪
Ва́ших би́тв.	´∪ ´

1869

Тарака́н	∪ ∪ ´
Как в стака́н	∪ ∪ ´
Попадёт –	∪ ∪ ´
Пропадёт,	∪ ∪ ´
На стекло́	∪ ∪ ´
Тяжело́	∪ ∪ ´
Не всползёт.	∪ ∪ ´
Та́к и я́:	◡ ∪ ´
Жи́знь моя́	◡ ∪ ´
Отцвела́,	∪ ∪ ´
Отбыла́;	∪ ∪ ´

1833

By contrast, the ternary dimeters seem much more natural for Russian verse. Indeed, the amphibrachic dimeter, with its second ictus falling on the fifth syllable of the line, is as long as the trochaic trimeter.

Similarly, the anapestic dimeter has as many syllables as the iambic trimeter. The following examples are by Nikolai Nekrasov and Rimma Kazakova, respectively:

Я е́хал к Росто́ву	∪–́∪∪–́∪
Высо́ким холмо́м,	∪–́∪∪–́
Лесо́к малоро́слый	∪–́∪∪–́∪
Тяну́лся на нём:	∪–́∪∪–́
Берёза, оси́на,	∪–́∪∪–́∪
Да е́ль, да сосна́;	∪–́∪∪–́
А сле́ва – доли́на,	∪–́∪∪–́∪
Как ска́терть, ровна́.	∪–́∪∪–́

                     1873

Что за глу́пая спе́шка,	∪∪–́∪∪–́∪
что за сме́рть на бегу́?	∪∪–́∪∪–́
Я, уби́тая пе́шка,	∪∪–́∪∪–́∪
ничего́ не могу́.	∪∪–́∪∪–́
Лакони́чна кавы́чка,	∪∪–́∪∪–́∪
то́чка стро́чек твои́х.	–́∪–́∪∪–́
Нелоги́чна привы́чка	∪∪–́∪∪–́∪
одному́ – за двои́х.	∪∪–́∪∪–́

                   [<1974]

Not surprisingly, both the amphibrachic and anapestic dimeters have been used more widely than either of the binary dimeters, and the anapestic dimeter is one of the common ternary meters. Dactylic dimeters, like other dactylic meters, are much less frequent than their amphibrachic and anapestic equivalents. Below are the opening lines of a poem by Nikolai Morshen:

Где́ под луно́ю	–́∪∪–́∪
Ка́мень беле́ет,	–́∪∪–́∪
Па́хнут землёю	–́∪∪–́∪
В па́рке алле́и.	–́∪∪–́∪
В ча́с полуно́чный	–́∪∪–́∪
Слы́шится гу́лко	–́∪∪–́∪
Зву́к одино́чный	–́∪∪–́∪
Из переу́лка:	–∪∪–́∪

                [<1959]

Poems in monometers are not only rare but belong more to the realm of curiosities than serious poetry. Among the few examples of such works are poems in Briusov's appropriately titled "Experiments" ("Opyty"). The trochees are written three to the line and the iambs four to the line.

Мо́ря вя́зкий шу́м, $\stackrel{\_}{\smile} / \stackrel{\_}{\smile} / \stackrel{\_}{}$
Вто́ря пля́ске ду́м, $\stackrel{\_}{\smile} / \stackrel{\_}{\smile} / \stackrel{\_}{}$
Зли́тся, – где́-то та́м... $\stackrel{\_}{\smile} / \stackrel{\_}{\smile} / \stackrel{\_}{}$
Мни́тся э́то – к на́м. $\stackrel{\_}{\smile} / \stackrel{\_}{\smile} / \stackrel{\_}{}$

И но́чи – коро́че, и те́ни – светле́й, $\smile \stackrel{\_}{} \smile / \smile \stackrel{\_}{} \smile / \smile \stackrel{\_}{} \smile / \smile \stackrel{\_}{}$
Щебе́чет, лепе́чет весе́нний ручей. $\smile \stackrel{\_}{} \smile / \smile \stackrel{\_}{} \smile / \smile \stackrel{\_}{} \smile / \smile \stackrel{\_}{}$

1918

Note that there is no difference between the iambic monometer and an amphibrachic monometer; both have stress on the second syllable of the "line." Similarly, the trochaic monometer is identical to a dactylic monometer, and, as noted earlier, the anapestic monometer is roughly equivalent to the trochaic dimeter. But the shortest lines of all can be found in Ilia Selvinsky's "Sonnet," written entirely in monosyllabic lines:

До́л
Се́д.
Шёл
Де́д.

Спе́д
Вёл –
Брёл
Всле́д.

Вдру́г
Лу́к
Ввы́сь:

Тра́х!
Ры́сь
В пра́х.
1927

Although long lines have been written since the very beginnings of Russian syllabo-tonic poetry, they never occurred in such variety as during the so-called Silver Age, when the symbolist poets led the revival of interest in poetic technique. Among the symbolists, Briusov and Konstantin Balmont are the most notable for their experiments with long lines, though such meters occur in the works of the other symbolists as well as in many of their contemporaries. Several futurist poets such as Maiakovsky and Igor Severianin also experimented with lines longer than those found in nineteenth-century practice.

While there is theoretically no limit to the length of a line, almost no ternary and only a handful of binary poems are written with lines containing more than eight feet. The most common of the long lines that appeared around the beginning of the twentieth century is the trochaic octameter, generally containing fifteen or sixteen syllables. Balmont, for instance, wrote over 150 poems in what might be called long meters, and of these more than 90 are in trochaic octameter.[121] Briusov, Sologub, Dmitry Merezhkovsky, Viacheslav Ivanov, and several other poets all used the meter as well.[122] The iambic octameter, while perhaps occupying a less salient position among the other iambic meters than does the trochaic octameter among the other trochees, is also not uncommon. The following excerpts are by Gumilev and Georgy Ivanov:

Соловьи́ на кипари́сах и над о́зером луна́,
Ка́мень чёрный, ка́мень бе́лый, мно́го
                                выпил я́ вина́.
Мне́ сейча́с буты́лка пе́ла гро́мче се́рдца
                                моего́:
Ми́р лишь лу́ч от ли́ка дру́га, всё ино́е
                                те́нь его́!

Виноче́рпия взлюби́л я не сего́дня, не
                                вчера́,
Не вчера́ и не сего́дня пья́ный с са́мого
                                утра́.
И хожу́ и похваля́юсь, что узна́л я
                                торжество́:
Ми́р лишь лу́ч от ли́ка дру́га, всё ино́е
                                те́нь его́!
                        [< 1921]

О́, пра́зднество на берегу́, в виду́
                                иску́сственного мо́ря,
Где разукра́шены пестро́ причу́дливые
                                корабли́.
Несётся ле́пет мандоли́н, и во́лны
                                пле́щутся, им вто́ря,
Раке́та лёгкая взлети́т и рассыпа́ется
                                вдали́.
                        [< 1916]

Both passages manifest a "strong" caesura in which the ictus immediately before the caesura is constantly stressed. As is common for the trochaic octameter, all the even ictuses in the Gumilev poem are stressed constantly, while the odd ictuses are relatively weak. On the other hand the iambic octameter has constant stresses only at the caesura and at the end of the line.

A variety of other long lines can be found as well: both iambic and trochaic poems occur in seven, nine, ten, and even twelve feet. Briusov

wrote some of the longest lines in Russian poetry: in the following
poems he used twelve-foot iambs and trochees respectively.

Я был простёрт, я был как мёртвый.   ⏑⊥⏑⊥⏑⊥⏑⊥‖⏑⊥⏑⊥⏑⊥⏑⊥⏑‖
  Ты богомольными руками мой стан   ⏑⊥⏑⊥⏑⊥⏑⊥
    безвольный обвила,
Ты распалёнными устами мне грудь   ⏑⊥⏑⊥⏑⊥⏑⊥‖⏑⊥⏑⊥⏑⊥⏑⊥⏑‖
  и плечи, лоб и губы, как красным   ⏑⊥⏑⊥⏑⊥⏑⊥
    углем, обожгла.

И, множа странные соблазны, меняя   ⏑⊥⏑⊥⏑⊥⏑⊥‖⏑⊥⏑⊥⏑⊥⏑⊥⏑‖
  лик многообразный, в меня впиваясь   ⏑⊥⏑⊥⏑⊥⏑⊥
    сотней жал,
Дух непокорный с башни чёрной ты   ⏑⊥⏑⊥⏑⊥⏑⊥‖⏑⊥⏑⊥⏑⊥⏑⊥⏑‖
  сорвала рукой упорной и с ним   ⏑⊥⏑⊥⏑⊥⏑⊥
    низринулась в провал.

             1907

Близ медлительного Нила, там, где   ⊥⏑⊥⏑⊥⏑⊥⏑‖⊥⏑⊥⏑⊥⏑⊥⏑‖
  озеро Мерида, в царстве пламенного   ⊥⏑⊥⏑⊥⏑⊥
    Ра,
Ты давно меня любила, как Озириса   ⊥⏑⊥⏑⊥⏑⊥⏑‖⊥⏑⊥⏑⊥⏑⊥⏑‖
  Изида, друг, царица и сестра!   ⊥⏑⊥⏑⊥⏑⊥
И клонила пирамида тень на наши   ⊥⏑⊥⏑⊥⏑⊥⏑‖⊥⏑⊥⏑⊥⏑⊥⏑‖
    вечера.   ⊥⏑⊥⏑⊥⏑⊥

         1906-7

When lines become this long, it is necessary to resort to special strata-
gems to hold the line together as a unit. The twelve-foot lines have two
caesuras—after the fourth and the eighth ictuses. The trochaic poem is
written in three-line stanzas in which the first two lines are twelve-foot
trochees and the last line an eight-foot trochee, thereby creating a
unique form of mixed meter. The poem also exhibits a complex pattern
of internal rhyme. The first cola in the first two lines of each stanza
rhyme with each other (N*íla* and liub*íla*). The second cola in the first
two lines rhyme not only with each other but also with the first colon of
the third line (Mer*ída*, Iz*ída*, piram*ída*). And the ends of all three lines
are joined by triple rhyme. The poem in twelve-foot iambs contains an
extra syllable at each caesura to create a line that is twenty-six (!) sylla-
bles long. In the second of the stanzas quoted here, the first colon of
each line rhymes with the second, though here Briusov is less consistent
and less intricate in his use of internal rhyme than in his trochaic poem.
While lines of this length are simply rhythmic tours de force, at least
some of the longer lines—especially the iambic and trochaic octam-
eters—are certainly viable meters for Russian poetry.

  Long ternaries are less common than the binaries; most of the ex-

amples again come from the period 1890–1930. As with the long bi-
nary lines, there is nearly always at least one caesura. In this dactylic
hexameter poem by Igor Severianin it appears after the third foot:

Блесткая аудитория, блеском ты зло отуманена!
Скрыт от тебя, недостойная, будущего горизонт!
Тусклые ваши сиятельства! Во времена Северянина
Следует знать, что за Пушкиным были и Блок и Бальмонт!

1913

$$\acute{-}\cup\cup\acute{-}\cup\cup\acute{-}\cup\cup\ \|\ \acute{-}\cup\cup\acute{-}\cup\cup\acute{-}\cup\cup$$

$$\acute{-}\cup\cup\acute{-}\cup\cup\acute{-}\cup\cup\ \|\ \acute{-}\cup\cup\acute{-}\cup\cup\acute{-}$$

$$\acute{-}\cup\cup\acute{-}\cup\cup\acute{-}\cup\cup\ \|\ \acute{-}\cup\cup\acute{-}\cup\cup\acute{-}\cup\cup$$

$$\acute{-}\cup\cup\acute{-}\cup\cup\acute{-}\cup\cup\ \|\ \acute{-}\cup\cup\acute{-}\cup\cup\acute{-}$$

The omission of stress on several ictuses within the line is a modern
feature of this poem, as is the very existence of a pure dactylic hex-
ameter. Although the imitations of the Greek and Latin hexameter based
on the dactylic hexameter were common enough in the eighteenth and
nineteenth centuries, the regular dactylic hexameter was virtually un-
known until the twentieth.[123]

Seven-foot and eight-foot ternary meters exist as well, although they
are extremely rare and, like the twelve-foot binary meters, should
probably be regarded as isolated experiments. Once again Balmont and
Briusov were the first (and very nearly the only) poets to attempt such
lines. The following seven-foot amphibrach is by Balmont and the
eight-foot anapest by Briusov:

Я знаю, что Брама умнее, чем все бесконечно-имянные боги.
Но Брама – индиец, а я – славянин. Совпадают ли наши дороги?
О, Брама – индиец, а я – скандинав, а я – мексиканец жестокий.
Я – эллин влюблённый, я – вольный араб, я – жадный, безумный,
стоокий.

1904

$$\cup\acute{-}\cup\cup\acute{-}\cup\ \|\ \cup\acute{-}\cup\cup\acute{-}\ \|\ \cup\cup\acute{-}\cup\cup\acute{-}\cup\cup\acute{-}\cup$$
$$\cup\acute{-}\cup\cup\acute{-}\cup\ \|\ \cup\acute{-}\cup\cup\acute{-}\ \|\ \cup\cup\acute{-}\cup\cup\acute{-}\cup\cup\acute{-}\cup$$
$$\acute{\cup}\acute{-}\cup\cup\acute{-}\cup\ \|\ \cup\acute{-}\cup\cup\acute{-}\ \|\ \cup\acute{-}\cup\cup\acute{-}\cup\cup\acute{-}\cup$$
$$\cup\acute{-}\cup\cup\acute{-}\cup\ \|\ \cup\acute{-}\cup\cup\acute{-}\ \|\ \cup\acute{-}\cup\cup\acute{-}\cup\cup\acute{-}\cup$$

Сладострастные тени на тёмной постели окружили, легли,
притаились, манят.
Наклоняются груди, сгибаются спины, веет жгучий,
тягучий, глухой аромат.

И, без си́лы подня́ться, без во́ли прижа́ться и вдави́ть
                                свои́ па́льцы в окру́жности пле́ч,
То́чно тру́п, наблюда́ю бессты́дные те́ни в раздража́ющем
                                        бле́ске куря́щихся све́ч.
                                                                    1895

∪∪‒∪∪‒∪‖∪‒∪∪‒∪‖∪∪‒∪∪‒∪∪‒∪∪‒

∪∪‒∪∪‒∪‖∪‒∪∪‒∪‖∪́∪‒∪∪‒∪∪‒∪∪‒

∪∪‒∪∪‒∪‖∪‒∪∪‒∪‖∪∪‒∪∪́‒∪∪‒∪∪‒

∪́∪‒∪∪‒∪‖∪‒∪∪‒∪‖∪∪‒∪∪‒∪∪‒∪∪‒

Both used two caesuras: Balmont's poem features a feminine caesura
after the second foot and a masculine caesura at the fourth ictus; also, in
the last two lines quoted he dropped a syllable immediately after the
second caesura. Briusov's anapestic line has feminine caesuras after the
second and fourth ictuses, and at the latter caesura he added an extra
syllable to the line. Neither poet used internal rhyme to emphasize the
caesuras; while the caesuras serve to divide the line into smaller intona-
tional units, the strongest syntactic break still comes at the end of the
line. Thus even these extremely long lines are meant to be considered as
integral lines rather than as composites of two or more shorter lines.
Still, among long ternary lines only the hexameters are a significant part
of the literary tradition.

THE STRONG CAESURA

The strong caesura is simply a caesura preceded by a constantly
stressed ictus.[124] It occurs regularly in all the types of long lines dis-
cussed in the previous section, though it also appears in shorter lines—
in particular, the binary tetrameters and hexameters. Of course the pres-
ence of any constant within the line affects a poem's rhythm, but the
strong caesura may introduce certain irregularities of its own: (1) the
caesura itself may shift between ictuses within a poem; (2) a syllable or
two may be constantly added or dropped at the caesura; or (3) the num-
ber of syllables at the caesura may vary in the course of a work.[125] Of
these irregularities, the most common is the second—the regular ex-
pansion or contraction of the line at the caesura. Examples include the
twelve-foot iambic and anapestic octameter poems by Briusov quoted in
the previous section, both of which add syllables at the caesura. The
stanza quoted from Balmont's poem in seven-foot amphibrachs illus-

trates the third of these unusual features; the last two lines (but not the first two) truncate a syllable at the caesura.

Attention to the strong caesura intensified at the end of the nineteenth and the beginning of the twentieth centuries, when "nonclassical" Russian meters such as *dol'niki* and accentual verse were first widely used. Poems with the strong caesura often occupy a transitional position between the classical and nonclassical meters. The works all maintain most of the qualities inherent in regular Russian classical verse, but those that add or subtract a syllable at the caesura violate the rule regarding fixed intervals between ictuses and thus represent a tentative step in the direction of the nonclassical verse forms.

Typical in this regard is the iambic tetrameter with strong caesura. The iambic tetrameter was normally not used with any caesura until the end of the nineteenth century; the form with strong caesura that appeared at that time contained strong stressing throughout the line. That is, in addition to the expected constant stresses at the second and fourth ictuses, stress on the other two was omitted only occasionally, as in this poem by Blok:

Я жду́ призы́ва, ищу́ отве́та,	∪́–∪́–‖∪́–∪́∪
Немѐет не́бо, земля́ в молча́ньи,	∪́–∪́–‖∪́–∪́∪
За жёлтой ни́вой – далѐко гдѐ-то –	∪́–∪́–‖∪́–∪́∪
На ми́г просну́лось моѐ воззва́нье.	∪́–∪́–‖∪́–∪́∪
Из отголо́сков далѐкой ре́чи,	∪–∪́–‖∪́–∪́∪
С ночно́го не́ба, с полѐй дремо́тных,	∪́–∪́–‖∪́–∪́∪
Всё мня́тся та́йны грядꙏу́щей встре́чи,	∪́–∪́–‖∪́–∪́∪
Свида́ний я́сных, но мимолѐтных.	∪́–∪́–‖∪–∪́∪

1901

Throughout this period stressing on the first and third ictuses was slightly less than 90 percent in such poems; by contrast, poems written in regular iambic tetrameter stressed the first ictus 83.5 percent of the time, the second 87.5 percent, and the third just 49.1 percent.[126] As the figures for the third ictus reveal most clearly, Blok's poem and others written with a strong caesura show a greatly reduced tendency toward regressive accentual dissimilation. In fact, the poems written with strong caesura at the beginning of the century have much higher average stressing throughout the line (just less than 94 percent) than do any of the other rhythmic variations for the iambic tetrameter with which poets have experimented over the years (cf. table 4, where average stressing is as low as 75.6 percent and never exceeds 81.5 percent).

The only type of strong caesura found regularly in the nineteenth century is the unrhymed trochaic tetrameter with dactylic caesura and dactylic clausula. This meter did not emerge from the Russian syllabotonic poetry tradition; rather, it represents a literary imitation of a Russian folk song meter, the 5+5 form, whose history was discussed in chapter 1 along with other folk meters.[127] As a result of its origins the classification of this meter has presented some difficulties, and many Russian scholars have preferred to interpret this line as based on a "five-syllable foot" with an obligatory stress on the third syllable. It is best, however, to view this folk meter as consisting of two five-syllable hemistichs, each of which has a constant *phrase* stress on the third syllable and optional *word* stresses on the first and fifth syllables. (In discussing folk meters it is important to consider phrase as well as word stresses.) Aleksei Koltsov popularized this meter during the 1830s in songs such as "The Forest" ("Les"):

Что́, дрему́чий ле́с,
Призаду́мался,
Гру́стью тёмною
Затума́нился?

Что́, Бова́-сила́ч
Заколдо́ванный,
С непокры́тою
Голово́й в бою́

1837

Each pair of lines can actually be written as one line. Stressing is constant on the third and eighth syllables; among all poems written in this meter, stressing on the first syllable of each hemistich runs to more than 40 percent, that on the fifth syllable of the line to 70 percent, and that on the last syllable to 30 percent.[128] The marked difference in stressing between the fifth and tenth syllables is evidence that the hemistichs are treated differently; if each of the five-syllable units belonged to a different line, then stressing on these two syllables should have been more or less equal.

While the strong caesura also occurs in iambic and trochaic hexameters and heptameters, it is used most consistently in the octameters and still longer lines. Indeed, the most common occurrence of the strong caesura is in the trochaic octameter with feminine caesura after the fourth ictus (cf. the poem by Gumilev quoted in the previous section).[129] Again, truncation or expansion may occur at the caesura. In long meters the constant stress at the caesura provides a fixed point that helps give the entire line a firm structure. Without such a feature, lines with eight or more ictuses would be difficult to write and even more difficult to declaim.

Poets have occasionally used two or more caesuras in a line. The extremely long meters—binary meters with more than eight feet and ternaries with more than six—are particularly likely to exhibit this rare feature; note that both the iambic and the trochaic twelve-foot poems by Briusov quoted in the previous section have two caesuras, as do Balmont's amphibrachic heptameter and Briusov's anapestic octameter. However, two caesuras are also found in lines with as few as six feet, especially in the poetry of Balmont and Igor Severianin, the two poets who experimented most widely with the strong caesura.[130] Balmont, in fact, was capable of using as many as three caesuras in a line; for instance, his poem "The Drop" ("Kaplia") was written in iambic octameter with three feminine caesuras (that is, with an extra syllable added to the line at each caesura). The expanded caesuras are by no means unusual for Balmont—in more than two hundred works he either added or dropped syllables at the caesura.[131] Igor Severianin was hardly less innovative in this regard, often employing a dactylic caesura (two extra syllables) and occasionally even a hyperdactylic (three extra syllables at the caesura).[132]

Both these poets were also among the few who frequently used the strong caesura in ternary meters. Of course since ternaries rarely omit stress within the line, any caesura is likely to be "strong," at least in the sense of being constantly stressed. However, Balmont and Igor Severianin often emphasized the caesura by adding or dropping syllables. The following poem by Igor Severianin is in anapestic tetrameter with dactylic caesura:

В па́рке пла́кала де́вочка:　　　　　　⏑⏑⏑́⏑⏑⏑́⏑⏑ ‖ ⏑⏑⏑́⏑⏑⏑́⏑⏑
　　　"Посмотри́-ка ты, па́почка,
У хоро́шенькой ла́сточки　　　　　　　⏑⏑⏑́⏑⏑⏑́⏑⏑ ‖ ⏑⏑⏑́⏑⏑⏑́⏑⏑
　　　перело́млена ла́почка, –
Я возьму́ пти́цу бе́дную и в плато́чек　⏑⏑⏑́⏑⏑⏑́⏑⏑ ‖ ⏑⏑⏑́⏑⏑⏑́⏑⏑
　　　уку́таю..."
И оте́ц призаду́мался, потрясённый　　⏑⏑⏑́⏑⏑⏑́⏑⏑ ‖ ⏑⏑⏑́⏑⏑⏑́⏑⏑
　　　мину́тою,
И прости́л все́ гряду́щие и капри́зы　　⏑⏑⏑́⏑⏑⏑́⏑⏑ ‖ ⏑⏑⏑́⏑⏑⏑́⏑⏑
　　　и ша́лости
Ми́лой ма́ленькой до́чери,　　　　　　⏑⏑⏑́⏑⏑⏑́⏑⏑ ‖ ⏑⏑⏑́⏑⏑⏑́⏑⏑
　　　зарыда́вшей от жа́лости.
　　　　　　1910

By using dactylic rhyme as well as the dactylic caesura, Igor Severianin expanded the anapestic tetrameter from a minimal number of twelve syllables (when used with masculine rhyme) to sixteen. In another poem, written in anapestic hexameter, Igor Severianin used two feminine caesuras throughout:

> До весны́ мы в разлу́ке. Повида́ться не мо́жем. Повида́ться нельзя́ нам.
> Ра́зве то́лько случа́йно. Ра́зве то́лько в теа́тре. Ра́зве то́лько в конце́рте.
> Да и то́ бесслове́сно. Да и то́ беспоклѡ́нно. Но зато́ – осия́нным
> И брилья́нтовым взо́ром обменя́ться успе́ем... как и сло́вом в конве́рте...
>
> 1911

```
∪∪⸴∪∪⸴∪ || ∪∪⸴∪∪⸴∪ || ∪∪⸴∪∪⸴∪
∪̆∪⸴∪∪⸴∪ || ∪̆∪⸴∪∪⸴∪ || ∪̆∪⸴∪∪⸴∪
∪∪⸴∪∪⸴∪ || ∪∪⸴∪∪⸴∪ || ∪∪⸴∪∪⸴∪
∪∪⸴∪∪⸴∪ || ∪∪⸴∪∪⸴∪ || ∪∪⸴∪∪⸴∪
```

Each of the three cola has seven syllables, and the resulting symmetry as well as the use of strong syntactic breaks at the caesuras reinforces the impression that the three parts of the line are distinct and equal units. The caesuras thus break the line down into smaller and easier to absorb segments; at the same time they make it easier to create the balance and symmetry that enable the line to be perceived ultimately as a unified whole.

Balmont used the caesura to shorten instead of lengthen the line in his poem "The Chase" ("Pogonia"). Each of the two caesuras is feminine and shortens the line by a syllable. Thanks to the exclusively masculine rhyme, each line contains seventeen syllables as opposed to the nineteen that normally would be the minimum for a poem written in dactylic heptameter:

> Че́й э́то то́пот? – Че́й э́то шёпот? – Че́й э́то све́тится гла́з?
> Кто́ э́то в кру́ге – в бе́шеной вью́ге – пля́шет и пу́тает на́с?
>
> Чьи́ э́то кры́лья – в дро́жи бесси́лья – бью́тся и сно́ва летя́т?
> Чьи́ э́то хо́ры? – Чьи́ э́то взо́ры? – Че́й э́то бле́щущий взгля́д?
>
> [1907]

```
⸴∪̆⸴∪ || ⸴∪̆∪⸴∪ | ⸴∪∪⸴∪∪⸴
⸴∪̆⸴∪ || ⸴∪∪⸴∪ || ⸴∪∪⸴∪∪⸴

⸴∪̆⸴∪ || ⸴∪∪⸴∪ || ⸴∪∪⸴∪∪⸴
⸴∪̆⸴∪ || ⸴∪̆∪⸴∪ || ⸴∪∪⸴∪∪⸴
```

The first and second cola in each line rhyme; that, combined with the dashes and truncations of syllables, causes the caesura to be especially prominent.

While most of the meters discussed earlier in this chapter are fairly easy to identify, the same is not always true of the strong caesura. If two extra syllables are added at the caesura to a poem written in binary meter, the line may simply appear to contain an extra foot. In such cases the constant stress on the ictus preceding the caesura provides the necessary clue. Also, poems that add or subtract a syllable at the caesura may, at first glance, appear to belong to one of the nonclassical verse forms. Here, the existence of the irregularity only at the caesura indicates that a strong caesura is causing the expansion or truncation. A further complication occurs when the caesura is variable, as with recent usage of binary strong caesuras in the poetry of Evtushenko and Voznesensky. To recognize poems with a strong caesura, to say nothing of the nonclassical verse forms, it is often necessary to examine more than just a line or two and to look for patterns that develop over an extended segment of the work.

PAEONS AND PENTONS

Trochees and iambs have an ictus every other syllable; dactyls, amphibrachs, and anapests every third syllable. Why not meters with an ictus every fourth or even fifth syllable? In fact, metrists have long discussed what would be a four-syllable foot (the paeon) and a five-syllable foot (the penton or *piatislozhnik*). Do such meters exist, or do lines called paeons and pentons represent variations of well-known verse forms?

The term *paeon* is taken from Greek and Latin metrics; Russian scholars talk of first, second, third, and fourth paeons, depending on which of the four syllables serves as the ictus.[133] "Pure" paeons—those with little or no hypermetrical stressing—would obviously be quite rare. Ternary meters are more likely to have hypermetrical stressing than binary meters, and paeons, with three unstressed syllables between ictuses, would require a poem consisting almost entirely of long words in order to avoid a significant amount of hypermetrical stressing. Briusov's "Experiments" included a couple of attempts at paeons with almost no hypermetrical stressing—"Spindles" ("Veretena") and "Storm from the Shore" ("Buria s berega")—but poems with stress only every fourth syllable are too infrequent and too obviously artificial to serve as the basis of a metrical form. In fact if paeons did exist, they would have to manifest frequent hypermetrical stressing. Also, unstressed ictuses within the line would be extremely rare:[134] they are not common in the ternary meters, where the omission of stress results in an interval of five unstressed syllables, and in paeons the interval would grow to a huge seven unstressed syllables (´∪∪∪–∪∪∪´).

However, the question immediately arises: do not the so-called paeons actually consist of iambs or trochees? The first and third paeons have a trochaic rhythm, the second and fourth iambic. Throughout his career Tomashevsky maintained that the number of syllables in a foot must be prime or the foot would break down into its constituent parts.[135] Other researchers have claimed that paeons simply "sound different" than iambs and trochees and that in any case the presence of constant stresses every fourth syllable distinguishes the paeons from binary meters.[136] A combination of evidence and practicality lends support to Tomashevsky on this issue. Consider the following stanza from a poem by Balmont:

Полным слёз, туманным взором	´∪´∪´∪´∪ ‖ ´∪´∪´∪´
я вокруг себя гляжу,	
С обольстительного Юга вновь	–∪´∪–∪´∪ ‖ ´∪´∪–∪´
на Север ухожу.	
И, как узник, полюбивший	–∪´∪–∪´∪ ‖ –∪´∪´∪´
долголетний мрак тюрьмы,	
Я от солнца удаляюсь,	´∪´∪–∪´∪ ‖ –∪´∪´∪´
возвращаясь в царство тьмы.	
[1894-95]	

This poem, like virtually all those in trochaic octameter, has constant stressing on the even ictuses and, partly for that reason, relatively light stressing on the others. Does this make it a poem in paeonic tetrameter? Probably not.

First, consider the pattern of hypermetrical stressing. In a four-syllable foot hypermetrical stressing would tend to fall most heavily on the syllable midway between the ictuses since consecutive stresses in Russian are less common than those with an interval of an unstressed syllable. Yet if the main metrical feature were only the constant stress on every fourth syllable, then a fair number of the hypermetrical stresses should appear on the other two syllables between the ictuses. However, such is not the case; if this stanza is regarded as an example of paeonic verse, then all eight of the "hypermetrical" stresses fall on odd syllables, just as in regular trochaic verse. Something similar occurs in the poem "Hoffmann" ("Gofman") by the contemporary poet Aleksandr

Kushner. The meter is either iambic hexameter or, as Boris Bukhshtab has claimed, a three-foot fourth paeon.[137] Analyzing the work as paeonic, Bukhshtab believes that many of the words at the second, sixth, and tenth syllables of the line are subordinated to words whose stresses fall on the ictuses (the fourth, eighth, and twelfth syllables). Thus he finds only fourteen stresses in all twenty-four lines occurring at syllables two, six, and ten. My own count shows about thirty-two stresses (which would be hypermetrical in a paeonic line) on the same syllables, and thus the paeonic rhythm of these lines may be a little less pure than he suggests. However, we both agree that only a handful of stresses do not occur on even syllables, that most of these stresses fall on the first syllable of the line, and that all the words involved in these cases are monosyllabic. In short, all the stressing in this poem meets the requirements for regular iambic hexameter poetry; the only unusual feature is the presence of constant stressing on the fourth and eighth syllables.[138] The strong tendency of hypermetrical stressing to fall on the even syllables, the lack of any stressing on the odd syllables involving words of two or more syllables, and the absence of any other feature that would be at odds with the rules for conventional iambic poetry all make a good case for claiming that the poem is written not in paeons but in iambs.

Second, if interpreted as regular binary meters, the poems that some metrists refer to as paeons follow the rule of regressive accentual dissimilation. While the constant ictuses obviously cannot vary in strength, these poems still have the predicted alternation of strong and weak ictuses, and the weak ictuses become less so toward the beginning of the line. Bailey's figures for more than three thousand lines written in trochaic octameter provide clear evidence for this phenomenon; the seventh or last of the odd ictuses is stressed least often, while the first ictus is stressed more than the other odd ictuses.[139]

Third, while the constants within the line clearly affect the rhythm, are they sufficient reason for assigning works to an entirely different kind of meter? Analyses of popular meters like the iambic tetrameter and pentameter have shown that a basic feature of the Russian meters is their ability to embrace a wide range of different stress patterns.[140] A given meter may "sound" different from era to era, from poet to poet, and from poem to poem. Thus talking of paeons seems a needless complication; lines with constant stresses every fourth syllable are simply rhythmic variations of the familiar binary meters.

The case for pentons (*piatislozhniki, piatidol' niki*) is, surprisingly, a bit stronger, though still not convincing.[141] Since the number five is prime, the five-syllable unit does not automatically break down into constituent parts. Also, the line most often described as a penton, the 5+5 meter, is a well-known verse form that owes its origins not to the traditions of syllabo-tonic poetry but to folk poetry. Still, more than half a century ago two of the pioneers of modern verse theory, Zhirmunsky and Tomashevsky, both pointed to the similarity of the "third penton" to the trochaic tetrameter with strong caesura (as this verse form was termed in the previous section).[142] As with the word *paeon*, *penton* is a term used to identify a line that can be described adequately as a rhythmic variation of a well-known meter. All examples of the penton—be they second, third, or whatever—upon closer examination turn out to be a type of strong caesura or some other established verse form.[143]

To end this series of metrical curiosities, it is fitting to mention still another oddity—the one-syllable foot. A line containing such "feet" could consist of nothing but monosyllabic words and would, for practical reasons, have to be quite short, as would any poem employing such a meter. Georgy Shengeli has found several examples of the one-syllable foot, but, as he points out, any meter that automatically excludes the 85 percent of Russian words with more than one syllable is not likely to develop very far.[144] All in all, the conventional binary and ternary meters appear to be adequate for describing the entire system of Russian classical poetry.

3

Nonclassical Verse

For a century and a half following the reforms of Trediakovsky and Lomonosov the overwhelming majority of Russian poems were written in the binary and ternary meters discussed in the previous chapter. Many of the scattered exceptions were translations that more or less followed the meter of the original. Until the end of the nineteenth century such poetry largely involved imitations of Greek and Latin meters—hexameters (including the elegiac distich) and logaoedic verse. These meters are "classical" in the sense of following Greek and Latin models, but within Russian verse tradition they are "nonclassical" since they do not adhere to the rules for binary or ternary meters. Around the beginning of the twentieth century, as part of a renewed interest in poetic technique poets began to experiment regularly with forms that were previously rare in Russian poetry. The *dol'nik*, various accentual meters, and free verse all entered the repertoire of Russian poets at more or less the same time. Of these forms, only the *dol'nik* quickly achieved full acceptance; today it is as much a part of Russian poetry as trochees or anapests.[1] Accentual meters and free verse remained less widespread; even though Maiakovsky helped popularize the use of accentual meters during the 1910s and 1920s, both they and free verse fell into disuse, only to be revived during the late 1950s and 1960s.[2]

Nonclassical Russian verse is distinguished from classical by its lack of a constant interval between the ictuses. Iambs and trochees maintain a one-syllable interval; for the ternary meters the interval is always two syllables. In the *dol'nik*, however, there are both one- and two-syllable intervals between the ictuses. Similarly, the imitations of Greek and Latin verse forms—hexameters and logaoedic verse—contain both one- and two-syllable intervals. Such poetry may, from the contempo-

126

rary standpoint, be considered special cases of the *dol'nik*.[3] For accentual meters the intervals between ictuses vary over a greater range than for the *dol'nik*, while the number of stresses per line is constant or nearly so (though, for instance, lines of four and three stresses may appear in regular alternation). In free verse neither the intervals between stresses nor the number of stresses per line serve as primary organizing features of the poetry.

The following discussion treats the various types of nonclassical verse in order of increasing "irregularity." The first section is devoted to the strictly organized hexameter and logaoedic forms; subsequent analyses deal with the *dol'nik*, accentual meters, and free verse. At the end of the chapter a brief discussion is devoted to polymetrical forms, that is, poems containing discrete sections written in different meters.

IMITATIONS OF GREEK AND LATIN VERSE FORMS

THE HEXAMETER (AND THE ELEGIAC DISTICH)

Although Lomonosov wrote a few lines of hexameter verse in his 1739 "Letter on the Rules of Russian Versification," it was his rival and co-developer of the Russian syllabo-tonic system, Trediakovsky, who was the first to use hexameters for major works. In particular, Trediakovsky's *Tilemakhida* (1766), a translation in hexameters of Fénelon's prose work *Les Aventures de Télémaque*, helped determine the subsequent fate of this meter in the Russian literary tradition.[4] The immediate reaction was negative; the translation was subjected to ridicule by Catherine the Great, who recommended it as a cure for insomnia, and by members of her court.[5] Partly for this reason hexameters were in disfavor for the remainder of the century; throughout the entire period poets other than Trediakovsky used this verse form fewer than ten times.[6] The hexameter was revived for another translation of a long work—Nikolai Gnedich's rendition of the *Iliad*. Since hexameters appear as well in Zhukovsky's well-known translation of the *Odyssey* and in several Russian versions of the *Aeneid*, the meter has become closely associated with translations of Greek and Latin epic poetry. The meter has also been used for original poetry dealing with classical themes and for translations from other languages. In this regard the Russian experience with hexameters is typical for writers in European languages; owing both to its somewhat irregular form and to its association with Greek and Latin works, the hexameter line has retained the feel of a borrowed form and has not been readily assimilated by most European poetic traditions.[7] Thus when Pushkin, apparently influenced by Gnedich's translation of the *Iliad*, started in 1829 to employ hexameters regularly (primarily within the elegiac distich), he reserved the meter for poems that were connected directly with classical themes or to which he wanted to impart the aura of antiquity.[8] Zhukovsky turned to hexameters for lighter verse and for poetic narratives as well as for translations, but he employed different rhythmic variations of the hexameter for the two types of poetry.[9] Zhukovsky lacked followers in this regard, and after 1850 the form appeared more and more rarely.[10] Some of Fet's translations are in hexameters, as are a few by several other poets active during the second half of the nineteenth century. Symbolist poets likewise translated works using this meter, but none of them employed it for their original poetry. And even in the case of translations only Briusov turned to it extensively. Thus since the mid-nineteenth century hexameters have been largely confined to translations, especially from Greek and Latin poetry, and poets have not been inclined to use them in other contexts. The prognosis would seem to be extremely limited application in the future as well.

The hexameter line has the following form:

$$-\left[\begin{array}{c}\smile\smile\end{array}\right]-\left[\begin{array}{c}\smile\smile\end{array}\right]-\left[\begin{array}{c}\smile\smile\end{array}\right]-\left[\begin{array}{c}\smile\smile\end{array}\right]-\smile\smile-\smile$$

(In describing the *dol'nik* and accentual meters, it is convenient to use a different type of schema, which both depicts ictuses and the range for the number of weak syllables between each ictus. In the case of hexameters, the form would be described as follows:

$$-2/1-2/1-2/1-2/1 \doteq 2 \doteq 1$$

However, for describing hexameters and logaoedic meters, which derive directly from Latin and Greek models, the breves and macrons conventionally used to depict meters in those languages seem more suitable.) As the name implies the hexameter line contains six ictuses, and as used by many Russian poets—notably in the translations of Gnedich and Zhukovsky—there are generally two weak syllables between each ictus. Thus individual lines are often equivalent to the dactylic hexameter. However, unlike regular dactyls, the hexameter may omit one of the two unstressed syllables after any of the first four ictuses, and some poets frequently take advantage of this feature. The end of the line has a fixed form: the fifth foot does not omit any syllables and is almost always stressed ($\stackrel{\angle}{} \cup \cup$), while the ending is feminine and unrhymed.

In the Greek and Latin hexameters, each of the first four feet was either a dactyl ($- \cup \cup$) or a spondee ($- -$). The final foot had two syllables and could be either a spondee or a trochee. The fifth foot was normally a dactyl, but in Greek poetry (and more rarely in Latin as well) it was sometimes replaced by a spondee, in which case the line itself was termed spondaic. (Russian poetry, by requiring that the fifth foot be dactylic, is closer to the Latin model in this regard.)[11] Since Greek and Latin poetry was based on length rather than stress and since on this basis a long vowel was considered to be the equivalent of two short vowels, a dactyl ($2+1+1=4$) and a spondee ($2+2=4$) were metrically identical. Russian vowels lack length as a distinctive feature, and therefore a two-syllable unit cannot be equivalent to a three-syllable unit. Furthermore, since Russian verse is based on stress and stressed vowels occur in Russian only once every 2.7 or 2.8 syllables, spondees (in Russian, two stressed syllables in a row) do not occur often in normal language usage. For this reason Trediakovsky created what he called the "dactylo-trochaic hexameter" (as opposed to the dactylo-spondaic hexameter of Greek and Latin); any of the first four feet could be either a dactyl or a trochee, and the last foot was always trochaic. His rules set forth the norms for the Russian hexameter, but with the establishment of the *dol'nik* in Russian poetry, it seems simpler to refer not to the replacement of one type of foot by another but to the use of either one-syllable or two-syllable intervals between ictuses.

In *Tilemakhida* Trediakovsky took full advantage of the opportunity to vary lines by using one-syllable as well as two-syllable intervals between ictuses. He occasionally placed as many as three one-syllable intervals within the first four feet, and more often than not he did so at least once or twice per line, as the following example shows:[12]

Бу́ря внеза́пна вдру́г возмути́ла
            не́бо и – мо́ре.
Вы́рвавшись, ве́тры свиста́ли
            уж-в-вервях и-парусах гро́зно;
Чёрные во́лны к бока́м
корабе́льным, как-мла́т прираж́ались,
Та́к что су́дно от те́х уда́ров шу́мно
            стена́ло.

$\stackrel{\angle}{}\cup\cup\stackrel{\angle}{}\cup\stackrel{\angle}{}\cup\cup\stackrel{\angle}{}\cup\cup\stackrel{\angle}{}\cup$

$\stackrel{\angle}{}\cup\cup\stackrel{\angle}{}\cup\cup\stackrel{\angle}{}\cup\cup\stackrel{\angle}{}\cup\cup\stackrel{\angle}{}\cup$

$\stackrel{\angle}{}\cup\cup\stackrel{\angle}{}\cup\cup\stackrel{\angle}{}\cup\cup\stackrel{\angle}{}\cup\cup\stackrel{\angle}{}\cup$

$\stackrel{\angle}{}\cup\stackrel{\angle}{}\cup\cup\stackrel{\angle}{}\cup\stackrel{\angle}{}\cup\stackrel{\angle}{}\cup\cup\stackrel{\angle}{}\cup$

То́ на-хребе́т мы-взбега́ем во́лн,
         то-низво́димся в бе́здну,
Мо́ре когда́, из-под-дна́ разлива́ясь,
         зия́ло глубя́ми.
Ви́дели бли́зко себя́ мы ка́мни
         остросуро́вы,
Я́рость о-ко́и вало́в сокруша́лась
         в ре́ве ужа́сном.
                           1766

Of the eight lines in this excerpt, only three take the form of regular dactyls; two others have a single one-syllable interval, lines 1 and 7 have two such intervals, and line 4 three. The use of many one-syllable intervals throughout *Tilemakhida* enabled Trediakovsky to avoid the often dull regularity of the iambic hexameter, the most common verse form employed in eighteenth-century serious poetry.

A natural question is Why were Trediakovsky's hexameters greeted with such disdain? The Russian scholar S. M. Bondi has offered a dual explanation. First, Trediakovsky's contemporaries disliked *Tilemakhida* for reasons other than its rhythm; his poetry had syntactically awkward lines, archaic language, and other weaknesses that made him an inferior poet to, say, Lomonosov. Second, readers probably had difficulty with the "irregularities" in Trediakovsky's hexameters. As already noted, Russian trochees and dactyls are not equivalent in the way that Greek and Latin spondees and dactyls were, so the varying intervals between ictuses could well have struck readers as odd—especially since by this time the vast majority of works were being written in regular binary or ternary meters.[13] But if the *Tilemakhida* did not win much praise in its day, neither it nor the hexameter were forgotten entirely. In 1801 Aleksandr Radishchev wrote "Tribute to the Dactylo-Trochaic Hero" ("Pamiatnik daktilokhoreicheskomu vitiaziu"), the last section of which is a defense of the meter employed by Trediakovsky in the *Tilemakhida*. Aleksandr Vostokov's influential "Essay on Russian Versification" ("Opyt o russkom stikhoslozhenii") includes a section on the hexameter; he particularly endorses the use of many one-syllable intervals between ictuses, finding that purely dactylic lines should be used sparingly.[14]

Meanwhile Gnedich was in the midst of translating the *Iliad*. He had begun to render the work in Alexandrines (iambic hexameters in which adjacent feminine rhymes alternate with adjacent masculine rhymes), but, largely owing to the advice of Sergei Uvarov, he threw out the six books he had translated and began again using hexameters. A polemic over the revival of hexameters arose at the time, with Vasily Kapnist, a leading poet of the day, attacking the hexameter and advocating a thirteen-syllable trochaic line based on folk verse. However, Gnedich continued to work with hexameters, and when his completed translation of the *Iliad* finally appeared in 1829 it was not only a huge success in its own right but also a model for subsequent translations of classical writers.[15]

Unlike Trediakovsky, Gnedich was cautious in using one-syllable intervals, and according to Bondi the relative smoothness of the rhythm may have helped Gnedich's translation achieve ready acceptance.[16] Zhukovsky's translation of the *Odyssey* goes still further in avoiding one-syllable intervals; the majority of his lines are simply regular dactylic hexameters with unrhymed feminine endings. Subsequently, however, the few poets who employed the hexameter line for translations once again began to exploit its rhythmic possibilities. To illustrate some basic features of the Russian hexameter, I have chosen three excerpts: the first is from Gnedich's translation of the *Iliad* (book 3), the second from Zhukovsky's rendition of the *Odyssey* (book 6), and the third from Briusov's translation of the *Aeneid* (book 2):

Та́к лишь на би́тву постро́ились о́ба наро́да с вождя́ми,
Тро́и сыны́ устремля́ются, с го́вором, с кри́ком, как пти́цы:
Кри́к тако́в журавле́й раздаётся под не́бом высо́ким,
Е́сли, избе́гнув и зи́мних бу́рь и дожде́й бесконе́чных,
С кри́ком стада́ми летя́т через бы́стрый пото́к Океа́на,
Бра́нью грозя́ и уби́йством мужа́м малоро́слым, пигме́ям,
С я́ростью стра́шной на ко́их с возду́шных высо́т напада́ют.
Но подходи́ли в безмо́лвии, бо́ем дыша́, аргивя́не.

                                    [1818]

```
´∪∪´∪∪´∪∪´∪∪´∪∪´∪
´∪∪´∪∪´∪∪´∪∪´∪∪´∪
´∪´∪∪´∪∪´∪∪´∪∪´∪
´∪∪´∪∪´∪´∪∪´∪∪´∪
´∪∪´∪∪´∪∪´∪∪´∪∪´∪
´∪∪´∪∪´∪∪´∪∪´∪∪´∪
‿∪∪´∪∪´∪∪´∪∪´∪∪´∪
```

Та́к постоя́нный в беда́х Одиссе́й отдыха́л, погружённый
В со́н и уста́лость. Афи́на же то́ю поро́й низлете́ла
В пышноустро́енный го́род любе́зных бога́м феаки́ян,
Жи́вших изда́вна в широкополя́нной земле́ Гипере́йской,
В бли́зком сосе́дстве с цикло́пами, ди́ким и бу́йным наро́дом,

С ни́ми всегда́ враждова́вшим, могу́ществом и́х превыша́я;
Но напосле́док боже́ственный во́ждь Навсифо́й посели́л их
В Схе́рии, ту́чной земле́, далеко́ от люде́й промышлённых.

                                                              1842-49

́∪∪́∪∪́∪∪́∪∪́∪∪́∪
́∪∪́∪∪́∪∪́∪∪́∪∪́∪
—∪∪́∪∪́∪∪́∪∪́∪∪́∪
́∪∪́∪∪—∪∪́∪∪́∪∪́∪
́∪∪́∪∪́∪∪́∪∪́∪∪́∪
́∪∪́∪∪́∪∪́∪∪́∪∪́∪
—∪∪́∪∪́∪∪́∪∪́∪∪́∪
́∪∪́∪∪́∪∪́∪∪́∪∪́∪

Смо́лкнули все́ и глаза́ устреми́ли, внима́нием по́лны.
На́чал с высо́кого та́к роди́тель Эне́й тогда́ ло́жа:

"Невырази́мую ско́рбь обнови́ть вели́шь ты, цари́ца,
То́, как троя́нскую мо́щь и слёз досто́йное ца́рство
Да́наи ниспрове́ргли, что са́м я ужа́сное ви́дел,
В чём сам уча́ствовал мно́го. Кто́, о тако́м повеству́я,
Бу́дь иль Мирми́донин о́н, иль До́лон, иль зло́го Ули́кса
Во́ин, от слёз усто́йт? А вла́жная но́чь с небоскло́на
Мчи́тся уже́, и ко сну́ зову́т заходя́щие звёзды.

                                                         [1910s]

́∪∪́∪∪́∪∪́∪∪́∪∪́∪
́∪∪́∪∪́∪́∪∪́∪∪́∪

—∪∪́∪∪́∪∪́∪́∪∪́∪
́∪∪́∪∪́∪́∪́∪∪́∪
́∪∪—∪∪́∪́∪́∪∪́∪
́∪∪́∪∪́∪́∪∪́∪∪́∪
́∪∪́∪∪́∪́∪∪́∪∪́∪
́∪∪́∪∪́∪́∪∪́∪∪́∪
́∪∪́∪∪́∪́∪∪́∪∪́∪

The first two examples show a marked divergence from Trediakovsky's
liberal use of one-syllable intervals between ictuses. Gnedich employed
the shorter intervals only twice in eight lines, while the entire excerpt
from Zhukovsky is regularly dactylic. In the entire translation Gnedich
used at least one of the shorter intervals in nearly 17 percent of the lines,
including 199 lines with two one-syllable intervals and 9 lines with three.
Zhukovsky, on the other hand, employed a single one-syllable interval in
only 1 percent of his lines and two such intervals in only three lines out
of the more than twelve thousand in the poem. Furthermore, Zhukovsky
limited these intervals largely to the beginning of the line; Gnedich also
placed more one-syllable intervals after the first ictus than after any

other, but his preference was not nearly so overwhelming.[17] Bondi, for one, regrets the preponderance of two-syllable intervals in both Gnedich and Zhukovsky. While he admits that Gnedich managed to avoid monotony in his hexameter by employing rhythmic devices other than varying the number of syllables between ictuses, he still finds that, in comparison to the hexameters used by Trediakovsky, these lines are "less flexible, less rich in resources, and less differentiated from the entire system of Russian classical verse."[18]

Zhukovsky, however, when employing the hexameter in works other than his translation of the *Odyssey*, used quite a few one-syllable intervals. Fet, who was very much a rhythmic innovator in his use of various meters, not only employed many one-syllable intervals but also concentrated them in the first and third feet of the line. He thereby created a distinct rhythmic effect, with the one-syllable intervals tending to alternate with those of two syllables.[19] Briusov, in his translation of the *Aeneid*, especially liked to use one-syllable intervals after the third ictus, as the above example illustrates. Seven of the nine lines have a one-syllable interval in that position, and only one line (the first) is regularly dactylic.

Neither Gnedich nor Zhukovsky omitted stresses at many ictuses, and when they did so, their tendency was to omit stress on the first ictus.[20] In this regard they followed the poetic practice for regular dactylic verse in the nineteenth century, which occasionally omits stress at the first ictus, but, like the other ternary meters, hardly ever does so within the line. In the examples above, Gnedich omitted a stress on the last line and Zhukovsky did so three times, though Zhukovsky may have believed that the compound words in lines 3 and 4 carried a secondary stress. Trediakovsky, on the other hand, often omitted stress on the first foot and occasionally within the line, but this practice became common again only from the time of Fet. In the example from Briusov, stress is omitted in the first ictus of line 3 and second ictus of line 5.

Poems employing the elegiac distich consist of hexameters in the odd lines alternating with pentameters. Like regular hexameters, this meter is normally unrhymed. The pentameter line adheres to the following schema:

$$-\left[\begin{smallmatrix} \smile\smile \\ \smile \end{smallmatrix}\right] - \left[\begin{smallmatrix} \smile\smile \\ \smile \end{smallmatrix}\right] \stackrel{\angle}{-} \| - \smile\smile - \smile\smile \stackrel{\angle}{-}$$

The intervals may consist of either one or two syllables in the first half of the line, with a caesura after the third ictus. The form for the second half of the line is fixed: both the intervals between the ictuses have two syllables, and the ending is always masculine. The name *pentameter* in Greek and Latin metrics derives from the presence of two-and-one-half feet on either side of the caesura: two full feet are followed by one long syllable or half of a four-unit foot such as a dactyl $(2+1+1)$ or spondee $(2+2)$. In Russian, of course, there are simply six ictuses, so the term *pentameter* is perhaps not entirely appropriate. The elegiac distich attained its greatest popularity during the first half of the nineteenth century when it was used primarily in shorter works by many poets including Pushkin and some of those in his pleiad.[21] Since then the form has largely fallen into disuse. An example of this meter is found in the following tribute to Gnedich by Pushkin's close friend Anton Delvig:

Му́за вчера́ мне, певе́ц, принесла́
   закоци́тную но́вость:
В тёмный неда́вно Айде́с те́нь
   славяни́на пришла́;
Та́м, окружённая со́нмом тене́й
   любопы́тных, пропе́ла
(Слу́шал и дре́вний Оме́р) пе́снь
   Илиа́ды твое́й.
Ста́рец наш, к пе́рсям вожа́того-ю́ноши
   сла́дко прини́кнув,
Вскри́кнул: "Во́т сла́ва моя́, во́т
   чего́ ве́ки я жда́л!"
     1821 or 1822

LOGAOEDIC VERSE

In Greek and Latin metrics the term *logaoedic* refers to the mixing of different feet on the line in specific stanzaic forms. Modern imitations of Greek and Latin logaoedic verse exist, but the term nowadays is more often applied to verse in which the ictuses always fall on the same syllables within the line, while the number of syllables between ictuses varies. That is, as in the *dol'nik* or hexameter, there may be one or two syllables between ictuses (or more rarely in logaoedic verse, zero or three syllables). It is possible for logaoedic verse to appear in regular alternation with another type of line, which may be a different logaoedic line or may be in an entirely different meter. Thus in the first of the following examples Marina Tsvetaeva employed a logaoedic tetrameter throughout; in the second she alternated a logaoedic tetrameter with the pattern ∪−∪∪−∪∪−∪́∪ and a logaoedic trimeter with the pattern

∪‒∪∪‒∪‒; and in the third she alternated a regular anapestic trimeter
and a logaoedic trimeter.[22]

Éсли душá родилáсь крылáтой –
Чтó ей хорóмы и чтó ей хáты!
Чтó Чингисхáн ей – и чтó – Ордá!
Двá на мирý у меня врагá,
Двá близнецá – неразрывно-слитых:
Гóлод голóдных – и сытость сытых!

                          1918

Знакóмец! Откóлева в нáши стрáны?
Котóрого вéтра клясть?
Знакóмец! С тобóю в любóвь не встáну:
Твоя воронáя мáсть.

Покáмест кострý воронóму – пыхать.
Красáвице – искра в глаз!
– Знакóмец! Твоя дорогáя прихоть,
А мóй дорогóй откáз.

                          1922

Ты меня никогдá не ослáвишь:
Моё имя – водá для ýст!
Ты меня никогдá не остáвишь:
Двéрь открыта, и дóм твой – пýст!

                          1919

Several different kinds of logaoedic meters should be differentiated
from each other as well as from binary meters with strong caesura on
the one hand and from the *dol'nik* on the other. As noted in chapter 2,
binary and ternary meters with strong caesura contain a constant stress
on the ictus preceding the caesura and may also consistently expand (or
contract) the line at that point. For instance, Zinaida Gippius, in her
iambic tetrameter poem "Non-Love" ("Neliubov'"), included an extra
syllable at the caesura:

Как вéтер мóкрый, ты бьéшься в стáвни,
Как вéтер чéрный, поёшь: ты мóй!
Я дрéвний хáос, я дрýг твой дáвний,
Твой дрýг единый, – открóй, открóй!

                          1907

Similarly, the following poem by Igor Chinnov might appear to be loga-
oedic but is actually in iambic hexameter with an extra syllable at each
of the two caesuras:

Одни́м заба́вы, други́м забо́ты. Зате́м забве́нье.
Да, жи́сть жестя́нка, да, жи́сть копе́йка, судьба́ инде́йка.
Да, хо́лод-го́лод. Не ра́дость ста́рость. (И но́чь, и о́сень).

                                                                            1965

    ◡́◡◡́◡ ‖ ◡́◡◡́◡ ‖ ◡́◡◡́◡
    ◡́◡◡́◡ ‖ ◡́◡◡́◡ ‖ ◡́◡◡́◡
    ◡́◡◡́◡ ‖ ◡́◡◡́◡ ‖ ◡́◡◡́◡

The schematic representation of ictuses and weak positions in such poems presents two main similarities with logaoedic verse: both one- and two-syllable intervals occur between ictuses, and the ictuses appear at the same positions from line to line. However, the presence of the strong caesura and the clearly binary or ternary impetus in each part of the line are reason enough to distinguish such works from poems written in logaoedic verse. The *dol'nik* and logaoedic verse are similar in that the variations between one- and two-syllable intervals are not tied to a caesura. However, in the *dol'nik* the sequence of ictuses and weak positions varies from line to line. Also, in logaoedic verse the number of syllables before the first ictus—that is, the anacrusis—remains constant throughout; in the *dol'nik* the anacrusis sometimes varies.[23] Still, the systems for the *dol'nik* and for modern logaoedic verse are basically similar; the development in the *dol'nik* has been toward a greater regularity in the lines, which makes them closer to logaoedic verse.[24] Conversely, most logaoedic verse could be treated as a subclass of the *dol'nik*.[25] My own preference, however, is to retain the term *logaoedic* to distinguish between the strictly organized logaoedic poems and the somewhat freer structure of the *dol'nik*.

The possible variations for logaoedic lines are numerous. A poem written in logaoedic trimeter has two main possibilities within the stem of the line ($-◡-◡◡-$ or $-◡◡-◡-$), but since the anacrusis may consist of zero, one, or two syllables, these two variations quickly become six. Also, since modern poets occasionally employ an interval between ictuses of zero or three syllables, still other types of lines can be found.[26] For lines with four ictuses the six variations within the stem of the line become eighteen when allowance is again made for the varying number of syllables that may precede the first ictus. Here too the occasional occurrence of a zero- or three-syllable interval between ictuses creates still more variations. For poems with five ictuses the basic possibilities expand to fourteen within the stem and forty-two in all.[27] And in mixed logaoedics any of these variations may be found in combination with some other logaoedic line or with lines written in a different type of meter.

Russian logaoedics in the eighteenth and early nineteenth centuries most often followed one of several stanzaic types from Greek and Latin poetry. Typical is this portion of Sumarokov's "Hymn to Venus" ("Gimn Venere"), which employs the Sapphic stanza:

Не проти́влюсь си́льной, боги́ня, вла́сти;	‿⏑‿⏑‿⏑⏑‿⏑‿⏑
Отвраща́й лишь то́лько любви́ напа́сти.	‿⏑‿⏑‿⏑⏑‿⏑‿⏑
Взо́р прельсти́в, мой ра́зум ты ве́сь плени́ла,	‿⏑‿⏑‿⏑⏑‿⏑‿⏑
Се́рдце склони́ла.	‿⏑⏑‿⏑
Хоть страши́мся к жи́зни прейти́ мяте́жной,	‿⏑‿⏑‿⏑⏑‿⏑‿⏑
Произво́льно же́ртвуем стра́сти не́жной.	‿⏑‿⏑‿⏑⏑‿⏑‿⏑
Ты́ простра́нной все́ю вселе́нной пра́вишь,	‿⏑‿⏑‿⏑⏑‿⏑‿⏑
Пра́здности сла́вишь.	‿⏑⏑‿⏑

[1755]

Here, as in his translations of Sappho's odes, Sumarokov allowed himself certain liberties with the rules of classical metrics. First, Sumarokov did not fulfill every ictus, whereas in Greek and Latin poetry each syllable represented by a macron had to be long. In this regard, of course, he followed the Russian practice of not necessarily stressing every ictus in the line. Second, Sumarokov employed rhyme, which is not normally found in the Sapphic stanza. Third, by the time of Horace the Sapphic stanza had come to contain a constant caesura after the fifth syllable in the three long lines; Sumarakov used a movable caesura, which appears usually after the sixth but sometimes after the seventh syllable.[28]

When the symbolist poets took up these forms at the beginning of the twentieth century, they paid closer attention to the metrical features of the original. For instance, here are the first two stanzas of a Sapphic ode as translated by Viacheslav Ivanov:

Мни́тся мне́: как бо́ги, блаже́н и во́лен,	‿⏑‿⏑‿⏑⏑‿⏑‿⏑
Кто́ с тобо́й сиди́т, говори́т с тобо́ю,	‿⏑‿⏑‿⏑⏑‿⏑‿⏑
Ми́лой в о́чи смо́трит и слы́шит бли́зко	‿⏑‿⏑‿⏑⏑‿⏑‿⏑
Ле́пет уми́льный	‿⏑⏑‿⏑
Не́жных у́ст!.. Улы́бчивых у́ст дыха́нье	‿⏑‿⏑‿⏑⏑‿⏑‿⏑
Ло́вит о́н... А я́, – чуть вдали́ зави́жу	‿⏑‿⏑‿⏑⏑‿⏑‿⏑
О́браз тво́й, – я се́рдца не чу́ю в пе́рсях.	‿⏑‿⏑‿⏑⏑‿⏑‿⏑
У́ст не раскры́ть мне!	‿⏑⏑‿⏑

1914

In this case neither the original nor the translation maintains a caesura. Ivanov avoided rhyme, and in the entire sixteen-line translation he omitted stress on only one ictus. Other common stanzaic forms from antiquity are the Alcaic and the Asclepiadean; Ivanov's use of the former is seen here in the first stanza from his translation of the poem "To Apollo" ("K Apollonu"):[29]

Когда́ роди́лся Фе́б-Аполло́н, ему́   ⏑‒⏑‒⏑‒⏑⏑‒⏑‒
Злато́ю ми́трой Зе́вс повяза́л чело́,   ⏑‒⏑‒⏑‒⏑⏑‒⏑‒
    И ли́ру да́л, и белосне́жных   ⏑‒⏑‒⏑‒_⏑‒⏑
Да́л лебеде́й с колесни́цей лёгкой.   ‒⏑⏑‒⏑⏑‒⏑‒⏑

1914

Note that both the Sapphic and Alcaic stanzas contain a majority of one-syllable intervals between the ictuses, and thus within the Russian poetic tradition they are more closely related to the binary meters. However, when the *dol'nik* appeared in Russian poetry at the beginning of the twentieth century, it favored two-syllable intervals and thus was based upon ternary meters. Since modern original poetry in logaoedic verse apparently developed from the *dol'nik* and thus contains many two-syllable intervals, a clear distinction can be made between the patterns prevalent in Greek and Latin logaoedic stanzas and those in the more recent original logaoedic verse.[30]

But even in the eighteenth century poets did not confine themselves to Greek and Latin logaoedics; they employed logaoedic lines of their own in a wide range of lengths and variations.[31] Again, Sumarokov was particularly interested in logaoedics, which appear in several of his songs; below is a brief excerpt from one of them:

Се́м-ка сплету́ себе́ вено́к   ‒⏑⏑‒⏑‒⏑‒
Я из лазу́ревых цвето́в,   ‒⏑⏑‒⏑_⏑‒
Бро́шу на чи́стый я пото́к,   ‒⏑⏑‒⏑‒⏑‒
Све́дать, мой ми́ленький како́в,   ‒⏑⏑‒⏑_⏑‒

Ту́жит ли в то́й он стороне́,   ‒⏑⏑‒⏑_⏑‒
Ча́сто ли мы́слит обо мне́.   ‒⏑⏑‒⏑_⏑‒

1765

Here too Sumarokov omitted stress on a number of ictuses. Logaoedic poems do not as a rule omit stresses as often as those written in regular binary meters; still, for logaoedics (and, as we shall see, for the *dol'nik*) the rhythmic inertia created by the poem as a whole is sufficiently strong so that the omitted stresses do not interrupt the flow.[32] In fact, as in binary meters, the absence of stress on certain ictuses allows for both diversity and individuality.

Original logaoedic verse became less common throughout the nineteenth century. One frequently quoted example is a poem by Fet; the first two stanzas appear to have been written in logaoedic tetrameter:

Изму́чен жи́знью, кова́рством наде́жды,	◡◡́◡◡́◡◡◡́◡◡◡́◡
Когда́ им в би́тве душо́й уступа́ю,	◡◡́◡◡́◡◡◡́◡◡◡́◡
И днём и но́чью смежа́ю я ве́жды	◡◡́◡◡́◡◡◡́◡◡◡́◡
И ка́к-то стра́нно поро́й прозрева́ю.	◡◡́◡◡́◡◡◡́◡◡◡́◡
Ещё темне́е мра́к жи́зни седне́вной,	◡◡́◡◡́◡◡◡́◡◡◡́◡
Как по́сле я́ркой осе́нней зарни́цы,	◡◡́◡◡́◡◡◡́◡◡◡́◡
И то́лько в не́бе, как зо́в задуше́вный,	◡◡́◡◡́◡◡◡́◡◡◡́◡
Сверка́ют звёзд золоты́е ресни́цы.	◡◡́◡◡́◡◡◡́◡◡◡́◡

Beginning with the third stanza, however, the pattern starts to break down, and the last two lines of that stanza are regular amphibrachs:[33]

И та́к прозра́чна огне́й бесконе́чность,	◡◡́◡◡́◡◡◡́◡◡◡́◡
И та́к досту́пна вся́ бе́здна эфи́ра,	◡◡́◡◡́◡◡◡́◡◡◡́◡
Что пря́мо смотрю́ я из вре́мени в ве́чность	◡◡́◡◡◡́◡◡◡́◡◡◡́◡
И пла́мя твоё узна́ю, со́лнце ми́ра.	◡◡́◡◡◡́◡◡◡́◡◡◡́◡

[1864]

The poem as a whole might better be termed four-stress *dol' nik*, but still it foretells developments at the beginning of the twentieth century. Even in the first two stanzas, only the one-syllable interval between the first and second ictuses differentiates the lines from regular amphibrachs; thus the logaoedic (or *dol' nik*) form is clearly based on ternary verse, as are the pioneering efforts at the *dol' nik* by Blok and his contemporaries.[34]

As noted above, twentieth-century logaoedics developed largely from the tendency for *dol' niki* to become more regular. When that regularity is taken to an extreme, as was frequently the case with Tsvetaeva, the result is logaoedic verse. While poets since her time have continued to prefer *dol' niki* over logaoedic verse, logaoedics continue to be written; this example is from a song by Aleksandr Galich, who used logaoedics frequently:

Как хоти́те, на доске́, на бума́ге,	◡◡◡́◡◡◡◡́◡◡◡́◡
Це́льным це́хом отмеча́йте, не ли́чно!	◡◡◡́◡◡◡◡́◡◡◡́◡
Мы ж рабо́таем на ве́сь наш социа́герь,	◡◡◡́◡◡◡◡́◡◡◡́◡
Мы ж проду́кцию даём на отли́чно!	◡◡◡́◡◡◡◡́◡◡◡́◡

И совсе́м мне, говорю́, не до сме́ху,   ᵕᵕ⊥ᵕᵕᵕ⊥ᵕᵕ⊥ᵕ
Э́то чьё же, говорю́, указа́нье,   ᵕᵕ⊥ᵕᵕᵕ⊥ᵕᵕ⊥ᵕ
Чтоб тако́му выдаю́щему це́ху   ᵕᵕ⊥ᵕᵕᵕ⊥ᵕᵕ⊥ᵕ
Не присва́ивать почётного зва́нья!"   ᵕᵕ⊥ᵕᵕᵕ⊥ᵕᵕ⊥ᵕ
                          [1960s]

When lines include at least one interval of three syllables, as is the case here, they appear to be based not so much on the tradition of *dol' niki* as on a kind of regularized accentual verse.[35] Be that as it may, even though classical logaoedics have gone the way of the hexameter and are met, if at all, only in an occasional translation, both uniform and mixed logaoedic verse have enjoyed something of a revival in the twentieth century as a result of the general interest in nonclassical meters.

THE *DOL' NIK*

The *dol' nik*, where the intervals between ictuses may consist of either one or two syllables, became a common verse form only in the twentieth century, but it has existed on the fringes of the Russian verse tradition ever since the reforms of Lomonosov and Trediakovsky. Indeed, Trediakovsky's hexameters, which allow either one or two weak positions after each of the first four ictuses, could be labeled a special form of the six-stress *dol' nik*. Similarly, logaoedic poetry can be categorized as highly "regularized" *dol' niki* in which the ictuses must always appear at the same position in the line. Zhukovsky used logaoedics and *dol' niki* in some of his translations from German;[36] later in the nineteenth century other Russian poets employed the *dol' nik* in translations of German poems that were themselves written in this type of meter. From about 1790 through 1840 many poets (including Radishchev, Vostokov, Pushkin, and Lermontov) experimented with imitations of folk meters that, like the *dol' nik*, allowed for a variable number of syllables between ictuses—though more often than not the fluctuation was greater than that allowed by the norms for the modern *dol' nik*. Also a few early examples of original literary poetry, such as Tiutchev's "Silentium!" and "Last Love" ("Posledniaia liubov'"), were written in what today would be considered *dol' niki*.[37]

Yet none of these efforts were sufficient to establish a viable tradition. For all the success enjoyed by the hexameter translations of Gnedich and Zhukovsky, their verses, it will be recalled, contained relatively few one-syllable intervals between ictuses and therefore were hardly distinguishable from regular dactylic poetry. The experiments by Pushkin and others with folk poetry found few reflections in works during the second half of the nineteenth century. Tiutchev's *dol'niki* sounded so abnormal to his contemporaries that no less a writer than Turgenev helped edit some of the "irregular" lines so that they would conform to regular syllabo-tonic practice.[38] And German *dol'niki* were often as not translated by regular anapests or, especially, amphibrachs; when the Russian translators did use the *dol'nik*, they generally favored the two-syllable rather than the one-syllable intervals that predominate in German.[39]

What is interesting here is not merely the failure of the *dol'nik* to become established despite the models of hexameter and logaoedic verse in addition to some well-known translations from the German, but also the predilection of most Russian poets to associate the *dol'nik* with ternary meters rather than with iambic or trochaic verse. Tiutchev, it is true, included *dol'nik* lines in poems that are otherwise iambic, but these are precisely the works that struck his contemporaries by their unusual rhythm. On the other hand, the occasional one-syllable intervals that dot the otherwise regularly dactylic lines in the translations of Gnedich and Zhukovsky did not unduly disturb their readers. In attempting to imitate the *dol'nik* meter of German poems, Russian translators imparted to their versions a ternary basis (owing to the abundance of two-syllable intervals) rather than the binary basis of the originals.[40] Just why "irregularities" were more acceptable in lines that were closer to ternary than to binary meters is open to speculation. Since the ternary meters began to approach the binary meters in popularity only during the second half of the nineteenth century, possibly they were considered less established and more amenable to experimentation than iambic or trochaic poetry.[41] Consequently, the appearance of occasional one-syllable intervals in ternary verse was considered to be less of a disruption than two-syllable intervals in the binary meters. Also, binary verse, with its frequent omissions of stress at the ictuses, already had the capability of creating a great deal of rhythmic variety; ternary poetry, on the other hand, had very few omitted stresses, and the use of one-syllable intervals could help ternary lines avoid a monotonous regularity. Finally, the *dol'nik*, with its variable number of syllables between ictuses, approximated the average number of syllables per stress in Russian better than the ternary meters. Be that as it may, when the *dol'nik* arose as an independent meter it had a ternary rather than a binary basis:

two-syllable intervals were used more frequently than one-syllable ones, and nearly all the ictuses were stressed.

More than any other poet, Aleksandr Blok was responsible for popularizing the *dol'nik* during the early period of its modern history. Gippius and Briusov (who coined the term; other metrists at the time frequently used *pauznik* instead) experimented with the *dol'nik* before Blok ever used the meter, but neither enjoyed Blok's reputation. Furthermore, Blok's *dol'nik* verse created a strong impact because he used the form intensely during a relatively brief period; of his fifty-odd *dol'nik* poems all but a handful were written during the years 1901–5.[42] By the 1910s numerous poets began to use the *dol'nik* extensively: Gumilev, Akhmatova, Kliuev, and Esenin, among others. At times, as in Esenin's poetry of the early 1920s, a poet favored *dol'niki* over all other meters.[43] Today the majority of poets employ the *dol'nik* in some of their poetry.[44]

During the early stages of the meter's development, the three-stress (a more precise name would be three-ictus) *dol'nik* was the favored line length. For example, it accounts for about 66 percent of Blok's poems in *dol'niki*, 75 percent of Gumilev's, and so forth. By the 1920s the four-stress *dol'nik*, either on its own or in regular alternation with the three-stress line, became common as well. Poems written entirely in *dol'niki* with two or with more than four ictuses are less frequent, though such lines can be found in the variable *dol'nik*, where the number of ictuses from line to line fluctuates. Since the three-stress *dol'nik* represents by far the most common line length written during the early stages of this meter's development and since this form has been studied most intensively, the bulk of the following discussion concentrates on this one meter while at the same time elucidating the salient features shared by other lengths of *dol'nik* lines. Toward the end of this section a few remarks are devoted to the special characteristics of the four-stress *dol'nik* and to some of the less common *dol'nik* meters.

The schema for the three-stress *dol'nik* is as follows:

$$0/2 - 1/2 - 1/2 \div 0/2$$

(where the solidus indicates the ranges of syllables). In certain ways *dol'niki* resemble regular syllabo-tonic poetry. They are most often rhymed, and the clausula may be masculine, feminine, or dactylic (longer endings, as in classical syllabo-tonic poetry, occur, but are relatively rare). Hypermetrical stressing is limited to monosyllabic or, when the interval between ictuses is two syllables, to disyllabic words. If hypermetrical stressing occurs on a word with two syllables, the unstressed syllable of the word may not correspond to an ictus.[45] As in both binary and ternary meters, hypermetrical stressing occurs most often on the anacrusis. Also, the only constant stress in *dol'niki* occurs on the final ictus of the line; any other ictus may be left unstressed. As a result, *dol'niki* have developed various rhythmical structures largely in keeping with the laws elucidated by Taranovsky to explain the rhythmic characteristics of Russian binary meters.[46]

At the same time *dol'niki* differ from classical Russian syllabo-tonic verse in two ways. First, the anacrusis may vary within a given poem: the number of syllables before the first ictus can range from zero to two (or zero to one, or one to two). In classical Russian verse, the anacrusis does not vary in binary poems and does so only rarely in ternary poems (which may then mix anapestic, amphibrachic, and dactylic lines within the same work). So here too is another link between the ternary meters and the *dol'nik*, though the variable anacrusis occurs much more frequently in the latter. Over the years, however, the majority of *dol'nik* poems have exhibited a constant anacrusis that most often consists of two syllables.[47] Second, the interval between ictuses fluctuates between one and two syllables, and occasionally "irregular" intervals of zero or three syllables turn up as well. As tables 19 and 22 demonstrate, true *dol'nik* lines have at least one interval between ictuses that differs from the others. In the three-stress *dol'nik* all the *dol'nik* variations either have one interval of two syllables and another of one syllable or, if the middle ictus is unstressed, have a single four-syllable interval (the unstressed ictus plus one plus two). A *dol'nik* poem may also have individual lines that are either binary or ternary in form; for instance in table 19, variations I, V, VIII, and XII are all ternary and, depending on the anacrusis, would be dactylic, amphibrachic, or anapestic. Thus a poem written in *dol'niki* may well have lines of different lengths. The stems of three-stress *dol'niki* can vary from five to seven syllables, and since the anacrusis can range from zero to two syllables, lines (exclusive of the clausula) may consist of anywhere from five to nine syllables.

Several problems in analysis arise from these differences. First, just where are the borders between *dol'niki* and regular syllabo-tonic poetry on the one hand and less regular accentual verse on the other? Particularly at the beginning of the century, many *dol'niki* poems had a high percentage of ternary lines. Yet ternary poems may themselves occasionally omit a syllable between ictuses. Conventionally, therefore, a poem with no more than 75 percent ternary lines will be assigned to the category of *dol'niki*; if the number of ternary lines exceeds that thresh-

TABLE 19

Rhythmic Variations of the Three-Stress *Dol'nik*

Number of Omitted Stresses	Number of Variation	Number of Syllables in Stem	Stem Form	Line Type	Example	Anacrusis in Example
0	I	7	´ 2 ´ 2 ´	ternary	Пáмятник Мéксике! Впрóчем	0 syllables
	II	6	´ 1 ´ 2 ´	*dol'nik*	почва в мёртвой корóсте	0 "
	III	6	´ 2 ´ 1 ´	*dol'nik*	кáждый вторóй—усáтый	0 "
	IV	5	´ 1 ´ 1 ´	binary	понялá свой юный дóлг	2 "
1	V	7	´ 2 — 2 ´	ternary	стéлющаяся полóго	0 "
	VI	6	´ 4 ´	*dol'nik*	сдéлаться обелúском	0 "
	VII	5	´ 1 — 1 ´	binary	от духóв и притирáний	2 "
1	VIII	7	— 2 ´ 2 ´	ternary	испепелённые скáлы	0 "
	IX	6	— 2 ´ 1 ´	*dol'nik*	а приглядúсь—жестóко	0 "
	X	6	— 1 ´ 2 ´	*dol'nik*	улыбáясь лукáво	0 "
	XI	5	— 1 ´ 1 ´	binary	и поцеловáвшей вóина	2 "
2	XII	7	— 2 — 2 ´	ternary	послеоперациóнная	0 "
	XIII	6	— 4 ´	*dol'nik*	—	
	XIV	5	— 1 — 1 ´	binary	—	

Sources: The three binary examples are from Gumilev's "Sestre miloserdiia" (1915), variation XII is from Voznesensky's "Zhizn' moia kochevaia" (1963), and the others are from Brodsky's "Meksikanskii romansero" (1975). The latter two poems are analyzed individually in tables 20 and 21. The numbering of the variations is based on the chart in Kolmogorov and Prokhorov, "O dol'nike sovremennoi russkoi poezii," p. 76. They just list ten variations; Bailey, "Blok and Heine," p. 7, divides their VIII into VIII and X, and their IX into IX and XI. I have divided their X into XII, XIII, and XIV.
Notes: When stress is lacking on the first ictus (VIII through XIV), certain variations become indistinguishable in poems with a variable anacrusis. Variations XII through XIV are theoretically possible but hardly ever found in practice.

The variations listed here represent only the different *stems*. Each stem may be preceded by zero, one, or two syllables, and these differences in the anacrusis may have an effect on the rhythm (see lines 4 and 5 of table 20).

old, then the work is considered to be written in a ternary meter, as a *transitional metrical form* between the ternary meter and *dol'niki*.[48] Similarly, if more than 25 percent of the lines contain intervals of either zero or more than two syllables, then the poem is written in accentual verse.[49] A second difficulty may occur in determining the rhythmic variation to which a given line belongs. Variations VIII through XI in table 19 are clearly distinguishable only when the anacrusis is constant; if it fluctuates variation VIII may be confused with X, and variation IX with XI. For instance, the sample line for variation VIII has the scheme $0 - 2 \acute{\,} 2 \acute{\,} 1$, but if the anacrusis were one instead of zero, it would belong to variation X: $1 - 1 \acute{\,} 2 \acute{\,} 1$. Even when the anacrusis is constant, problems may arise within the line either because of words with dual stress patterns or because of hypermetrical stressing. Consider the following line: *Pokuda ia byl s toboiu.* Here the anacrusis is one syllable and the first and third stresses are easy to determine, but the line may be assigned either to variation II or III, depending on whether *ia* or *byl* is given the metrical stress. A reasonable rule in such cases is to let the part of speech be the determining factor: nouns are more strongly stressed than adverbs, verbs more than pronouns, etc. If a poem is composed in the variable *dol'nik* and also lacks a constant anacrusis, it may be difficult to distinguish, say, a three-stress *dol'nik* line from a four-stress. Take the line *Tsélyi dén ia brodíl v toské.* This could either be variation III of three-stress *dol'niki* with a two-syllable anacrusis and hypermetrical stressing on the first syllable ($\acute{2} \acute{\,} 2 \acute{\,} 1 \acute{\,}$), or it could be variation VI of the four-stress line with a zero anacrusis ($0 \acute{\,} 1 \acute{\,} 2 \acute{\,} 1 \acute{\,}$). In fact, it comes from a poem by Gumilev written entirely in the three-stress *dol'nik*, but in a different context it could be ambiguous.[50]

The three-stress *dol'nik* has been employed in a wide variety of rhythmic structures. The opening lines of this early poem by Blok are fairly typical both of his usage and of *dol'niki* in general during the earliest period of their development:

Вхожу́ я в тёмные хра́мы,	$1 \acute{\,} 1 \acute{\,} 2 \acute{\,} 1$
Соверша́ю бе́дный обря́д.	$2 \acute{\,} 1 \acute{\,} 2 \acute{\,}$
Та́м жду́ я Прекра́сной Да́мы	$\acute{1} \acute{\,} 2 \acute{\,} 1 \acute{\,} 1$
В мерца́ньи кра́сных лампа́д.	$1 \acute{\,} 1 \acute{\,} 2 \acute{\,}$
В тени́ у высо́кой коло́нны	$1 \acute{\,} 2 \acute{\,} 2 \acute{\,} 1$
Дрожу́ от скри́па двере́й.	$1 \acute{\,} 1 \acute{\,} 2 \acute{\,}$
А в лицо́ мне гляди́т, озарённый,	$2 \acute{\,} 2 \acute{\,} 2 \acute{\,} 1$
То́лько о́браз, лишь со́н о Не́й.	$\acute{2} \acute{\,} 2 \acute{\,} 1 \acute{\,}$

1902

TABLE 20

Stressing in the Three-Stress *Dol'nik*

		Stressing (by ictus)			Average Stressing
	Anacrusis	I	II	III	
1. Blok (1901–20)	both 2-syllable and variable	100%	99.4%	100%	99.8%
2. Gumilev (1905–21)	2-syllable	99.8	83.9	100	94.6
3. Tsvetaeva (1915–26)	2-syllable	99.5	64.4	100	88.0
4. Ivask (1961–64)	0-syllable	72.0	69.5	100	80.5
5. Ivask (1960–65)	1-syllable	96.2	59.7	100	85.3
6. Voznesensky (pre-1972)	variable	96.3	74.7	99.2	90.0
7. Voznesensky (pre-1972)	0-syllable	87.5	62.5	100	83.3
8. Voznesensky ("Zhizn' moia kochevaia"— 40 lines)	0-syllable	87.5	65.0	100	84.2
9. Brodsky ("Meksikanskii romansero"—112 lines)	variable (0/1)	78.6	95.5	100	91.4

Sources: Line 1 is from Bailey, "Blok and Heine," p. 7; line 2 from Sampson, "*Dol'niks* in Gumilev's Poetry," pp. 25–27 (based on the twenty-four poems that Gumilev wrote in the three-stress *dol'nik* with a constant two-syllable anacrusis); line 3 is from G. S. Smith, "Logaoedic Metres in Tsvetayeva," p. 348 (based on the thirteen poems employing what Smith calls the "minor variant" of the particular line, or poems in which at least 25 percent of the lines exhibit variation VI); lines 4 and 5 are from Bailey, "*Dol'niki* of George Ivask," pp. 160–64; lines 6 and 7 are from Bailey, "Voznesenskij," pp. 166–67; and lines 8 and 9 contain my own calculations.

Two lines (the first and third of the second stanza) are ternary; four are variation II and two are III. The anacrusis fluctuates between one and two syllables, and within the entire sixteen-line poem all the ictuses are stressed. As line 1 of table 20 shows, even this brief example bears a close resemblance to Blok's general practice. Nearly all his lines belong to one of the first three variations, with nearly 50 percent belonging to variation II. Of Blok's approximately 650 lines written in the three-stress *dol'nik*, about 75 percent belong to one of the *dol'nik* variations (mostly II and III, with a very few VI), nearly 25 percent are ternary (I), only several lines are binary (IV), and a handful are irregular. The excerpt above is atypical, however, in that Blok used a two-syllable anacrusis nearly twice as often as the one-syllable.[51]

The profile of Blok's usage is similar to that for the entire 1890–1910 period.[52] First, the early *dol'niki* have a clear ternary basis. Ternary lines (primarily variation I) comprise about 33 percent of the total lines in *dol'niki* for these years, while binary lines are rare—few poets used them more than 2 or 3 percent of the time. Second, the two fully stressed *dol'nik* variations (II and III) are common; together they account for more than 50 percent of the lines, with II generally used more frequently than III. Unstressed ictuses are rare, and the anacrusis, as often as not, is variable.

M. L. Gasparov, in his massive study of fifty thousand three-stress *dol'nik* lines in works by 101 poets, has distinguished three basic traits in the evolution of the *dol'nik*.[53] First, over time *dol'nik* poems have tended to contain increasingly more lines that belong to one of the main *dol'nik* variations (II, III, and VI). Consequently, *dol'niki* appear to be less an offshoot of ternary meters and are more clearly perceived as an independent meter. Variation I continues to be used and is quite common in the poetry of certain contemporary poets (e.g., Evtushenko), but many other poets employ it only sparingly (cf. lines 4–9, table 21). Binary lines have become still rarer than before and are totally absent from the work of many poets, while irregular lines are also less frequent. Second, much like regular binary and ternary poems, many *dol'nik* works now have the same number of syllables in all lines, from the first syllable through the last ictus. The isosyllabism partly results from the tendency to favor *dol'nik* variations, since all have precisely six syllables in the stem. Another factor is the growing use of a constant anacrusis; if the lines are only in *dol'nik* variations and maintain a constant anacrusis, they will all be the same length. Third, *dol'nik* poems often show an anapestic rhythm, thanks both to the frequency of a two-

TABLE 21

Rhythmic Variations in the Three-Stress *Dol'nik*

	I	II	III	IV	V	VI	VII	VIII	IX	X	XI	Other
1.	23.2%	43.0%	31.8%	0.6%	1.0%	0.6%	1.8%	—	—	—	—	0.8%
2.	4.7	33.5	42.1	1.8	—	13.0	—	—	0.5%	0.1%	0.1%	1.9
3.	—	—	63.9	—	—	35.6	—	—	4.9	—	—	—
4.	—	21.9	19.5	—	—	30.5	—	—	0.8	23.2	—	—
5.	5.4	23.0	32.9	0.8	2.5	40.2	1.2	0.4%	1.2	3.1	1.7	3.3
6.	7.5	13.7	48.6	—	3.8	20.8	—	1.9	10.6	0.4	—	0.6
7.	—	5.0	37.5	—	—	33.1	—	—	10.0	—	—	2.5
8.	—	5.0	50.0	—	—	32.5	—	—	10.0	—	—	—
9.	1.8	37.5	34.8	—	1.8	2.7	—	4.4	3.6	13.4	—	—

Sources: See table 20.

Note: The column "Other" indicates rare instances of variations XII through XIV and, more often, irregular lines that do not adhere to the norms for the three-stress *dol'nik*.

syllable constant anacrusis and to the preference of many poets for variation III over variation II. As a result the beginning of many lines is anapestic $(2-2-)$, and only toward the end is the rhythm altered by a one-syllable interval.

To these three features can be added a fourth: *dol'niki* have come to exhibit more clearly defined rhythmical structures. As Gasparov notes, the percentage of lines with an omitted stress has gone from less than 2 percent during the early history of the meter to nearly 25 percent in more recent years.[54] Variation VI is by far the most widely used of those that omit a stress (cf. table 21), but variations IX and X appear as well. The resulting rhythms have by now developed to the extent that it is possible to talk of individual manners in the use of rhythmic structures and to analyze the effect of the anacrusis on the choice of variations.[55] The appearance of definite rhythmic structures is further evidence that *dol'-niki* have become fully established as independent meters.

One consequence of these developments has been a marked change in the use of the different rhythmic variations. If variations I, II, and III accounted for more than 90 percent of the lines during the early years of the twentieth century, in recent years variation I has fallen to 10 percent of the total and variation II to a bit more than that. The most popular variations have become III—used in nearly 50 percent of the lines—and VI, which appears in about 20 percent. The lines with two omitted stresses (variations XII through XIV) continue to exist more in theory than in practice, and all the binary types taken together (variations IV, VII, and XI) add up to less than 1 percent of the lines. The remaining variations (V, VIII, IX, and X) are used sporadically; some occur often in particular poems or groups of poems, but they are rare in the works of many poets.[56]

Gasparov has attempted to distinguish three main types of three-stress *dol'nik* poems, which he has named after the poets who were among the first to employ each form. In the "Esenin" type, variations I and III predominate; in the "Gumilev," variations III and II; and in the "Tsvetaeva," variations III and VI. While the Tsvetaeva type reflects the greatest evolution of *dol'niki* and the Esenin type the least, no single type has ever gained universal favor; all three can still be found in the works of contemporary poets. The most important models in more recent times, however, seem to be the rhythmic patterns favored by Gumilev and Tsvetaeva, as in this excerpt from Gumilev's "Madaga-skar" and this brief poem by Tsvetaeva:

А в роско́шной фо́рме гуса́рской   2 – 1 – 2 – 1
Благоскло́нно на ни́х взира́л   2 – 2 – 1 –
Короле́вы мадагаска́рской   2 –   4   – 1
Са́мый пре́данный генера́л.   2 –   4   –

Между ни́х быки́ Томата́вы,   2 – 1 – 2 – 1
Схо́жи с гру́дою тёмных камне́й,   2 – 2 – 2 –
Пожира́ли жи́рные тра́вы   2 – 1 – 2 – 1
Благово́ньем по́лных поле́й.   2 – 1 – 2 –

И вздыха́л я, заче́м плыву́ я,   2 – 2 – 1 – 1
Не оста́нусь я зде́сь заче́м: 2 – 2 – 1 –
Неуже́ль и зде́сь не спою́ я   2 – 1 – 2 – 1
Са́мых лу́чших мои́х поэ́м?   2 – 2 – 1 –

                    [< 1921]

Не возьмёшь моего́ румя́нца –   2 – 2 – 1 – 1
Си́льного – как разли́вы ре́к!   2 – 2 – 1 –
Ты́ охо́тник, но я́ не да́мся,   2 – 2 – 1 – 1
Ты́ пого́ня, но я́ е́смь бе́г.   2 – 2 – 1 –

Не возьмёшь мою́ ду́шу жи́ву!   2 – 2 – 1 – 1
Та́к, на по́лном скаку́ пого́нь –   2 – 2 – 1 –
Пригиба́ющийся – и жи́лу   2 –   4   – 1
Перекусы́вающий ко́нь   2 –   4   –

                    1924

The Gumilev poem contrasts with Blok's "Vkhozhu ia v temnye khramy" in several ways. First, as in most of Gumilev's poems written with the three-stress *dol'nik*, "Madagaskar" has a constant two-syllable ana-crusis.[57] Second, variation I is significantly rarer in Gumilev's poetry than in Blok's; it appears in just one of the twelve lines quoted here (the sixth) and in less than 5 percent of all Gumilev's three-stress lines (cf. lines 1 and 2 in table 21). Third, Gumilev allows more unstressed ic-tuses. In Blok's *dol'niki*, as in nineteenth-century ternary poetry, unful-filled ictuses within the line were a great rarity, but Gumilev's poems, largely owing to his use of the sixth variation, have a second ictus that is clearly weaker than either the first or the third. The rhythmic structure with its alternation of strong and weak ictuses is in keeping with the law of regressive accentual dissimilation. Otherwise Gumilev's poetry is distinctive, as Gasparov has noted, for its abundance of lines in varia-tions II and III. Here they appear in nine of the twelve lines (75 per-cent), about the same percentage as in all his three-stress *dol'nik* poetry. Tsvetaeva's poem presents a markedly different rhythm. Variations I and II are completely absent, and all but the second line (variation IX) were composed in variations III or VI. The poem exhibits all the developments that *dol'niki* have undergone: the use of only *dol'nik* variations, a constant two-syllable anacrusis, isosyllabism, and a well-defined rhythmic structure. The second line not only falls outside the pattern of the rest of the poem, it also contains a hypermetrical stress on *sil'nogo*, a three-syllable word. Since hypermetrical stressing in the *dol'nik* is limited to words of one or two syllables, the stress here is actually nonmetrical (though some would interpret this phenomenon as involving a shift of the ictus to the anacrusis).[58] In any case, this stress is in keeping with Tsvetaeva's general tendency to place strong emphasis on the beginning of her lines. Otherwise, Tsvetaeva's near-exclusive use of variations III and VI in poems with this form makes it possible to classify them as a type of logaoedic verse.[59] At the very least, Tsvetaeva and the handful of other poets who employed a similar rhythm wrote poetry that should be termed a highly "regularized" form of the *dol'nik*.[60]

By no means all poets have taken "regularity" to the extreme practiced by Tsvetaeva. George Ivask's *dol'niki* present the same basic picture as Tsvetaeva's: isosyllabism, a constant anacrusis, and exclusively *dol'nik* variations. But rather than limit himself to two of the variations, he used all five of the basic *dol'nik* lines. Of particular interest is the rhythm of his poems with a zero anacrusis; these not only contrast with the poems that have a one-syllable anacrusis, but also display a rhythm quite close to that of poetry in trochaic trimeter, with the first ictus about as weak as the second (table 20, lines 4, 5).[61] Andrei Voznesensky's practice resembles Tsvetaeva's in that he shows a clear preference for variations III and VI (these two variations comprise about 70 percent of his lines), but he too makes use of many other variations, including ternary and a very few binary lines (table 21, lines 6, 7). As with Ivask, the anacrusis affects the rhythm of his works, though the differences in Voznesensky's case are not so pronounced.[62] The opening lines of the following poem illustrate Voznesensky's three-stress *dol'nik*; as lines 7 and 8 of table 20 show, the poem's rhythmic structure and use of different variations are similar to Voznesensky's overall writing of the three-stress *dol'nik* with a zero anacrusis.

Жи́знь моя́ кочева́я	0 ⌣́ 1 ⌣́ 2 ⌣́ 1
ста́ла мое́й плани́дой...	0 ⌣́ 2 ⌣́ 1 ⌣́ 1
Пти́цы крича́т над Ни́дой.	0 ⌣́ 2 ⌣́ 1 ⌣́ 1
Ста́нция кольцева́ния.	0 ⌣́ 4 ⌣́ 2

Сто́нет в сетя́х капро́новых	0 ∸2∸1∸2
в о́блаке пу́ха, кри́ка	0∸2∸1∸1
кры́льями трехметро́выми	0∸ 4 ∸2
у́зкая журавли́ха!	0∸ 4 ∸1

1963

Owing to the frequency of variation VI, most poems written in the three-stress *dol' nik* have a strong first and a somewhat weaker second ictus; thus their rhythm is much like that of the iambic trimeter. Ivask's use of a first ictus that is as weak as the second for his poems with a zero anacrusis is a natural result of the laws governing Russian meters and shows a further development in the tendency of *dol' niki* to form their own rhythmic structures. Nor have all the possibilities been exhausted; as poets continue to write *dol' niki*, still other structures can be expected to appear. One example is the unusual rhythm of Joseph Brodsky's "Mexican Romancero" ("Meksikanskii romansero") from the cycle called *Mexican Divertimento* (*Meksikanskii divertisment*):

Что́-то внутри́, похо́же,	0∸2∸1∸1
сорвало́сь, раскло́лось.	0−1∸2∸1
Произнося́ "о Бо́же",	0−2∸1∸1
слы́шу со́бственный го́лос.	0∸1∸2∸1
Та́к страни́цу мара́ешь	0∸1∸2∸1
ра́ди ме́лкого чу́да.	0∸1∸2∸1
Та́к при э́том взира́ешь	0∸1∸2∸1
на себя́ ниотку́да.	0−1∸2∸1

1975

Brodsky himself has claimed that the rhythm of this poem echoes that of the Spanish ballad.[63] The rhythm also represents a new departure for the Russian *dol' nik* in that it displays a weak first but a strong second ictus (table 20, line 9). Since lines with a zero anacrusis predominate throughout (and are the only kind found in the above excerpt), the weakening of the first ictus may not be totally unexpected but the strong second is quite unusual. Usually when numerous stresses are omitted throughout the poem, variation VI, which lacks stress on the second ictus, is far more frequent than it is here. Another interesting feature is the interplay between variations II and III. While the number of both variations in the poem as a whole is nearly equal, variation III is more frequent in the first half of the poem and II in the second. A detailed analysis reveals finer distinctions: Brodsky divided the poem into seven four-stanza sections, and certain of these have distinctive rhythmic structures. For instance, of the sixteen lines making up the section from which the above excerpt was taken, ten belong to variation II, three to variation X, and just two to variation III; in an earlier section eleven lines are in variation III and only three in II.

To date, studies of the four-stress *dol'nik* have not succeeded in elucidating as clear a picture of its rhythmic patterns. Even Gasparov's survey of over 43,000 four-stress lines in the work of some ninety-two poets is less authoritative than his study of the shorter line.[64] For one thing, he does not examine the anacrusis, which plays an important part in determining the rhythm of individual poems. For another, specific trends in the usage and evolution of the larger line are harder to discern. Yet some general observations are possible.

First, as table 22 makes clear, a wide number of theoretically possible forms exist: forty-eight, as opposed to fourteen for the three-stress line, again without allowing for different lengths of the anacrusis. As with the three-stress *dol'nik*, some of the variations practically never occur. All the variations of the four-stress line with stress omitted on at least the first two ictuses (variations XXXIX through XLVIII) belong more to the realm of theory than practice, as do all but one of those with stress omitted on consecutive internal ictuses (variations XXI through XXIV). Once again binary lines are largely avoided, and ternary lines are much more acceptable. Unlike the three-stress line, ternary variations have not declined significantly in popularity; in Gasparov's survey, one of the two most common lines is variation I, the fully stressed ternary line. Variation IV, the most widely used, has what might be called a ternary impetus, with the two-syllable intervals occurring after the first two ictuses and the single one-syllable interval occurring only at the end of the line. The fully stressed variations (except for variation VIII—the purely binary line) are all among the more common, as are some of the variations with stress omitted on the third ictus. Only a few variations account for the vast majority of all lines: of the "correct" *dol'nik* lines in Gasparov's survey, the two variations marked A on table 22 comprise nearly 50 percent of the lines, and the ten marked either A or B appear in about 90 percent.

Second, stresses are once again omitted at ictuses more frequently than in ternary poems but less so than in binary, and the resulting rhythmic structures tend to adhere to the main laws governing Russian meters. Overall, the correct *dol'nik* lines in Gasparov's survey show a stressing over the line of 93.6 percent, 97.1 percent, 85.6 percent, and

TABLE 22

Rhythmic Variations of the Four-Stress *Dol'nik*

Number of Omitted Stresses	Number of Variation	Number of Syllables in Stem	Stem Form	Line Type	Frequency
0	I	10	´2´2´2´2´	ternary	A
	II	9	´1´2´2´2´	*dol'nik*	B
	III	9	´2´1´2´2´	*dol'nik*	B
	IV	9	´2´2´1´2´	*dol'nik*	A
	V	8	´1´1´2´2´	*dol'nik*	B
	VI	8	´1´2´1´2´	*dol'nik*	B
	VII	8	´2´1´1´2´	*dol'nik*	B
	VIII	7	´1´1´1´2´	binary	C
1	IX	10	´2—2´2´	ternary	D
	X	9	´—4—2´	*dol'nik*	C
	XI	9	´2—2´1´	*dol'nik*	D
	XII	8	´1—1´2´	*dol'nik*	D
	XIII	8	´—4—1´	*dol'nik*	C
	XIV	7	´1—1´1´	binary	D
1	XV	10	´2´2—2´	ternary	C
	XVI	9	´1´2—2´	*dol'nik*	C
	XVII	9	´2´—4—´	*dol'nik*	B
	XVIII	8	´1´—4—´	*dol'nik*	B
	XIX	8	´2´1—1´	*dol'nik*	C
	XX	7	´1´1—1´	binary	D
2	XXI	10	´2—2—2´	ternary	X
	XXII	9	´—7—´	*dol'nik*	X
	XXIII	8	´—6—´	*dol'nik*	D
	XXIV	7	´1—1—1´	binary	X

1	XXV	10	─ 2 ́ 2 ́ 2 ́ 2 ́	ternary	C
	XXVI	9	─ 1 ́ 2 ́ 2 ́ 2 ́	*dol'nik*	D
	XXVII	9	─ 2 ́ 1 ́ 2 ́ 2 ́	*dol'nik*	C
	XXVIII	9	─ 2 ́ 2 ́ 1 ́ 2 ́	*dol'nik*	B
	XXIX	8	─ 1 ́ 1 ́ 2 ́ 2 ́	*dol'nik*	D
	XXX	8	─ 1 ́ 2 ́ 1 ́ 2 ́	*dol'nik*	D
	XXXI	8	─ 2 ́ 1 ́ 1 ́ 2 ́	*dol'nik*	D
	XXXII	7	─ 1 ́ 1 ́ 1 ́ 2 ́	binary	X
2	XXXIII	10	─ 2 ́ 2 ́ 2 ─ 2 ́	ternary	D
	XXXIV	9	─ 1 ́ 2 ́ 2 ─ 2 ́	*dol'nik*	X
	XXXV	9	─ 2 ́ 4 ─ 2 ́	*dol'nik*	C
	XXXVI	8	─ 1 ́ 4 ─ 2 ́	*dol'nik*	D
	XXXVII	8	─ 2 ́ 1 ─ 1 ─ 2 ́	*dol'nik*	D
	XXXVIII	7	─ 1 ́ 1 ─ 1 ─ 2 ́	binary	X
2	XXXIX	10	─ 2 ─ 2 ́ 2 ─ 2 ́	ternary	X
	XL	9	─ 4 ─ 2 ́	*dol'nik*	X
	XLI	9	─ 2 ─ 1 ─ 1 ─ 2 ́	*dol'nik*	X
	XLII	8	─ 1 ─ 1 ─ 2 ─ 2 ́	*dol'nik*	X
	XLIII	8	─ 4 ─ 1 ─ 2 ́	*dol'nik*	X
	XLIV	7	─ 1 ─ 1 ─ 1 ─ 2 ́	binary	X
3	XLV	10	─ 2 ─ 2 ─ 2 ─ 2 ́	ternary	X
	XLVI	9	─ 7 ─ 2 ́	*dol'nik*	X
	XLVII	8	─ 6 ─ 2 ́	*dol'nik*	X
	XLVIII	7	─ 1 ─ 1 ─ 1 ─ 2 ́	binary	X

Sources: The chart is based on Kolmogorov and Prokhorov, "O dol'nike," p. 77, but, as in table 19, variations are added for all lines in which the first ictus is unstressed. Hence 48 variations are shown as opposed to 34. The frequency column is based on data provided in Gasparov, "Chetyrekhiktnyi dol'nik," pp. 256–57.

Note: A, over 20 percent; B, 2–12 percent; C, 0.5–1.9 percent; D, 0.05–0.4 percent; X, trace or not found.

100 percent.[65] As the law of regressive accentual dissimilation predicts, stressing is weakest on the next-to-last ictus, second strongest on the second ictus from the end, and so forth. But the broad statistics conceal much variety among individual poets and poems. Roughly, it is possible to distinguish two extremes in the usage of the four-stress *dol'nik*. One of these, the more "conservative" trend, involves a large number of ternary lines (variation I) and relatively few omitted stresses. The other, a more "innovative" type, contains a higher number of *dol'nik* variations among the fully stressed lines and also employs more lines with omitted stresses.[66] While no boundary appears to exist between the two types, most poets write fairly consistently according to the norms of one type or the other. Surprisingly, Maiakovsky was among the more "conservative" users of this verse form. For the most part the four-stress *dol'nik* appears in portions of his polymetrical works or in combination with the three-stress *dol'nik*; his one poem written entirely with the four-stress *dol'nik* is "I Love" ("Liubliu"), from which the following lines are taken:[67]

Я в ме́ру любо́вью бы́л одарённый.	1 ́2 ́1 ́2 ́1
Но с де́тства	
людье́	
труда́ми муштро́вано.	1 ́2 ́1 ́2 ́2
А я́ –	
убёг на бе́рег Рио́на	1 ́1 ́1 ́2 ́1
и шля́лся,	
ни чёрта не де́лая ро́вно.	1 ́2 ́2 ́2 ́1
Серди́лась ма́ма:	
"Мальчи́шка парши́вый!"	1 ́1 ́2 ́2 ́1
Грози́лся папа́ша по́ясом вы́стегать.	1 ́2 ́1 ́2 ́2
А я́,	
разживя́сь трехрублёвкой фальши́вой,	1 ́2 ́2 ́2 ́1
игра́л с солдатьём под забо́ром в "три́ ли́стика".	1 ́2 ́2 ́2 ́2

1922

Within this excerpt the anacrusis is always one syllable, three of the lines (4, 7, and 8) are simply regular amphibrachs, three others belong to variation III, and no stresses are omitted. In the poem as a whole over 90 percent of the lines are fully stressed, and nearly as many have a one-syllable anacrusis (the rest have a zero anacrusis).[68] Akhmatova's "By the Very Edge of the Sea" ("U samogo moria") displays a more "innovative" rhythm:

Бу́хты изре́зали ни́зкий бе́рег,	0 ́2 ́2 ́1 ́1
Ды́мное со́лнце упа́ло в мо́ре.	0 ́2 ́2 ́1 ́1
Вы́шла цыга́нка из пеще́ры,	0 ́2 ́1 ́1 ́1

Па́льцем меня́ к себе́ помани́ла:	0 ‿ 2 ‿ 1 ‿ 2 ‿ 1
"Что́ ты, краса́вица, хо́дишь бо́са?	0 ‿ 2 ‿ 2 ‿ 1 ‿ 1
Ско́ро весёлой, бога́той ста́нешь.	0 ‿ 2 ‿ 2 ‿ 1 ‿ 1
Зна́тного го́стя жди́ до Па́схи,	0 ‿ 2 ‿ 1 ‿ 1 ‿ 1
Зна́тному го́стю кла́няться бу́дешь;	0 ‿ 2 ‿ 1 ‿ 2 ‿ 1
Ни красото́й твое́й, ни любо́вью,	0 — 2 ‿ 1 ‿ 2 ‿ 1
Пе́сней одно́ю го́стя прима́нишь".	0 ‿ 2 ‿ 1 ‿ 2 ‿ 1

1914

In this passage none of the lines are ternary and the favorite variations
are III and IV. The entire poem contains two distinct fragments and sev-
eral scattered lines in three- or two-stress *dol'niki*, but over 80 percent
of the lines are four-stress.[69] Nearly 40 percent of the poem's lines be-
long to variation IV, only about 2 percent to variation I (the fully
stressed ternary line; as opposed to over 25 percent in Maiakovsky's "I
Love"), and more than 25 percent contain at least one omitted stress (cf.
lines 3 and 9 above). Most of the lines have a zero anacrusis (though it
varies), while the clausula is always feminine and unrhymed.

A third and related feature is the great variety in the rhythmic struc-
tures employed by individual poets. Thus a still more "innovative" ex-
ample of the four-stress *dol'nik* can be found in Boris Slutsky's poem,
"N. N. Aseev at Work" ("N. N. Aseev za rabotoi"). The twenty-six lines
include at least one instance of each of the eight fully stressed variations
as well as at least one omitted stress in more than 33 percent of the lines;
in all, this relatively short poem contains thirteen variations and ends
with an eight-line sequence which only two are fully stressed:

И все́ пова́дки –	1 ‿ 1 ‿ 4 ‿ 1
пенсионе́ра,	
И всё поведе́ние –	1 ‿ 2 ‿ 4 ‿
старика́	
Стано́вятся по́ступью пионе́ра,	1 ‿ 2 ‿ 4 ‿ 1
Кото́рая, как изве́стно, легка́.	1 ‿ 4 ‿ 2 ‿
И стро́фы равня́ются – ро́та к ро́те,	1 ‿ 2 ‿ 2 ‿ 1 ‿ 1
И сви́щут, сло́вно в лесу́ соловьи́,	1 ‿ 1 ‿ 2 ‿ 2 ‿
И всё э́то пи́шется на оборо́те	1 ‿ 2 ‿ 2 – 2 ‿ 1
Отло́женной почему́-то статьи́.	1 ‿ 4 ‿ 2 ‿

[< 1963]

The poem as a whole has nearly equal stressing on the first two ictuses
(96.1 percent and 92.7 percent) and distinctly weaker stressing on the
third (73.1 percent), which represents a more level version of the stress-
ing pattern that predominated in the Russian iambic tetrameter during
the early part of the nineteenth century (table 4, line 2).

The four-stress line is particularly frequent in alternation with the three-stress *dol'nik*. Eduard Bagritsky used this type of mixed meter in a pair of long poems called "Night" ("Noch'") and "The Last Night" ("Posledniaia noch'"). As in Akhmatova's "By the Very Edge of the Sea," the lines are unrhymed. Omitted stresses are common in both the four-stress and three-stress lines, as the following example from "The Last Night" illustrates:

Грядущий убийца дремал пока,   1 ⌣ 2 ⌣ 2 ⌣ 1 ⌣
голову положив   0 ⌣   4   ⌣
На юношески твёрдый кулак   1 ⌣ 1 – 1 ⌣ 2 ⌣
В коричневых волосках.   1 ⌣   4   ⌣

. . . .

В Одессе каштаны оделись в дым,   1 ⌣ 2 ⌣ 2 ⌣ 1 ⌣
И море по вечерам,   1 ⌣   4   ⌣
·Хрипя, поворачивалось на оси,   1 ⌣ 2 ⌣ 2 – 2 ⌣
Подобное колесу.   1 ⌣   4   ⌣

                    1932

Both works have a variable anacrusis, though lines with a one-syllable anacrusis predominate. As expected, stressing is lowest on the next-to-last ictus: 69.4 percent in the four-stress line and 73.1 percent in the three-stress.[70] Thus, each line length assumes a definite rhythmic structure; that of the four-stress *dol'nik* is much like the Slutsky poem quoted above, while the pattern for the three-stress resembles Voznesensky's use of the meter with a variable anacrusis (table 20, line 6).

Dol'nik lines other than those with three- or four-stresses occur occasionally. The two-stress line, especially when it has a variable anacrusis, can avoid monotony more easily than the very short classical meters. Interestingly, a few examples of the two-stress *dol'nik* can be found in the nineteenth century as well as in the twentieth. Below are lines taken from Fet's "When the rooster" ("Kogda petukh") and, as a more modern example, from a poem by Elagin:

Чу! Слышу, вздох   1 ⌣ 1 ⌣
Ко мне несётся   1 ⌣ 1 ⌣ 1
С мягкого ложа,   0 ⌣ 2 ⌣ 1
Где при серебряной   0 ⌣ 2 ⌣ 2
Луне белеют   1 ⌣ 1 ⌣ 1
Младые ланиты,   1 ⌣ 2 ⌣ 1
Покрытые первым   1 ⌣ 2 ⌣ 1
Шёлковым пухом,   0 ⌣ 2 ⌣ 1
                [1840]

Како́й я хозя́ин   1 ⌣ 2 ⌣ 1
Колу́ и двору́?   1 ⌣ 2 ⌣
Так во́т припа́ян   1 ⌣ 1 ⌣ 1
Остро́жник к ядру́.   1 ⌣ 2 ⌣

Мой до́м – берло́га,   1 ⌣ 1 ⌣ 1
Мой до́м – нора́,   1 ⌣ 1 ⌣
Где над поро́гом   1 – 1 ⌣ 1
Те́нь топора́.   0 ⌣ 2 ⌣

[< 1982]

Lines with more than four ictuses, of course, have a long tradition in the
hexameter and in certain classical logaoedic forms. Poets also occasion-
ally employ a variable *dol'nik* in which the number of ictuses per line
varies irregularly. In this lyric Blok used lines that contain anywhere
from two to five ictuses:

Блесну́ло в глаза́х. Метну́лось в мечте́.   1 ⌣ 2 ⌣ 1 ⌣ 2 ⌣
Прильну́ло к дрожа́щему се́рдцу.   1 ⌣ 2 ⌣ 2 ⌣ 1
Кра́сный с ко́зел спрыгну́л – и на све́тлой черте́   0 ⌣ 1 ⌣ 2 ⌣ 2 ⌣ 2 ⌣
Распахну́л каре́тную две́рцу.   2 ⌣ 1 ⌣ 2 ⌣ 1

Ни́щий по́днял дрожа́щий фона́рь: 0 ⌣ 1 ⌣ 2 ⌣ 2 ⌣
Афи́ша на мо́кром столбе́...   1 ⌣ 2 ⌣ 2 ⌣
Ступи́ла на све́тлый тротуа́р,   1 ⌣ 2 ⌣ 2 ⌣
Исче́зла в толпе́.   1 ⌣ 2 ⌣

Лу́ч дождли́вую мглу́ пронза́л –   0 ⌣ 1 ⌣ 2 ⌣ 2 ⌣
Боги́ня вступи́ла в скле́п...   1 ⌣ 2 ⌣ 1 ⌣
Гори́, маскара́дный за́л!   1 ⌣ 2 ⌣ 1 ⌣
Зде́сь ни́щий во мгле́ осле́п.   í ⌣ 2 ⌣ 1 ⌣

1904

Note that the *ua* in *trotuar* (line 7) was probably regarded as a diph-
thong by Blok; in his *Poeticheskii slovar'* (p. 104), A. P. Kviatkovsky
cites another instance in which Blok treats *trotuar* the same way. The
poem has a definite ternary impetus: four of the lines (2, 6–8) are regu-
lar amphibrachs, and none of the remaining lines have more than a
single one-syllable interval between ictuses. As is typical for Blok, all
the lines are fully stressed. A more recent use of variable *dol'nik* can be
seen in the first half of this poem by Brodsky:

Ниотку́да с любо́вью, надца́того мартобря́,   2 ⌣ 2 ⌣ 2 ⌣ 4 ⌣
дорого́й уважа́емый ми́лая, но нева́жно   2 ⌣ 2 ⌣ 2 ⌣ 2 – 1 ⌣ 1
да́же кто́, и́бо че́рт лица́, говоря́   2 ⌣ 2 ⌣ 1 ⌣ 2 ⌣
открове́нно, не вспо́мнить уже́, не ва́ш, но   2 ⌣ 2 ⌣ 2 ⌣ 1 ⌣ 1
и ниче́й ве́рный дру́г вас приве́тствует с одного́   2 ⌣ 2 ⌣ 2 ⌣ 4 ⌣
из пяти́ контине́нтов, держа́щегося на ковбо́ях;   2 ⌣ 2 ⌣ 2 ⌣ 2 – 2 ⌣ 1

Я люби́л тебя́ бо́льше, чем а́нгелов и самого́,   2 ‑ 2́ ‑ 2 ‑ 2 – 2 ‑
и поэ́тому да́льше тепе́рь от тебя́, чем от ни́х обо́их;   2 ‑ 2 ‑ 2 ‑ 2 ‑ 2 ‑ 1 ‑ 1
                                                    1975-76

Here the lines are longer than in the quotation from Blok, ranging from four to six ictuses, and fewer than half the lines are fully stressed. The variable *dol'nik* with longer lines has become an important meter in recent years. Brodsky may well have adapted it from modern English practice, which would indicate that it did not so much develop out of the Russian tradition as result from a sudden innovation.[71]

While the *dol'nik* has only recently been studied to the degree that it deserves, it has clearly been an important part of the Russian verse tradition since the beginning of the century. The different rhythmic variations that occur within the four- and three-stress lines and the experiments with the variable *dol'nik* are evidence that they have become fully recognized as an independent verse form. Their popularity with Russian poets is firmly established and likely to continue.

ACCENTUAL VERSE

The broad term *accentual* actually embraces two quite distinct verse forms. Strict accentual verse (which most Russian scholars currently refer to as the *taktovik*) consists of poems with a fixed number of ictuses per line and a limited range in the number of syllables allowed between ictuses: for most poems written in strict accentual verse there may be anywhere from one to three syllables between each ictus. Loose accentual verse (which Russian scholars often call "accentual verse" or "pure accentual verse") need show only a certain regularity in the number of stresses per line and allows for complete freedom in the number of syllables between stresses. Since the intervals between ictuses are still regulated in strict accentual verse, it is also possible to distinguish hypermetrical stressing and occasional cases of unstressed ictuses. In other words, strict accentual verse maintains some interplay between meter and rhythm; loose accentual verse, like free verse, has a structure provided by the line (along with, in many cases, rhyme and stanzaic form).[72]

While the terms *strict accentual verse* and *loose accentual verse* are awkward, they show the relationship between these two types of poetry and at the same time help avoid confusion with earlier terms. *Taktovik* (strict accentual verse) is easier to write, but because it derives from the temporal theories of A. P. Kviatkovsky which are no longer generally accepted by metrists, it seems best avoided.[73] Terms such as *accentual verse* or *pure accentual verse* (loose accentual verse) are too vague; strict accentual verse is also "accentual," while the word *pure* may incorrectly imply that loose accentual verse is necessarily organized according to a fixed number of stresses per line.

STRICT ACCENTUAL VERSE

While strict accentual verse (the *taktovik*) became an established literary meter only at the beginning of the twentieth century, much folklore—especially *byliny*—was composed in this form years earlier. Throughout the nineteenth century poets frequently used what today would be labeled strict accentual verse in their imitations of folklore.[74] Pushkin, for instance, utilized strict accentual verse in both "Songs of the Western Slavs" ("Pesni zapadnykh slavian") and "Tale of the Fisherman and the Fish" ("Skazka o rybake i rybke").[75] Below is an excerpt from one of the "Songs" called "Marko Iakubovich":

У воро́т сиде́л Ма́рко Якубо́вич;	2 ⌣ 2 ⌣ 3 ⌣ 1
Перед ни́м сиде́ла его́ Зо́я,	2 ⌣ 1 ⌣ 3 ⌣ 1
А мальчи́шка и́х игра́л у поро́гу.	2 ⌣ 3 ⌣ 2 ⌣ 1
По доро́ге к ни́м идёт незнако́мец,	2 ⌣ 3 ⌣ 2 ⌣ 1
Бле́ден о́н и чуть но́ги воло́чит,	2 ⌣ 2 ⌣ 2 ⌣ 1
Про́сит он напи́ться, ра́ди бо́га.	2 ⌣ 1 ⌣ 3 ⌣ 1
Зо́я вста́ла и пошла́ за водо́ю	2 ⌣ 3 ⌣ 2 ⌣ 1
И прохо́жему вы́несла ко́вшик,	2 ⌣ 2 ⌣ 2 ⌣ 1
И прохо́жий до дна́ его́ вы́пил.	2 ⌣ 2 ⌣ 2 ⌣ 1
Во́т, напи́вшись, говори́т он Ма́рке:	2 ⌣ 3 ⌣ 1 ⌣ 1
"Э́то что́ под горо́ю там ви́дно?"	2 ⌣ 2 ⌣ 2 ⌣ 1
Отвеча́ет Ма́рко Якубо́вич:	2 ⌣ 1 ⌣ 3 ⌣ 1
"То кладби́ще на́ше родово́е".	2 ⌣ 1 ⌣ 3 ⌣ 1

1834

As is generally the case with either kind of accentual verse and with free verse, it is necessary to look at a sizable excerpt to gain a proper appreciation of a work's rhythmic qualities. A three- or four-line segment may appear to be far more (or less) regular rhythmically than the entire poem. In "Songs" as a whole most of the lines fit the following pattern: 2 ⌣ 1/3 ⌣ 1/3 ⌣ 1. There are three metrical stresses per line, a strong tendency to use a two-syllable anacrusis, and an unrhymed feminine clausula. About 30 percent of the lines resemble trochaic pentameter (that is, all the intervals between ictuses consist of either one or three syllables), and a few less are anapestic (all the intervals contain precisely two syllables).[76] Here lines 2, 6, 10, 12, and 13 are trochaic; lines 5, 8, 9, and 11 are anapestic. The remaining lines in this example contain one two-syllable and one three-syllable interval; these are accentual. The total number of syllables on each line remains within a very narrow range: just ten or eleven syllables, most often ten. The presence of regular binary or ternary lines within accentual verse is common in the literary tradition as well; however, most modern poems in strict accentual verse show more variety in the anacrusis, in the clausula, and in the number of syllables per line than does this poem.

The literary tradition of strict accentual verse in Russian—as opposed to imitations of folk meters—arose in Russia during the 1890s and 1900s. Its earliest practitioners include Sologub, Blok, Balmont, and Mikhail Kuzmin. However, strict accentual verse, like the four-stress *dol'nik*, became an established meter only during the 1910s and 1920s when it appeared in the works of Maiakovsky, Nikolai Aseev, Sasha Cherny, Valentin Goriansky, Georgy Ivanov, and Kliuev, among others.[77] Some of these poets (Maiakovsky, Cherny, and Goriansky) contributed regularly to the journal *Satirikon*, which served as the focal point for the development of this meter. At the very least, Goriansky used the meter more often than any other poet of the 1910s, and Maiakovsky's practice ultimately had an important influence on other poets. Even at this time strict accentual verse remained a minor form, appearing in only about 2 percent of all poetry.[78] The *Satirikon* poets used it mainly in highly satirical and colloquial works. By the mid-1930s it fell into disuse and appeared only in isolated poems until the 1960s. While still one can hardly call it a common meter, it occurs every so often in the work of several poets—most notably Robert Rozhdestvensky, who has probably written more strict accentual verse than any other postwar poet.

In strict accentual verse, unlike the *dol'nik*, the four-stress line is more common than the three-stress; sometimes four- and three-stress lines alternate within a given poem. The form for the four-stress meter is as follows:

$$- 1/3 - 1/3 - 1/3 \doteq$$

Both the anacrusis and the clausula, which are omitted from this schema, generally contain from zero to two syllables, though sometimes more. The anacrusis usually varies, and most poems written in strict accentual verse are rhymed. Some of the intervals between ictuses may fall outside the range of one to three syllables, but usually no more than 10 percent will do so. (This requirement is not very restrictive; even in prose about 75 percent of the intervals between stresses naturally fall into the range of one to three syllables.)[79] Another type of strict accentual verse allows for intervals that vary between zero and two syllables, but examples are so rare that the discussion may safely be limited to the kind with intervals of one to three syllables. The number of stresses that actually appear on the line may vary slightly. Omitted stresses at the ictuses are rare, occurring, according to one study, on only about 2 percent of the lines. On the other hand, more than 33 percent of the lines contain hypermetrical stressing.[80]

Like the *dol'nik*, strict accentual verse allows for lines that are in keeping with one of the more "regular" meters: in this case, binary, ternary, and the *dol'nik*. The number of possible rhythmic variations is large. Even if variations in the anacrusis and the rare lines with omitted stresses are ignored, there are 9 basic variations for the three-stress line and 27 for the four-stress. However, since intervals of both zero and four stresses sometimes occur, the number of theoretically possible variations rises to 25 for the three-stress line and 125 for the four-stress.

As might be expected, it is not always easy to distinguish strict accentual verse from its neighboring types. The *dol'nik* may have occasional three-syllable intervals, but when the number of lines containing intervals of other than one or two syllables exceeds about 25 percent, the poem is considered to be written in strict accentual verse. Poems are categorized as loose accentual verse if they fulfill either of two conditions: (1) when the number of intervals that fall out of the range of one to three syllables exceeds about 15 percent; or (2), as happens more often, when over 10 percent of the lines deviate from the particular number of metrical stresses that occur throughout the poem. The discussion here will focus on works that fall safely within the confines of strict accentual verse, but borderline cases do occur. In such instances it is probably safest to label the poem a transitional metrical form and deal with it accordingly.

Since so many rhythmic variations are available for use in strict accentual verse, the differences in rhythmic structure from poem to poem and, in particular, from poet to poet may be great indeed. In most instances line endings are emphasized to provide a regular organizational device for the otherwise fluid verse, hence the rarity both of unrhymed poems and enjambment.[81] It is not possible to talk definitively about any "evolution" in the usage of strict accentual verse; too few poems have been written in the meter to decide what changes may depend on a broad evolutionary trend and what apparent differences may simply result from the chance use of certain rhythmic structures among the many that are theoretically available. Still, sufficient data are now available that a given poem or poems can be compared with other works in this meter.[82]

To see what the study of a poem might reveal, let us take a close look at two works in the three-stress meter. Below is the first half of Kuzmin's poem "In the Theater" ("V teatre"):

Переходы, коридоры, уборные,	2⌣3⌣2⌣2
Лестница витая, полутёмная;	0⌣3⌣3⌣2
Разговоры, споры упорные,	2⌣1⌣2⌣2
На дверях занавески нескромные.	2⌣2⌣2⌣2
Пахнет пылью, скипидаром, белилами,	2⌣3⌣2⌣2
Издали доносятся овации,	0⌣3⌣3⌣2
Балкончик с шаткими перилами,	1⌣1⌣3⌣2
Чтоб омотреть на полу декорации.	2⌣2⌣2⌣2
Долгие часы ожидания,	0⌣3⌣2⌣2
Болтовня с маленькими актрисами,	2⌣0⌣4⌣2
По уборным, по фойе блуждание,	2⌣3⌣1⌣2
То в мастерской, то за кулисами.	0⌣2⌣3⌣2

1907

This excerpt contains no omitted stresses and relatively little hypermetrical stressing. Only one line of the twenty-four in the entire poem (the last) does not have three metrical stresses and has been omitted from the analysis. As the types of nonclassical verse become less regular, incorrect lines become more frequent and should not be unexpected. However, one out of twenty-four is still well under 10 percent, so the poem stays within the confines of strict accentual verse. Intervals between ictuses range from zero to four syllables, though forty-four out of forty-six (just under 96 percent) are within the norm of one to three syllables. The anacrusis varies from zero to two syllables; the clausula consists of two syllables throughout this excerpt owing to the dactylic rhymes, but in the rest of the poem dactylic and feminine rhymes alternate. The most common type of line in this poem is accentual (all the lines with one two- and one three-syllable interval as well as the line with a zero- and a four-syllable interval), but others fit the pattern for binary (all one- and three-syllable intervals), ternary (both two-syllable intervals), and *dol'nik* lines. Problems in determining stress are relatively few. Hypermetrical stressing occurs on the first word of line 5 and again within line 12. In strict accentual verse hypermetrical stressing is found most often in the anacrusis and usually involves words of one or two syllables. While the metrical stresses primarily fall on strongly stressed words (nouns, adjectives, and independent verbs), the hypermetrical stresses will, as often as not, appear on pronouns, auxilliary verbs, and other words that are only weakly stressed.[83] Here in fact nearly all the metrical stresses are on strongly stressed words, while one of the hypermetrical stresses is on a word that is normally only weakly stressed (*to*) and the other is on a strongly stressed word. Statistics for the poem as a whole are as follows:

	No. of Syllables					
	0	*1*	*2*	*3*	*4*	Average
Anacrusis	9	4	10	0	0	1.04
Clausula	0	5	18	0	0	1.78
Intervals	1	8	22	14	1	2.00 (1st)
						2.26 (2d)
Stem	(range: 6–9 syllables)					7.26
Line	(range: 8–12 syllables)					10.08
Line types	binary, 5; ternary, 5					
	dol'nik, 4; accentual, 9					

These data can be compared both to Kuzmin's other poems in three-stress accentual verse and to works by other poets.[84] The poem turns out to be fairly typical for Kuzmin. The clausula in his works tends to be longer than in most poets', largely because of the frequency with which he used dactylic rhyme, but the clausula here is long even by his standards. The lines, partly as a result of the long clausula, are longer than usual. Kuzmin typically made his second intervals longer, on the average, than his first (though not all poets do so), and, like virtually all the poets who employ this meter, he used two-syllable intervals more often than any other. Thus the most distinctive feature of this poem is the clausula, which in turn affects several other elements of the poem. Kuzmin, like most of his contemporaries, employed similar rhythmic structures for nearly all his poems written in strict accentual verse; the greater differences appear to be from writer to writer rather than from poem to poem. Individual poets generally do not write enough accen-

tual verse to develop different kinds of rhythmic structures for it, as
some poets have done, for instance, with certain of the iambic meters or
even with the *dol'nik*.

The second example of three-stress accentual verse is taken from
Novella Matveeva's poem, "The Conjurer" ("Fokusnik"):

А́х ты, фо́кусник, фо́кусник-чуда́к!	2 ⌣ 2 ⌣ 3 ⌣
Ты́ чуде́сен, но хва́тит с на́с чуде́с.	2 ⌣ 2 ⌣ 3 ⌣
Переста́нь!	
Мы пове́рили и та́к	2 ⌣ 2 ⌣ 3 ⌣
В поросёнка, упа́вшего с небе́с.	2 ⌣ 2 ⌣ 3 ⌣
Да и вни́з головой на потолке́	2 ⌣ 2 ⌣ 3 ⌣
Не сиди́ – не расхо́дуй вре́мя зря!	2 ⌣ 2 ⌣ 3 ⌣
Мы́ ведь ве́рим,	
Что у тебя́ в руке́	2 ⌣ 4 ⌣ 1 ⌣
В тру́бку свёрнуты стра́ны и моря́.	2 ⌣ 2 ⌣ 3 ⌣

1962

This poem can be discussed briefly, owing to the extreme regularity of
its rhythm. Of the twenty lines in the entire work, seventeen have the
pattern 2 ⌣ 2 ⌣ 3 ⌣. The main stress problem here (and in many other
poems) is how to treat monosyllabic pronouns and other weakly stressed
words. In the classical meters and the *dol'nik* I consider such words
stressed only when they coincide with an ictus. But for the less-regu-
lated meters where the intervals between stresses may be large, the rule
is to consider them stressed if they are not adjacent to a stressed syllable
or if they are set off by punctuation. Here the first *ty* is not considered
stressed; the second is. Some prefer to treat such words differently, but
the effect is largely on the amount of hypermetrical stressing that will
be found in the poem; as has already been noted, these weakly stressed
words do not often appear at the ictus in strict accentual verse. Hyper-
metrical stressing is common in Matveeva's poem, and it occurs largely
where it is to be expected: in the two-syllable anacrusis and in the three-
syllable interval that occurs between the second ictus and the third. The
most irregular line in the poem has four strong stresses and eleven syl-
lables; the other two lines that fall outside the predominant rhythm (in-
cluding the third line in the second stanza quoted above) still have ten
syllables. The constant placement of the metrical stresses at the same
positions in all but three of the lines brings the work close to modern
logaoedic verse, along the lines of the song by Galich quoted above.

Poems written in four-stress strict accentual verse also reveal great
varieties in their rhythmic structure. Again it will be useful to look at

two examples. The first is taken from Sasha Cherny's "Second Epistle" ("Poslanie vtoroe"):

Курза́льные ба́рышни, и жёны, и ма́тери!	1 2 3 2 2 2
Как ва́с нетру́дно смеша́ть с проститу́тками,	1 1 2 2 2 2
Как ме́лко и ти́нисто в ва́шем фарва́тере,	1 2 2 2 2 2
Наби́том глу́постью и предрассу́дками...	1 1 2 2 2 2
Фальши́вит му́зыка. С крова́вой оби́дою	1 1 3 2 2 2
Ка́тится со́лнце за мо́ре вече́рнее.	0 2 2 2 2 2
Встреча́юсь су́мрачно с курси́сткой Ли́дою –	1 1 3 1 2 2
И вла́сть уны́ния больне́й и безме́рнее...	1 1 3 2 2 2
Опя́ть о Ду́ме, о жи́зни и ро́дине,	1 1 2 2 2 2
Опя́ть о при́нципах и то́чках зре́ния...	1 1 3 1 2 2
А я́ вздыха́ю по чёрной сморо́дине	1 1 2 2 2 2
И по́лон жёлчи, и по́лон презре́ния...	1 1 2 2 2 2

1908

Cherny's poem may be analyzed in a fashion similar to that of Kuzmin's "In the Theater," but only the most salient features will be listed. Intervals between ictuses range from one to five syllables, though in 116 out of 119 cases (over 97 percent) the range is between one and three. Most are either one or two syllables, which accounts for the predominance of *dol'nik*-type lines. Just less than half of the poem's forty lines are *dol'niki* (here lines 2, 4, 9, 11, and 12), and eleven others are ternary (here lines 3 and 6). The anacrusis is primarily one syllable, though for the entire poem the range is zero to two syllables; rhyming throughout is dactylic. The average length of the lines is 12.78 syllables (range: 11 to 16), which is a little longer than usual for poems in this meter and probably results from the constant two-syllable clausula. The stressing is regular; hypermetrical stressing is virtually absent from the poem, and omitted stresses are equally rare—though one is omitted in the fourth line quoted above. Probably the most notable quality of the poem is its definite ternary basis, a feature found in many early works employing either the *dol'nik* or strict accentual verse. About 60 percent of the intervals contain two syllables, and at one point in the poem seven out of eight consecutive lines are ternary.

Contrast the rhythm of Cherny's poem with the first half of a poem by Robert Rozhdestvensky:

Взя́л биле́т до ста́нции	
Пе́рвая любо́вь.	2 1 2 3
Взя́л его́ нега́данно.	
Шутя́.	

Невзначай.   2́ ‒ 1 ‒ 3 ‒ 2 ‒
Нé было попýтчиков.
Бы́л ды́м голубóй.   0 ‒ 3 ‒ 3 ‒ 2 ‒
Сигарéты кѝслые.
                    И крéпкий чáй.   2 ‒ 1 ‒ 3 ‒ 1 ‒
А ещё шатáлась
монотóнная мглá.   2 ‒ 1 ‒ 3 ‒ 2 ‒
А ещё задýмчиво
гудéл паровóз...   2 ‒ 1 ‒ 3 ‒ 2 ‒

Тáм, на э́той стáнции,
                    вершѝна былá.   2́ ‒ 1 ‒ 3 ‒ 2 ‒
Тёплая вершѝна.
До сáмых звёзд.   0 ‒ 3 ‒ 2 ‒ 1 ‒
Ты́ её по ѝмени сейчáс не зовѝ,   2́ ‒ 1 ‒ 3 ‒ 2 ‒
хоть онá остáлась –
                    лицóм на зарю́...   2 ‒ 1 ‒ 2 ‒ 2 ‒
Встáл я у поднóжия
                    Пéрвой любвѝ.   0 ‒ 3 ‒ 2 ‒ 2 ‒
Пýсть не поднимýсь ужé –
так посмотрю́.   0 ‒ 3 ‒ 1 ‒ 3 ‒
                              [<1966]

Line endings here are established by rhyme; therefore two or more
graphic lines may sometimes indicate a single line of verse. Purely
accentual lines predominate; the most frequent rhythmic variation is
2 ‒ 1 ‒ 3 ‒ 2 ‒. Two-syllable intervals between stresses remain the most
common, but now both one-syllable and three-syllable intervals are not
far behind. Lines with exclusively two-syllable intervals—that is, ter-
nary lines—are absent from the poem. The stems of the lines average
out to be a bit longer than in the Cherny poem, but the lines in their
entirety are shorter (an average of 11.54 syllables) because of the exclu-
sively masculine rhyme. A noticeable quality, as in the Matveeva poem
discussed earlier, is the relative uniformity of line lengths. Even though
the anacrusis may have either zero or two syllables, the rest of the line
tends to compensate for this difference rather than exaggerate it. All but
two of the lines in the poem have either eleven or twelve syllables.
Stressing is also quite regular; each of the ictuses in the poem is
stressed, and the hypermetrical stressing that does occur is largely con-
fined to the anacrusis.

It may be useful to summarize the relationship among the four main
types of meter in Russian: binary (iambs and trochees), ternary (dac-
tyls, amphibrachs, and anapests), *dol' niki*, and strict accentual verse.
The following table illustrates the main qualities of each:[85]

Type of Verse	All or Nearly All Ictuses Usually Stressed	Constant Number of Syllables between Ictuses
Binary	no	yes
Ternary	yes	yes
Dol'niki	no	no
Strict accentual	yes	no

Rhythmic variety is most readily obtained either by omitting certain stresses at the ictuses (except for the last, which is constantly stressed in all Russian meters) or by varying the number of syllables between the ictuses. The constant number of syllables between ictuses is, of course, the main feature that distinguishes classical from nonclassical Russian verse. The tendency for ternary meters to stress virtually all the ictuses has weakened slightly in the twentieth century, but even so the interaction between meter and rhythm in ternary meters is much weaker than in modern *dol'niki* and still weaker than in the binary meters. Even though the earliest *dol'niki* had a ternary basis (and, like ternary meters, rarely omitted stresses at the ictuses), they now share neither major feature with ternaries: *dol'niki* have a variable number of syllables between the ictuses, and unstressed ictuses are no longer rare. Strict accentual verse offers the sharpest contrast to binary meters, which were the favorite verse form of nearly every poet until the beginning of the twentieth century. This may help explain why strict accentual verse has taken longer than the *dol'nik* to become established.

LOOSE ACCENTUAL VERSE

While nineteenth-century imitations of Russian folk poetry written in what now may be called strict accentual verse were not uncommon, only a few utilized loose accentual verse, which was almost totally absent from literary verse prior to 1890.[86] Like strict accentual verse, however, loose accentual verse became an established verse form during the early part of the twentieth century. The meter came to be used fairly regularly during the 1910s and 1920s by some of the futurist poets (most prominently Maiakovsky) and by others as well, including Esenin and Selvinsky.[87] By the 1930s interest in loose accentual verse dropped sharply; it has been revived to a moderate degree during recent decades.

The problem of defining accentual verse, and in particular of determining the border between loose accentual verse and free verse, still has not been resolved. Even among scholars who fully accept the existence of strict accentual verse (the *taktovik*) as an independent type of meter, there is little agreement as to precisely which of the remaining poems should be termed "accentual" and which "free." Some would make rhyme virtually the sole factor in assigning poems to one category or the other. Thus A. L. Zhovtis believes that any poem rhymed throughout is not really "free." [88] Similarly, Gasparov calls rhymed poems in which the number of syllables between stresses varies widely and the number of stresses per line does not appear to be regulated *raeshnyi stikh*. The term is borrowed from the folk *raeshnik*—a rhymed couplet with no discernible meter. Gasparov considers *raeshnyi* verse a form of accentual verse and contrasts it with free (*svobodnyi*) verse, which he defines as unrhymed. [89] Yet another scholar specifically includes all unrhymed verse with a variable number of accents per line under the rubric of free verse. [90] According to this definition, unrhymed variable iambs (*vol'nye iamby*) or unrhymed variable anapests would qualify as free verse. However, some have argued that even if a poem is rhymed it can still be written in free verse so long as it lacks any tendency toward a particular number of stresses per line and has irregular intervals between stresses. [91] I prefer to accept this latter view. To call a poem with no predominant number of stresses per line "accentual" is not describing it in any meaningful way. "Free" verse within the context of Russian poetry basically means nonmetrical. Since meter involves some regularity in the alternation of stressed and unstressed syllables or in the number of stresses per line (or both), a poem can be "free" and still rhymed. On the other hand a poem in variable iambs, even if it is unrhymed, still has meter and therefore is not free. Meter and rhyme are two of the organizing features that may or may not be present in a work of verse; others include syntactic parallels, sound harmony (such as alliteration), and anaphora. To say that a Russian poem is written in free verse means only that it lacks meter; it may still possess rhyme or any of the other devices used to structure poetry. [92]

Rhyme historically has played a prominent role in the Russian verse tradition, and it is understandable why some have tried to make it a distinguishing feature between accentual and free verse. In fact, the presence or absence of rhyme may help decide whether a poem is written in loose accentual or in free verse, but only, as will be discussed below, in a few marginal cases.

In strict accentual verse no more than 10 percent of the lines will deviate from a particular number of metrical stresses, and no more than 15 percent of the intervals between stresses will fall outside the range of one to three syllables (in a few poems, zero to two syllables). Loose accentual verse can therefore be of two kinds:

(1) poems in which the number of strong stresses per line is still nearly constant (or varies to some regular pattern, such as 4-3-4-3), but in which a large number of the intervals fall outside the range of one to three syllables; or

(2) poems in which the number of stresses per line varies, but in which at least about half the lines still have the same number of strong stresses per line.

The term *strong stresses* is meant to exclude monosyllabic pronouns, adverbs, and auxillary verbs that appear adjacent to the stressed syllable of another word.

Rhyme is not crucial for poems in the first category; if the number of stresses per line is a near constant, the poems are clearly accentual whether or not rhyme is present. The second category presents more of a problem. The nonclassical meters exist as a continuum. While most poems fit clearly into one classification or another, other works fall near the boundaries of the categories. The border between loose accentual and free verse is particularly vague; it is not always easy to determine just when the number of stresses per line is organized in some way and when it is not. Intuitively, poems with rhyme seem more "organized" than those that lack rhyme; therefore when rhyme is not present, even if half the lines have the same number of stresses, the poem may still not appear to be accentual. In general, it is best to look for a greater degree of accentual regularity in unrhymed poems before calling them "accentual"—roughly 75 percent of the lines should have the same number of strong stresses, or perhaps 90 percent or more of the lines should contain either of two numbers of stresses. These criteria are offered more as guidelines than as firm rules; in some instances the decision may be left to the reader's judgment. When a poem is difficult to classify, trying to pin a label on it is less important than understanding why it does not fit comfortably into any one category.

Loose accentual verse displays only a limited degree of organization. The number of syllables between stresses may vary freely; as a result there are no metrical "expectations" for the positioning of stressed and unstressed syllables. Once again individual lines may be written according to the norms of regular binary or ternary verse, but others show a much less regular alternation of stressed and unstressed syllables. When the number of stresses per line varies, there will be a tendency toward a regular sequence of longer and shorter lines. Rhyme and the division into stanzas, when present, can also help create a structure for the work.[93] For instance, long lines may cluster toward the beginning or end of a stanza or rhyming lines both may be of a particular length.

Two major problems frequently arise in analyzing loose accentual verse. First, what constitutes a line division is not always clear. Some poets set individual words or phrases on separate lines, and if the rhyme itself is irregular in some way—possibilities include occasional unrhymed lines, the use of internal rhyme, and so forth—determining the end of a line may involve some guesswork.[94] Second, stress, as in strict accentual verse, can be ambiguous. The problem of strong and weak stresses has already been discussed, but there are also words that may be stressed on either of two syllables, neologisms for which the proper stressing must be deduced, and questions of whether to count secondary stresses on extralong coined compounds.

Several examples indicate some of the problems that can arise when attempting to identify or analyze loose metrical verse. Below is a passage from part 2 of Maiakovsky's *A Cloud in Trousers* (*Oblako v shtanakh*):

Ýлица мýку мóлча пёрла.	0 ⌣ 2 ⌣ 1 ⌣ 1 ⌣ 1
Крúк торчкóм стоя́л из глóтки.	0 ⌣ 1 ⌣ 1 ⌣ 1 ⌣ 1
Топóрщились, застря́вшие поперёк гóрла.	1 ⌣ 3 ⌣ 4 ⌣ 0 ⌣ 1
пýхлые taxí и костля́вые пролётки.	0 ⌣ 3 ⌣ 2 ⌣ 3 ⌣ 1
Грýдь испешехóдили.	
Чахóтки плóще.	0 ⌣ 3 ⌣ 3 ⌣ 1 ⌣ 1
Гóрод дорóгу мрáком зáпер.	0 ⌣ 2 ⌣ 1 ⌣ 1 ⌣ 1
И когдá –	
всё-таки! –	
вы́харкнула дáвку на плóщадь.	2 ⌣ 0 ⌣ 2 ⌣ 3 ⌣ 2 ⌣ 1
спихнýв наступúвшую на гóрло пáперть,	1 ⌣ 2 ⌣ 3 ⌣ 1 ⌣ 1
дýмалось:	
в хóрах архáнгелова хорáла	0 ⌣ 2 ⌣ 2 ⌣ 4 ⌣ 1
бóг, огрáбленный, идёт карáть!	0 ⌣ 1 ⌣ 3 ⌣ 1 ⌣
А ýлица присéла и заорáла:	1 ⌣ 3 ⌣ 4 ⌣ 1
"Идёмте жрáть!"	1 ⌣ 1 ⌣

1914-15

On the whole, Maiakovsky wrote a fairly "regular" form of accentual verse, and his later poetry is still more organized than his earlier work.[95]

His poetry shows a definite preference for a particular number of stresses on each line (generally four or a four-three alternation), but there are still enough lines with varying numbers of stresses to place his poems in the second category of loose accentual verse. Within this excerpt the range of stresses is two to five, but nine out of twelve lines have precisely four. In *A Cloud in Trousers* more than 50 percent of the lines have precisely four stresses, while in Maiakovsky's later poetry the figure can reach more than 70 percent.[96] A characteristic of Maiakovsky's poetry is the wide variation in line lengths, and even within this brief excerpt the range is four to fifteen syllables. While most of the intervals are from one to three syllables, no fewer than five contain either zero or four. One-syllable and three-syllable intervals are particularly common, a reflection of the tendency toward a binary rhythm in this passage. Thirty-three percent of the lines (2, 5, 10, and 12) are iambic or trochaic. However, Maiakovsky frequently changed the rhythm by creating individual sections or subsections with varying percentages of binary, ternary, or *dol'niki* line types.[97]

Since the number of syllables between stresses may fluctuate widely, and since individual lines may be written according to the norms of more regulated meters, loose accentual verse has the potential for exhibiting many distinct rhythmic structures. In the following passage from "Pugachev," Esenin shared Maiakovsky's preference for the four-stress line and yet created quite a different rhythm:

Где́ он? Где́? Неуже́ль его́ не́т?	0⌣1⌣2⌣2⌣
Тяжеле́е, чем ка́мни, я нёс мою́ ду́шу.	2⌣2⌣2⌣2⌣1
А́х, давно́, знать, забы́ли в э́той стране́	2⌣2⌣1⌣2⌣
Про отча́янного негодя́я и жу́лика Хлопу́шу.	2⌣5⌣2⌣3⌣1
Сме́йся челове́к!	
В ваш хму́рый ста́н	0⌣3⌣1⌣1⌣
Посыла́ются замеча́тельные разве́дчики.	2⌣4⌣4⌣2
Бы́л я ка́торжник и ареста́нт,	0⌣1⌣5⌣
Бы́л уби́йца и фальшивомоне́тчик.	0⌣1⌣6⌣1
Но всегда́ ведь, всегда́ ведь, ра́но ли, по́здно ли,	2⌣2⌣1⌣2⌣2
Расставля́ет распла́та капка́ны те́рний.	2⌣2⌣2⌣1⌣1
Закова́ли в коло́дки и вы́рвали но́здри	2⌣2⌣2⌣2⌣1
Сы́ну крестья́нина Тверско́й губе́рнии.	0⌣2⌣3⌣1⌣2

1921

The immediately obvious difference is Esenin's preference for longer lines. The intervals between stresses are from one to six syllables (as opposed to Maiakovsky's zero to four), and one-syllable intervals are much less frequent here than in the excerpt from Maiakovsky. Even the shortest of the lines (1 and 7) have nine syllables, while the longest (4) has seventeen. No lines have fewer than three stresses; in this work Esenin employed lines with three or fewer stresses much less often than Maiakovsky, and lines with five or more stresses much more often.[98] The lines in this segment show a ternary, specifically an anapestic impetus. The second and eleventh lines are in anapestic tetrameter, and several other lines have a single one-syllable interval between stresses to deviate from what would otherwise be regular anapests (3, 9, and 10). While it is not exactly correct to speak of "hypermetrical" stressing in loose accentual verse (since any interval between stresses is permissible and the number of stresses per line may vary, it is difficult to specify just where the ictuses might be located), nonetheless certain stresses probably should not be counted among the poem's "strong" stresses. In particular, the stress on *ego* in line 1 receives a weaker stress than the obligatory stress on the rhyme word *net*; the stress on *moiu* in line 2 is weaker than that on the adjacent syllable of *dushu*, and in a regular anapestic tetrameter poem this stress clearly would be hypermetrical. Esenin also made his three-stress lines about as long as his four-stress lines by placing especially large intervals between stresses. The five- and six-syllable intervals in lines 7 and 8 are long enough to account for an "omitted" stress and make these two three-stress lines plausible variations of his four-stress lines. Both this passage and that from Maiakovsky illustrate the main characteristics of accentual verse:

(1) the lack of firm rules governing the placement (and at times the number) of stresses on the line;

(2) a certain regularity that can be perceived both in the numbers of stresses (for the second category of loose accentual verse) and sometimes in the creation of rhythmic structures that seem to be based on regular binary, ternary, or *dol'niki* poetry;

(3) the likelihood, especially in longer works, that poets will vary the rhythm from one segment of the work to the next.

Unrhymed accentual verse is rare; most such works cross the border into the realm of free verse. However, this poem from Kuzmin's *Alexandrian Songs* (*Aleksandriiskie pesni*), many of which are indeed written in free verse, is quoted in its entirety as an illustration of this form:

Я спра́шивал мудрецо́в вселе́нной:	1 ⌣ 4 ⌣ 1 ⌣ 1
"заче́м со́лнце гре́ет?	1 ⌣ 0 ⌣ 1 ⌣ 1
заче́м ве́тер ду́ет?	1 ⌣ 0 ⌣ 1 ⌣ 1
заче́м лю́ди родя́тся?"	1 ⌣ 0 ⌣ 2 ⌣ 1

Отвечали мудрецы́ вселе́нной: 2 ́ 3 ́ 1 ́ 1
– со́лнце гре́ет затем, 0 ́ 1 ́ 2 ́
чтоб созрева́л хле́б для пи́щи 3 ́ 0 ́ 1 ́ 1
и что́бы лю́ди от зара́зы мёрли. 1 ́ 1 ́ 3 ́ 1 ́ 1
Ве́тер ду́ет затем, 0 ́ 1 ́ 2 ́
чтоб приводи́ть корабли́ к при́стани да́льней, 3 ́ 2 ́ 0 ́ 2 ́ 1
и чтоб песко́м засыпа́ть карава́ны. 3 ́ 2 ́ 2 ́ 1
– Лю́ди родя́тся зате́м, 0 ́ 2 ́ 2 ́
чтоб расста́ться с ми́лою жи́знью 2 ́ 1 ́ 2 ́ 1
и чтоб от ни́х роди́лись други́е для сме́рти. 3 ́ 1 ́ 2 ́ 2 ́ 1

"Почему́ же бо́ги так всё созда́ли? 2 ́ 0 ́ 2 ́ 1 ́ 1
– Потому́ же, 2 ́ 1
почему́ в тебя́ вложи́ли жела́нье 2 ́ 1 ́ 1 ́ 2 ́ 1
задава́ть пра́здные вопро́сы. 2 ́ 0 ́ 3 ́ 1

[1905]

The poem was written in three- and four-stress accentual verse. More than 90 percent of the lines display one of these two stresses; in fact, only one line, the sixteenth, has neither three nor four stresses. Intervals between stresses range from zero to four syllables; of particular interest is the frequency of contiguous strong stresses—no fewer than seven. If the number of stresses were equal throughout, it could be said that the poem was written in the minor form of strict accentual verse in which all or nearly all the intervals range between zero and two syllables. The opening sequence of seven consecutive lines with three stresses and, with the exception of line 16, the slight variation throughout in the number of stresses per line combine to give the poem an accentual regularity that distinguishes it from Kuzmin's works in free verse. For the sake of contrast, one such poem is analyzed in the following section.

FREE VERSE

As is clear from the discussion of loose accentual verse, the definition of free verse presents more difficulties than might at first be expected. The two poems with rhyme analyzed below are specifically excluded from the category of free verse by some.[99] And one theory, already discussed, holds that all unrhymed poems with a varying number of stresses per line are written in free verse.[100] The very term *free verse* is perhaps unfortunate; at first glance it seems to imply a poetry free from all restraints, but poetry without any formal restraints is the same as prose. A more accurate term might be *freed verse*, for such poetry has abandoned one or more of the main organizing elements that are operative within a given poetic tradition. It is necessary, therefore, to consider the background against which free verse has arisen in a particular language and then to specify precisely from what poetry has been freed.[101] The Russian classical syllabo-tonic tradition was based on meter. In each of the meters ictuses could appear only at certain positions within the line, and the number of syllables between the ictuses was a constant. In the nonclassical meters established around the beginning of the twentieth century the metrical constraints were loosened: the number of syllables between ictuses was no longer fixed and the anacrusis could vary, consequently the ictuses could appear at different positions from line to line. Free verse within the Russian tradition was another form of reaction against metrical constraints, but instead of relaxing the constraints, it abandoned them. Therefore, Russian free verse is *nonmetrical* poetry, works in which neither the number of stresses per line nor the number of unstressed syllables between stresses are regulated in any consistent way throughout the poem. Free verse may or may not be rhymed; as it happens, most Russian works in free verse are not rhymed, but a fair number are. At least one scholar has set up different categories to distinguish between rhymed free verse (*svobodnyi rifmennyi stikh*) and unrhymed (*verlibr*).[102] Most Russians, however, use *svobodnyi stikh* and *verlibr* (from the French *vers libre*) interchangeably.[103] And while rhymed free verse may deserve special attention, it still shares with other free verse the main trait of nonmetricality; there does not seem to be any need to set up a separate category for it. Therefore I will use the term *free verse* for all nonmetrical poetry, whether or not it is rhymed.

The sometimes hazy boundary separating accentual from free verse has already been discussed. It can also be difficult to determine the boundary between free verse and prose, especially a highly stylized prose that seems to be as carefully wrought as free verse. The essential distinction between the two genres is division into lines, or verses. The orthography, which signifies the author's intention, represents the minimal requirement for free verse.[104] Beyond that it is difficult to isolate features that are common to all free verse. One longtime investigator has defined its main quality as follows: "Free verse is constructed upon the repetition of various kinds of phonetic essences that change at irregular intervals; the components of the repetition . . . can be phonemes, syllables, feet, stresses, clausulae, words, groups of words, and phrases."[105] The point is that many different kinds of repetition or parallelism may operate within the same poem. Some lines may be in regular binary or ternary verse, groups of lines may be linked by anaphora, several other lines may rhyme, and so forth. While this statement helps explain what goes on in free verse, as a definition it seems too restrictive. The requirement that the types of repetition vary eliminates from the category of free verse poems with rhyme throughout. Also, individual lines may not exhibit any kind of repetition; the formula can be said only to describe a general tendency for lines in free verse. Another definition claims that free verse is based on "intonational waves" that follow the rhythms of speech.[106] This is probably a reasonable description of at least some works in free verse. All the less-regulated types of Russian poetry (strict and loose accentual verse, as well as free verse) are particularly well suited for reproducing the intonation of ordinary speech. Not just the rhythm but also the syntax and the vocabulary may sometimes be more "conversational" than "literary." However, this definition is too narrow to account for all works in free verse. A more inclusive description of free verse is that it is organized in some way, though not according to the kinds of limits on stress placement or syllable count that lend themselves to metrical analysis. Instead, the poet replaces metrical organization with any one of several other organizing features. If more than one organizing feature appears, no one of these necessarily predominates throughout the poem. The result is a type of writing that is denser and more tightly organized than most prose writing but that in most cases requires the graphic division into lines to distinguish it from stylized prose.

Like the other nonclassical forms, free verse has existed in Russian poetry almost since the beginning of the syllabo-tonic era, but it has been used systematically only in the twentieth century. The earliest examples of Russian free verse are generally considered to be several of Sumarokov's translations from the Psalms.[107] During the nineteenth century a limited amount of original verse but a fair number of translated poems were rendered in unrhymed, variable, nonclassical meters. For the most part these works now appear to have been written in unrhymed variable *dol'niki*, though within the context of nineteenth-century poetry they would have appeared relatively "free" and can be considered an intermediate step in the development of Russian free verse.[108] Of particular importance in this regard were some original verses and translations by Fet, one of the most innovative poets of the time when it came to experiments with form, and the translations of Mikhail Mikhailov.

Among the first to write free verse in the contemporary sense was
Zinaida Gippius. But as with the other nonclassical verse forms, Blok
was to prove more influential. His handful of free verse poems were
composed during the first decade of the twentieth century and played a
major role in creating an awareness of the possibilities inherent in this
type of poetry.[109] The other important founder of the free verse tradition
in Russian poetry was Kuzmin; his *Alexandrian Songs*, composed circa
1905 and published together in his first collection of poetry (1908), con-
tain one of the more extensive applications of free verse in the history of
Russian poetry.[110] Not long afterward Velimir Khlebnikov began to write
both rhymed and unrhymed free verse. And so the tradition continued,
although less extensively, in various poems or sections of poems through-
out the 1920s.[111] Like both strict and loose accentual verse, free verse
almost disappeared from view from the 1930s until the end of the 1950s;
perhaps the only poet to use free verse in more than a poem or two dur-
ing those years was the little-known Kseniia Nekrasova. Since the late
1950s free verse has again been revived and seems to be growing more
popular. Evgeny Vinokurov and Vladimir Soloukhin are two poets who
have written a significant number of works in free verse, and many
others have tried it occasionally. Still, free verse remains a minor form
in Russian, accounting for perhaps 1 or 2 percent of all poetry. It also
remains somewhat controversial, with a few poets embracing it enthusi-
astically, others more reservedly, and still others not finding it a fruitful
course for Russian poetry to follow.[112]

At least three approaches have been taken in analyzing Russian free
verse, sometimes in isolation and sometimes in combination with each
other.[113] One method looks at the work statistically, counting the number
of syllables per line, the length of the anacrusis and the clausula, and the
number of syllables in the intervals between stresses.[114] The analysis
then resembles that for loose metrical verse. A second method examines
the types of repetition and parallelism that occur within the poem and
describes where and how often each occurs.[115] A third classifies the
work according to certain features that may or may not be present:
rhyme, stanzas, wide diversity in line lengths, many types of repetitions
(as opposed to just one or two), and so forth.[116] For any given work one
approach may prove superior to the others.

Two examples of poems written in free verse with rhyme are an ex-
cerpt from Khlebnikov's "The Crane" ("Zhuravl'") and the first two-
thirds of Leonid Martynov's "Cords" ("Vervi"):

Что? Ма́льчик бре́дит на-яву́?	0 ⌣ 0 ⌣ 1 ⌣ 3 ⌣
Я ма́льчика зову́.	1 ⌣ 3 ⌣
Но о́н молчи́т и вдру́г бежи́т: каки́е стра́шные	1 ⌣ 1 ⌣ 1 ⌣ 1 ⌣ 1 ⌣ 1 ⌣ 3 ⌣
скачки́!	
Я ме́дленно достаю́ очки́.	1 ⌣ 4 ⌣ 1 ⌣
И то́чно: тру́бы подыма́ли свои́ ше́и,	1 ⌣ 1 ⌣ 3 ⌣ 2 ⌣ 0 ⌣ 1
Как на стене́ те́нь па́льцев ворожеи́.	3 ⌣ 0 ⌣ 0 ⌣ 3 ⌣ 1
Так де́лаются подви́жными дото́ле неподви́жные	1 ⌣ 4 ⌣ 3 ⌣ 3 ⌣ 4 ⌣ 1 ⌣ 1
на боло́те вы́пи,	
Когда́ опа́сность минова́ла.	1 ⌣ 1 ⌣ 3 ⌣ 1
Среди́ камыше́й и озёрной ки́пи	1 ⌣ 2 ⌣ 2 ⌣ 1 ⌣ 1
Пти́ца-расте́ние главо́ю закива́ла.	0 ⌣ 2 ⌣ 3 ⌣ 3 ⌣ 1
Но что́ же? Ска́чет вдоль реки́ в како́м-то ви́хре	1 ⌣ 1 ⌣ 3 ⌣ 1 ⌣ 1 ⌣
Желе́зный, ки́сти руки́ подо́бный, крю́к.	1 ⌣ 1 ⌣ 2 ⌣ 1 ⌣ 1 ⌣
Сто́я над волна́ми, когда́ они́ сти́хли,	0 ⌣ 3 ⌣ 2 ⌣ 1 ⌣ 0 ⌣ 1
О́н походи́л на пода́рок на па́мять костяку́ ру́к!	0 ⌣ 2 ⌣ 2 ⌣ 2 ⌣ 3 ⌣ 0 ⌣
[1908-9]	

В магази́не	2 ⌣ 1
Хозя́йственных изде́лий	1 ⌣ 3 ⌣ 1
Я поду́мал, что вы́ставлены каки́е-то	2 ⌣ 2 ⌣ 4 ⌣ 5 ⌣ 3 ⌣ 1
произведе́ния скульпту́ры,	
Но на са́мом де́ле э́то бы́ли ра́зных сорто́в	2 ⌣ 1 ⌣ 1 ⌣ 1 ⌣ 1 ⌣ 2 ⌣
Виты́е верёвочные фигу́ры	1 ⌣ 2 ⌣ 4 ⌣ 1
С несомне́нными при́знаками носо́в и рто́в.	2 ⌣ 2 ⌣ 4 ⌣ 1 ⌣
Не́которые	0 ⌣ 4
Напомина́ли	3 ⌣ 1
Ли́ц, свя́занных ра́зными обстоя́тельствами.	0 ⌣ 0 ⌣ 2 ⌣ 4 ⌣ 3
Не́которые, бу́дто бы и не вия́сь, и ничего́ не боя́сь,	0 ⌣ 4 ⌣ 5 ⌣ 3 ⌣ 2 ⌣
Напомина́ли свя́занных да́нными обяза́тельствами.	3 ⌣ 1 ⌣ 2 ⌣ 4 ⌣ 3
Сло́вом, вме́сте с прямо́й тут была́ и обра́тная	0 ⌣ 1 ⌣ 2 ⌣ 2 ⌣ 2 ⌣ 2 ⌣
свя́зь.	
Не́которые ве́рви	0 ⌣ 4 ⌣ 1
Кре́пки, как не́рвы,	0 ⌣ 2 ⌣ 1
Ли́бо арка́ны на ше́ю врага́м,	0 ⌣ 2 ⌣ 2 ⌣ 2 ⌣
А потому́ и даю́т, наве́рно,	3 ⌣ 2 ⌣ 1 ⌣ 1
Как бы са́ми связа́ть себя́ по рука́м и нога́м.	2 ⌣ 2 ⌣ 1 ⌣ 2 ⌣ 2 ⌣
1965	

The Khlebnikov poem exhibits certain regularities: the lines tend to have four or five stresses, several lines within this excerpt (such as the first three) are iambic, and the rhymes are adjacent or alternating. At the same time the number of stresses within the excerpt varies from seven to two (and elsewhere in the poem there are lines with only one stress), and the iambic lines are scattered—they never occur frequently enough to become predominant. In several cases the assignment of stress is problematical. The word *volnámi* in the next-to-last line could just as well be *vólnami*. At the beginning of the tenth line *ptitsa* has been given an independent stress, although here it is part of a compound word. *Vorozheia* is normally end-stressed, but the iambic rhythm of the line, the rhyme with *shéi*, and the possibility that Khlebnikov was influenced by the masculine *vorozhéi* have all led me to place the stress on the next-to-last syllable of this word at the end of line 6. The anacrusis varies, though it most often contains one syllable. The number of syllables per line within this excerpt varies from six to twenty-three, while the intervals between stresses range from zero to four syllables. The poem is divided into stanzas, but these are of irregular length. The main organizing features of the poem include rhyme (the most predominant device); the sporadic use of iambic lines, which acts as a kind of rhythmic leitmotif throughout; and the occasional rough grouping of lines by number of stresses (for instance, the last four lines here all have five or six stresses).

The Martynov poem is considerably less regular. The first two lines in each of the first two stanzas lack rhyme and are much shorter than those that follow. Perhaps the two should be considered as one line or even part of the third line, but in the absence of any solid evidence it seems safest to accept the author's line division as is (albeit Martynov would often put the first word of a poem on a separate line even when using one of the classical meters). Line lengths and intervals between stresses again vary widely, and only two lines, the fourteenth and fifteenth, fit within one of the classical meters (both are dactylic). As in the Khlebnikov poem, there is a tendency to group longer and shorter lines together. Rhythmically, the third stanza with its short lines and preponderance of two-syllable intervals between stresses is distinct from the first two. Another organizing feature, not fully evident in this excerpt, is the use of *nekotorye* and *napominali*, singled out at the beginning of the second stanza, to begin several other lines throughout the poem.

Since Blok and Kuzmin were the two most significant practitioners of free verse at the beginning of the century, it is worth looking at excerpts of works by both. Below are the first dozen lines of a poem by Blok, followed by an excerpt from Kuzmin's *Alexandrian Songs*:

Она́ пришла́ с моро́за,	1 ́ 1 ́ 1 ́ 1
Раскрасне́вшаяся,	2 ́ 3
Напо́лнила ко́мнату	1 ́ 2 ́ 2

Ароматом воздуха и духов,   2 ⌣ 1 ⌣ 4 ⌣
Звонким голосом   0 ⌣ 1 ⌣ 2
И совсем неуважительной к занятиям   2 ⌣ 3 ⌣ 3 ⌣ 2
Болтовнёй.   2 ⌣

Она немедленно уронила на пол   1 ⌣ 1 ⌣ 4 ⌣ 1 ⌣ 1
Толстый том художественного журнала,   0 ⌣ 1 ⌣ 1 ⌣ 5 ⌣ 1
И сейчас же стало казаться,   2 ⌣ 1 ⌣ 2 ⌣ 1
Что в моей большой комнате   2 ⌣ 1 ⌣ 0 ⌣ 2
Очень мало места.   0 ⌣ 1 ⌣ 1 ⌣ 1

1908

Как люблю я книги (моих друзей),   0 ⌣ 1 ⌣ 1 ⌣ 2 ⌣ 1 ⌣
тишину одинокого жилища,   2 ⌣ 2 ⌣ 3 ⌣ 1
и вид из окна   1 ⌣ 2 ⌣
на дальние дынные огороды!   1 ⌣ 2 ⌣ 4 ⌣ 1
Как люблю пестроту толпы на площади,   0 ⌣ 1 ⌣ 2 ⌣ 1 ⌣ 1 ⌣ 1 ⌣ 2
крики, пенье и солнце,   0 ⌣ 1 ⌣ 2 ⌣ 1
весёлый смех мальчиков, играющих в мяч!   1 ⌣ 1 ⌣ 0 ⌣ 3 ⌣ 2 ⌣
Возвращенье домой   2 ⌣ 2 ⌣
после весёлых прогулок,   0 ⌣ 2 ⌣ 2 ⌣ 1
поздно вечером,   0 ⌣ 1 ⌣ 2
при первых звёздах,   1 ⌣ 1 ⌣ 1
мимо уже освещённых гостинниц   0 ⌣ 2 ⌣ 2 ⌣ 2 ⌣ 1
с уже далёким другом!   1 ⌣ 1 ⌣ 1 ⌣ 1

[1905]

Both Blok and Kuzmin lack the great disparity in line lengths typical of
Khlebnikov and Martynov.[117] Short lines occur in their work, but neither
resorts to the extremely long lines (eighteen or more syllables) that are
found in the poems discussed above. The Blok and Kuzmin poems,
however, display their own share of diversity. While lines with three and
four stresses are the most common in Blok's poem, the range for the
poem is one to five (one to four in this excerpt).[118] Individual lines may
have been written according to the norms of a particular classical meter,
but the meters vary: the first line is iambic trimeter, the third amphi-
brachic dimeter, the fifth trochaic dimeter, the ninth trochaic hexameter
(with two consecutive omitted stresses), and the twelfth trochaic trim-
eter. The anacrusis varies freely from zero to two syllables, and the
clausula may have anywhere from zero to three syllables. Intervals be-
tween stresses range from zero to five syllables. Stanzas vary in length,
and their boundaries correspond to the ends of sentences or particular
thoughts. Similarly, line boundaries are used to highlight individual
words or phrases. Since stanzas and lines are not subject to the limita-
tions of a particular rhyme or rhythmic scheme, it is easier for poets to

use stanza and line demarcations for putting special emphasis on the semantic aspects of the work. Perhaps for this reason some researchers have claimed that free verse in Russian often occurs in the more meditative or "philosophical" poems.[119] Such may sometimes be the case, though free verse, especially in recent years, seems to be employed in many different types of works.

The Kuzmin poem shows even less diversity in line length than the Blok poem; the lines all have between two and five stresses, and the number of syllables per line varies only between four and twelve. Still, there is much greater variety in stressing than in the poem by Kuzmin cited earlier as an example of loose accentual verse. There, seventeen of eighteen lines had either three or four stresses; here, no such regularity prevails. In both instances, however, Kuzmin used anaphora as an important organizing feature of the poem. In this work the phrase *Kak liubliu* (cf. lines 1 and 5 of the excerpt) begins each of the poem's five complete sentences. In the poem discussed previously the words *zachem* and *chtob* occur at the beginning of successive lines. Thus even though one poem appears to be more tightly organized accentually than the other, Kuzmin employed similar techniques when writing both and may well have felt that both utilized the same verse form.

Among the more recent practitioners of free verse, only Vinokurov has received extensive attention.[120] Most of his poems in free verse date from the early 1960s and show many of the same tendencies already discussed: occasional lines in various classical meters along with many others less regular, wide variations in numbers of syllables and stresses per line, varying anacrusis and clausula, and both line and stanzaic boundaries determined by syntactic or semantic considerations rather than the requirements of rhyme or meter. Below is the beginning of one poem in free verse; it contains more long lines than usual for Vinokurov but it is otherwise typical of his works:

Весна́. Мне пятна́дцать ле́т. Я пишу́ стихи́.	1 ́2 ́1 ́2 ́1 ́
Я собира́юсь е́хать в Соко́льники,	0 ́2 ́1 ́2 ́2
Что́бы броди́ть с записно́й кни́жкой	0 ́2 ́2 ́0 ́1
По сыры́м тропи́нкам.	2 ́1 ́1
Я выхожу́ из пара́дного.	0 ́2 ́2 ́2
Кирпи́чный коло́дец двора́.	1 ́2 ́2 ́
Я поднима́ю глаза́: та́м, вдалеке́, в про́руби,	0 ́2 ́2 ́0 ́2 ́0 ́2
Мерца́ет, как вода́, голуба́я бесконе́чность.	1 ́3 ́2 ́3 ́1
Но я ви́жу и друго́е.	2 ́3 ́1

В ка́ждом окне́ я ви́жу же́нские но́ги.	0 ‑ 2 ‑ 1 ‑ 1 ‑ 2 ‑ 1
Мо́ют о́кна. Идёт весе́нняя сти́рка и мо́йка,	0 ‑ 1 ‑ 2 ‑ 1 ‑ 2 ‑ 2 ‑ 1
Весёлые поломо́йни! Они́, как гре́ческие	1 ‑ 4 ‑ 2 ‑ 1 ‑ 3 ‑ 2
пра́зднества,	
В по́ру сбо́ра виногра́да!	0 ‑ 1 ‑ 3 ‑ 1
Оголя́ются ру́ки. Зашпи́ливаются узло́м	2 ‑ 2 ‑ 2 ‑ 5 ‑ 0 ‑ 2
во́лосы.	
Подтыка́ются подо́лы. Сверка́ют ло́кти	2 ‑ 3 ‑ 2 ‑ 1 ‑ 3 ‑ 1
и коле́ни.	

1962

To conclude the description of nonclassical verse forms it is worth summarizing several features common to the history of *dol'niki*, the two varieties of accentual verse, and free verse. First, all the forms occur in Russian poetry written well before the twentieth century, though most are limited to translations and imitations of folk verse. Second, all the nonclassical forms entered the basic repertoire of Russian poetry at about the same time, roughly between the mid-1890s and 1910. Third, while others employed nonclassical verse more often and in some instances earlier, Aleksandr Blok played a central role in popularizing the various kinds of nonclassical poetry among Russian poets. Fourth, even though only *dol'niki* among the nonclassical forms have enjoyed continued wide usage throughout the twentieth century, all types of Russian nonclassical verse are being written, and poets appear to be experimenting more frequently with some of the less regulated forms, especially free verse.

WORKS IN MORE THAN ONE METER

Poems categorized as multimetrical are not necessarily nonclassical; they may be written in classical meters, nonclassical meters, or both. Although some types of multimetrical poems are related to either mixed or variable (*vol'nyi*) meters, there are some basic differences. In particular, multimetrical poems may contain meters of different types. That is, they may combine iambs and anapests; trochees and *dol'niki*; or iambs, amphibrachs, and strict accentual verse. Mixed and variable meters join lines of different lengths in a regular (for the mixed meters) or irregular (for the variable meters) alternation, but the lines are all of the same metrical type: one poem may contain iambic tetrameter and iambic trimeter lines, another *dol'niki* lines with anywhere from two to four stresses.

Three kinds of multimetrical poems can be distinguished as follows:
(1) transitional metrical forms, in which several lines do not corre-
spond to the poem's predominant meter;
(2) compound meters, in which at least two kinds of line in at
least two different metrical types alternate according to an invariant
schema;
(3) polymetrical compositions, in which integral segments of a
poem are each written in a different meter.
The first and third kinds occasionally refer to poems in which, like those
in variable and mixed meters, all the lines are of the same metrical type;
however, all three categories can include poems that are written in dif-
ferent types of meters. As already noted, all the meters in these cases
may be classical, all may be nonclassical, or both classical and non-
classical meters may be combined.

TRANSITIONAL METRICAL FORMS

The term *transitional metrical forms* (*perekhodnye metricheskie
formy*) appeared in the discussion of mixed classical meters and else-
where to describe a poem that has a few lines written in a meter other
than the one used in most of its lines. The most thorough discussions of
transitional metrical forms have appeared in articles by the Russian
scholar P. A. Rudnev.[121] The upper limit for lines outside the main meter
is conventionally set at 25 percent; once the number of nonconforming
lines exceeds that threshold, the poem is no longer a "transitional"
form but passes over into a different meter. Thus a twenty-four-line
poem in which twenty of the lines are in iambic tetrameter and the re-
mainder in iambic pentameter and trimeter would be a transitional met-
rical form between iambic tetrameter and variable iambs. If only fifteen
of the lines are in iambic tetrameter and the rest in pentameter and trim-
eter, then the poem is written in variable iambs, since the most frequent
meter lies below the 75 percent threshold. Rudnev does not cite any
minimal requirements for transitional metrical forms. Such a broad use
of the term provides a useful label for distinguishing completely regular
poems from all others. However, twentieth-century poets, particularly
when utilizing the nonclassical meters, often employ only one or two
lines that do not fit in with the rest of the poem.[122] An example is
Kuzmin's "In the Theater," analyzed above as an example of three-stress
strict accentual verse. There just one line of twenty-four, the last, does

not belong to the main meter. In cases where the irregular lines are rare—no more than one or two in a short poem and under 5 percent in a longer poem—it is possible to analyze the regular lines and leave the others to one side. Once the frequency of irregular lines moves beyond 5 percent and particularly as it starts to approach 25 percent, the entire poem must be treated as a transitional form. Thus while poems with one or two irregularities and those with significant numbers of irregularities may both be called transitional metrical forms for the purpose of categorization, only in the latter case do the nonconforming lines affect the entire analysis.

Transitional metrical forms that are within the classical syllabo-tonic system generally fall on the border between a given meter and the variable form for that line type: for instance, a transitional metrical form between trochaic pentameter and variable trochees or between anapestic trimeter and variable anapests. The border may also be between a mixed and a variable form, say a poem written basically in alternating iambic tetrameter and trimeter but with a few lines of another length. Examples of transitional metrical forms in the syllabo-tonic meters are common in nineteenth- as well as in twentieth-century poetry. The following example appears in a poem by Tiutchev:

Не говори: меня́ он, как и пре́жде, лю́бит,	∪‒∪∸∪‒∪‒∪‒∪∸∪
Мно́й, как и пре́жде, дорожи́т...	∸‒∪∸∪‒∪∸
О не́т! Он жи́знь мою́ бесчелове́чно гу́бит,	∪∸∪∸∪‒∪∸∪‒∪∸∪
Хоть, ви́жу, но́ж в руке́ его́ дрожи́т.	∪∸∪∸∪∸∪∸∪∸
То́ в гне́ве, то в слеза́х, тоску́я, негоду́я,	∸∪∸∪∸∪‒∪‒∪‒∪∸∪
Увлечена́, в душе́ уязвлена́,	∪‒∪∸∪‒∪‒∪∸
Я стра́жду, не живу́... им, и́м одни́м живу́ я –	∪∸∪‒∪∸∪∸∪‒∪‒∪∸∪
Но э́та жи́знь!.. О, ка́к горька́ она́!	∪∸∪∸∪∸∪‒∪∸

[1851 or 1852]

The poem is written basically in a mixed meter, with iambic hexameter and pentameter lines alternating, but the second line is in iambic tetrameter. Therefore the poem is written in a transitional metrical form between mixed iambs (hexameter and pentameter) and variable iambs.

Poems that are transitional between one of the classical meters and nonclassical verse forms are essentially a twentieth-century phenomenon. Particularly common are poems written largely in one of the ternary meters but containing a few lines in *dol'niki*:

Что зате́ял ты, Ро́к? не игро́й ли	∪∪∸∪∪∸∪∪∸∪
На аре́не веко́в за́нят ты́?	∪∪∸∪∪∸∪∸∪∸

Толпы бросил ты к Савонароле,   ◡◡◡◡–◡◡◡◡
Руки, в знаке креста, подняты.   ◡◡◡◡◡◡◡◡

И от воли ль твоей, от речей ли   ◡◡◡◡◡◡◡◡◡◡
Исступленца, что длань распростёр.   ◡◡◡◡◡◡◡◡
Возложил Сандро Боттичелли   2 ́ 1 ́ 2 ́ 1
Картины свои на костёр?   1 ́ 2 ́ 2 ́

                         1921

The first half of Briusov's "Botticelli" opens with six consecutive lines of anapestic trimeter. The seventh is a three-stress *dol'nik*, and the eighth is amphibrachic in form. The same ratio holds for the rest of the poem: of its sixteen lines, two are *dol'nik*, two are in amphibrachic trimeter, and twelve anapestic trimeter.[123] But in describing such works it is unnecessary to make overly fine distinctions among secondary meters. Since *dol'nik* meters may include at least some lines that use ternary meters, it seems more concise and, I believe, more accurate to identify the secondary meter in this poem as three-stress *dol'nik* for all four of the nonanapestic lines. Therefore the poem can be categorized as a transitional metrical form between anapestic trimeter and the three-stress *dol'nik*.

Transitional metrical forms totally within the nonclassical meters are sometimes analogous to the forms that usually occur within the classical meters—that is, on the border between a given meter and the variable form for that type, say between the four-stress *dol'nik* and variable *dol'nik*. Of particular interest are poems in which one or more of the intervals between stresses falls outside the normal range for the main meter. In these cases the poems conbine features of two different metrical types:

Но найду, и нищий, дорогу,   2 ́ 1 ́ 2 ́ 1
Выходи, морозное солнце!   2 ́ 1 ́ 2 ́ 1
Проброжу весь день ради бога,   2 ́ 1 ́ 2 ́ 1
Ввечеру постучусь в оконце...   2 ́ 2 ́ 1 ́ 1

И откроет белой рукою   2 ́ 1 ́ 2 ́ 1
Потайную дверь предо мною   2 ́ 1 ́ 2 ́ 1
Молодая, с золотой косою,   2 ́ 3 ́ 1 ́ 1
С ясной, открытой душою.   0 ́ 2 ́ 2 ́ 1

                         1903

In the seventh line of this excerpt from a poem by Blok, one of the intervals is three syllables whereas the norm for *dol'niki* is only one or two syllables. Therefore the poem can be said to be a transitional form between the three-stress *dol'nik* and strict accentual verse, though as has already been noted, poems in *dol'niki* and in both kinds of accentual verse frequently exhibit at least occasional irregularities. Only when the irregularities become more than occasional is the border between two of the nonclassical forms approached.

COMPOUND METERS

To date compound meters have been by far the least common type of multimetrical verse; the only poet who has used the form extensively is Tsvetaeva.[124] Compound meters are roughly analogous to mixed meters; that is, lines in different meters appear according to a regular, repeated pattern. The sequence recurs at the level of the stanza, so lines at a specific place in the stanzas all contain the same meter. In mixed meters the lines are all of the same general type, say iambic tetrameter and trimeter. In compound meters the lines are of different types, say iambs and anapests or trochees and *dol'niki*.

The sequence may involve a simple alternation, as in Briusov's "To Damascus" ("V Damask"), where the dactylic trimeter appears in the odd lines of each stanza and iambic dimeter in the even lines:

Гу́бы мои́ приближа́ются	⊥∪∪⊥∪∪⊥∪∪
К твои́м губа́м,	∪⊥∪⊥
Та́инства сно́ва сверша́ются,	⊥∪∪⊥∪∪⊥∪∪
И ми́р как хра́м.	∪⊥∪⊥
Мы, как священнослужи́тели,	⊥∪∪–∪∪⊥∪∪
Твори́м обря́д.	∪⊥∪⊥
Стро́го в вели́кой оби́тели	⊥∪∪⊥∪∪⊥∪∪
Слова́ звуча́т.	∪⊥∪⊥

1903

At other times the alternation is more complex and can involve nonclassical as well as classical meters. The first two stanzas of Tsvetaeva's "A Letter" ("Pis'mo") each have amphibrachic dimeter in lines 1 and 3, iambic dimeter in 2 and 4, and the three-stress *dol'nik* (or logaoedic verse of the form 1 ⊥ 2 ⊥ 1 ⊥) in lines 5 and 6.

Так пи́сем не жду́т,	∪⊥∪∪⊥
Так жду́т – письма́.	∪⊥∪⊥
Тряпи́чный лоску́т,	∪⊥∪∪⊥
Вокру́г тесьма́	∪⊥∪⊥
Из кле́я. Внутри́ – словцо́.	1⊥2⊥1⊥
И сча́стье. – И э́то – всё.	1⊥2⊥1⊥

Так счáстья не ждýт,   ∪⏜∪∪⏜
Так ждýт – концá: ∪⏜∪⏜
Солдáтский салют   ∪⏜∪∪⏜
И в грýдь – свинцá   ∪⏜∪⏜
Трй дóльки. В глазáх красно́.   1⏜2⏜1⏜
И тóлько. – И это – всё.   1⏜2⏜1⏜

                                1923

The final two stanzas of this poem each have four lines in alternating
amphibrachic dimeter and iambic dimeter; in other words, they are like
the first two stanzas but with the final two lines truncated. Tsvetaeva's
cultivation of compound meters is in keeping with her tendency to seek
rhythmic diversity by creating complex and carefully organized struc-
tures. Often Tsvetaeva's forms regulate the alternation of stressed and
unstressed syllables in a fashion even stricter than is found in the regular
classical meters.[125] While no other poet has used compound meters so
systematically, the term remains useful for describing a small but dis-
tinct class of Russian poems.

POLYMETRICAL COMPOSITIONS

The definition of *polymetrical compositions* (*polimetricheskie kom-
pozitsii*), like that of *transitional verse forms*, owes much to the work of
P. A. Rudnev, who has analyzed polymetrical compositions by several
poets.[126] The term is used to describe works that contain distinct seg-
ments written in different meters; sometimes a poem will contain one or
more segments in prose.[127] Works containing a single segment that devi-
ates from the main meter on either side of it require special attention. If
the segment appears to be an integral part of the poem, then the work is
polymetrical. However, if the segment is an insertion that is written in a
different manner—for instance, the song in chapter 3 of Pushkin's *Eu-
gene Onegin*, written in trochaic trimeter rather than in the iambic te-
trameter of the poem's main body—then the work is generally not
perceived as polymetrical.[128] Both short and long poems may be poly-
metrical, though shorter works are more likely to contain only two or
three segments (and hence just one or two changes of meter) while nar-
rative poems and plays may involve dozens of changes and many differ-
ent meters.

Although polymetrical compositions have become more widespread
in the twentieth century, they were hardly rare in the nineteenth. They

appear among the works of Pushkin, Lermontov, Tiutchev, Fet, Katenin, Pavlova, and Nekrasov, among many others.[129] Karolina Pavlova's long work, *A Double Life* (*Dvoinaia zhizn'*), is particularly interesting for combining passages of poetry with long passages in prose; she and Nekrasov were two poets who made particularly extensive use of polymetrical compositions.[130] In the twentieth century Blok, Bely, Briusov, Maiakovsky, and Tsvetaeva all wrote numerous polymetrical compositions. As in the nineteenth century, authors naturally use the form in drama (all the original plays by Blok and Innokenty Annensky are polymetrical) and in narrative poems (such as Blok's "The Twelve" as well as works by both Tsvetaeva and Maiakovsky).[131] Children's poetry frequently makes use of polymetrical compositions as well; this tendency likewise goes back to the nineteenth century (cf. Nekrasov's "Uncle Iakov") and is reflected especially in the poetry of Kornei Chukovsky and Agniia Barto.[132] Polymetrical compositions remain common today; Voznesensky, for instance, has used them in all his longer poems and even in 15 percent of his shorter works.[133] Their most important use in recent years has been by writers like Bulat Okudzhava, Vladimir Vysotsky, and Aleksandr Galich for songs meant to be accompanied by a guitar.

The simplest kinds of polymetrical compositions involve only a single change in meter. In Karolina Pavlova's "Moscow" the two meters are furthermore both iambic: iambic pentameter in the first four stanzas and iambic tetrameter in the last seven. Below are the fourth and fifth stanzas from that poem:

И го́род та́м пала́тный и собо́рный,
Раски́нувшись широ́ко в ширине́,
Блиста́л внизу́, как бы нерукотво́рный,
И что́-то вдру́г просну́лося во мне́.

Москва́! Москва́! что в зву́ке э́том?
Како́й отзы́в серде́чный в нём?
Заче́м так сро́ден о́н с поэ́том?
Так вла́стен о́н над мужико́м?

1844

Other poems involve several changes and different types of classical meters. Ivan Nikitin's "The Master" ("Khoziain") begins with a long section in iambic tetrameter, followed by much shorter passages in dactylic tetrameter, mixed amphibrachs (tetrameter and trimeter in a 4-4-3-3 alternation), and a return to dactylic tetrameter. The poem's

meter then goes back to the original—iambic tetrameter. The following
excerpt includes all three of the poem's meters:

Твоя́ слеза́ на кро́вь похо́дит...   ◡⏦◡⏦◡⏦◡⏦◡
Пла́чь бо́льше!.. В во́здухе чума́!..   ⏦◡⏦◡⏦◡⏦◡⏦
Люби́мый сы́н в моги́лу схо́дит,   ◡⏦◡⏦◡⏦◡⏦◡
Друго́й давно́ сошёл с ума́.   ◡⏦◡⏦◡⏦◡⏦

Во́т он сиди́т на лежа́нке просто́рной,   ⏦◡◡⏦◡◡⏦◡◡⏦◡
Го́ло остри́жен, и бле́ден, и хи́л;   ⏦◡◡⏦◡◡⏦◡◡⏦
Па́лку, как скри́пку, к плечу́ прислони́л,   ⏦◡◡⏦◡◡⏦◡◡⏦
Бро́вью и гла́зом мига́ет прово́рно,   ⏦◡◡⏦◡◡⏦◡◡⏦◡
Пра́вой руко́ю и взад и вперёд   ⏦◡◡⏦◡◡⏦◡◡⏦
Во́дит по па́лке и пе́сню поёт: ⏦◡◡⏦◡◡⏦◡◡⏦
"На ста́ром курга́не, в широ́кой степи́,   ◡⏦◡◡⏦◡◡⏦◡◡⏦
Прико́ванный со́кол сиди́т на цепи́.   ◡⏦◡◡⏦◡◡⏦◡◡⏦
Сиди́т он уж ты́сячу ле́т,   ◡⏦◡◡⏦◡◡⏦
Всё не́т ему́ во́ли, всё не́т!   ⏦◡◡⏦◡◡⏦

                                            1861

Of course polymetrical compositions, particularly in the twentieth cen-
tury, are not limited to classical meters. They may be written entirely in
nonclassical meters (though such works are relatively rare) or they may
combine both classical and nonclassical meters, as in the two works dis-
cussed below.[134]

   In all polymetrical compositions, no matter what their length or met-
rical make-up, the change in meter is often directly motivated by the
poem's content. It may signal a new mood, a different speaker, or an-
other topic. At times each meter becomes associated with a particular
subject or personage. For instance, in Annensky's "The Birth and Death
of a Poet" ("Rozhdenie i smert' poeta") the legendary singer of tales,
Baian, employs three-stress strict accentual verse with unrhymed dac-
tylic endings—a meter reminiscent of folk verse:[135]

Над Москво́ю ста́рой златогла́вою   2⏦1⏦3⏦2
Не звезда́ в полу́ночи зате́плилась,   2⏦1⏦3⏦2
Над её садо́чками зелёными,   2⏦1⏦3⏦2
Ой зелёными садо́чками кудря́выми   2⏦3⏦3⏦2
Молода́я зо́рька разгора́лася.   2⏦1⏦3⏦2

The various voices and choirs are then given their own meters, such as
iambic tetrameter and amphibrachic dimeter:

         Х о р
Среди́ изме́н, среди́ моги́л   ◡⏦◡⏦◡⏦◡⏦
Он, улыба́ясь, сы́пал ро́зы,   ⏦◡⏦◡⏦◡⏦◡
И в чи́стый жѐмчуг перели́л   ◡⏦◡⏦◡⏦◡⏦
Поэ́т свои́ немы́е слёзы.   ◡⏦◡⏦◡⏦◡⏦◡

Д р у г о й   г о л о с
О, сви́ток печа́льный!   ⏑́⏑⏑⏑́⏑
Безу́мные стро́ки,   ⏑́⏑⏑⏑́⏑
Как го́сть на пиру́   ⏑́⏑⏑⏑́
В небра́чной оде́жде,   ⏑́⏑⏑⏑́⏑
Чита́ю и пла́чу...   ⏑́⏑⏑⏑́⏑

1899

Semen Kirsanov's "Dolphiniad" ("Del'finiada") shows a still more developed system of metrical changes. The poem includes a variety of iambic and trochaic meters, one nonclassical meter, and sections in prose. The narrator speaks in iambic tetrameter:

Спаса́ясь от земны́х оби́д,   ⏑́⏑−⏑́⏑⏑́
я грёб оди́н в откры́том мо́ре   ⏑́⏑⏑́⏑⏑́⏑
без маяка́ на кругозо́ре,   ⏑−⏑⏑́⏑−⏑́⏑
далёким бе́регом забы́т.   ⏑́⏑⏑́⏑−⏑́

The dolphins' thoughts are given in trochaic hexameter:

— Мы́ не лю́ди,
        мы́ не ры́бы,
               мы́ дельфи́ны,   ⏑́⏑⏑́⏑⏑́⏑⏑́⏑⏑́⏑
мы́ дета́ли
        позоло́ченной лепни́ны,   ⏑́⏑⏑́⏑−⏑́⏑⏑−⏑́⏑
среди о́бразов орли́ных,
              среди льви́ных   −⏑́⏑⏑−⏑́⏑−⏑−⏑́⏑
украша́ем ва́ши кре́сла
                мы́ — дельфи́ны.   −⏑́⏑⏑́⏑⏑́⏑⏑́⏑

The introduction to the mock-biblical section appears in a kind of strict accentual verse (or perhaps logaoedic) of the form $1-2-0\overset{\text{-}}{}$, with masculine endings in the first and third lines of each stanza and feminine endings in the second. The first and third lines of each stanza rhyme as do the second lines of consecutive stanzas:

"В нача́ле пошёл лёд, $1\overset{\text{-}}{}2\overset{\text{-}}{}0\overset{\text{-}}{}$
и ста́ли тону́ть зве́ри, $1\overset{\text{-}}{}2\overset{\text{-}}{}0\overset{\text{-}}{}1$
и тре́снул земно́й свод. $1\overset{\text{-}}{}2\overset{\text{-}}{}0\overset{\text{-}}{}$

Поки́нул нору́ кро́т, $1\overset{\text{-}}{}2\overset{\text{-}}{}0\overset{\text{-}}{}$
покры́лся водо́й бе́рег; $1\overset{\text{-}}{}2\overset{\text{-}}{}0\overset{\text{-}}{}1$
мы ста́ли вяза́ть плот. $1\overset{\text{-}}{}2\overset{\text{-}}{}0\overset{\text{-}}{}$

1970

In the biblical section the elders speak in iambic pentameter and the offspring in iambic dimeter; the language of the dolphins is presented "directly" (it consists of Russian words written backward) in what appears to be trochaic dimeter, albeit with a couple of irregular lines.

   As with transitional metrical forms, the use of nonclassical verse in polymetrical compositions became a regular occurrence only during the twentieth century. Furthermore, twentieth-century poets have tended to use nonclassical meters relatively more often within their polymetrical works than in those that contain just one meter. For lines in works that employ a single meter, Blok, Bely, and Briusov all used nonclassical verse about 10 to 15 percent of the time. In their polymetrical compositions, however, the amount of nonclassical verse rises to 40 to 50 percent.[136] Tentative evidence points to a broader use of polymetrical compositions in more recent years when they appear both in numerous long poems and in the lyric poetry of certain poets. The twentieth century has, then, witnessed not only an expansion in the variety of regularly used verse forms but has also seen them combined within works in ever more complex ways.

4

Rhyme and Stanzaic Forms

DEFINITIONS OF RHYME

Like many literary phenomena, rhyme is easy to recognize but resists adequate definition. When a definition is attempted, two problems are presented immediately. First, a formula must be arrived at that is specific enough to be meaningful yet broad enough to include all the forms of rhyme. Simply saying that rhyme involves an identity of sounds from the final stressed syllables to the ends of two or more lines is not sufficient. Rhyme can occur at the beginning of or within the line.[1] While identity of sounds describes so-called exact rhyme, much Russian rhyme, especially in twentieth-century poems, is based more on a similarity than an identity of sounds. Second, the concept of what is and is not rhyme, and in particular the parameters of exact rhyme, may change from one era to the next.[2] Unstressed *o* and *a*, which readily rhyme in contemporary practice, were scrupulously not rhymed by poets in the eighteenth and the beginning of the nineteenth centuries. Different literary traditions may also impose their own standards on rhyme. In English a masculine rhyme ending in a vowel (an "open" masculine rhyme) requires only identity of the vowel sounds. *Sea* and *tea* are exact rhymes to the English ear, as are *go* and *foe* or *pie* and *spy*. Only the last of these would be considered an acceptable exact rhyme for Russian poetry, which in the case of open masculine rhymes also requires identity of the supporting consonant (*opornaia soglasnaia*).[3] Therefore all Russian poets would accept водá / кудá as a perfectly exact rhyme, but nearly all (at least until the twentieth century) would have rejected водá / глазá.

Clearly, no brief definition can be totally satisfactory, but for studying Russian rhyme a modified version of the definition suggested by David Samoilov—whose book on Russian rhyme, now in its second edition, represents the fullest treatment of the topic to date—will serve our needs: Rhyme involves words containing identical or similar sounds from (and sometimes before) the last stressed syllable to the end. The rhyme words occur at regular intervals, most often at the line endings, and they generally aid in both the semantic and euphonic organization of the poem.[4] Samoilov would insist that rhymes occur only at the ends of lines, and he would omit my *generally*, but on the whole my revisions do not affect his major points. Several implications of this description should be noted. First, while rhymes appear regularly, they are not necessarily present throughout a poem. It is possible, to take what is perhaps the most common instance, for a poem's even lines to rhyme while the odd ones do not. Second, exact rhyme is only a particular case; similarity of sounds as well as identity can lead to rhyme. Third, the definition recognizes the possibility of "enrichment"—the similarity or identity of sounds before the final stressed vowel.

This formula also says something about the function of rhyme. Poetry of course can exist without rhyme, and serious English poetry today is as often as not unrhymed. While unrhymed poems are found in Russian as well, they are infinitely less common. Certainly rhyming has become "freer" (in the sense of less exact) among many poets, just as many twentieth-century meters are less restrictive than the classical iambs and trochees. But the overwhelming majority of Russian poems written today are metrical, and so too they are rhymed. Perhaps because rhyme continues to be so much a part of the poetic tradition, those poets who have written about rhyme believe it plays a semantic as well as a euphonic role in their poetry. Maiakovsky, whose innovations in rhyme were as striking as those of any modern poet, claimed that he began to create the line only after he had decided on the main word or rhyme. Furthermore, he believed there was a semantic affinity between rhymed words that served to link lines and hence the entire poem.[5] Similarly, Samoilov talks of the "associative power" of rhyme and how it serves both to organize the poem and underline its meaning.[6] In an interesting essay the linguist Dwight Bolinger has pointed out that sets of words beginning or ending with the same sound often have—or at least seem to have—similar meanings, even when they are not related etymologically. His examples include a list of words ending with the *-ash* sound (crash, bash, mash, gnash, smash, etc.) as well as a chart illustrating how a multilevel chain of association is built through both opening and concluding sounds (shudder, shutter, mutter, stutter, mumble, stumble, stammer, yammer, etc.).[7] As Bolinger warns, a mere similarity in sounds will not always suggest a semantic relationship (never/clever), but by highlighting individual words rhyme can strengthen, and in some instances create, an affinity between them.

The semantic role rhyme plays in a poem is closely related to two other roles it can play. Rhyme, by its insistence on the regular occurrence of at least a similarity between phonemes, helps create the sound texture for the poem as a whole. Other factors may be significant—assonance, consonance, the patterning of closely related sounds throughout a line or stanza—but rhyme frequently becomes the most salient feature drawing attention to the sound quality of a poem. Maiakovsky's interest in reading his poetry aloud, in how it would be perceived aurally, no doubt helps explain his search for original rhymes. But even for poets whose practice is more traditional, rhyme focuses attention on how the words of a poem sound as well as on what they mean.

Finally, rhyme helps to organize the poem. When used consistently at the end of lines, rhyme demarcates line boundaries—a purpose that may not seem all that crucial to the reader of a poem in iambic pentameter but a definite service to the person hearing a Krylov fable in variable iambs. Without rhyme only pauses in the reader's voice would indicate where the breaks between lines should be.[8] More generally, rhyme words, because of their prominence and regular occurrence, impose a kind of order on any poem in which they appear.[9] Note that it is impossible to separate the three roles played by rhyme; any discussion of one must necessarily deal to some extent with the others.[10]

The terminology used to discuss rhyme is often confusing. Russian scholars usually speak of *exact rhyme* (*tochnaia rifma*), but the term is not universal; English critics have used *correct rhyme*, *perfect rhyme*, *full rhyme*, *proper rhyme*, *pure rhyme*, *true rhyme*, and a host of others.[11] Meanwhile Russian sources show some disagreement about both classifying and naming the various types of rhyme other than exact. In general, research on Russian rhyme has lagged behind that on meters. While great progress was made in defining and classifying the newer types of meters during the 1960s, little research on the problems of rhyme was begun until a decade later. Of particular interest has been the production of rhyme "dictionaries," which provide the raw information needed to speak about the nature and development of Russian rhyme.[12] But problems of classification have not yet been entirely solved. In the following pages, therefore, I shall attempt to describe and label each of the main types of Russian rhyme and show where my usage of certain terms may differ from previous usage.

One area of general agreement is the use of small and capital letters

to distinguish masculine (*a*), feminine (*A*), dactylic (*A'*), and hyper-
dactylic (*A''*) rhymes. The second rhyme in a stanza is indicated by
some form of the letter *b*, the third by *c*, and so forth. Unrhymed lines
are usually referred to by *x*, *X*, *X'*, or *X''*, depending on whether the
final stress of the line falls on the last syllable, or one, two, or three
syllables earlier.[13] Only small letters are used to describe an abstract
rhyme pattern in which the length of the clausula is not important.
(Since feminine and longer rhymes are much less common in English,
the description of English stanzas usually employs only small letters and
does not distinguish between masculine rhymes and those of more than
one syllable.) While stanzaic forms are discussed in detail in the second
half of this chapter, here it will be useful to mention the most common
rhyme combinations: adjacent (*aabb*), alternating (*abab*), and enclosed
(*abba*). By far the most common stanza in Russian is the quatrain with
alternating masculine and feminine rhymes (*aBaB* or *AbAb*, with the
latter predominating).

INTERNAL RHYME

Later it will be simplest to limit the discussion to rhyme that occurs
at the ends of lines, but in rare instances rhyme also occurs between a
word at a rhythmic break within the line and a word at the end of the
line. In Russian poetry one of the few writers to cultivate this form of
rhyme was Balmont:

Ускользáющая пéна... Поминýтная измéна...	A — A
Жáжда вы́рваться из плéна, внóвь извéдать гнёт окóв.	A — b
И в тумáнности далёкой, оскорблённый, одинóкий,	C — C
Ищет гéний светлоóкий неизвéстных берегóв.	C — b

[<1898]

From a glance at the line endings (second column above), the odd lines
appear to be unrhymed. But the internal rhymes are quickly evident,
especially if the poem is read aloud. The end of the first line rhymes
with the caesura in the first and second lines, while the end of the third
rhymes with the caesura in the third and fourth. The constant rhyme at
the caesura as well as the length of the lines cause them to sound like
pairs of lines joined together on the page. If the stanza is considered to
have eight lines instead of four it would yield a rhyme scheme of *AAAb-
CCCb*—unusual but resembling that found in some poems by Joseph
Brodsky.

However, Balmont also used internal rhyme more subtly:

То́лько вспы́хнет Ве́спер, то́лько ме́сяц гля́нет,	A
То́лько но́чь наста́нет ра́ннею весно́й, –	A—b
Се́рдце жа́ждет чу́да, но́чь его́ обма́нет,	A
Се́рдце умира́ет с га́снущей луно́й.	b

[< 1898]

In this stanza, and in the other two in the poem as well, the first and
third lines rhyme with the caesura of the second. Here the format does
not cause double lines to masquerade as single. The internal rhyme
simply creates another type of regularity in the poem through the con-
sistent though unexpected repetition of sounds at the same point in each
stanza.

Internal rhyme is not limited to the caesura. For instance, consider
yet another passage from Balmont:

Приди́ – и она́ обоймёт, заласка́ет тебя́,	a
Себя́ не жале́я, терза́я, бы́ть мо́жет, губя́,	a—a
Но всё же она́ поцелу́ет тебя́ – не любя́.	a·a

[< 1898]

In each of the three stanzas of this poem he used a single masculine
rhyme for the three lines, and on the third he created an inner rhyme
between the final two stressed words. In this stanza, though not in the
other two, the first word of the second line also forms a rhyme, though
whether it is meant to rhyme with the end of the first line—the so-called
link rhyme—or the end of the second is difficult to tell. Such a random
internal rhyme, which is not part of any pattern, is a factor in the sound
texture of a poem, but it falls outside the work's rhyme scheme.[14] One of
the few other poets to use internal rhyme throughout entire works was
Briusov. Such curiosities can be found among modern poets as well,
but the story of Russian rhyme is largely that of end rhyme.[15]

EXACT RHYME AND APPROXIMATE RHYME

Exact rhyme requires acoustic identity from the final stressed vowel
to the end of the line, with the additional requirement in Russian that if
a masculine rhyme ends in a vowel the preceding consonants must also
be identical. These requirements would seem relatively straightforward,
but as a result of changes in orthography, pronunciation, and poetic
tradition the boundaries separating exact rhymes from approximate
rhymes have not remained constant. In the 1920s Viktor Zhirmunsky, in

his pioneering work on Russian rhyme, suggested a distinction among exact, approximate, and inexact rhyme that, with certain modifications, continues to be used today.[16] The term *approximate* is limited to feminine or longer rhymes. It refers to instances when (1) the only difference between two rhymed words is in a vowel following the final stressed vowel; (2) one of the words ends in a й and the other does not; and (3) the unstressed vowels are pronounced the same but are spelled differently (мáло/сначáла),[17] though many scholars prefer to categorize this last phenomenon as exact rhyme. Inexact rhyme would then involve any differences, no matter how minor, in the consonants after the stressed vowel. Thus пéла/дéлал is an inexact rhyme, and so is отцóв/любóвь.

There is some justification for making this distinction between approximate and inexact rhymes since most innovations in rhyme practice during the twentieth century have involved consonants, which therefore seem more important than vowels in creating unusual rhymes.[18] Still, any classification seems suspect that would label the rhyme Рúга/кнúгу as approximate while assigning the rhyme отцóв/любóвь to the category "inexact" and that would also call certain acoustically exact rhymes approximate.

I propose, therefore, to use a somewhat different system, doing away with the term *inexact*, which carries with it unfortunate negative connotations. Rhymes that are not exact are not imperfect rhymes, they merely represent an alternative type of sound correspondence between words. I shall speak of exact rhymes, liberties within the system of exact rhyming, and approximate rhymes. Exact rhymes are those whose sounds are the same, even if the spelling differs. Approximate rhyme is based on a similarity rather than an identity of sound. The allowable liberties that have been employed in all periods, even by poets who essentially adhere to a system of exact rhyming, are limited to small sets of exceptions that generally derive from older forms of spelling or pronunciation.

EXACT RHYME AND THE TRADITIONAL EXCEPTIONS

The system of exact rhyme in Russian has always included the rhyming of unvoiced consonants with their voiced equivalents that have been devoiced at the end of a word (обéд/лéт) and the rhyming of the vowel pairs that reflect the hardness or softness of a preceding consonant (теля́та/утра́та).[19] Even though ы and и are not identical phonetically, they are the same phoneme in Russian and are rhymed as a matter of course by all poets. Since the soft sign that appears after a sibilant has no effect on the pronunciation, pairs such as крадёшь/нож also rhyme exactly. Similarly, silent consonants, such as a *t* between an *s* and an *n*, do not affect the quality of a rhyme: стра́стный/прекра́сный.

Among the permissible liberties, the most common are the following:

(1) Truncation of final й in feminine rhymes. Originally this was limited to situations in which one of the rhymed words was an adjective in -ый or -ий (по́лный/во́лны), but it was eventually extended to other parts of speech and other vowels before the й (си́лой/уны́ло).[20] In the twentieth century this deletion sometimes occurs in masculine rhyme pairs, where it is much more perceptible and is better considered a form of approximate rhyme.

(2) Rhyming of -ый and -ий with -ой. In the late eighteenth and early nineteenth centuries adjectives such as кра́сный and ти́хий could be written with the ending -ой as well (the -ый is of Church Slavonic origin, while -ой is Russian). Under the influence of the orthography, poets came to treat these endings equally; thus Lermontov rhymed не́жный not only with мяте́жный but also with мяте́жной. Even poets like Baratynsky, whose rhyme practice was so strict that he avoided rhymes with a deleted й, still felt no compunction about rhyming unstressed -ый and -ой.[21] Such rhymes continued even after the spelling -ой was no longer permissible in the nominative masculine singular form of stem-stressed adjectives.

(3) Rhyming of к, г, and х. In some words the gutteral stop г was pronounced as a fricative, while Russians with a south Russian or Ukrainian accent regularly pronounced it as a fricative. Therefore poets came to rhyme г with х (друг/дух). At the same time poets continued to rhyme г and к in final position (друг/звук). Most likely by analogy (if г and х rhyme, and г and к rhyme, then so must х and к), rhymes of the sort дух/звук also occur.

(4) Rhyming of final hard and soft consonants. Rhymes like отцо́в/любо́вь, which some scholars would classify as inexact rhyme, can be found in the poetry of Derzhavin, Batiushkov, and their contemporaries. This one rhyme seems to have originated from a particular dialectical pronunciation, but other rhymes involving hard and soft consonants (следи́т/жи́ть; чуде́с/здесь) can also be found in the nineteenth century.[22]

(5) Open masculine rhymes. Normally, masculine rhymes ending in a vowel must have the same supporting consonant (страна́/спина́), but there have always been a few common exceptions to this rule. The preceding consonants may differ if they form a voiced/unvoiced pair (нога́/строка́). More commonly, the consonants may be different but "related" soft consonants (especially two different sonorants: заре́/огне́). Finally, a soft consonant and a plain й may serve as the supporting consonants (люблю́/ловлю́/пою́; твоя́/дитя́).[23]

APPROXIMATE RHYME

Approximate rhyme is not the exclusive property of modern literary poets. It is to be found in proverbs, riddles, and other types of folk verse, while even within the literary tradition an eighteenth-century figure like Derzhavin could employ approximate rhyme more frequently than many a twentieth-century writer. Nor is approximate rhyme at all peculiar to Russian poetry. Since the early years of the twentieth century many American and British poets who employ rhyme have used approximations that would have seemed unusual even to a Maiakovsky. Most of what is commonly called "near rhyme" in American poetry can be traced back to Emily Dickinson, who often based her rhymes on minimal similarities. In her rhyme pairs the only repeated sound might be the rhymed vowels (these/weep) or a final consonant (clock/tick).[24]

Russian poets have often compensated for the lack of identity after the stressed vowel by increasing the similarity to the left of it. This rhyme "enrichment" may also occur in exact rhyme, and perhaps the first detailed discussion of this phenomenon appeared in an article by Briusov on the "leftness" of Pushkin's rhymes.[25] Elsewhere Briusov also pointed to enrichment as a key feature of twentieth-century poetry, which, he believed, had come to employ a whole new system of rhyming.[26] More recent scholars agree on the importance of enrichment for modern poets; as a result of the greater similarity in sounds before the stressed vowel and the decrease after it, the focus has shifted from the very end of the line to a section that includes the syllable or two before the rhymed vowel.[27] Some would further distinguish between rich rhyme, which includes a consonant or two before the stressed vowel (си́ла/спроси́ла: капри́з/сюрпри́з) and "deep" or "super-rich" rhyme, for which the sound identity embraces at least a full syllable before the stressed vowel (роково́й/веково́й).[28] For our purposes, however, when speaking of enrichment we should bear in mind that it may extend well back into the line.

One type of approximate rhyme involves a difference in vowels that appear after the stressed vowel. Such rhyming can be found as far back as the first half of the nineteenth century, though the poet who cultivated such rhymes most consciously was Aleksei K. Tolstoi. His 1859 letter to B. M. Markevich in which he defended himself against Turgenev's charge of using lame (*khromye*) rhymes constitutes one of the most important statements on rhyme by any nineteenth-century poet and is worth quoting at length (the emphasis throughout is his):

> In my opinion, the *vowels* at the end of a rhyme, *if they are not stressed*, are totally indistinguishable and of no significance. Only consonants count, and they form the rhyme. Безмо́лвно and во́лны rhyme, in my opinion, far better than ша́лость and мла́дость or гру́зно and дру́жно, where the vowels are completely identical. It seems to me that only an inexperienced ear could demand identity of vowels, and it does so because it makes concessions to sight. . . . *Approximate* rhyme *within certain limits* does not frighten me at all.[29]

At one point in his letter Tolstoi drew back somewhat from the sweeping statement quoted here. He believed that any of the vowels that can follow a hard consonant, rhyme with each other. And he was willing to rhyme any of the vowels that follow soft consonants but unwilling to mix the two. Thus the rhymes стремни́ны/доли́ну and уче́нье/значе́нью were acceptable to him but not переме́ны/значе́нью.[30] Note too that all these rhymes are feminine; the syllable immediately following the stress is the weakest in Russian words, and therefore the differences are not that noticeable. Still, in his direct advocacy of rhymes that were clearly not exact Tolstoi gave an impetus to changes in Russian rhyme practice and helped pave the way for the more drastic experiments of the twentieth century.

Modern approximate rhyme, however, largely arises from differences in the consonants that follow the stressed vowel in the words that are rhymed. These differences may be of three kinds.[31]

(1) The most common is *truncation*, in which one of the words lacks one or more consonants that are present after the stressed vowel in the other. The truncation most often occurs at the end of a word, but it may take place within it as well. Some examples from Kliuev: нос/мост, изво́за/гро́зам, кра́е/вдува́ет (all final consonants); па́стбище/кла́дбище, пусты́нный/обши́рный (internal consonants); ро́ще/

ро́пщет (both final and internal). Truncation, particularly when it occurs at the end of a rhyme word, is related to the rhymes lacking a final й that were described earlier as the first of the traditional exceptions to the requirement for exact rhyme. While the deletion of a consonant other than й is felt more strongly, this type of rhyme had a precedent and is also less radical than the other kinds of approximate rhyme involving consonants. Therefore it both appeared earlier and became more widely used than the others.

(2) Also used often, especially by certain contemporary poets, is the *substitution* of one consonant for another; all these examples are from a single poem by Viktor Sosnora, "Fountain of Tears" ("Fontan slez," 1965): ястреба́ми/истребля́ли, слеза́ми/сказа́ла, са́м/сам теса́л, кла́д/гла́з, стра́ху/стра́жу, смоли́ли/моли́твой. Two traits of substitution are evident here. First, it is common to substitute closely related consonants for each other. Here half the instances involve a switch between the resonants л and м; in the fourth pair the д and з are both dentals. Second, the differences in consonants after the stressed vowels are to an extent compensated for by enrichment before them— all examples of the "leftness" found in much modern rhyme. Note the repetition of стреб in the first example, the кл and гл in the fourth (where к/г form a voiced/voiceless pair), стр in both words of the fifth, and so forth. In every case the approximate rhymes in this poem are accompanied by some enrichment. While enrichment is not a requirement for instances of substitution (or truncation), and enrichment occurs with exact rhyme as well, for much modern rhyme the segment of the line immediately preceding the rhymed vowel has become as important as that after the vowel.

(3) *Transposition* of two or more consonants is more complex than the previous two types of rhyme and therefore is found more rarely. At the same time it can be particularly effective. Samoilov finds that successful transpositions are perhaps the most elegant of all rhymes.[32] The following examples are from Tsvetaeva:

стра́хами/са́харной	кни́га/насти́гну	бе́режной/безде́нежью
у́мер/трю́ме	по́просту/про́пасти	вы́мысел/яви́лись мы

In most of these examples a consonant appears before the stressed vowel in one word and after both the vowel and another consonant in the other. In both rhyme pairs from the last column the transposition takes place entirely after the stressed vowel. Note that since the same sounds are retained albeit in a different order, enrichment is less important than in the case of deletion or substitution.

All these types of approximate rhyme may appear either on their own or in combination with others. In the first of the transpositions listed above, note that the final consonants in the two words, while closely related, are not identical (м and н). Tsvetaeva in fact frequently combined transpositions with substitutions (мéста/тéсно or the more extreme тысяче/сыщика) or truncation (лóтос/прóпасть, пóиски/покóится).[33]

These last few examples in particular illustrate the system of rhyme at work in the twentieth century. It would be wrong to think that modern rhyming is based on less of a similarity in sounds than predominated when exact rhyme was the norm. If anything, combinations like стрáху/стрáжу and кнѝга/настѝгну, as much as they might have grated on the ear of a nineteenth-century listener, involve a more profound correspondence than many exact rhymes. While certainly some of the approximations—such as a few of the truncations as well as the consonances that are discussed below—are reminiscent of the minimal rhyming toward which English poetry has moved since the time of Emily Dickinson, the overall impression left by modern Russian poetry is quite different. Russian poets have supplemented the principle of exact rhyme with the principle of approximate rhyme. If the former held that there should be sound identity between the rhymed words from the stressed vowel to the end, the latter implies that there must be sound similarity in the vicinity of the rhymed vowels. As with classical and nonclassical meters, two types of rhyming now exist side by side. Some poets continue to follow nineteenth-century practice, some apply the new techniques only occasionally, while still others use it in most of their work.

While the new type of rhyming is largely based on the approximate rhymes described above, four other kinds of such rhyme, all virtually unknown in Russia prior to the twentieth century, have played roles as well.

Heterosyllabic (*neravnoslozhnye*) rhymes are rhymed words that have a different number of syllables after the stress. Maiakovsky was particularly inclined to use heterosyllabic rhymes, and they are also found in the works of contemporary poets such as Voznesensky.

рáструбы/я́стреб	надкýсанный/искýсство
подсýживает/пссýдной	кадýшку/контýженный

All these examples are from the poem "Vanka the Avant-Gardist" ("Van'ka-avangardist," 1971); it is worth comparing them to several from Maiakovsky:[34]

а́втора/за́втра	ну́жна/дю́жина	во́рот/бо́рт
до́рого/восто́рга	ора́торов/психиа́тров	ну́жная/у́жинаю

The most common type of heterosyllabic rhyme combines one word with a dactylic and one with a feminine ending, though other pairings (feminine and masculine, hyperdactylic and dactylic, hyperdactylic and feminine) sometimes occur. To this extent the two sets of examples are similar. In Maiakovsky's rhymes the "missing" syllable is more often the most weakly pronounced syllable of the word—the syllable immediately following the stressed vowel. Also, while Maiakovsky occasionally included other kinds of approximation in his heterosyllabic rhymes,[35] in most instances the only deviation from nineteenth-century practice is in the unequal number of syllables. In the first of the four rhymes by Voznesensky the final syllable, not the syllable immediately after the rhymed vowel, has been dropped. In the other three instances the sounds following the rhymed vowels differ to such a degree that it is impossible to specify which syllable is lacking. Most of the sound similarities occur *before* the rhymed vowels. Here Voznesensky, like other contemporary poets, has taken an innovation introduced earlier in the century and developed its possibilities still further.

A second kind of rhyme, heteroaccentual (*raznoudarnaia*), occurs when the rhymed vowel is stressed in one word but not in the other. Heteroaccentual rhymes do not appear often in the work of contemporary poets, though they enjoyed a certain vogue in the 1910s. The first poet to use them in any quantity was Khlebnikov; however, the true master of the form was Anatoly Mariengof:[36]

пе́пел/капе́лл	бо́ли/ли́к	мешки́/ка́мешки
сосу́ды/суда́	шпа́лам/попола́м	дно́/хо́лодно

The term *heteroaccentual rhyme* actually describes two phenomena. One is *wrenched rhyme*, in which the stress of a rhyming polysyllabic word does not correspond to the last ictus of the line. In the first two columns above the rhymes are of this sort: if the stress of one word in the pair falls on an ictus, then stress in the other word clearly does not. The other phenomenon, *unstressed rhyme*, describes a pair in which the stress of one word falls on an ictus before the last ictus in a line. For the

examples in the third column, in either an iambic or trochaic poem
the first word would coincide with the last ictus of the line, while stress
on the second word would fall on the next-to-last ictus. Note that hetero-
accentual rhymes in Russian are analogous to English *eye rhymes*,
where a similarity in spelling masks a difference in pronunciation:
prove/love; home/come.[37]

The third kind—consonances, or rhymes with different stressed
vowels—are also rare in Russian; the following are by Blok:[38]

ро́зах/ри́зах   со́лнце/се́рдце
даю́т/ле́т   при́свистом/ше́лестом

As with most other approximate rhymes, consonances tend to compen-
sate for the lack of identity in sounds from the stressed vowel by em-
ploying enrichment, as in the first two rhyme pairs above.

The fourth type involves changes that have occurred in the twentieth
century in the requirements for masculine rhymes. Masculine rhymes
ending in a vowel must normally have the same supporting consonant,
though as we have seen, even in the nineteenth century the consonants
could be a voiced/unvoiced pair or two related soft consonants. In the
twentieth century the strictures on these rhymes are sometimes ignored:
ты́/попы́, лицо́/плечо́, налицо́/ушло́, небеса́/ушла́.

In the first two of these examples from Tsvetaeva's cycle "Epitaph"
("Nadgrobie," 1935) the supporting consonants are still phonetically
similar, but the only relationship between the last two is that both conso-
nants are hard. Such pairings are often called poor (*bednaia*) or inade-
quate (*nedostatochnaia*) rhyme.[39] (However, in English poetry, it will be
recalled, such rhymes are exact.) I prefer to avoid terms with such pe-
jorative overtones and therefore suggest the phrase *minimum rhyme* to
describe rhyme pairs in which only a single phoneme matches at the end
of the words. Also, masculine rhymes now occur with a deleted й,
which in the nineteenth century was found only in feminine rhymes.
Pasternak employed косе́й/красе́, крупо́й/По́, прямо́й/трюмо́.
More recently, Iunna Morits has used the same type of rhyme: воско-
во́й/нико́го.

SPECIAL PHENOMENA

Five other categories of rhyme, all but one in existence since the
nineteenth century, should be mentioned as well. Three by definition in-

volve exact rhyme; a fourth can be used with either exact or approximate rhyme; while the fifth is a direct product of modern developments in rhyme.

The first two are *homonym rhyme* and *repetend rhyme*. Both terms mean that the two words in a rhyme pair sound alike. In the case of homonyms, however, the words have different meanings; repetend rhymes are based on pairings of the same word. The latter often occurs in refrains or with other conscious efforts to emphasize a single word, as in this stanza by Slutsky:

Э́то я́, го́споди!	A′
Го́споди – э́то я́!	b
Сле́ва мои́ това́рищи,	X′
спра́ва мои́ друзья́.	b
А посерёдке, го́споди,	A′
я́, самоли́чно – я́.	b
Неуже́ли, го́споди,	A′
не призна́ешь меня́?	b

[<1977]

In the poem's subsequent stanzas the first four and the last four lines contain different sets of rhymes. If that were the case here, only the fifth and seventh lines would contain a repetend rhyme. But with the given rhyme scheme a triple repetend occurs on lines 1, 5, and 7 and a regular repetend on lines 2 and 6. Homonym rhymes, while they often border on puns (whether intentional or not), are by their very nature more interesting; the first pair of rhymes in this passage by Pasternak offers an example:

Уже́ я позабы́л о дне́,	a
Когда́ на океа́нском дне́	a
В зия́ющей япо́нской бре́ши	B
Суме́ла различи́ть депе́ша	B
(Како́й учёный водола́з)	c
Кла́сс спру́тов и рабо́чий кла́сс.	c

1923-28

Echo rhyme occurs when the final portion of one rhyme word includes all the sounds of the other. While the rhymes must be absolutely exact, the use of two different words helps avoid the dullness that could result from frequent use of repetend rhyme. The following examples are all from Fet:

и́вы/изви́вы	ве́к/челове́к	э́ти/де́ти	стороне́/оне́
о́ко/высо́ко	со́н/вознесён	и́х/свои́х	лазу́рной/у́рной

Fourth is *compound (broken) rhyme*—when the stressed vowel of at least one member of the rhyme set occurs in a word other than the last one on the line. In practical terms this means that two words rather than one are involved in the rhyme. Compound rhymes can be found in the nineteenth century, though they were largely limited to instances when the second word was a particle or a pronoun. On the rare occasions when the second word was a noun, the stress usually had been shifted back to an accompanying preposition, as in the last of these examples from Lermontov:[40]

печа́ли/тебя́ ли   ничего́ я/поко́я   цвели́ мы/пали́мы
иди́ же/побли́же   где́ ты/ле́ты   на́ сто/ба́ста

In the twentieth century the frequency of compound rhymes in the work of certain poets has become much higher than it was for poets writing during the nineteenth century. Parts of speech other than pronouns and particles have come to be used regularly, and many of the rhymes are approximate as well as exact. The first to employ the new compound rhyming extensively was Khlebnikov.[41] Among the contemporary poets who have used compound rhymes often, Joseph Brodsky is notable for achieving some original effects. Sometimes, like other poets, he creates interesting approximate rhyme (за́ два/за́втра); at other times the rhyme itself is technically not compound, but enrichment occurs over two or three words (октября́/ох ты бля́). Brodsky particularly likes to use compound rhymes along with enjambment; that is, the final word of the line will be a conjunction or a preposition. Occasionally these rhymes are approximate, but more often they are exact. The following stanza, which has both an unusual length for modern Russian poetry and an unusual rhyme scheme, is from "December in Florence" ("Dekabr' vo Florentsii"); one of the rhymes in the first rhyme triplet and two in the second are compound:

Гла́з, мига́я, загла́тывает, погружа́ясь в сырье́	A
су́мерки, как табле́тки от па́мяти, фонари́; и	A
твой подъе́зд в двух́ мину́тах от Синьори́и	A
намека́ет глу́хо, спустя́ века́, на	B
причи́ну изгна́нья: вблизи́ вулка́на	B
невозмо́жно жи́ть, не пока́зывая кулака́; но	B
и нельзя́ разжа́ть его, умира́я,	C
потому́ что сме́рть – это всегда́ втора́я	C
Флоре́нция с архитекту́рой Ра́я.	C

                                    1976

Shadow (tenevaia) rhyme results directly from the increase in both prevalence and kinds of approximate rhyme.[42] The borders between rhyme sets (that is, the groups of two or more words that form a given rhyme) have sometimes become more difficult to determine. Consider the following stanza from a poem by Iunna Morits:

Но́чью бу́дут холода́.	a
В си́нем су́мраке окна́	b
Намеча́ется звезда́,	a
Намеча́ется луна́.	b

　　　[< 1974]

The first and third as well as the second and fourth lines form exact rhyme, but today it is not rare to find masculine rhymes with different supporting consonants. In other words, given current rhyme practice, all four of these lines could be considered to rhyme with each other. While the rhyme scheme of the stanza appears to be *abab*, the *a* rhyme set forms a shadow rhyme with the *b* set. In the following stanza from a poem by Igor Severianin the shadow rhyme is more subtle:

Мне́ не́ в чем ка́яться, Росси́я, пред тобо́й:	a
Не предава́л тебя́ ни мы́слью, ни душо́й,	a
А е́сли в чу́ждый кра́й физи́чески ушёл,	b
Давно́ уж по́нял я́, как то́ нехорошо́...	b

　　　　　　1939

In this example does the third line rhyme with the first two (substitution) or with the fourth (deletion)? The analogy with the other stanzas in the poem reveals that paired adjacent rhyme occurs throughout, and therefore the rhyme scheme for this stanza must also be *aabb*. However, deciding on the basis of this stanza would be difficult because the pattern *aaaa* would be just as reasonable. Shadow rhyme extends the effect of regular rhyme; the similarity between words that actually belong to different rhyme sets may help bring out a semantic connection between the words or the entire lines that belong to both sets. At the very least, shadow rhyme creates yet another kind of sound texture in the poem.

HISTORY OF RUSSIAN RHYME

The previous sections have already offered a rough picture of how Russian rhyme evolved over the years. Rhyme was reasonably exact in the eighteenth century, after the syllabo-tonic reform, but was most

strict during the beginning of the nineteenth century. Some loosening of
the requirements for rhyme began to take effect around the middle of
that century, until at the beginning of the twentieth century a system
of approximate rhyme evolved. Over the years this new type of rhyme
has become both more widespread in its usage and more varied in its
manifestations.[43]

The poets most closely associated with important changes in rhyme
practice (such as Lermontov, Nekrasov, Aleksei K. Tolstoi, Blok, and
Maiakovsky) are largely the same individuals who introduced the most
important metrical and rhythmic innovations as well. Experiments with
the one aspect of verse have generally been accompanied by experi-
ments with the other. Blok's poetry provides a graphic example: his
"new" rhymes occurred most often precisely during those years (espe-
cially 1905–7) when he was also trying out new meters.[44] Both before
and after this period his practice was more traditional.

Two terms have gained wide currency among historians of Russian
verse practice. The phrase "decanonization of exact rhyme," coined by
Zhirmunsky, is often used to describe the broad development that took
place from the early nineteenth century until the early twentieth.[45] More
recently Roman Jakobson has spoken of rhyme as being less gram-
matical, thus characterizing the increasing reluctance of poets to base
too much of their rhyming on the relatively easy correspondences cre-
ated by pairing words—especially verbs—that have the same gram-
matical ending.[46]

The changes that have taken place in rhyme practice are in fact of two
distinct types. These processes have sometimes taken effect separately
and sometimes in conjunction with each other. First, there has been a
growing interest in approximate rhyme—Zhirmunsky's decanonization
of exact rhyme. However, the progression was not always steady: in the
eighteenth century Derzhavin used more approximate rhyme than did
most poets for the next several generations. Second, the nature of exact
rhyme has changed. There has been, as Jakobson would say, a tendency
for rhyme to become "antigrammatical"; thus verbal rhymes, for in-
stance, are used much less often than they were in the eighteenth cen-
tury. Certainly one way to avoid grammatical rhymes is to use more ap-
proximate rhyme, but poets also moved in this direction by broadening
the liberties allowed in exact rhyme. A contrary development in exact
rhyme during the nineteenth century was the increasingly wide use of
dactylic rhyme, which, at the start anyway, tended to be both exact and

grammatical—that is, it ran counter to the prevalent trend. In short, rhyme practice was dynamic and at times seemed to be going in several directions at once.

The importance of rhyme in the Russian poetic tradition remains virtually undiminished to the present day. In English literature, and in many other traditions as well, rhyme is less prevalent in the twentieth century than it was earlier.[47] But in Russia both blank verse and free verse remain relatively rare.

EARLIEST RHYMES AND THE EIGHTEENTH CENTURY

The origin of rhyme in world literature remains vague, despite attempts to trace it back through Persian literature to a Chinese source.[48] No doubt influences of certain ancient literatures upon others played some role in the development of rhyme, but the pleasing effect that can be attained through sound repetitions is sufficiently striking to make it likely that rhyme may have arisen more or less spontaneously in several different literatures at various times.

Any argument for a spontaneous origin of rhyme in Russian would have to be based on the existence of rhymes in folk verse. The major genres of Russian folk poetry, most notably the *bylina*, are basically unrhymed, though it is possible to find what has been dubbed *embryonic rhyme*. The term mostly describes occasional rhymes that arise, partly by chance, through the use of words with the same grammatical endings at the end of two or more consecutive lines, though it sometimes applies to more complex and more clearly intentional attempts at rhyme as well.[49] Spoken verse, which is found in the minor genres—proverbs, sayings, riddles—employs rhyme often (ко́нчил де́ло—гуля́й сме́ло) and also makes use of approximate rhyme (ста́рость—не ра́дость, with both transposition and substitution). The *chastushka*, the most modern of the folk verse genres, contains rhymes as well. Even though this form arose only in the nineteenth century when literary rhyme was already well developed, the type of rhyming it employs is more like that found in other short folk verse rather than in the literary tradition. In particular the *chastushka* uses much approximate rhyming, which was not then common in any but folk poetry.[50]

While the rhymes found in folk poetry may have had an indirect influence on Russian poets, literary rhyme largely came into Russia along with the various systems of versification. Already the *virshi*—the couplets that appeared in Russia through the influence of Polish and Ukrainian poetry—employed adjacent rhyme. The rhyme was primarily though not exclusively exact, and it was based on grammatical parallelism—the homoeoteleuton. Indeed, the requirement of grammatical identity appears to have been stronger than that of sound identity.[51] When syllabic poetry became entrenched during the seventeenth century, it brought along from Polish the characteristic paired feminine rhymes. The rules for rhyming appear to have been vague; some approximate rhyming occurred along with exact, and in some cases arbitrary shifts in word stress were necessary to create the desired feminine line endings. For that matter, not all the rhymes were even feminine. Alternating feminine rhyme entered Russian literature abruptly during the 1730s when it appeared in the work of Trediakovsky, Kantemir, and Prokopovich.[52] Antiokh Kantemir attempted to establish a more orderly rhyme system by stipulating only a small number of permissible approximate rhymes and decrying the practice of arbitrary stress shifts.[53] Much of what Kantemir advocated appeared in the rhyme practice of syllabo-tonic poets who otherwise had little use for Kantemir's syllabic poetry. Kantemir recognized the existence of masculine and dactylic as well as feminine rhymes, even though he used the latter exclusively. He preferred using identical supporting consonants in open masculine rhymes, saw the value of enrichment, and allowed for the truncation of й after ы. In particular, he based rhyme more on sound than on spelling; he noted that а and я rhyme, as do ы and и, and had no difficulty with rhyming voiced and unvoiced consonants.[54]

Lomonosov formally established the main principles of Russian exact rhyme with one exception—he did not insist on the identity of the supporting consonants in open masculine rhyme. He rhymed г and х, and he allowed for the deletion of й after ы and, more rarely, и in feminine rhymes. A handful of his rhymes may be considered approximate, but these are isolated exceptions. An original feature of his work is the regular appearance of masculine rhymes that frequently alternate with feminine—a pattern of rhyming that remains predominant to this day. Lomonosov recognized dactylic rhymes in theory but not in practice— they did not become common until the nineteenth century—and he relied heavily on grammatical rhymes, as did most of his contemporaries.[55]

Perhaps the most exact rhymer of the eighteenth century was Sumarokov, whose rhyming practice was still more regular than that of Lomonosov. Yet there are interesting features to be found in his rhyme as well, most notably his apparently conscious efforts at enrichment by rhyming words whose consonants immediately preceding the rhymed vowels were identical.[56]

An anomalous trend in the development of Russian rhyme occurs in the poetry of Derzhavin, who truncated consonants (во́лн/зво́н, да́р/ ла̄вр), substituted one consonant for another, and was one of the first to rhyme hard and soft final consonants (даро́в/любо́вь).[57] Derzhavin was not without influence; several minor poets of the early nineteenth century frequently used approximate rhyme, and it can be found in the poetry of Batiushkov, Zhukovsky, and the young Pushkin as well. Derzhavin wrote at a time when syllabo-tonic poetry was still young and the new tradition for creating rhymes was not yet firmly established. Even though most rhyme was exact, a major figure such as Derzhavin could set off on his own and cause others to follow his example. The situation remained unsettled into the early part of the nineteenth century, when exact rhyme became the definite norm.

Throughout the eighteenth century and well into the 1820s poets remained reluctant to employ rhymes in which one of the words had an unstressed a after the rhyme vowel and the other an unstressed o. Baratynsky and Delvig avoided such rhymes entirely, while Zhukovsky and Iazykov allowed them only a few times.[58] The rhyming of e and и in unstressed position was also quite rare until the time of Lermontov and Tiutchev.[59] The reluctance of poets to rhyme sounds that are totally identical is not easy to explain, and there are nearly as many answers as there are scholars who have investigated the problem. Zhirmunsky saw as crucial the influence of the orthography on rhyme practice of the time. Tomashevsky objected to this view by pointing out that in other instances (e.g., voiced/voiceless pairs in final word position) poets would rhyme identical sounds that were represented by different letters; he suggested that a and o were in fact pronounced differently in the eighteenth century, since the syllable-by-syllable pronunciation of Old Church Slavonic recitation was still the norm for poetry. Roman Jakobson has stated that a and o were not rhymed at first because early rhyme was largely grammatical and that such rhymes became common only when the shift to "antigrammatical" rhyme had begun. The Soviet critic Zapadov has claimed that no single principle was operative during the eighteenth century, for the system of rhyme in a given work largely depended on the genre in which it was written. Still others have addressed this matter as well.[60] My belief is that some combination of the reasons given by Zhirmunsky, Tomashevsky, and Jakobson may be necessary to explain the restriction. Just because the orthography did not inhibit certain kinds of rhymes does not mean it could not have been a factor in preventing others, and the persistence of an older pronunciation norm for poetry is quite possible even though difficult to prove. Jakobson's contribution may be the most significant since the movement away from grammatical rhyme was necessary before rhymes involving *o* and *a* could become common. While Zapadov implies a greater significance for genre distinctions in determining rhyme practice than seems to have been the case, he is right to point out the complexity of the matter and the possibility that different norms may have been in effect simultaneously. What is most instructive in this controversy, however, is the plethora of factors that could influence rhyme practice. As a result definite answers are hard to determine, but at least one can become aware of and to some extent evaluate the range of possibilities.

THE NINETEENTH CENTURY

The 1820s and the 1830s marked the high point of exact rhyme. Pushkin, after his lycée period, virtually abandoned approximate rhymes. Baratynsky's rhymes were still more conservative, as he was one of the few poets to avoid rhyming ы and ый. But even while these poets were still active, changes began to take place within exact rhyme. Unstressed *o* and *a* were rhymed more frequently. Zhukovsky employed dactylic rhymes and wrote poems in nothing but masculine rhyme, and the alternation of masculine and feminine rhymes in poems became less of a norm.[61] Lermontov and Tiutchev introduced still more developments. Lermontov turned to dactylic rhyme still more often, a few times writing poems with such rhymes exclusively, and he often deleted й in feminine rhymes—not just after ы but also after и and о.[62] He showed a special liking for triple rhymes—where there are three words in the rhyme set—in addition to the more usual paired rhymes.[63] His masculine rhymes ending in vowels were somewhat freer than those of most previous poets; often й was rhymed with a soft sonorant.[64] Tiutchev, whose rhymes were nearly always exact, nevertheless helped establish some of the tendencies that were important for the future of Russian rhyme. Like Lermontov, he frequently employed rhyme triplets. He liked masculine rhyme and used it exclusively in some better-known poems such as "Silentium!" and "A Dream at Sea" ("Son na more"). To a much greater degree than, say, Pushkin or Baratynsky, Tiutchev relied on sound rather than orthographic identity to create rhyme. Thus he paired поколе́ний/пе́ней, больши́е/стихи́я, and, especially, words with unstressed *o* and *a*: ма́ло/ста́ла, роково́го/покро́ва. While absolute identity in spelling was never a requirement for rhyme, Tiutchev expanded the range of spelling differences between unstressed vowels. The sole requirement was that they still sound alike, and with Aleksei K. Tolstoi even that principle was abandoned. Both Tiutchev and Lermontov furthered the process of "degrammatization," as poets toward midcentury made a greater effort to avoid grammatical rhymes in general and the "easy" verbal rhymes in particular.

The other two major names in the history of nineteenth-century rhyme are Nekrasov and Tolstoi. Nekrasov was the first poet to use dactylic rhymes in quantity. While they were noticeable in Lermontov's work, still they accounted for less than 1 percent of the total. In Nekrasov's work they represented more than 7 percent—more than eleven hundred rhyme sets.[65] Much of the dactylic rhyme in Nekrasov resulted from his interest in folk poetry, more specifically from his frequent use of the diminutives that characterize popular Russian speech. Thus endings like -ушка and -ёхонько frequently appear in his rhyme words and are responsible for much dactylic rhyme. At the same time his dactylic rhymes tend to be conservative: they are nearly always exact, and since they are rather long can seem monotonous in too great numbers. But Nekrasov did use approximate rhyme, especially when the clausula was feminine. He substituted related consonants for each other: сле́по/не́бо, любе́зный/небе́сный. Truncations also occur: приве́та/оде́том, весь/весть. He was the first poet after Derzhavin to show such an interest in approximate rhyme, and in this way he was a forerunner of the major changes that took place at the beginning of the twentieth century.[66]

Aleksei K. Tolstoi's main contribution has already been discussed: he was the first poet for whom unstressed vowels after the last stress could be mixed almost at will. The only restriction was that the consonants preceding the vowels in the two words must both be either hard or soft. By allowing for still greater differences after the final stressed vowel, Tolstoi made it less likely that rhymes would be purely grammatical and thus furthered a process that had begun with the preceding generation.

THE TWENTIETH CENTURY

The innovations that appeared in rhymes by poets like Lermontov, Nekrasov, and Tolstoi did not achieve universal acceptance; while certain changes—such as the rhyming of *o* and *a* and of other unstressed vowels that sounded alike—were widely adopted, others remained tentative. Not all poets rhymed post-tonic vowels as freely as Tolstoi, and many employed dactylic rhymes only sparingly. Similarly, when modern rhyme came into being during the age of symbolism, not every poet rushed to use it. And as in the nineteenth century, not all the changes emerged at once. Briusov and Blok expanded the range of approximate rhyme and used many rhymes that would have been quite unusual in the nineteenth century. Only with the futurists, however, are approximate rhymes so pervasive that they can be said to form an entire system. And, some would argue, certain contemporary poets have introduced further modifications that involve not just approximate rhyme but a greater use of compound rhyme and, especially, enrichment. To a still greater extent rhyme has come to be based on a similarity of sounds between entire words or phrases at the end of the line rather than between the segments that begin with the final stressed vowel.

At the beginning of the century Briusov and Blok did the most to introduce new methods of rhyming. Briusov employed substitutions of all sorts, including those involving consonants not at all related to each other (ве́чер/ме́чет). He also used truncation, some heterosyllabic rhyme, and a number of very long rhymes (spread over four or more syllables). At the same time his unusual rhymes are confined to relatively few works. His experiments in rhyme, like those involving meter and rhythm, seem to have been part of his conscious efforts to test the possibilities of verse; the modern rhyme never became an integral part of his poetic practice. On the other hand, new rhyme techniques are a regular feature in Blok's poetry, especially during the first decade of the twentieth century. His approximate rhymes are mostly feminine and tend to involve truncation of a consonant (вы́шел/повы́ше), though substitution occurs as well (ги́мна/ди́вно).[67] Transposition often occurs in conjunction with one of the other forms of approximate rhyme (оби́тели/ги́бели), and Blok's efforts to find harmonies throughout his rhyming words rather than just from the stressed vowel on show that his concept of rhyme was quite modern.[68]

During the 1910s approximate rhyme became widespread. Akhmatova, whose rhymes are somewhat more conservative than those found among many of her contemporaries, still used numerous truncations: сух́ую/целу́ют, па́мять/пла́мя. Khlebnikov, Pasternak, and Maiakovsky all expanded the frontiers of rhyme. Khlebnikov was one of the first to employ consonance rhyme (да́нь/де́нь), and he also liked to use homonyms, which in his case often involve words that are spelled differently even though they sound alike: ногóй/нагóй. His compound rhymes are original in that the second element may be a noun, verb, or some archaic form (óсп иди/гóсподи, бóзи ми/óзими); in the nineteenth century the second element was almost always a pronoun or particle.[69] Pasternak liked to use truncation in his masculine rhymes, where the difference between the two words is more clearly heard than would be the case with feminine rhyme: обо всéх/в овсé, здéсь/звездé, спит/в степи. He often used transposition to create quite unusual rhymes: чирикнув/черникой, кварц/лекáрств, ехидной/панихиды. His compound rhymes are not numerous, but those he used are usually based on some form of approximate rhyme: прорицáнья/лицá нет, Homo Sápiens/зá пояс. Pasternak also employs much enrichment: in the majority of his approximate rhymes the sounds before the stressed vowels contribute as much to the overall sound texture as those after them.

Maiakovsky is generally regarded as the single most important figure for securing the acceptance of modern rhyme. Not that his own contribution was so original—his main types of approximate rhyme can all be found earlier or at least in the work of his contemporaries. Nor is his influence as significant as might at first appear; his manner of rhyming (as opposed to the types of rhymes he used), like his manner of using meter and rhythm, is sufficiently idiosyncratic that few could imitate him. However, he is important for the significance he attached to the meanings of his rhymed words, as well as for the sheer quantity of his approximate rhymes and for the extreme nature of the effects that he created. Almost 50 percent of his rhymes are approximate, a figure that no earlier poet even remotely approached. (By comparison, only about 15 percent of Khlebnikov's rhymes are approximate.) Everything else about his rhymes is equally remarkable. He used a large number of dactylic rhymes (about 20 percent in some works) and a correspondingly low number of masculine. At times more than 10 percent of his rhymes were heterosyllabic, and compound rhymes are even more numerous.[70] Maiakovsky's favorite type of approximate rhyming was truncation, which sometimes affected three or more consonants: судá/госудáрств, кляче/делячеств, к вискý/искýсств. Note that the heterosyllabic rhymes he liked are related to deleted rhymes, for in both cases one rhyme word contains fewer elements after the stressed vowel than the other word.[71] His rhyme practice, for all its extremes in individual

cases, was based largely on differences in the syllable appearing imme-
diately after the stressed syllable. That is, he usually truncated conso-
nants in feminine rhymes; the "missing" syllable in his heterosyllabic
rhymes is most often that appearing right after the stressed vowel. Many
of the differences are mitigated by their appearance in the most weakly
pronounced syllable of the word. When combined with his frequent use
of enrichment, this technique has the effect of underscoring the basic
sound similarity between his rhymed words rather than detracting
from it.

Other major poets of the period—Kuzmin and Tsvetaeva—also fur-
thered a new approach to rhyming, but enough has been said to give a
general picture of modern rhyme. It is, first of all, oriented toward
sound similarity rather than identity, and in many cases the sounds be-
fore the stressed vowel (as a result of enrichment) are as important or
more so for creating the rhyme than those afterward. Second, modern
rhyme is often longer than nineteenth-century rhyme: while Nekrasov's
7 percent figure for dactylic rhyming was high for the nineteenth cen-
tury, it would be by no means unusual in the twentieth. Third, the ten-
dency is to avoid grammatical rhyme; sound similarities in the roots of
words gain at the expense of similarities in the endings. Fourth, much
modern rhyme is strikingly original. The transpositions, substitutions,
compound rhymes, and heterosyllabic rhymes all allow for the juxta-
position of words for which similarity in sound might not have been im-
mediately evident.

Has rhyme evolved since the 1920s? Some critics would answer yes,
that the rhymes found in the works of poets such as Voznesensky—who
does not mind using repetend rhyme, or writes poems in which rhyme
appears only occasionally, or creates rhymes in which the sound simi-
larity ends at the stressed vowel instead of beginning there—prove that
rhyming in the poetry of the 1960s and 1970s is different from that of
the 1920s.[72] All evidence indicates, however, that the techniques of con-
temporary poets are not completely new; as with meter, existing meth-
ods have simply become more prevalent or perhaps have been modified
slightly. Certain poets who have come to the fore during the past decade
or two pay more attention to substitution and transposition and less to
truncation of consonants than, say, Maiakovsky, but the essence of
rhyme has not drastically changed. The minimal sound similarities
found in some rhymes by poets such as Voznesensky represent an ex-
treme; the similarities are not likely to be an "innovation" in the sense of

opening up new directions for poets. Nor has the "old" rhyme disappeared. Some poets, like Pasternak, returned to a heavier reliance on traditional rhyming after a period of youthful experimentation. Among the younger poets some take advantage sparingly, if at all, of the possibilities offered by modern rhyme. As with meter, where both accentual meters and the traditional syllabo-tonic forms coexist and are used in varying proportions by different poets, so too there are now two systems of rhyming in Russian poetry.

Several excerpts from poems of different eras may help illustrate the development of Russian rhyme.

Я здесь, от суетных оков освобождённый,	A
Учуся в истине блаженство находить,	b
Свободною душой закон боготворить.	b
Роптанью не внимать толпы непросвещённой,	A
Участьем отвечать застенчивой мольбе	c
И не завидовать судьбе	c
Злодея иль глупца в величии неправом.	D
Оракулы веков, здесь вопрошаю вас!	e
В уединеньи величавом	D
Слышнее ваш отрадный глас;	e
Он гонит лени сон угрюмый,	F
К трудам рождает жар во мне,	g
И ваши творческие думы	F
В душевной зреют глубине.	g

1819

The first of these excerpts is from "The Village" ("Derevnia") by Pushkin, who uses exact rhymes. The only noteworthy features occur in the A and F rhyme sets, but both are among the liberties commonly found in the system of exact rhyme that prevailed in Pushkin's day. Note that all the rhymes are masculine or feminine, much (but not all) of the rhyming is grammatical, and in this particular excerpt there is almost no enrichment.[73]

This excerpt, from Nekrasov's early poem "The Drunkard" ("P'ianitsa"), employs rhyme somewhat differently:

Всё, что во сне мерещится,	A′
Как будто бы назло,	b
В глаза вот так и мечется	A′
Роскошно и светло!	b
Всё – повод к искушению,	C′
Всё дразнит и язвит	d
И руку к преступлению	C′

Нетвёрдую мани́т...   d
А́х! е́сли б ча́сть ничто́жную!   E′
Стару́шку полечи́ть,   f
Сестра́м бы не роско́шную   E′
Обно́вку подари́ть!   f

1845

Nekrasov relied heavily on grammatical rhyme in this passage, but here
and in many of his poems dactylic rhymes appear. Equally important
are the instances of approximate rhyme in two of the three dactylic
rhymes (A' and E'); in both cases the different consonants that appear
after the rhyme vowel are closely related, but even so they represent a
tentative step in the direction that would be taken by twentieth-century
poets.

By the time of Maiakovsky rhyme had evolved markedly:

Пристаёт ковче́г.
            Сюда́ луча́ми!   A
Пристань.
        Эй!
            Кида́й кана́т ко мне́!   b
И сейча́с же
            ощути́л плеча́ми   A
тя́жесть подоко́нничьих камне́й.   b
Со́лнце
            но́чь пото́па вы́сушило жа́ром.   C
У окна́
            в жару́ встреча́ю де́нь я.   D
То́лько с гло́буса – гора́ Килиманджа́ро.   C
То́лько с ка́рты африка́нской – Ке́ния.   D′
Го́лой голово́ю гло́бус.   E
Я́ над гло́бусом
            от го́ря го́рблюсь.   E
Ми́р
        хоте́л бы
            в э́той гру́де го́ря   F
настоя́щие обла́пить гру́ди-го́ры.   F

1923

Not all of Maiakovsky's rhymes are unusual; certainly the A rhyme here
would have been acceptable to all poets at all times. Still, the rhyming is
quite varied. The b rhyme involves truncation of final й in a masculine
rhyme; the C rhyme similarly uses truncation of a final consonant; and
the D rhyme is both heterosyllabic and compound. The E rhyme man-
ages to combine truncation (of the letter r), transposition (of the l), and
substitution (of hard l and s for their soft counterparts). All but the D

rhyme contain at least some enrichment, and in the last two lines it is difficult to tell whether the rhyme should be considered feminine, as marked here, or hyperdactylic (гру́де го́ря / гру́ди-го́ры).

Voznesensky's rhymes are every bit as unusual as Maiakovsky's:

Как арха́нгельша времён	a
на стенны́х часа́х над ры́нком	B
ба́ба вы́вела: "Ремо́нт",	a
сня́вши стре́лки для почи́нки.	B
Ве́рьте тёте Мо́те –	A
Вре́мя на ремо́нте.	A
Вре́мя на ремо́нте.	A
Ме́длят сбро́сить кро́ны	B
про́секи лимо́нные	B'
в сла́достной дремо́те.	A
Фи́льмы поджеймсбо́ндили.	A'
В тви́сте и нерво́зности	B'
же́нщины – вне во́зраста.	B'
Вре́мя на ремо́нте.	A
Сно́ва клёши в мо́де.	A
Но́вости тира́жные –	B'
ка́к позавчера́шние.	B'
Та́к же тягомо́тны.	A

1969

Here rhyming has come a long way from the days of Nekrasov; while the substitution involving ж and ш in the *B'* rhyme of the last stanza is approximate, it seems almost exact in comparison with the other rhymes. Truncation is common in the passage, and heterosyllabic rhyming occurs in both the third and fourth stanzas. The third stanza also offers an example of shadow rhyme: ремонте could rhyme just as well with the second line of the stanza as with the last. In light of Voznesensky's rhyme practice, it would not be unreasonable to suggest that all four lines in the stanza are rhymed. Both here and in the Maiakovsky poem it is possible to perceive a twentieth-century influence in the choice of rhyme words. While foreign words sometimes appeared in rhymes even in Pushkin's day, now more geographical terms (as in the Maiakovsky poem) and neologisms (поджеймсбо́ндили) can be found. Once again, some exact rhyme occurs in the poem, even though none is quoted here. Enrichment abounds, but there is less similarity in the endings than in those quoted from Maiakovsky. A much larger sampling from both poets would show that Maiakovsky gave the segment before the rhyme vowel about as much importance as what comes afterward; in Voznesensky's work, and in that of other modern poets as well, the sounds before the stressed vowel are sometimes more important for creating the rhyme than what appears in the ending.

UNRHYMED VERSE

While most Russian poetry since the days of syllabic poetry (and before) has been rhymed, some unrhymed verse has appeared regularly from the eighteenth century on. Kantemir's syllabic poem "To Elizabeth I" ("Elizavete Pervoi") employed unrhymed verse, and in syllabotonic poetry it was used by Sumarokov for some parodies that he wrote in the 1750s.

The term *blank verse* (*belyi stikh*) is frequently used to describe unrhymed poetry, though some prefer to reserve the term for certain verse forms. In particular, Western critics have frequently limited the category of blank verse to poems written in unrhymed iambic pentameter.[74] This form was widely used in English and German poetry, especially for verse drama, and through the influence of poets in both traditions it also became important in the history of Russian literature. However, Russian has always used unrhymed lines with other types of meters. Therefore blank verse refers to all unrhymed metrical poetry; it does not include free verse, even though that too usually lacks rhyme.

The first literary blank verse was Italian, and the eleven-syllable unrhymed lines were called *versi sciolti* (literally, verse loosened or set free). From there unrhymed poetry passed into the English tradition during the sixteenth century, where the word *blank* indicated that the poetry lacked the adornment of rhyme. French, where the tradition never really took hold, borrowed the term *vers blanc*. While *blanc* may mean empty or unmarked in French, Russians simply interpreted the word to mean white; hence, *belyi stikh*.[75]

The blank verse that has been written in Russian can be divided roughly into four groups:[76]

(1) Imitations of Greek and Latin verse forms. Of greatest importance here are the hexameter and its companion, the elegiac distich. Although both were quite common from the establishment of the syllabotonic tradition until the middle of the nineteenth century, since then they have been used, when at all, almost exclusively in translations. Below are the opening lines of a poem by Fet that employs the elegiac distich:

Стра́нное чу́вство како́е-то в не́сколько дне́й овладе́ло
Те́лом мои́м и душо́й, це́лым мои́м существо́м:
Ра́дость и све́тлая гру́сть, благотво́рный поко́й и жела́нья
Де́тские, ре́звые – са́м да́же поня́ть не могу́.

[1847]

(2) Imitations of folk verse. This group of works includes actual folk stylizations as well as poems that simply contain folk motifs. Since rhyme was not common in the major genres of Russian folk poetry, poets have often believed that by omitting rhyme they could make their own works more closely resemble folklore—thus Pushkin's "Tale of the Fisherman and the Fish" ("Skazka o rybake i rybke"), Lermontov's "Song of the Merchant Kalashnikov" ("Pesnia pro . . . kuptsa Kalashni-kova"), Nekrasov's *Who Can Live Well in Russia?* (*Komu na Rusi zhit' khorosho*), and many of Koltsov's songs are all unrhymed. Similarly, imitations or direct translations of foreign folk verse are frequently un-rhymed—for example, the majority of Pushkin's "Songs of the Western Slavs" ("Pesni zapadnykh slavian") as well as Akhmatova's precise translations of the Serbo-Croatian *deseterac* (a ten-syllable line with a caesura after the fourth syllable).[77] The unrhymed clausula is often dac-tylic, as in much folk poetry, while the meters tend to be trochaic or strict accentual verse, again in imitation of folk models. Typical is this excerpt written in trochaic tetrameter with unrhymed dactylic clausula from Karamzin's "Ilia Muromets":

Ви́тязь Ге́снера не чи́тывал,
но, име́я се́рдце не́жное,
любова́лся красото́ю дня;
ти́хим ша́гом е́хал по́ лугу
и в душе́ свое́й чувстви́тельной
же́ртву у́треннюю, чи́стую,
приноси́л царю́ небе́сному.

1794

(3) The most important use of blank verse has been in poems em-ploying the unrhymed iambic pentameter. The form was prominent in the work of Shakespeare, Milton, and many other English poets; from the second half of the eighteenth century the form has been equally im-portant in German poetry. Particularly influential on Russian poets was its use in verse dramas by both English and German writers. Thus it appears in Zhukovsky's translation of Schiller's *Die Jungfrau von Or-leans* (1817–21), while Pavel Katenin's play *The Feast of John Lackland*

(*Pir Ioanna Bezzemel'nogo*, 1820) may have been the first original dramatic work in Russian where the meter appears.[78] Pushkin's *Boris Godunov* was written in iambic pentameter with caesura, though from the late 1820s on most works in this meter, including Pushkin's own *Little Tragedies* (*Malen'kie tragedii*), lack the caesura. Throughout the nineteenth century the unrhymed iambic pentameter remained the predominant form for Russian verse drama; it was used in Aleksei K. Tolstoi's historical trilogy on Ivan the Terrible and his successors, in Ostrovsky's historical plays, and in many other works. Somewhat later, in Annensky's polymetrical verse dramas, the unrhymed iambic pentameter appeared in the majority of lines. It has also been used in many nondramatic works, for example, in Blok's cycle "Free Thoughts" ("Vol'nye mysli"). Many poets such as Arseny Tarkovsky who nearly always prefer to employ rhyme, still use this form for the occasional lyric poem:

Стол повернули к свету. Я лежал
Вниз головой, как мясо на весах,
Душа моя на нитке колотилась,
И видел я себя со стороны:
Я без довесков был уравновешен
Базарной жирной гирей.

      Это было
Посередине снежного щита,

     [< 1962]

(4) Blank verse is also found in lyric poetry that employs meters other than the iambic pentameter. The number of unrhymed works may be modest when compared to the total amount of Russian poetry or to the frequency of unrhymed verse in other traditions, but blank verse is still sufficiently common to have appeared in nearly all the meters that have been used in Russian poetry. The following examples demonstrate the range of unrhymed poetry written in Russian: the first excerpt, from a poem by Aleksandr Mezhirov, is in iambic trimeter; the second, from a work by Voloshin, in variable trochees; and the third, from the concluding half of a polymetrical poem by Slutsky, in unrhymed three-stress *dol'niki* (three stanzas) and anapestic trimeter alternating with anapestic dimeter (last stanza).

Тишайший снегопад –
Дверьми обидно хлопать.
Посередине дня
В столице как в селе.

Тишайший снегопад,
Закутавшийся в хлопья,
В обувке пуховой
Проходит по земле.

[< 1976]

Лихорадка с зыбкими руками,
Лихорадка в буйный свой поток меня
Увлекает и несёт, как камень, по дорогам.
Разум меркнет,
Сердце рвётся к славе или преступленью,
И на дикий зов единокупной силы
Я бегу из самого себя.

1917

Научился и чай и сахар
на свои покупать на кровные,
и без чаевых обходиться.

А когда не умел заработать
ни на чай, ни на сахар,
я без чаю сидел и без сахару,
но не брал чаевые.

[< 1977]

INTRODUCTION TO STANZAIC FORMS

A stanza is a cluster of lines that serves as a structural segment in a poem. The same pattern of rhyme (or clausulae) and meter is usually repeated in each stanza of a given work, though on occasion different types of stanzas are combined in the same poem. The borders between stanzas are indicated both graphically, by extra spacing, and rhythmically, by clear breaks in both syntax and intonation. Enjambment between stanzas may occur, though it is relatively uncommon and is an especially strong disruption in the poem's intonational and syntactic organization.

Four main characteristics describe a given stanza: the number of lines, the order of the rhyme, the kinds of clausula (masculine, feminine, dactylic), and the meter (or meters). The third feature is important in Russian, where poems written with a single kind of clausula are more the exception than the rule. It is much less so in, say, English, where most rhymes are masculine and variations in the clausula are less likely to be carefully regulated throughout a work. The number of lines may vary from two on up. Attempts have been made to define an upper limit for the length of stanzas, but it is difficult to decide where the theoretical maximum lies.[79] In practice, most stanzas in modern poems are from two to eight lines in length, with the quatrain—the four-line stanza—by far the favorite among Russian poets. Stanzas exceeding the length of a sonnet (fourteen lines) are rare. Rhymes may be alternating, adjacent, or enclosed; in stanzas with more than four lines some combination or multiple of these types must obviously occur—for instance, a six-line stanza of *AbAbCC* with both alternating and adjacent rhyme. Not all the lines of a stanza have to rhyme; the pattern *xaxa* occurs often in both Russian and English quatrains. Furthermore, even unrhymed poems sometimes maintain a clear division into stanzas. In most stanzas the same meter occurs in every line, but regularly alternating line lengths (such as iambic tetrameter and iambic trimeter) are fairly common. In such schemes the shorter line, which provides a stopping point in the rhythmic movement of the stanza, usually follows the longer line. As noted at the beginning of chapter 2, such alternations may be quite complex, involving three or more different types of lines, as long as the same pattern is repeated from stanza to stanza.

From the early days of Russian syllabo-tonic poetry until well into the nineteenth century, alternating feminine and masculine rhyme predominated. For a time Russian poets also adhered to the French rules of alternance: if two neighboring lines had the same clausula (masculine or feminine) they had to rhyme with each other; also, any lines appearing between two rhymed lines had to employ the same rhyme. Thus *aBaB*, *abba*, and *abbba* were proper sequences, but not *abcabc*, where two different rhymes appear between each of the rhyme pairs. The rules had already loosened by the time of Pushkin, who generally observed the first rule within stanzas but not at their borders. Poems written entirely with, for instance, alternating masculine rhymes began to appear during this period as well, thus ignoring the first rule entirely. Along with a general lessening of interest in stanzaic forms, these French rules lost importance over the first half of the nineteenth century.[80]

The effect of stanzaic structure on the semantic, rhythmic, and sound structure of a poem is often evident, though few systematic studies of this topic have been conducted. The end of the stanza, with its natural tendency to create a break in the syntax and the intonation, is often marked by the use of adjacent rhyme, the appearance of a summarizing phrase, or the shortening of the final line.[81] The beginning of a stanza may be similarly emphasized, while the use of framing techniques or repetitions can strengthen the inner coherence of the stanza and play a role in the work's general structure.[82] Also, the rhythmic impulse may vary from line to line within the stanza; relatively little poetry has been studied from this viewpoint, but it has been shown that at least in some instances stressing is lighter toward the end of the stanza than at the beginning.[83] Other research has shown that adjacent rhyme pairs in a given stanza are likely to resemble each other more than alternating pairs.[84]

In general, however, research on stanzaic forms in Russian has been late getting started. While the basic classification scheme for stanzaic forms goes back to Tomashevsky's extensive analysis of Pushkin's stanzaic forms (published posthumously in 1958), few careful investigations had been conducted on the works of other poets until the publication of metrical handbooks for nineteenth-century poets.[85] Meanwhile, even the attempt to describe stanzaic forms involves several problems that have yet to be satisfactorily resolved. One difficulty occurs when a poem is heterostanzaic, that is, when the stanzas in a poem vary according to the number of lines, rhyme scheme, or some other characteristic. A scheme for describing heterostanzaic poems of one poet may be unnecessarily detailed (or not detailed enough) when applied to the works of another.[86] Second, it is not easy to decide whether certain short poems that are not divided graphically should be regarded as stanzaic or nonstanzaic. Tomashevsky set an arbitrary dividing point at eight lines: undivided poems of that length or less are called single-stanza poems, while longer works—except for some traditional forms like the sonnet—are called nonstanzaic.[87] But there are longer poems that maintain a regular pattern throughout (for instance, alternating *abab* rhyme), and only the graphic divisions on the page keep them from qualifying as regular quatrains. What to do in all these cases? As Tomashevsky recognized, no firm boundary exists between stanzaic and nonstanzaic poetry; still, it seems more consistent to treat all poems without graphic divisions between stanzas as nonstanzaic and to ignore Tomashevsky's category of single-stanza poems. Third, nonstanzaic poetry deserves special attention. In most cases it tends to group lines in certain ways through rhyming and can be, even if somewhat loosely, categorized according to those patterns.

Still, Tomashevsky's classification, if modified slightly, remains useful. The main categories are stanzaic poems (from two-line stanzas on up, with all stanzas in the poem identical), heterostanzaic poems, nonstanzaic poems, and unrhymed poetry. Subcategories describe length, clausula, rhyme scheme, and meter. Thus within four-line stanzas each rhyme scheme and clausula pattern is listed separately. Not only are *AbbA* stanzas distinguished from *AbAb*, but *AbAb* are distinguished from *aBaB*. Furthermore, *aBaB* stanzas in iambic tetrameter are grouped apart from *aBaB* stanzas in, say, iambic pentameter. Certain traditional forms such as terza rima and sonnets are usually distinguished from other types of stanzas that contain the same number of lines.[88]

HISTORY

The history of Russian stanzaic forms differs sharply from the changes that took place in meter and rhyme. While new kinds of meter and rhyme developed and became widespread during the twentieth century, stanzaic forms are now less varied than they were in the eighteenth century. But this case is not one of a simple inverse relationship—a greater variety in meter and rhyme being compensated for by simpler stanzaic forms. Rather, the turn away from wide experimentation with types of stanzas occurred during the first half of the nineteenth century, when *dol'niki* and modern rhyme were still largely unknown. A few changes within the classical syllabo-tonic system occurred at that time: previously rare meters such as the trochaic pentameter came into use, and some experiments in rhyme took place. Perhaps the interest in other formal aspects of the poem partially explains the decreased attention to stanzaic variety during that one period. At the beginning of the twentieth century, along with other formal innovations, certain poets—including Viacheslav Ivanov, Kuzmin, and Voloshin—began to revive stanzaic forms that had long been neglected. However, in this one area the experiments did not take hold; despite a handful of exceptions contemporary poets rely heavily on the familiar quatrain for most of their stanzaic poetry.

Throughout the late eighteenth and early nineteenth centuries Russian poets experimented widely with the so-called traditional forms, some of which are quite complex in their formal requirements.[89] In many instances stanzaic forms were closely related to the genre of a particular poem. Thus odes were normally written in a particular ten-line stanza and ballads in an eight-line stanza. Poets writing long works often carefully selected a stanza; sometimes they would invent a new form for their poem (the outstanding example being Pushkin's Onegin stanza), while other times they would adopt a form found in a similar type of work.[90] When all the various subcategories are considered, nearly seven hundred kinds of stanzas were employed during the eighteenth and early nineteenth centuries.[91] Of these, more than 66 percent were used just once, and the ten that occurred most often account for more than 50 percent of the stanzaic poems from this period. During the first half of the nineteenth century both the interest in traditional forms (except perhaps for the sonnet) and the connection of genres with particular stanzaic forms gradually faded. Quatrains, already the most common stanza length in the eighteenth century, became still more predominant. In the eighteenth century 40 percent of all poems were written in quatrains; in Lermontov's work the figure attained 60 percent; in Nekrasov's it passed 75 percent.[92] The picture changed only briefly around the turn of the century. Besides the traditional forms that occurred in the works of Viacheslav Ivanov and others, innovative linked stanzas (where the two lines of a given rhyme set appear in different stanzas) can be found among the works of Briusov, Balmont, and Blok. A typical, if complex, pattern is *abac bdbc dedf*—the last lines of paired stanzas rhyme while the second line of each stanza rhymes with the first and third lines of the next.[93] The poets' successors, however, while taking innovations in metrics and rhyme even further, showed little inclination to pursue work on stanzaic forms. Surveys of twentieth-century poetry have found that nearly 90 percent of the stanzaic poems simply employed quatrains.[94] Although quatrains can be divided into numerous subcategories according to the meter and rhyme scheme, the figures indicate that recent poets have tended to experiment in areas other than the stanzaic configuration of their poetry. Among contemporary authors, Joseph Brodsky stands out as one of the few who has cultivated a wide range of stanzaic forms, devoting as much attention to this aspect of his poetry as to its other formal features.

TRADITIONAL FORMS

Stanzas written in traditional forms all have strictly defined patterns and are often referred to as "fixed" forms (*tverdye formy*). Many are sufficiently complex to require a poetic tour de force, and in any case only a few of the less restrictive fixed forms have been used regularly since the eighteenth century. Traditional forms are very important in certain literatures. The seventeen-syllable haiku, with its lines of five, seven, and five syllables, has played a significant role in the history of

Japanese poetry. The ruba'i, well known throughout the world thanks to *The Rubáiyát of Omar Khayyám*, is found in the poetry of the Near and Middle East; it is a quatrain that usually rhymes *aaxa*, more rarely *aaaa*. The ghazal, another Eastern form, generally consists of five to twelve couplets; the two lines in the first couplet rhyme, and they in turn rhyme with the second line in the remaining couplets, so the scheme is *aa xa xa xa*. Translations of both the ruba'i and ghazal—and for that matter of other Eastern forms—are not uncommon in Russian poetry.[95] Original poetry employing these stanzas is much rarer, though the ghazal enjoyed some popularity at the beginning of the twentieth century. Kuzmin, for instance, composed a large series of ghazals that appeared in his second book of verse *Autumn Lakes* (*Osennie ozera*), and they were also employed by Viacheslav Ivanov and Briusov. Certain forms such as the Sapphic and Alcaic stanzas were borrowed from ancient Greek and Latin poetry. These stanzas also have a strict rhythmic form that places them in the category of logaoedic verse. They appeared in Russian poetry during the eighteenth and early nineteenth centuries; a few instances of their use can be found in work from the beginning of the twentieth century as well.

Some complicated forms adopted from French poetry likewise occur in eighteenth-century works with some frequency, but only sporadically in later poetry.[96] The most common is the triolet, which enjoyed a brief revival during the 1910s, owing in part to Fedor Sologub whose 178 triolets make up the greater portion of his *Earthly Charms* (*Ocharovaniia zemli*), volume 17 of his collected works:

Де́нь то́лько к ве́черу хоро́ш,	a
Жи́знь те́м ясне́й, чем бли́же к сме́рти.	B
Зако́ну му́дрому пове́рьте –	B
Де́нь то́лько к ве́черу хоро́ш.	a
С утра́ уны́ние и ло́жь	a
И копоша́щиеся че́рти.	B
Де́нь то́лько к ве́черу хоро́ш,	a
Жи́знь те́м ясне́й, чем бли́же к сме́рти.	B

1913

The usual form of the triolet is *abaaabab*; just two rhymes occur, and all the underlined *a*s consist of the same line, as do the underlined *b*s.[97] Sologub preferred to make the third line into a *b* rhyme instead of an *a*, but otherwise he adhered closely to the norms for the triolet. He and others who composed triolets tended to use relatively short lines, in particular the iambic tetrameter, though longer lines appeared as well. So-

logub did not always repeat the exact first and second lines later in the
stanza, but at the very least the rhyme word in the first, fourth, and sev-
enth lines is always the same, as it is in the second and eighth. The key
to writing successful triolets is making the repeated lines sound natural,
causing them to contribute to the development of the poem. Those in-
stances where Sologub allowed variations in the normally repeated lines
may have resulted from his perception that the lines were not succeeding
in this function.

The triolet is in fact a simpler variant of other two-rhyme stanzaic
forms such as the rondel and the rondeau.[98] The rondel contains thirteen
or fourteen lines in the pattern *abba abab abbaa* (*b*); again, the under-
lined letters indicate repetitions of entire lines. The rondeau comes in
several versions; most frequently it had fifteen lines, of which the ninth
and fifteenth were a refrain (*r*) formed from the first half of the first line.
The three stanzas of a rondeau poem would normally follow the pattern
aabba aabr aabbar. Several poets of the early twentieth century wrote
stylizations of these forms, which otherwise were found only in the
eighteenth and first half of the nineteenth centuries, as in this example
of a rondeau by Katenin:

Фанта́зия, злато́е сновиде́нье,	A
Усла́да чу́вств, рассу́дка обольще́нье,	A
Цве́т, ра́дуга, бле́ск, ро́скошь бытия́,	b
Легка́, как пу́х, светла́, как то́к ручья́,	b
И Ди́ево люби́мое рожде́нье.	A
Но во́т лежи́т тяжёлое творе́нье,	A
Без ри́фм и сто́п, нескла́дных стро́к сплете́нье	A
И названа́ в стиха́х галиматья́:	b
Фанта́зия.	r
С чего́ баро́н, нам издаю́щий чте́нье,	A
Хвали́л её? что ту́т? своя́ семья́?	b
Зло́й у́мысел? насме́шка? заблужде́нье?	A
Вопро́с мудрён, а про́сто разреше́нье:	A
У вся́кого баро́на е́сть своя́	b
Фанта́зия.	r

1836

Writing when this form had already fallen out of use, Katenin took a
few liberties with the structure. He moved what would normally be the
last line of the first stanza into the second stanza, and he made the
rhyme scheme of lines 11 through 14 (*bAAb*) the inverse of the expected
AbbA. The iambic pentameter with caesura, used here, was the favored

meter for Russian versions of the rondeau. The refrain word, *fantaziia*, was probably meant to be pronounced with a secondary stress on the last syllable in order to echo the *b* rhyme.

Even more complex was the sestina—six six-line stanzas, followed by a three-line conclusion, or envoi. The six end words of the first stanza were used again in each subsequent stanza according to a fixed formula (usually 6-1-5-2-4-3). In the final three-line stanza the six words were repeated in their original order, with one of the words appearing in the middle and at the end of each line. Note that this is normally an unrhymed stanzaic form, though occasionally poets have written rhymed sestinas. Thus Lev Mei's 1851 "Sekstina" employs a set of three masculine rhymes and another set of three feminine rhymes so despite all the scrambling the lines continue to rhyme. A more traditional approach is found in the first three stanzas of another "Sestina" by Viacheslav Ivanov; note that each stanza repeats the end words of the previous stanza according to the formula 6-1-5-2-4-3:

1

У зы́блемых набáтом Океáна
Утёсов, самоцве́тные пеще́ры
Тая́щих за гряда́ми ко́см пурпу́рных, –
Мы́ сму́глых до́лов разлюби́ли лáвры,
Следя́ вало́в по гу́лкой ме́ли ру́ны,
И го́рьких у́ст нам разверзáлись ги́мны.

2

Как благове́ст, пылáли в ду́хе ги́мны
Отзы́вных у́з набáтам Океáна,
Обе́тные в пескáх зыбу́чих ру́ны;
И влáжные внимáли нам пеще́ры,
И ве́щее чело́ венчáли лáвры,
По тёрнам Вáкх горе́л в плющáх пурпу́рных.

3

Но трáуром пови́ты трáв пурпу́рных,
Крести́лись вы́ в купе́лях го́рьких, ги́мны!
И на челе́ не со́лнечные лáвры –
Сплетáлся тёрн с обры́вов Океáна,
Что заливáет жáдные пеще́ры
И тёмные с песко́в смывáет ру́ны.

[< 1910]

All the stanzaic forms discussed so far are best regarded as literary curiosities; since the early nineteenth century they have been found only in the occasional stylization. Four other traditional forms have, however, had a continuing influence on Russian poetry. Three derive from foreign models while the fourth—the Onegin stanza—became an instantaneous "traditional" form when it appeared in Pushkin's verse novel.

TERZA RIMA

Terza rima (*tertsiny*) achieved renown in Dante's *Divine Comedy* and has been used regularly ever since in many European literatures. The rhyme scheme is *aba bcb cdc . . . yzy z*. The middle line of each stanza rhymes with the first and third lines of the next; the final single line of the poem rhymes with the middle line of the last stanza. Italian poets employed an eleven-syllable line for the terza rima; in Russia the usual meters have been the iambic hexameter and, as illustrated here in the final stanzas of a poem by Balmont, the iambic pentameter:

> Последний стон. Дороги нет назад.
> Кругом, везде, густеют властно тени.
> Но тучи торжествующе горят.
>
> Горят огнём переддремотной лени
> И, завладев всем царством высоты,
> Роняют свет на дольние ступени.
>
> Я вас люблю, предсмертные цветы!
>   [1900]

While the terza rima has appeared occasionally in Russian poetry since the 1820s and 1830s, it is most often found in conscious stylizations or in translations either from Dante or from other writers who employed the form.

OTTAVA RIMA

Like terza rima the ottava rima (*oktava*) is Italian in origin. It apparently developed as a folk verse form, becoming a popular literary meter after it was used by Boccaccio in his fourteenth-century works *Teseida* and *Filostrato*. It too is found in various European poetic traditions; Byron's use of it in *Beppo* and *Don Juan* inspired Pushkin to adopt it for *Little House in Kolomna* (*Domik v Kolomne*). Ottava rima consists of a threefold alternation of one rhyme pair followed by a concluding couplet: *abababcc*. In Russian practice the stanza generally alternates

masculine and feminine rhymes and is written in iambic pentameter or
hexameter. Pushkin's octaves alternated stanzas in *AbAbAbCC* and
aBaBaBcc, thus adhering to the French requirement of alternance even
at the borders of stanzas. The same pattern is found in Pushkin's "Au-
tumn" ("Osen'") written in iambic hexameter, and his examples strongly
influenced subsequent Russian poems in this form.[99] Many poets in-
cluding Aleksei K. Tolstoi, Sologub, and Briusov have used ottava
rima. Below are the opening stanzas of Fet's "The Dream" ("Son"):

1

Мне не спалось. Томителен и жгуч	a
Был тёмный воздух, словно в устьях печки.	B
Но всё я думал: сколько хочешь мучь,	a
Бессонница, а не зажгу я свечки.	B
Из ставень в стену падал лунный луч,	a
В резные прорываяся сердечки	B
И шевелясь, как будто ожило	c
На люстре всё трехгранное стекло,	c

2

Вся зала. В зале мне пришлось с походу	A
Спать в качестве служащего лица.	b
Любя в домашних комнатах свободу,	A
Хозяин в них не допускал жильца,	b
И, указав мне залу по отводу,	A
Просил ходить с парадного крыльца.	b
Я очень рад был этой благодати	C
И поместился на складной кровати.	C

[1856]

SONNET

The sonnet also originated in Italy, appearing as far back as the thir-
teenth century, and was popularized in the poetry of both Dante and
Petrarch. It too became widely used throughout Europe, becoming an
especially significant mode in English poetry; Shakespeare, Donne,
Milton, Wordsworth, and Keats are some of the poets for whom it was a
favorite form. In Russia the sonnet has been by far the most prevalent
traditional form. It is found in the works of Trediakovsky and Sumaro-
kov, remained common throughout the nineteenth century, was used ex-
tensively by several poets at the beginning of the twentieth (Viacheslav
Ivanov, Voloshin, Igor Severianin), and is seen in works written up to
the present day.

As could be expected the form developed a number of variations, both from one literature to the next and within given traditions. The sonnet contains fourteen lines, most often divided into an octave and a sextet. In the Italian version, often called the Petrarchan sonnet, the rhyme scheme is *abbaabba cdecde*. The sextet may also rhyme *ccdeed* or according to another pattern that avoids a final rhymed couplet. The more common form in English, which has difficulty sustaining the large rhyme sets required by the Petrarchan octave, is *abab cdcd efef gg*: in other words, it breaks down into three quatrains followed by a concluding couplet. The Italian sonnets were usually written in an eleven-syllable line, the English in iambic pentameter, and the Russian in iambic hexameter or, more commonly after the eighteenth century, pentameter. Russian poets have employed numerous rhyme schemes. Frequently they adhere to the Petrarchan model, as in this poem by Igor Severianin:

Рассказчику обыденных историй	A
Суждён в удел оригинальный дар,	b
Вручённый одному из русских бар,	b
Кто взял свой кабинет с собою в море...	A
Размеренная жизнь – иному горе,	A
Но не тому, кому претит угар,	b
Кто, сидя у стола, был духом яр,	b
Обрыв страстей в чьём отграничен взоре...	A
Сам, как Обломов, не любя шагов,	c
Качаясь у японских берегов,	c
Он встретил жизнь совсем иного склада,	D
Отличную от родственных громад,	e
Игрушечную жизнь, чей аромат	e
Впитал в свои борта фрегат "Паллада".	D

1926

The pure English form is largely reserved by Russian poets for translations, as in Samuil Marshak's well-known versions of Shakespeare's sonnets. Not infrequently Russian poets have experimented with original rhyme schemes. In the following work, part of a sonnet cycle, Novella Matveeva followed the Petrarchan sonnet in maintaining the original rhyme pair over the first eight lines, but her rhyme scheme more nearly resembles the English sonnet.

Мы только женщины – и, так сказать, "увы!".	a
А почему "увы"? Пора задеть причины.	B
"Вино и женщины" – так говорите вы,	a
Но мы не говорим: "Конфеты и мужчины".	B

Мы отличаем вас от булки, от халвы,   a
Мы как-то чувствуем, что люди – не ветчины,   B
Хотя, послушать вас, лишь тем и отличимы,   B
Что сроду на плечах не носим головы.   a

"Вино и женщины"? – Последуем отсель!   c
О женщина, возьми поваренную книжку,   D
Скажи: "Люблю тебя, как ягодный кисель,   c
Как рыбью голову! Как заячью лодыжку!"   D

По сердцу ли тебе привязанность моя?   E
Ты не пирог? Не сыр? Ты – человек? А я?   E

1965

The use of sonnets in cycles is not rare, although unlike terza rima or ottava rima the sonnet form is most often used singly to create a given poem. More closely linked than most poetic cycles is the so-called crown of sonnets, usually consisting of seven sonnet stanzas. The first line of each sonnet repeats the last line of its predecessor, and the last line of the final sonnet repeats the first line of the sonnet that begins the sequence. A complex variant of the crown was used by several Russian poets early in the twentieth century. It contains fifteen sonnets and follows the pattern of the shorter crown, with the last line of the fourteenth repeating the first line of the poem. The fifteenth stanza, called the *magistral'*, repeats the first lines of the previous fourteen sonnets in order. Many poets, including Viacheslav Ivanov, Balmont, Briusov, Voloshin, and Ilia Selvinsky, have written such "crowns" in Russian. Evidence of the form's popularity was the appearance of entire volumes by individual poets containing only sonnets: Konstantin Balmont's *Sonnets of the Sun, Honey, and Moon* (*Sonety solntsa, meda, i luny*, 1917) with more than 250 sonnets or, a more recent example, Valery Pereleshin's *Ariel* (1976) with about 170 sonnets composed between 1971 and 1975. Each volume includes one crown. Furthermore, not long ago two large collections of Russian sonnets appeared in a single year.[100]

ONEGIN STANZA

Because the Onegin stanza is a native Russian form and lacks the long history and foreign origin of other traditional stanzas, classifying it as a traditional form might be debatable. Still, once the Onegin stanza was introduced it was used by other poets throughout the nineteenth century and since has continued to appear in various imitations and par-

odies. Like the sonnet the Onegin stanza contains fourteen lines, but the
rhyme scheme is unique: *AbAb CCdd EffE gg*. Furthermore, it employs
iambic tetrameter rather than the longer lines typical of the sonnet.

Прошла́ любо́вь, яви́лась Му́за,	A
И прояснился тёмный у́м.	b
Свобо́ден, вно́вь ищу́ сою́за	A
Волше́бных зву́ков, чу́вств и ду́м;	b
Пишу́, и се́рдце не тоску́ет;	C
Перо́, забы́вшись, не рису́ет	C
Близ неоко́нченных стихо́в	d
Ни же́нских но́жек, ни голо́в;	d
Пога́сший пе́пел уж не вспы́хнет,	E
Я всё грущу́; но слёз уж не́т,	f
И ско́ро, ско́ро бу́ри сле́д	f
В душе́ мое́й совсе́м ути́хнет:	E
Тогда́-то я́ начну́ писа́ть	g
Поэ́му пе́сен в два́дцать пя́ть.	g

1823

The differences between Pushkin's stanza and the Petrarchan sonnet are
self-evident. The Onegin stanza more closely resembles the Shake-
spearian sonnet, especially in its use of seven rhyme sets and a conclud-
ing couplet. However, rather than rely on alternating rhyme throughout,
Pushkin resorted to all three possible types of rhyme in a quatrain: alter-
nating, adjacent, and enclosed.

The stanza suited Pushkin's needs extremely well. On the one hand,
like any stanza, it offers a fixed structure that imparts a sense of regu-
larity and unity to a longer work. On the other, its rhyme pattern and
length help avoid monotony. The rhymes change from quatrain to qua-
train, and by varying the syntactic breaks and other structural features
Pushkin was able to make the stanzas sound different from each other.
Most often a strong break occurs after the fourth line, thus the first
quatrain tends to form a separate unit. As in the above example, the
syntax sometimes helps set off the concluding couplet, which may pro-
vide a pointed or witty summary to the stanza. Frequently the breaks
create different groupings such as 4-4-3-3. Thus, while both the rhyme
scheme and the size of the stanza are fixed, the inner make-up is flex-
ible. The length also enabled Pushkin to make each stanza into a the-
matic whole. Often a general topic continues for several stanzas or
more, but even in these instances the particular item treated within a
given stanza usually forms a self-contained unit. Enjambment between

stanzas is rare: there are only about ten in the entire novel, and these are perceived as particularly sharp interruptions in the rhythm. The closing couplet, with its adjacent masculine rhymes, provides a strong sense of closure and helps underline the independence of each stanza.[101]

The Onegin stanza was invented by Pushkin expressly for his novel. He may have been inspired to write a long stanzaic poem by Byron, whose *Childe Harold's Pilgrimage* greatly influenced Pushkin around the time he began *Eugene Onegin*. But Byron's work contained the nine-line Spenserian stanza (*ababbcbcc*), which apparently did not interest Pushkin.[102] The sonnet no doubt provided Pushkin with the idea for a fourteen-line unit, yet the particular rhyme scheme he used has been found by scholars in earlier works only as seemingly chance occurrences in the midst of long poems. (For instance, it is in Byron's *The Bride of Abydos* and even in one fourteen-line segment of Pushkin's *Ruslan and Liudmila*.)[103] There is no specific model for the Onegin stanza.

After *Eugene Onegin* Pushkin experimented with the stanza in "The Genealogy of My Hero" ("Rodoslovnaia moego geroia"), an eight-stanza fragment from the uncompleted narrative poem *Ezerskii*. Lermontov used the form in a couple of lyric poems and also in several of his longer works, most notably *The Tambov Treasurer's Wife* (*Tambovskaia kaznacheisha*).[104] Other nineteenth-century poets used the form less often, though Iazykov's "Linden Trees" ("Lipy") is of interest because its Onegin stanzas employ the iambic pentameter.[105] Later poets preferred the original iambic tetrameter, which appears in Viacheslav Ivanov's "Infancy" ("Mladenchestvo") and in Voloshin's "Fragments from Epistles" ("Otryvki iz poslanii"). As with terza rima, the form is readily recognizable to all readers of poetry; perhaps for this reason poets usually acknowledge their source, either directly at the beginning of the poem or indirectly through references to Pushkin.

THE MAIN STANZAIC FORMS

In this section each of the more common stanza lengths, from two lines to eight, is treated separately. While the quatrain is by far the most common stanzaic form used in Russian poetry, others with even numbers of lines have also been popular. Those with odd numbers of lines have achieved less favor: only the three- and five-line forms are found at all regularly. Stanzas longer than eight lines occur much more rarely in

the twentieth century than they did in the late eighteenth and early nine-
teenth centuries; they are therefore examined as a group.

COUPLETS

Two lines is the minimum requirement for a stanza; units of this size
are basically limited to adjacent rhyme, as in this excerpt from a poem
by Georgy Ivanov:

Наконец-то повеяла мне золотая свобода,	A
Воздух полный осеннего солнца и ветра и мёда.	A
Шелестят вековые деревья пустынного сада,	B
И звенят колокольчики мимо идущего стада	B
И молочный туман проползает по низкой долине...	C
Этот вечер однажды уже пламенел в Палестине.	C

1920

A danger for any poem written in a long series of couplets is monotony.
The simplicity of the rhyme scheme does not seem adequate to sustain
a work with more than a few stanzas, though couplets have been used
effectively in lyrics up to twenty or thirty lines in length. Sometimes
couplets are hard to distinguish from other forms. Consider Belyi's "Au-
tumn" ("Osen' "):

Мои пальцы из рук твоих выпали.	A′
Ты уходишь – нахмурила брови.	B
Посмотри, как берёзки рассыпали	A′
Листья красные дождиком крови.	B
Осень бледная, осень холодная,	C′
Распростёртая в высях над нами.	D
С горизонтов равнина бесплодная	C′
Дышит в ясную твердь облаками.	D

1906

Here and at other times Belyi created linked couplets by using alternat-
ing rhyme. If the poem lacked graphic divisions after the first and third
couplets, it would be natural to see it as consisting of two quatrains. In
doubtful instances it is nearly always wise to accept the intentions of the
poet. The graphic divisions in this case are supported by the strong syn-
tactic break at the end of each couplet; therefore the organizing units of

the poem seem to be two-line stanzas, despite the interlocking rhyme
scheme.

TERCETS

Three-line stanzas are generally linked through the rhyme pattern,
much as in the terza rima. Unlike that traditional form, however, other
three-line stanzas are usually linked only in pairs. Note the opening
stanzas of this poem by Briusov:

На берегу́ Мерца́ющих Озёр	a
Есть вы́ступы. Оди́н зову́т Прокля́тым.	B
Та́м смо́трит из воды́ уны́лый взо́р.	a
Зде́сь вхо́дит в во́лны у́зкая коса́;	c
Пройди́ по не́й до кра́я пред зака́том,	B
И ты́ уви́дишь стра́нные глаза́.	c
И́х цве́т зелёный, но светле́й воды́,	d
И́х выраже́нье – сме́сь тоски́ и стра́ха;	E
Они́ гляди́т весь ве́чер до звезды́	d
И, исчеза́я, вспы́хивают вдру́г	f
Бесцве́тным бле́ском, как проста́я бля́ха.	E
Темне́ют во́ды; ту́скло всё вокру́г.	f

                                       1898

The other possibility is to continue the same rhyme throughout each
stanza. Thus the poem employs a series of triple adjacent rhymes, as in
this work by Balmont:

Как стра́шно-ра́достный и бли́зкий мне́ приме́р,	a
Ты́ всё мне чу́дишься, о ца́рственный Бодле́р,	a
Любо́вник у́жасов, обры́вов и химе́р!	a
Ты́, па́вший в про́пасти, но жа́ждавший верши́н,	b
Ты́, ви́девший лазу́рь сквозь тя́жкий жёлтый спли́н,	b
Ты́, ме́жду ва́рваров зало́жник-властели́н!	b

                                       1899

QUATRAINS

Owing to their popularity, quatrains have been written with virtually
every type of meter and clausula combination. Still, only three possible
rhyme combinations exist:

Я завещаю вам шиповник,   A
Весь полный света, как фонарь,   b
Июньских бабочек письмовник,   A
Задворков праздничный словарь.   b

[< 1966]

Я не хочу ни власти над людьми,   a
Ни почестей, ни войн победоносных.   B
Пусть я застыну, как смола на соснах,   B
Но я не царь, я из другой семьи.   a

[< 1962]

Мы звёзды меняем на птичьи кларнеты   A
И флейты, пока ещё живы поэты,   A
И флейты – на синие щётки цветов,   b
Трещотки стрекоз и кнуты пастухов.   b

[< 1966]

The first of these excerpts from poems by Arseny Tarkovsky represents
the most typical of all Russian stanzas: an iambic tetrameter quatrain
with alternating *AbAb* rhyme. The inverse type of alternating rhyme,
aBaB, is also quite common, though the favored stanzaic forms for
quatrains and for stanzas of other lengths are generally those that end
with the shorter rhyme. Thus *A'BA'B* is also found more often than
AB'AB'. The second example, written in iambic pentameter, illustrates
another popular rhyme scheme, though enclosed rhymes are not em-
ployed as often as alternating ones. The two-line interval between the *a*
rhyme is more difficult to sustain and is perceived as less natural than
alternating rhyme. The third quotation is written with adjacent rhyme.
As with couplets, much depends on the graphic division between stan-
zas; theoretically, little distinguishes a quatrain in adjacent rhyme from
a pair of couplets. Usually, however, poets who place adjacent rhymes in
quatrains will avoid consistently strong syntactic breaks between the
second and third lines.

FIVE-LINE STANZAS

While much rarer than quatrains, five-line stanzas have been em-
ployed on occasion by most Russian poets. The most common forms are
AbAAb (*aBaaB*) and *AbbAb* (*aBBaB*). The following examples are by
Boris Poplavsky and Anna Akhmatova, respectively:

Розовеющий призрак зари   a
Возникал над высоким строеньем.   B

Га́сли в мо́кром саду́ фонари́,   a
Я моли́лся любви́... Озари́!   a
Безмяте́жным свои́м озаре́ньем.   B

По горба́тому мо́сту во тьме́   a
Проходи́ли высо́кие лю́ди.   B
И вдого́нку уше́дшей весне́,   a
Безвозме́здно лете́л на коне́   a
Жёсткий сви́ст соловьи́ных прелю́дий.   B

1927

Проро́чишь, го́рькая, и ру́ки урони́ла,   A
Прили́пла пря́дь воло́с к бескро́вному челу́,   b
И улыба́ешься – о́, не одну́ пчелу́   b
Румя́ная улы́бка соблазни́ла   A
И ба́бочку смути́ла не одну́.   b

Как лу́нные глаза́ светлы́, и напряжённо   A
Далёко ви́дящий останови́лся взо́р.   b
То мёртвому ли сла́достный уко́р,   b
Или живы́м проща́ешь благоскло́нно   A
Твоё изнеможе́нье и позо́р?   b

1921

Note that the most popular rhyme schemes are asymmetrical; both begin
with an alternation but then avoid either a regular alternation (of the
type *ababa*) or an enclosed triple rhyme (*abbba*). Both also end with an
alternation; a concluding adjacent rhyme would tend to single out the
final couplet. Such line pairs are common at the end of longer stanzas,
but less so in this shorter form. Of course other combinations are pos-
sible and sometimes occur. At first glance it might appear that five-line
stanzas are limited to two rhyme sets, but by linking or chaining stanzas
it is possible to use three different rhymes in each stanza. Blok, who
like his fellow symbolists paid much attention to stanzaic forms, em-
ployed this device more than once:

Всё б тебе́ жела́ть весе́лья,   A
Се́рдце, зо́лото моё!   b
От похме́лья до похме́лья,   A
От приво́лья вно́вь к приво́лью –   C
Беспеча́льное житьё!   b

Но низка́ земна́я ке́лья,   A
Бле́дно зо́лото твоё!   b
В ча́с разгу́льного весе́лья   A
Вдру́г нама́шет страстно́й бо́лью,   C
Чёрным кры́льем воронье́!   b

1908

SIX-LINE STANZAS

Six-line stanzas are more common than the five-line forms and of-
fer numerous possibilities for combining rhymes. Sometimes a stanza
will be based on just two sets of rhymes, as in this poem by Natalia
Gorbanevskaia:

В седо́й прови́нции свинцо́вый океа́н	a
коло́тится о су́мрачный бето́н.	b
Ело́вый Но́вый го́д не ле́чит ста́рых ра́н,	a
отло́жим всё, как пре́жде, на пото́м,	b
отки́нем, отшвырнём, отбро́сим, как стака́н,	a
небью́щимся не звя́кнувший стекло́м.	b

1977

More often, six-line stanzas contain three rhymes. Even without consid-
ering different placements of masculine, feminine, and dactylic rhymes
in the stanza, there are theoretically fifteen different ways in which three
rhyme sets fit into a six-line stanza. In practice the most common have
been those that either begin or end with a rhymed couplet, as in the fol-
lowing examples by Kazakova and Pleshcheev:

Росси́ю де́лает берёза.	A
Смотрю́ споко́йно и тверёзо,	A
ещё не зна́я отчего́,	b
на ле́с с лило́винкою у́тра,	C
на то́, как то́ненько и му́дро	C
берёза вре́зана в него́.	b

[between 1965 and 1969]

Была́ пора́: свои́х сыно́в	a
Отчи́зна к би́тве призыва́ла	B
С толпо́й несме́тною враго́в,	a
И ра́ть за ра́тью восстава́ла,	B
И бо́дро шла́ за ра́тью ра́ть	c
Геро́йской сме́ртью умира́ть.	c

[1858]

The first example consists of an adjacent rhyme followed by an enclosed
rhyme; in the second, the adjacent rhyme comes at the end and is pre-
ceded by an alternating rhyme. The second pattern, with its concluding
couplet (already seen in the ottava rima and the Onegin sonnet) provid-
ing a forceful ending, is perhaps the most common. As in the examples
here, couplets at the beginning of the stanza are more often than not
feminine and those at the end masculine. Kuzmin, whose verse experi-

ments did not ignore stanzaic forms, created one of the more unusual six-line stanzas:

Бере́менная Ра́я,	A
Суббо́ту пригото́вь:	b
Всё вы́мети,	C′
Всё вы́чисти,	C′
Чтоб оживи́лись вно́вь	b
Мы за́пахами ра́я.	A

1929

He used feminine, masculine, and dactylic rhymes in the one stanza, while ordering the rhymes in the second half to form a mirror image of the first.

SEVEN-LINE STANZAS

Seven-line stanzas are unusual in Russian. English poetry—which through Byron and other poets influenced the use of stanzaic forms in Russian—has long employed a seven-line stanza of the pattern *abab-bcc*; indeed, the form goes back to Chaucer, who used it in *Troilus and Criseyde* as well as in several other works. This particular form, however, did not find favor in Russia, though Lermontov, who used a wide range of stanzaic forms throughout his career, created a seven-line stanza for his famous poem "Borodino": *AAbCCCb*. Over a century later Pavel Antokolsky borrowed the stanza for a quite different poem:

Ко́нчен де́нь. И в балага́не жу́тком	A
Я воспо́льзовался промежу́тком	A
Ме́жду "сто́лько све́та" и "ни зги́".	b
Ко́нчен де́нь, изображённый ре́зко,	C
По́лный ви́зга, дре́безга и тре́ска.	C
Он непро́чен, как сыра́я фре́ска,	C
От кото́рой сы́плются куски́.	b

1966

EIGHT-LINE STANZAS

Sometimes eight-line stanzas are constructed as double quatrains, with a rhyme scheme such as *ababcdcd* or *abbacddc*. The chief reason for selecting eight-line instead of four-line stanzas often seems to be thematic; the longer stanzas enable the poet to complete a single topic or idea before moving on to a new point in the next stanza. Mandelshtam occasionally used stanzas of this type, as in "Tristia":

Я изучи́л нау́ку расстава́нья   A
В простоволо́сых жа́лобах ночны́х.   b
Жую́т волы́, и дли́тся ожида́нье,   A
После́дний ча́с виги́лий городски́х;   b
И чту́ обря́д той петуши́ной но́чи,   C
Когда́, подня́в доро́жной ско́рби гру́з,   d
Гляде́ли в да́ль запла́канные о́чи   C
И же́нский пла́ч меша́лся с пе́ньем му́з.   d

1918

The ottava rima, with its alternating rhyme followed by a concluding couplet, is only one of many possible forms that break away from the quatrain pattern. Joseph Brodsky has devised an intricate eight-line stanza that consists of two triple rhymes punctuated by a third rhyme in the fourth and eighth lines. His "Speech on Spilled Milk" ("Rech' o prolitom moloke") contains this stanza with feminine rhymes throughout (*AAABCCCB*). In "1972" the rhymes are dactylic (though in some stanzas the *B* rhyme is feminine):

Пти́ца уже́ не влета́ет в фо́рточку.   A′
Деви́ца, как зве́рь, защища́ет ко́фточку.   A′
Подскользну́вшись о вишнёвую ко́сточку,   A′
я не па́даю: си́ла тре́ния   B′
возраста́ет с паде́ньем ско́рости.   C′
Се́рдце ска́чет, как бе́лка, в хво́росте   C′
рёбер. И го́рло поёт о во́зрасте.   C′
Э́то – уже́ старе́ние.   B′

1972

The eight-line stanza was the usual form of the French ballade, which became well known in the fifteenth century thanks largely to the works of François Villon. The rhyme scheme was *ababbcbc*, with the last line repeated as a refrain at the end of each stanza. The French ballade normally had three full stanzas followed by a four-line envoi; the same rhymes were used from stanza to stanza. Eighteenth-century Russian poets expressed some interest in this form as they did in so many other foreign models.[106] A more modern instance is this opening of a five-stanza ballade by Pasternak. He reversed the usual order for the *c* and *b* rhymes in the second half of each stanza, but he maintained the same rhymes throughout the five stanzas and used a refrain:

Дрожа́т гаражи́ автоба́зы,   A
Нет-не́т, как ко́сть, взблеснёт костёл.   b
Над па́рком па́дают топа́зы,   A
Слепы́х зарни́ц бурли́т котёл.   b
В саду́ – таба́к, на тротуа́ре –   C

Толпа́, в толпе́ – гуде́нье пчёл.   b
Разры́вы ту́ч, обры́вки а́рий,   C
Недви́жный Дне́пр, ночно́й Подо́л.   b

"Пришёл", – лети́т от вя́за к вя́зу,   A
И вдру́г стано́вится тяжёл   b
Как бы дости́гший вы́сшей фа́зы   A
Бессо́нный за́пах матио́л.   b
"Пришёл", – лети́т от па́ры к па́ре,   C
"Пришёл", – стволу́ лепе́чет ствол.   b
Пото́п зарни́ц, гроза́ в разга́ре,   C
Недви́жный Дне́пр, ночно́й Подо́л.   b

                                   1930

LONG STANZAS

As with most of the less usual stanzaic forms, the longer stanzas
were in use during the late eighteenth and early nineteenth centuries,
were revived to some extent around the beginning of the twentieth, and
have become relatively uncommon in contemporary poetry. Nine-line
stanzas, like the seven-line, never became popular in Russia, though
they too were found in a well-known English variant, the Spenserian
stanza. The rhyme scheme of *ababbcbcc* was the French ballade stanza
with an extra line added to create a concluding couplet.[107] This is also
the stanza of Byron's *Childe Harold's Pilgrimage*. But Pushkin rejected
this model for *Eugene Onegin*, while Lermontov's "The Dying Gladia-
tor" ("Umiraiushchii gladiator"), a reworking of several stanzas from
Byron's poem, contains stanzas of different lengths. In the stanzas that
do have nine lines Lermontov did not imitate the rhyme scheme of the
original,[108] although elsewhere he created a nine-line stanza of his own:

Он бы́л рождён для сча́стья, для наде́жд   a
И вдохнове́ний ми́рных! – но безу́мный   B
Из де́тских ра́но вы́рвался оде́жд   a
И се́рдце бро́сил в мо́ре жи́зни шу́мной;   B
И ми́р не пощади́л – и бо́г не спа́с!   c
Так со́чный плод до вре́мени созре́лый   D
Между цвето́в виси́т осироте́лый,   D
Ни вку́са он не ра́дует, ни гла́з;   c
И ча́с их красоты́ – его́ паде́нья ча́с!   c

                                   1832

A rare contemporary instance of a nine-line stanza is Brodsky's "De-
cember in Florence" ("Dekabr' vo Florentsii") with its three triple
feminine rhymes: *AAABBBCCC*.

Except for the sonnet and the Onegin stanza, the only long stanzaic form that achieved popularity in Russia was that for the ode:

Я в свет исшёл, и ты со мною;	A
На мышцах нет моих заклеп;	b
Свободною могу рукою	A
Прияти данный в пищу хлеб.	b
Стопы несу, где мне приятно;	C
Тому внимаю, что понятно;	C
Вещаю то, что мыслю я.	d
Любить могу и быть любимым;	E
Творю добро, могу быть чтимым;	E
Закон мой – воля есть моя.	d

1781–83

As this stanza from Radishchev's "Liberty" ("Vol'nost'") illustrates, the normal meter for the ode was iambic tetrameter. The rhyme scheme generally caused the stanza to form a 4+6 structure, with a definite break after the alternating rhyme of the opening quatrain.[109] Unlike the sonnet, the ode has not proved to be a lasting form. It was popular during the eighteenth and well into the nineteenth century, but by the 1850s it had already largely fallen into disuse.

Poems with still longer stanzas are not hard to find, especially in poetry from the first half of the nineteenth century. Most, however, are isolated instances. Even the poets who used them rarely repeated their experiments. Examples include the following eleven-line stanza by Küchelbecker and the twelve-line stanza by Baratynsky:

Венчав Александра главой своих сил,	a
Славяне и русы отважной рукою	B
Сражали соседей за светлой Невою:	B
Но город великий татарам служил.	a
Пусть ужас наслала святая София	C
На дикую душу злодея Батыя, –	C
Орда не ярилася в древних стенах,	d
Не пали священные храмы во прах	d
Зажжённые светочем брани:	E
Но всех ослепляющий страх	d
В Сарай отправляет позорные дани.	E

[1824]

Есть бытие; но именем каким	a
Его назвать? Ни сон оно, ни бденье;	B
Меж них оно, и в человеке им	a
С безумием граничит разуменье.	B
Он в полноте понятья своего,	c
А между тем, как волны, на него,	c
Одни других мятежней, своенравней,	D

Виде́ния бегу́т со все́х сторо́н,   e
Как бу́дто бы свое́й отчи́зны да́вней   D
Стихи́йному смяте́нью о́тдан о́н;   e
Но иногда́, мечто́й воспламене́нный,   F
Он ви́дит све́т, други́м не открове́нный.   F

[1827]

OTHER ASPECTS OF STANZAIC STRUCTURES

LARGE RHYME SETS

Usually each rhyme set includes just two rhyming words, such as the sets *A* and *b* in an *AbAb* quatrain. In many of the longer stanzas, rhyme sets of three or four words are common. But much larger rhyme sets are possible in either stanzaic or nonstanzaic poems. One of the four "fragments" about Blok in Pasternak's "Wind" ("Veter") is based on just two rhyme sets. The last fourteen of the twenty-four lines are given below:

Но о́н не доде́лал уро́ка.   A
Упрёки: лентя́й, лежебо́ка!   A
О де́тство! О шко́лы моро́ка!   A
О пе́сни поло́лок и слу́г!   b

А к ве́черу ту́чи с восто́ка.   A
Обло́жены се́вер и ю́г.   b
И ве́тер жесто́кий не к сро́ку   A
Влета́ет и ре́жется вдру́г   b
О ко́сы косцо́в, об осо́ку,   A
Резу́чую гу́щу излу́к.   b

О де́тство! О шко́лы моро́ка!   A
О пе́сни поло́лок и слу́г!   b
Широ́ко, широ́ко, широ́ко   A
Раски́нулись ре́чка и лу́г.   b

1957

In all there are thirteen *A* rhyme words and eleven *b*. Large rhyme sets are by no means peculiar to modern poets; in one poem by Pushkin thirty of the sixty-three lines employ the same rhyme.[110] While very large rhyme sets may sometimes be intended as a tour de force, they can help create a tightly knit structure and add to a work's intensity.

HETEROSTANZAIC FORMS

Stanzas within a given poem may differ from each other in any of four ways. In order of increasing perceptibility they are as follows:

(1) differences in the clausula (*aBBa* and *AbbA*)
(2) changes in the rhyme scheme (*AbAb* and *AbbA*)
(3) varying numbers of lines from stanza to stanza
(4) shifts in the meter

Various combinations of changes may occur, so the list of possible categories is quite large.[111] The first appears to have only a slight effect; yet even a switch in the order of masculine and feminine rhymes can change the rhythmic impulse, as in Tiutchev's "Noon" ("Polden'"):

Лениво дышит полдень мглистый,	A
Лениво катится река,	b
И в тверди пламенной и чистой	A
Лениво тают облака.	b
И всю природу, как туман,	a
Дремота жаркая объемлет,	B
И сам теперь великий Пан	a
В пещере нимф покойно дремлет.	B

[1820s]

A change in the rhyme scheme tends to be more noticeable; here Blok went from enclosed rhyme to alternating and back again:

Шар раскалённый, золотой	a
Пошлёт в пространство луч огромный,	B
И длинный конус тени тёмной	B
В пространство бросит шар другой.	a
Таков наш безначальный мир.	a
Сей конус – наша ночь земная.	B
За ней – опять, опять эфир	a
Планета плавит золотая...	B
И мне страшны, любовь моя,	a
Твои сияющие очи:	B
Ужасней дня, страшнее ночи	B
Сияние небытия.	a

1912

Usually these changes are more likely to occur in short poems; when creating longer works most poets seem to prefer holding to an established pattern. Needless to say there are exceptions. Joseph Brodsky's "The Thames at Chelsea" ("Temza v Chelsi") contains seventy-two lines broken down into six twelve-line stanzas, no two of which are identical. Four different rhyme schemes are used; when the rhyme schemes are alike, differences occur in the clausula.

When the number of lines varies, deciding whether the poem is stanzaic or nonstanzaic can be problematic. Once again, establishing a firm rule is impossible, though changes in size that do not follow any systematic order indicate a nonstanzaic work. Voznesensky's "At the Lake" ("Na ozere") clearly is stanzaic; only the third of its five stanzas differs from the rest in length. The middle three stanzas are below:

Я проснусь и промолвлю: "Да здррра-	a
вствует бодрая температура!"	B
И на высохших после дождя	a
громких джинсах – налёт перламутра.	B
Спрыгну в сад и окно притворю,	a
чтобы бритва тебе не жужжала.	B
Шнур протянется	
в спальню твою.	a
Дело близилось к сентябрю.	a
И задуматься было ужасно,	B
что свобода пуста, как труба,	a
что любовь – это самодержавье.	B
Моя шумная жизнь без тебя	a
не имеет уже содержанья.	B

1973

The extra *a* line in the middle stanza occurs at the precise center of the poem; it thus calls attention to the poem's halfway point and signals the shift to a more serious mood. A more complex change in stanza length occurs throughout Evtushenko's "Golden Gate" ("Zolotye vorota"). The stanzas vary from seven to eleven lines, but all contain only two rhyme sets. The *B* set always has just two lines in iambic trimeter, one coming at or near the middle of the stanza and the other at the end. The remaining lines all employ the *a* rhyme and are in iambic tetrameter. Following are two of the stanzas:

Был краток их сиянья час.	a
Сгущались тучи, волочась,	a
но, зыбким золотом лучась,	a
мерцали те ворота	B
над чернотой прозрачных чащ,	a
как свежевытертая часть	a
старинного киота.	B
И тихо верили сердца,	a
что если с детскостью лица,	a
а не с нахальством пришлеца	a
чуть-чуть коснуться багреца	a
мизинцем удивлённым,	B
то наподобие ларца	a

в рука́х дару́ющих творца́   a
воро́та э́ти до конца́   a
откро́ются со зво́ном.   B

1967

A change in meter from one stanza to the next may be slight—for
example, a shift from iambic tetrameter in the even lines and trimeter in
the odd to the reverse. Or a poem with iambic hexameter and trimeter
lines in the pattern 6-6-6-3 may have a stanza with all hexameter lines.
A more radical change occurs when a poem contains two or more types
of meter—polymetrical compositions. An example is the following ex-
cerpt from a poem by Tsvetaeva in which she used the same rhyme
scheme throughout but alternated trochaic tetrameter and amphibrachic
dimeter stanzas.

Как по льсти́вой по трости́   a
Ро́сным би́сером плеща́,   b
Зарабо́тают персты́...   a
Ша́г – поду́шками глуша́,   b

Лежи́ – да не дви́нь,   a
Дрожи́ – да не гри́нь.   b
Волы́нь-перелы́нь,   a
Хвалы́нь-завира́нь.   b

1923

NONSTANZAIC POEMS

More often than not, nonstanzaic poems show certain tendencies in
the pattern of their rhymes; few works are totally "free" in their rhyme
patterns.[112] In many cases nonstanzaic poems exhibit a regular rhyme
scheme:

И когда́ друг дру́га проклина́ли   A
В стра́сти, раскалённой добела́,   b
О́ба мы́ ещё не понима́ли,   A
Как земля́ для дву́х люде́й мала́,   b
И что па́мять я́ростная му́чит,   C
Пы́тка си́льных – о́гненный неду́г! –   d
И в ночи́ бездо́нной се́рдце у́чит   C
Спра́шивать: о, где́ уше́дший дру́г?   d
А когда́ сквозь во́лны фимиа́ма   E
Хо́р греми́т, лику́я и грозя́,   f
Смо́трят в ду́шу стро́го и упря́мо   E
Те́ же неизбе́жные глаза́.   f

1909

Akhmatova's poem could conceivably have been written as three qua-
trains, but the poet's own choice of layout is usually decisive for classi-
fying a poem. Furthermore, most nonstanzaic poems, especially longer
works, tend to exhibit a different syntactic structure than stanzaic po-
etry. The rhyme groupings are less likely to be set off by definite syntac-
tic breaks; the flow of the work is more readily maintained. In the ex-
ample here there is less of a break between the fourth and fifth lines than
would probably occur had the poem been written in quatrains. Non-
stanzaic forms are particularly suited therefore to narrative poems; the
majority of such works by Pushkin, Lermontov, and Nekrasov were
nonstanzaic.[113]

As noted earlier, Tomashevsky and most later Soviet scholars refer to
poems with eight lines or less as single-stanza poems. My preference is
to call very short poems (two to four lines) by a descriptive name—for
example, couplet or quatrain. But these too are nonstanzaic, as are
poems of five to eight lines with no graphic break, such as this piece by
Baratynsky:

Как описа́ть тебя́? я, пра́во, са́м не зна́ю!	A
Вчера́ заду́мчива, я по́мню, ты была́,	b
Сего́дня ве́трена, заба́вна, весела́;	b
Во всём, что лишь в тебе́ встреча́ю,	A
Непостоя́нство примеча́ю, –	A
Но постоя́нно ты мила́!	b

[1819]

Except for their length, nothing seems to distinguish short nonstanzaic
poems from their longer counterparts.

In the longer poems, however, predominant rhyme schemes usually
emerge. Some poems such as this one by Pushkin are based primarily
on couplets:

Моё собра́нье насеко́мых	A
Откры́то для мои́х знако́мых:	A
Ну, что за пёстрая семья́!	b
За ни́ми где́ ни ры́лся я!	b
Зато́ кака́я сортиро́вка!	C
Во́т Гли́нка – бо́жия коро́вка,	C
Во́т Качен
о́вский – зло́й пау́к.	d
Во́т и Свиньи́н – росси́йский жу́к.	d
Во́т О́лин – чёрная мура́шка,	E
Во́т Ра́ич – ме́лкая бука́шка.	E
Куда́ их мно́го набрало́сь!	f
Опря́тно, за стекло́м и в ра́мах,	G

Они́, пронзённые наскво́зь,   f
Рядко́м торча́т на эпигра́ммах.   G

                                    1829

The greatest number of nonstanzaic poems tend to use four-line group-
ings, as in the Akhmatova poem quoted above. That work's neat division
into quatrains is not typical of the longer poems that favor quatrains.
Rather, such poems often show a fair amount of variety in their rhyme
units, more so than the poems based on couplets. For instance, of the
294 lines in Nekrasov's "The Poet and the Citizen" ("Poet i grazhda-
nin"), there are 52 four-line units, 24 couplets, 4 units with five lines,
and 3 with six.[114]

In some works no one type of rhyme scheme stands out.[115] In the fol-
lowing excerpt from a poem by Kuzmin it is difficult to see any pre-
ferred pattern:

Ско́к, ско́к!   a
Лакиро́ванный ремешо́к   a
Кре́пче затяни́,   b
Герме́с!   c
Внизу́, в тени́ –   b
Лёс...   c
Да́льше – мо́ря,   D
С не́бом спо́ря,   D
Голубе́ет ро́г чуде́с.   c

                                    1926

Overall the poem uses more couplets than other combinations, but the
use of alternating rhyme and large rhyme units (lines 3 through 9 must
be treated together here) makes for a work in which the rhyme varies
freely.

Longer nonstanzaic works usually contain graphic breaks every so
often. The divisions help signal shifts in the narrative or subject matter.
Depending on the nature of the poem, these sections are usually re-
ferred to as "verse paragraphs" or "chapters." In any case, the very ir-
regularity in their size and structure makes it impossible to call them
stanzas.

UNRHYMED AND PARTIALLY RHYMED POEMS

Unrhymed poems, like rhymed, may be either stanzaic or nonstan-
zaic.[116] Rhyme is only one of the organizing features in stanzas; even if

it is absent, meter, size, and a regular pattern in the sequence of clausulae may combine to serve the same organizing function as rhymed stanzas. For instance, in this poem by Apollon Maikov the first two lines of each stanza were written in amphibrachic tetrameter and have feminine endings; the third line was written in amphibrachic trimeter with a masculine ending.

Люблю́ тебя́, ме́сяц, когда́ озаря́ешь   X
Толпу́ шаловли́вых краса́виц, иду́щих   X
   С ночно́го купа́нья домо́й!   x

Прекра́сен ты, во́здух, неся́ издалёка   X
С венко́в их роско́шных волну́ арома́та,   X
   Их на́м возвеща́я прихо́д.   x

1862

Unrhymed stanzas may be quite long: Gumilev's "Sudan" contains eight stanzas, each with thirteen lines. The last line of each stanza has a masculine ending (thereby providing a sense of closure to each stanza), while the other lines are feminine; the meter is anapestic trimeter.

Ах, наве́рно, сего́дняшним у́тром   X
Сли́шком гро́мко звуча́т бараба́ны,   X
Крокоди́льей обтя́нуты ко́жей,   X
Сли́шком зво́нко взыва́ют колду́ньи   X
На утёсах Нуби́йского Ни́ла,   X
Потому́ что сжима́ется се́рдце,   X
Ло́б горя́ч и глаза́ потемне́ли   X
И в мечта́х оживлённая при́стань,   X
Голоса́ смуглоли́цых матро́сов,   X
В пе́нных кло́чьях весёлое мо́ре,   X
А за мо́рем уще́лье Дарфу́ра,   X
Галере́и-леса́ Кордофа́на   X
И вели́кие во́ды Борну́.   x

[<1921]

Finally, many poems mix rhymed and unrhymed lines according to some regular pattern. As noted earlier, quatrains in which only the even lines rhyme are common in English poetry, and they occur in Russian poetry as well. Other combinations sometimes can be found; for example, here Kuzmin employed a five-line stanza in iambic pentameter with masculine rhyme linking the first and last lines. The middle three lines each have a feminine clausula but are unrhymed:

Припа́дочно заколоти́лся джа́з,   a
И Ми́цци ди́ко завизжа́ла: "Ла́зарь!"   X

К стене́ прили́пли декольте́ и фра́ки,   X
И на гита́ры не́гры засмотре́лись,   X
Как бу́дто ви́дели их в пе́рвый ра́з...   a

– Но Ми́цци, Ми́цци, что́ смути́ло ва́с?   a
Ведь э́то бра́т ваш Ви́лли. Не узна́ли?   X
Он да́же не перемени́л костю́ма,   X
Похо́дка та́ же, то́т же ро́ст, причёска,   X
Оттёнок то́т же серова́тых гла́з. –   a

                              1928

Thus rhymed, unrhymed, and partially rhymed verse all offer rich possibilities for stanzaic forms. Even though most contemporary poets rarely venture beyond the familiar quatrain in their stanzaic poetry, it would not be surprising to see a revival of interest in longer and more complex stanzas.

5

Secondary Rhythmic Features

IN RUSSIAN POETRY, rhythm, it will be recalled, is primarily determined by stress. Each main meter exhibits a certain number of rhythmic variations, and the rhythmic impulse of the poem is determined both by the total number of each variation as well as by the way in which the variations are ordered. Compilations of the figures for the frequency of each variation and for stressing at the ictuses may then be used for determining the characteristic rhythms of a given poet, genre, or period. Yet two lines with exactly the same placement of stresses may read differently as a result of "secondary" features that affect the rhythm. All of these features are, for one reason or another, difficult to quantify as unambiguously as word stress; therefore it is much less convenient to make broad claims regarding their function. At the same time they often significantly affect a given line or work and thus should be kept in mind when analyzing individual poems.

WORD BOUNDARIES

The word boundary is the secondary feature most closely related to the stressing of a line. (By *word* I mean a word plus any proclitics or enclitics; thus a one-syllable preposition, for instance, is counted as part of the following word.) The maximum number of word boundaries in a line (if hypermetrical stresses are ignored) is equal to the number of ictuses minus one. That word boundaries influence the reader's perception is clear; compare modulations (a) and (h) in table 23.[1] All eight modulations are for the fully stressed rhythmic variation of the iambic tetrameter. In (a) all the interior word boundaries are masculine, that is, the stress falls on the last syllable of the word. In (h) all the boundaries fall on the next-to-last syllable of the words, and therefore the endings are all feminine. The intervening six modulations contain a mixture of

TABLE 23
Word Boundaries in the Fully Stressed Iambic Tetrameter

Word Boundary	Rhythmic Modulation	Example
∪́|∪ ́|∪ ́|∪ ́ (∪) M M M	(a)	Она́ поёт в печно́й трубе́. Они́ давно́ меня́ томи́ли:
∪ ́|∪́|∪ ́|∪ ́ (∪) F M M	(b)	Безу́мных гла́з твои́х мечи́. Коме́та! Я́ прочёл в свети́лах
∪ ́|∪ ́|∪́|∪ ́ (∪) M F M	(c)	Звездо́й крова́вой ты́ текла́, Что я́ уви́дел дно́ стака́на,
∪ ́|∪́|∪́|∪ ́ (∪) F F M	(d)	То пре́жде я́влен ли́к змеи́, За две́рью пла́чет тво́й ребёнок.
∪ ́|∪ ́|∪ ́∪|∪ ́ (∪) M M F	(e)	Я́ всё скова́л в возду́шной мгле́. Она́ идёт неслы́шным ша́гом.
∪ ́∪|∪́|∪ ́∪|∪ ́ (∪) F M F	(f)	Надме́нный вздо́х истле́вших у́ст: И лжи́вый бле́ск созве́здий ми́лых
∪ ́|∪ ́∪|∪́∪|∪ ́ (∪) M F F	(g)	И клю́ч пору́чен то́лько мне́! Кого́ бича́ми вы́гнал го́лод
∪ ́∪|∪́∪|∪́∪|∪ ́ (∪) F F F	(h)	Иль э́то то́лько сни́тся мне́? Не ме́дли, в тёмных те́нях кро́ясь,

Sources: The ordering of the rhythmic variations follows that of Shengeli, *Traktat o russkom stikhe*, pp. 139–40. The examples are all from Blok's cycle "Gorod" (1904–8).
Notes: Capital letters indicate the type of word boundary; M = masculine, F = feminine. For each pair of examples the top phrase shows the rhythmic modulation with a masculine line ending, the bottom with a feminine.

feminine and masculine word boundaries, and thus differences among them are less distinct though generally noticeable. Except for (a) and possibly (h), a poet is not likely to consciously use one modulation of the fully stressed iambic tetrameter rather than another; still, the types of modulations that finally appear in a poem can point to subtle aspects of its rhythmic organization.

The number and variety of rhythmic modulations is impressive. Those in table 23 are only found in the fully stressed line; the types of lines that omit one or more stresses have rhythmic modulations of their own. There are four for the second rhythmic variation (stress omitted at the first ictus), eight for each of the third and fourth variations, six for the fifth, four for the sixth, two for the seventh, and one for the eighth—a total of forty-one modulations for the iambic tetrameter alone. Note that the omission of stress within the line allows for dactylic (two syllables after the stress) and even hyperdactylic endings (three or more syllables).

It is possible to determine how many rhythmic modulations exist, at least in theory, for any type of meter.[2] As with rhythmic variations, some are virtually (or entirely) absent from actual poems, while others are extremely rare. Iambic and trochaic trimeter both have 11 modulations, the binary pentameters already have 153 modulations, and the hexameters 571. (All these numbers, as well as the 41 for the tetrameter, assume obligatory stress on the last ictus; otherwise, the totals would be still larger.) Most scholars have calculated word boundaries for the ternary meters under the assumption that each ictus is always stressed. As a result the numbers for the ternaries are more modest, but still substantial: 9 modulations for the trimeters, 27 for the tetrameters, and 81 for the pentameters.[3]

But the issue is more complex than even these figures indicate. Let us turn again to table 23, which includes examples of lines with both masculine and feminine clausulae, thus doubling the number of modulations to sixteen. Most scholars simply do not consider hypermetrical stressing, which greatly increases the number of possible modulations, or clausulae longer than feminine.

The vast number of modulations makes it difficult to carry out broad studies of word boundaries.[4] Perhaps for this reason investigations in recent years have dealt only sporadically with word boundaries despite the extensive descriptions of them in pioneering works by Tomashevsky, Shengeli, Jakobson, and Taranovsky.[5] An effort some years back to include the strength of word boundaries as part of an elaborate system of verse notation proved cumbersome; the authors themselves seemed to favor a simplified method that merely indicated the location of word boundaries in the line.[6]

When word boundaries are discussed, the effort is usually to analyze their placement and consequent effect on a given poem rather than to gather statistical evidence. Tomashevsky offered several general observations. He noted that masculine word boundaries are normally pronounced more sharply but that they also meld readily into the following word if the words involved are related grammatically—for instance, a noun and an adjective. (Note the beginning of the top example for the (c) modulation in table 23.) Nonetheless, masculine endings are felt strongly at the end of the line, where they may help impart a sense of closure. Feminine word boundaries sound smoother, but the words are less likely to lose their independence (see the beginnings of both examples in the (f) modulation). Dactylic endings, which do not occur among the modulations for the fully stressed binary lines, may give a certain solemnity to the passage.[7]

A brief analysis of two poems will illustrate how an examination of word boundaries can be useful. The following poems are by Mandelshtam; the rhythmic variations are indicated by roman numerals (see table 3, chapter 2), while, as in Shengeli, capital letters indicate the types of word boundaries (D=dactylic; H=hyperdactylic) within lines:

Как ко́ни ме́дленно ступа́ют,	∪–́∣–́∪–∣∪–́∪	IV	F	D
Как ма́ло в фонаря́х огня́!	∪–́∪∣–∪–́∣∪–́	III	F	M
Чужи́е лю́ди, ве́рно, зна́ют,	∪–́∪∣–́∪∣–́∪∣–́	I	F F F
Куда́ везу́т они́ меня́.	∪–́∣∪–́∣∪–́∣∪–́	I	M M M
А я́ вверя́юсь и́х забо́те.	∪–́∣∪–́∪∣–́∣∪–́∪	I	M F M
Мне хо́лодно, я спа́ть хочу́.	∪–́∪∣∪–́∣∪–́	III	D	M
Подбро́сило на поворо́те,	∪–́∪–∣∪–∪–́∪	V	D
Навстре́чу звёздному лучу́.	∪–́∪∣–́∪–∣∪–́	IV	F	D
Горя́чей головы́ кача́нье,	∪–́∪∣–∪–́∣∪–́∪	III	F	M
И не́жный лёд руки́ чужо́й,	∪–́∪∣–́∣∪–́∣∪–́	I	F M M
И тёмных е́лей очерта́нья,	∪–́∪∣–́∪∣–∪–́∪	IV	F F
Ещё неви́данные мно́й.	∪–́∣∪–́∪–∪∣–́∪	IV	M H

1911

О времена́х просты́х и гру́бых	–́–∪–́∣∪–́∣∪–́∪	II	(M) M M
Копы́та ко́нские твердя́т,	∪–́∪∣–́∪–∣∪–́	IV	F	D
И дво́рники в тяжёлых шу́бах	∪–́∪–∣∪–́∪∣–́∪	III	D	F
На деревя́нных ла́вках спя́т.	∪–∪–́∪∣–́∪∣–́	II	F F
На сту́к в желе́зные воро́та	∪–́∣∪–́∪–∣∪–́	IV	M D
Привра́тник, ца́рственно лени́в,	∪–́∪∣–́∪–∣∪–́	IV	F	D
Вста́л, и звери́ная зево́та	–́∣–∪–́∪–∣∪–́∪	VI	(M) D
Напо́мнила тво́й о́браз, ски́ф,	∪–́∪–∣∪–́∪∣–́	III	D	F
Когда́ с дряхле́ющей любо́вью,	∪–́∣∪–́∪–∣∪–́∪	IV	M D
Меша́я в пе́снях Ри́м и сне́г,	∪–́∪∣–́∪∣–́∣∪–́	I	F F M
Ови́дий пе́л арбу́ воло́вью	∪–́∪∣–́∣∪–́∣∪–́∪	I	F M M
В похо́де ва́рварских теле́г.	∪–́∪∣–́∪–∣∪–́	IV	F	D

1914

In the first example the ending of the initial stanza is conspicuous. The last two lines are fully stressed but the word boundaries are the exact opposite; note that the concluding line of the stanza contains the "sharper" masculine word endings throughout as well as in the rhyme word. In the third stanza Mandelshtam again used the same rhythmic form in the two concluding lines but assigned them virtually opposite modulations. The two stanzas are also alike in that the first word boundary, which is often perceived more strongly than the others in a line, is feminine in the first three lines and masculine in the last. The situation in the second poem is different, primarily because the use of rhythmic variations has changed—there are only two fully stressed lines as opposed to four in the first poem. Yet some of the structural features are repeated. Here too the first and third stanzas seem the more tightly organized, while the middle stanza, which is the most lightly stressed, lacks distinctive parallels in the use of rhythmic modulations. In the first stanza the feminine word boundaries of the last line mirror the masculine word boundaries of the poem's opening line. The same two lines are roughly parallel in the third stanza, as are the middle two. The second poem also contains no fewer than eight dactylic word boundaries; if Tomashevsky's suggestion regarding the synaesthetic quality of dactylic endings is accepted, then the endings are in keeping with the mood of the poem. Interestingly, the modulations tend to pair lines that are not rhymed; here the alternating lines of each stanza rhyme, but all the comparisons occur between either adjacent lines or lines at the extreme ends of the stanza.

POETIC SYNTAX

Probably the first time most people become aware of what is conventionally called "poetic license" is when they try to cope with the irregular word order that appears now and then in virtually all metrical poetry. (In free verse, where there is no meter to interfere with normal syntax, unusual word order is generally less frequent.) Poetic and prose syntax are not quite the same. The main stress in prose phrases is logical, that is, it falls most strongly on the words that are crucial for the meaning or are emphasized by the syntactic structure. In metrical poetry the key determinant is not the phrase but the verse line. Its composition is determined by various poetic features—primarily meter and end rhyme, but in some cases also parallelism, internal rhyme, the use of a caesura, and so forth.[8] Phrase stress or logical stress loses some of its significance, since the structure of the verse line determines the placement of stress and will single out words according to its own rules.[9] Poetic syntax usually does not differ drastically from prose syntax, for if it were to do so the poems would become difficult to comprehend and could seem awkward—as in some of Trediakovsky's poetry where his efforts to follow metrical rules caused him to take great liberties with the syntax. More often the metrical and rhythmic features of the poetry interact with the norms for prose syntax, stretching them somewhat and creating word placements or structures that in a typical prose work would be regarded as highly unusual if not ungrammatical.[10]

The chief characteristics of poetic syntax are not difficult to list and in some cases may be obvious. Sentences in poetry tend to be shorter and less complex than those in prose.[11] As in prose, the sentences in a poem can be broken down into various *syntagms*, or speech units, which are defined as the minimally sized groupings of words that (1) create a semantic whole, (2) are linked syntactically, and (3) are part of the same intonational construction (e.g., subject and predicate, prepositional phrase, etc.). But in poetry the structure of the syntagms as well as the divisions between them are affected by the nature of the poem's line. Sometimes "false" syntagms appear when a group of words seems unified by its location on a single line but in fact does not form a syntactic unit. Furthermore, the length of the poetic line tends to influence the way in which the syntagms join together.[12]

Perhaps the most common and the most easily recognized feature of Russian poetic syntax is its inclination to employ inversion.[13] Changes in the customary word order are by no means impossible or even all that unusual in prose; certain types of inversion, such as the reversal of subject and predicate, are about equally common in either genre. But other kinds of inversion, such as reversal of noun and adjective, are far more typical of poetry.[14] In addition, inversions are sufficiently frequent in poetic syntax to be stylistically neutral in most cases, whereas similar inversions in a work of prose would be evidence of a special stylistic effect.[15] For that matter, some of the more complex inversions that occur in poetry would be ungrammatical in a work of prose. The basic kinds of inversion can be seen in the following poem by Aleksandr Mezhirov:

В жи́зни па́рка наме́тилась ве́ха,
Та́, кото́рую ве́к предрека́л:
Ремонти́руем ко́мнату сме́ха,
Выпрямля́ем пове́рхность зерка́л.

Нам оши́бки вскрыва́ть не впервы́е,
Мы́, позо́рному сме́ху назло́,
Зеркала́ выпрямля́ем кривы́е,
Ста́вим в ра́мы прямо́е стекло́.

Пусть не сли́шком толпа́ весели́тся,
Переста́нет бессмы́сленно ржа́ть, –
Совреме́нников до́блестных ли́ца
Никому́ не дади́м искажа́ть!

[<1975]

The mildest form of inversion, that of subject and predicate, occurs in the first line. In the next-to-last line there is a double inversion: the adjective and noun are in reverse order, while *litsa* belongs at the beginning of the line rather than at the end. For that matter, to establish a "normal" word order the poem's last two lines would have to change places. The most distinctive inversion occurs earlier, in the third line of the second stanza. Here the noun and adjective are not only switched around but are separated by another word. Such an inversion would be impossible in prose.

Many if not most inversions result from the exigencies of meter and rhythm, yet they often affect the way in which a given line or passage is perceived.[16] In cases such as this last example, the inversion serves to isolate a specific word (most often an adjective) and thereby emphasize it. Frequently, the unusual word order resulting from an inversion forces a slower reading and results in greater attention to individual words. Also, the surprising contiguity of certain words implies semantic links that would otherwise not arise, or the word order itself has semantic implications. Here, for instance, the delay of the final verb, *to distort* until the end of the last line makes it stand out more than if a normal word order were used.[17]

Of the other features that may be cited under the heading of syntax, three are especially deserving of separate mention: parallelism, enjambment, and closure.

PARALLELISM

Parallelism frequently serves as a central organizing principle in many poetic traditions, including Russian, where grammatical parallelism was often used to link successive lines in folk poetry.[18] Almost any repetition of the same or comparable elements may be considered an instance of parallelism, though for singling out significant parallel structures in poetry it may be best to rely on a stricter definition: parallel lines in verse are identical in some way, and the nonidentical segments occupy the same position in each line.[19] Still, many types of parallelism exist; for example, rhyme is an obvious instance of sound parallelism. Here, however, I am concerned with parallel structures, that is, repetitions of words, phrases, or grammatical forms in the analogous positions of verse lines.[20] Most often the repetitions occur between lines, but on occasion it is possible to find entire stanzas that

show a distinct parallel relationship.[21] Similarly, in poetry that observes
a caesura it is possible to talk of parallels within lines as well. Probably
the most frequent form of parallelism is anaphora—the appearance of
the same word or group of words at the beginnings of lines. Other types
include parallels at the ends of lines (sometimes called epiphora) and
various kinds of "ring" structures in which beginnings and endings are
linked. (These may range from using the same phrase at the beginning
of one line and end of the next to repeating the opening words of a poem
at the very end.)[22] Note too that certain traditional stanzaic forms are
based on repetitions or the use of parallel structures (for instance, the
triolet and rondel).

The use of parallelism is best illustrated by a complete poem:

> Всё, как бывало, весёлый, счастливый,
> Ленты твоей уловляю извивы,
> Млеющих звуков впивая истому;
> Пусть ты летишь, отдаваясь другому.
>
> Пусть пронеслась ты надменно, небрежно,
> Сердце моё всё по-прежнему нежно,
> Сердце обид не считает, не мерит,
> Сердце по-прежнему любит и верит.
>
> Тщетно опущены строгие глазки,
> Жду под ресницами блеска и ласки, –
> Всё, как бывало, весёлый, счастливый,
> Ленты твоей уловляю извивы.

1887

Fet, as here, often relied on more than one type of parallelism in his
poems. The obvious instance above is the anaphora with *serdtse* in the
second stanza. Anaphora often is based upon function words such as
conjunctions and prepositions; when a noun or verb is involved, the
word itself clearly receives special emphasis. In this case the threefold
repetition of *heart* draws attention to both that word and the central
stanza. Anaphora also occurs between the fourth and fifth lines of the
poem, thereby providing a link between the two stanzas and also creat-
ing a sharp break between *pust'* and the anaphora that follows. Further-
more, the last two lines of the middle stanza, with the same opening
words and a pair of verbs at the end of each, are closely parallel. The
particularly tight structure underscores the emotional climax that occurs
at this point. The poem ends with the same two lines that began it; abso-
lute identity, strictly speaking, belongs more to the realm of repetition

than parallelism, but the effect is similar. In this case it underscores the network of parallel structures (only the most salient of which are discussed here) largely responsible for the poem's effectiveness.

ENJAMBMENT

Normally the end of the verse line is accompanied by a syntactic break—the end of a sentence, clause, or phrase. In the case of enjambment, the significant break occurs within the line rather than at the end. Enjambment has been present in Russian poetry since the days of syllabic versification. Kantemir described the phenomenon in detail and believed that it embellished the poetic work.[23] The practice fell into disrepute during the early days of the syllabo-tonic tradition because poets were at first leery of harming the integrity of the verse line. By the time of Pushkin, however, enjambment had become a common device for varying the syntactic rhythm of the poem. It has proved appropriate for creating a heightened emotional quality (Pushkin resorted to frequent enjambment when describing the mad Evgeny in *The Bronze Horseman*) or for establishing a conversational tone (cf. the opening stanza of *Little House in Kolomna*).[24]

Enjambment may be of several kinds, listed here in order of decreasing strength. If the line boundary (1) splits a word, or (2) separates a proclitic or enclitic from the main word, or (3) directly divides a syntagm, then enjambment always occurs, even if there is no definite break within either of the two lines. Enjambment may also arise when (4) a word from one syntagm is "left behind" on the previous line because of an inversion (see below for an example), or (5) the end of the line coincides with the end of a syntagm but a stronger break occurs within one of the two lines.[25] Each of these last two cases requires a syntactic break within one of the two lines for enjambment to occur.[26]

The following passages, by Voznesensky, Brodsky, and Tsvetaeva, offer examples of all five types:

Я проснусь и промолвлю: "Да здрррá-
вствует бодрая температура!"
И на высохших после дождя
громких джинсах – налёт перламутра.

1973

Одиночество учит сути вещей, ибо суть их то же
одиночество. Кожа спины благодарна коже

спинки кресла за чувство прохлады. Вдали рука на
подлокотнике деревенеет. Дубовый лоск
покрывает костяшки суставов. Мозг
бьётся, как льдинка о край стакана.

1975

Рас-стояние: вёрсты, мили...
Нас рас-ставили, рас-садили,
Чтобы тихо себя вели,
По двум разным концам земли.

Рас-стояние: вёрсты, дали...
Нас расклеили, распаяли,
В две руки развели, распяв,
И не знали, что это – сплав

Вдохновений и сухожилий...
Не рассорили – рассорили,
Расслоили...
              Стена да ров.
Расселили нас, как орлов-

Заговорщиков: вёрсты, дали...
Не расстроили – растеряли.
По трущобам земных широт
Рассовали нас, как сирот.

Который уж – ну который – март?!
Разбили нас – как колоду карт!

1925

The first example illustrates the unusual splitting of a word over two
lines (type 1). The third and fourth lines contain an example of type 4,
in which enjambment results from inversion. The line breaks at the end
of a syntagm, but the word *vysokhshikh* is "left behind" while the rest of
its syntagm appears on the next line—and a strong syntactic break oc-
curs within that line. Brodsky frequently separates prepositions from
nouns (type 2), as in lines 3 and 4 in the second example. Between the
last two lines he divides a syntagm (type 3), and he employs type 5 at
the end of line 4, which ends with a noun-adjective unit but has a much
stronger syntactic break within the line. Enjambment occurs at the end
of every line within the stanza until the final period. Elsewhere in the
same poem there is enjambment between stanzas, as in the third ex-
ample here. There is strong enjambment (in one case splitting a hyphen-
ated word) between the second and third as well as the third and fourth
stanzas. Enjambment between stanzas is often perceived as a stronger
disruption than that between lines; thus, it will be recalled, Pushkin em-

ployed enjambment between stanzas only a handful of times in *Eugene Onegin*. Besides lines and stanzas, there is still a third place at which enjambment may occur. Normally, poems written with a caesura contain a syntactic break at that point in the line; the absence of a break (for types 1 through 3) or the shift of that break to another position (types 4 and 5) leads to enjambment. Even though Tsvetaeva's poem lacks a caesura after a fixed syllable, the lines show a strong tendency to divide into two roughly equal halves. When the expected break does not occur (as in the last line of the first stanza), the effect is similar to that of enjambment in poems that formally observe a caesura.

The location of the inner break, which is obligatory for types 4 and 5, serves as the basis for a further classification of enjambment as *rejet*, *contre-rejet*, and *double rejet*. The Brodsky example contains instances of all three. If the inner syntactic break occurs near the beginning of the second line, with the bulk of the phrase on the first line, the enjambment is called *rejet* (see lines 1 and 2 of the Brodsky fragment). *Contre-rejet* (lines 4 and 5) is the opposite: the bulk of the phrase carries over onto the second line, with a break near the end of the first. When breaks occur both near the end of the first line and the beginning of the second (lines 5 and 6), the term *double rejet* is sometimes used.

POETIC CLOSURE

Closure is not necessarily the same as ending. Presumably all poems must have a last line, and in coming to it the reader arrives at the end of the poem. But closure implies something else—a sense of finality and at the same time of wholeness, of the poem as a finished, integral work. This quality is not present in all poetry. Indeed, some modern poetry purposefully avoids a perception of closure. Barbara Herrnstein Smith, in her fine monograph on this topic, describes closure as follows:

> Closure occurs when the concluding portion of a poem creates in the reader a sense of appropriate cessation. It announces and justifies the absence of further development; it reinforces the feeling of finality, completion, and composure which we value in all works of art; and it gives ultimate unity and coherence to the reader's experience of the poem by providing a point from which all the preceding elements may be viewed comprehensively and their relations grasped as part of a significant design.[27]

Closure may be confined to either the formal or thematic aspects of a poem, or it may involve a combination of the two.[28] Here the concern is with the formal elements, which may be divided roughly into five categories:

(1) Perhaps the most noticeable is repetition, either of a previous line (or group of lines) or of an entire stanza. A common device in this regard is the use of a ring structure—when the beginning of a poem recurs at the end (e.g., Fet's "Vsë, kak byvalo" quoted in the section on parallelism).[29] Refrains, which occur when one or more lines are repeated at regular intervals (and are often set off metrically from the rest of the work), are most frequently used to indicate closure for stanzas. At the same time, a thematic development in the main text or even a slight change in the refrain may enable it to provide a sense of closure for an entire work.[30]

(2) Some changes in the stanzaic form may mark closure. For instance, in the Tsvetaeva poem quoted in the previous section the final two-line stanza stands in contrast to the series of four-line stanzas that precede it.

(3) The rhyme scheme may also play a role. Consider the following poem by Gleb Gorbovsky:

Навеселе́, на ди́вном веселе́
я находи́лся в но́чь под понеде́льник.
Заговори́ли зве́ри на земле́,
запе́ли тра́вы, ка́мни загалде́ли...
А челове́к – обу́гленный пенёк –
торча́л траги́чно и не без созна́нья,
как фантасти́чно бы́л он одино́к,
загля́дывая в се́рдце мирозда́нья...
Навеселе́, на ди́вном веселе́
я спа́л и пла́кал, жа́луясь Земле́.

1961

The pattern of alternating rhymes concludes with a final rhymed couplet. The switch to a rhymed couplet, especially when the endings are masculine, is a favorite device of poets for emphasizing the ends of stanzas as well as of entire poems. Several of the traditional stanzaic forms (the English sonnet, the Onegin stanza) as well as some of the more popular rhyme schemes for stanzas of six or more lines make use of such couplets.

(4) Closure sometimes involves a change in the meter. Again, the Tsvetaeva poem serves as an example. The first sixteen lines are written in three-stress *dol'niki* (which are sufficiently regular to be classified as logaoedic verse—the ictuses occur at the same positions in each line),

and the anacrusis contains two syllables. The last two lines suddenly switch to four-stress *dol' niki* with a one-syllable anacrusis.

(5) Changes in the rhythm often provide a more subtle form of closure. For instance, enjambment between the final two lines or the use of heavily stressed lines at the end of a poem may impart a sense of completion or finality. A conspicuous example of such closure occurs at the end of a poem by Morshen:

Но что́ у на́с в наш ча́с осе́нний
Еди́ный вызыва́ет вздо́х?
Лири́ческого тяготе́нья
Где вы́сший це́нтр для все́х эпо́х,
Оме́га все́х пересече́ний?

Жи́знь? сме́рть? любо́вь? Бы́ть мо́жет, Бо́г?

[< 1979]

SOUND REPETITIONS

Western scholars sometimes group nearly all forms of sound repetition under the single category of alliteration.[31] However, *alliteration* will be used here in the somewhat narrower sense—as applying to sounds that recur at the beginnings of words. (As such, it is less important in Russian than in English or German, where stress on the initial syllable is more common and gives it prominence.)

Со́лнце по́лное пали́ло,
пелена́я ци́трус.
Ни́мфа Э́хо полюби́ла
ю́ного Нарци́сса.

Ку́дри кру́глые. Краса́вец!
Полюби́ла ни́мфа.
Ко́нчиков кудре́й каса́лась,
как престу́пник ни́мба.

1964

The fifth and seventh lines in this passage from Sosnora's "Echo" are indicative of the striking effects that may be achieved through alliteration, though in the fifth line the alliteration is strengthened by other sound correspondences as well. Less immediately obvious is the alliteration of the consonant *p* that begins three of the first four words in the poem.

Assonance, or the repetition of vowel sounds, is not always as readily perceived:

Крестья́нина я о́тдал в повара́:
Он уда́лся; хоро́ший по́вар – сча́стье!
Но ча́сто отлуча́лся со двора́
И зва́нью неприли́чное пристра́стье
Име́л: люби́л чита́ть и рассужда́ть.
Я, утомя́сь грози́ть и распека́ть,
Оте́чески посёк его́, кана́лью,
Он взя́л да утопи́лся: ду́рь нашла́!
Живя́ согла́сно с стро́гою мора́лью,
Я никому́ не сде́лал в жи́зни зла́.

1847

However, the emphasis on the vowel *a* in this excerpt from Nekrasov's "A Moral Person" ("Nravstvennyi chelovek") is hard to ignore. In particular, all the stressed vowels in the third line are *a*, as are the stressed vowels in the words that immediately precede and follow that line. Furthermore, the rhymed vowels in all ten lines of the stanza are *a*s. Strictly speaking, assonance is based on stressed vowels, but unstressed vowels can contribute to the effect: again in line 3, since unstressed *o* is pronounced the same as *a*, nearly all the vowel sounds in that line are similar.

Finally, a broad class of repetitions contribute to the sound texture of a poem:

Застона́л я от сна́ дурно́го
И просну́лся, тя́жко скорбя́;
Сни́лось мне́ – ты лю́бишь друго́го,
И что о́н оби́дел тебя́.

Я бежа́л от мое́й посте́ли,
Как уби́йца от пла́хи свое́й,
И смотре́л, как ту́скло блесте́ли
Фонари́ глаза́ми звере́й.

[1917]

In the first line of "The Dream" ("Son") Gumilev uses the *s-t-n* sound group to great effect; in fact, the *s-n* combination recurs in the next two lines as well. In the seventh line the sounds *s-t-l* are important, appearing in each of the three main words in that line.[32] Sound texture is closely related to the sound similarities that occur in rhyme. These repetitions too may be exact, but—as in modern rhyme—they may also involve various types of transpositions and substitutions (especially, again as in rhyme, of related consonants).

Sound repetitions were first analyzed in some detail by Osip Brik, who pointed out the various combinations and permutations that may occur when groups of consonants are repeated.[33] But while he showed how these repetitions may spread over more than one line and shed light on the great variety they involve, he ignored vowels and confined himself largely to classifying and listing examples of the repetitions; he says little about their effect.[34] His work has been influential to the extent it has made scholars aware that sound texture exists and should be considered in the analysis of poetry. However, until recently few attempts were made among scholars of Russian verse to carry Brik's findings further. Now efforts are under way to look at the semantic effect of such repetitions. One direction has been to extend the concept of "anagrams," developed by Ferdinand de Saussure in posthumously published writings, to the study of Russian poetry.[35] Saussure's idea is that certain groups of letters may function as anagrams for key words. Not all instances of sound correspondence are based on an anagram, and when they arise they may well be due as much to intuitive processes as to a conscious effort. A likely case occurs in the above work by Nekrasov. The repetition of the *ch-a-s-t* sounds in lines 3 and 4 provides an echo for the ironic use of *schast'e* at the end of line 2. A second approach has been to examine what is called "paronymous attraction."[36] A comparable effect was described some years ago for English words: a similarity in sounds may make words appear to be semantically related even if their derivations are quite different.[37] As discussed in chapter 4, the phenomenon occurs naturally with many rhyme pairs. It also arises in most instances where sound texture is carefully developed throughout a passage. However, it came into being as a conscious device largely through the experiments carried out by the futurists, most notably Maiakovsky and Khlebnikov.[38] Paronymous attraction may be said to function as a crucial element in the poetics of Khlebnikov, who was forever searching out semantic relationships between historically unconnected words that share certain sound similarities. It now turns up regularly in the works of contemporary poets, for whom the sound innovations of the futurists are a part of the poetical heritage. A possible example is the *kudri kruglye* in Sosnora's "Echo."

INTONATION

Over the years much has been written about intonation in Russian poetry, by which scholars have meant the tone, the speed of reading, the melodic quality of the verse, the use of pauses, and so forth. In all like-

lihood interest in intonation dates from the appearance of a study by
Boris Eikhenbaum, *The Melodics of Russian Lyric Poetry*, in which he
distinguished three types of lyric verse: melodic (*napevnyi*), rhetorical
(*deklamativnyi* or *ritoricheskii*), and conversational (*govornoi*).[39] His
study is in fact devoted to delineating the first of these, in particular as it
appears in the poetry of Zhukovsky and Fet; the other two types are
barely mentioned. Still, the distinction remains in vogue to the present
day, so it is worth looking at the three types:

О ты, чьей памятью кровавой
Мир долго, долго будет полн,
Приосенён твоею славой,
Почий среди пустынных волн...
Великолепная могила!
Над урной, где твой прах лежит,
Народов ненависть почила,
И луч бессмертия горит.

                                            1821

Наталья Павловна к балкону
Бежит, обрадована звону,
Глядит и видит: за рекой
У мельницы коляска скачет,
Вот на мосту — к нам точно... нет,
Поворотила влево. Вслед
Она глядит и чуть не плачет.

Но вдруг... о радость! косогор;
Коляска набок. — Филька! Васька!
Кто там? скорей! Вон там коляска:
Сейчас везти её на двор
И барина просить обедать!
Да жив ли он?.. беги проведать!

                                            1825

"Куда, куда вы удалились,
Весны моей златые дни?
Что день грядущий мне готовит?
Его мой взор напрасно ловит,
В глубокой мгле таится он.
Нет нужды: прав судьбы закон.
Паду ли я, стрелой пронзённый,
Иль мимо пролетит она,
Всё благо: бдения и сна
Приходит час определённый;
Благословен и день забот,
Благословен и тьмы приход!

                                            1826

All three excerpts, from works by Pushkin, are written in iambic tetrameter; thus the differences in the ways these works sound are not a
function of meter. The first is in the rhetorical manner, which is perhaps
the easiest to distinguish; it was particularly common during the late
eighteenth and early nineteenth centuries when more declamatory poems
such as odes were in fashion. The use of direct address, exclamations,
and an elevated vocabulary are all typical; enjambment is relatively
rare. The second passage illustrates the conversational type, which is by
far the most common among contemporary poets. Although the excerpt
here is filled with exclamations and questions that might be thought
more typical of the other two styles, the tone is nonetheless conversational. The wide variations in sentence length, the more prosaic vocabulary, the frequent intonational breaks within lines as well as enjambment, and the incomplete sentences (ellipses) all contribute to the work's
intonation.[40] The third type, the melodic, did not appear very often in
Pushkin's poetry after his youthful infatuation with Zhukovsky's writings, but it turned up in *Eugene Onegin* when Pushkin imitated his
character Lensky's romantic manner. The questions in this last excerpt
were typical of Zhukovsky's "melodic" verse as well, but the key element is symmetry. The stanza tends to break down into symmetrical
portions, and the syntactic structure in comparable units is often parallel—indeed, parallelism is the basis for most melodic verse. Note the
anaphora (as well as parallel syntactic structures) in the last two lines,
while the twelve lines of the stanza devoted to Lensky's writing break
down into two six-line units, each of which may again be divided: 2+1
and 2+1 in the first half, 2+2+2 in the second. Repetition of identical
or at least corresponding lines (i.e., refrains) is also typical of melodic
verse.

   Of course the three examples chosen here all offer clear-cut representations of the particular styles. In such cases conclusions about the intonational manner are easy to reach, but a mere listing of traits common
to one type of intonation or another is not adequate for categorizing
poems. The problem is twofold. Virtually all the devices may be found
with each type of intonation; thus while parallelism is particularly important for melodic verse, it is not at all uncommon in rhetorical poetry
and may be found as well in much of the work usually labeled conversational (for instance, most of Pushkin's mature poetry). Also, the intonation of a poem is determined primarily through the general meaning of
the text and the emotional tones that the words themselves establish; the

various formal elements play only a supporting role.[41] It seems best to talk of intonation as a complex phenomenon that is dependent upon a poem's content, the poet's style, and specific contributory formal elements; as part of a specific analysis or an attempt to characterize a poet's manner it may be useful, but as a way to categorize poems it offers less promise.[42]

ORTHOGRAPHY

Orthography in poetry applies to two related topics: the graphic layout of a poem on the page, and the use of punctuation and special typographical effects. I shall say just a word about the latter at the end of this section, but the former—layout of verse on the page—is of some interest for twentieth-century poetry.

Since ancient times poems in most languages have generally been printed on the page by verse lines. Occasionally, efforts to create designs with the printed word have been in fashion. In Russian poetry, examples of such efforts can be found among the very first poems in the literary tradition; Simeon Polotsky occasionally wrote works in the shape of roses or hearts. Much later Valery Briusov experimented with geometrical shapes.[43] Somewhat more radical distortions of the usual layout (and of typography) are found among many poems by the futurists, for whom the printing of a poem sometimes blended with graphic art.[44] More recently Andrei Voznesensky composed *Izopy* (an acronym based on *izobrazitel'naia poeziia*—literally, graphic poetry), a work intended solely for the eye and not the ear.[45] However, graphic poetry amounted to a serious tradition in modern times only among certain of the futurists; experiments like those of Voznesensky are basically curiosities.

More important has been the tendency to segment the line on the printed page, with the various parts either placed one directly beneath the other in a column (*stolbik*) or intended to form a shape like that of a stepladder (*lesenka*). Belyi was the greatest innovator in this regard; he was particularly taken by the way in which the unusual line segmentation could lead to a change in emphasis and a consequent change in meaning.[46] Maiakovsky, however, was the poet who actually popularized the new forms. Below are examples of both his *stolbik* and *lesenka* forms; the rhyme scheme indicates where the ends of lines occur.

А теперь
попробуй.
Су́нь ему́ "Ана́тэм".   A
В но́рах ми́стики вели́ ему́ мы́шиться.   B′
Тепе́рь
у него́
душа́ кана́том,   A
и хоть гво́здь вбива́й ей –
ка́ждая мы́шца.   B

Ему́ ли
ны́ть
в кварти́рной я́ме?   A
А така́я
нра́вится мане́ра вам: B′
не́жность
из па́мяти
вы́рвать с корня́ми,   A
го́ловы скрути́ть ору́щим не́рвам.   B

[1914]

По провода́м
       электри́ческой пря́ди –   A
я зна́ю –
    эпо́ха
      по́сле па́ра –   B
здесь
  лю́ди
    уже́
      ора́ли по ра́дио,   A′
здесь
  лю́ди
    уже́
      взлета́ли по а́эро.   B′
Здесь
  жи́знь
    была́
      одни́м – беззабо́тная,   C′
други́м –
  голо́дный
    протя́жный во́й.   d
Отсю́да
  безрабо́тные   C′
в Гудзо́н
  кида́лись
    вниз голово́й.   d

[1925]

The young Maiakovsky, no doubt under the influence of Belyi, favored
the column form from the very start of his career. In early 1923 he

abruptly switched to the stepladder layout, possibly again after reading
Belyi and probably as a result of seeking a new manner for his long and
complex *About This* (*Pro eto*).[47] The influence of Maiakovsky and his
contemporaries does not extend to all recent poets; Akhmadulina pre-
fers the more conventional format, Vinokurov employs the *lesenka* only
sparingly—sometimes just in a few lines of a given poem. On the other
hand, Voznesensky has used these layouts extensively and is capable of
combining columns and stepladders in a single poem.[48] For Robert
Rozhdestvensky the stepladder and column layouts are crucial aspects of
the poetic method; in "Dispute" ("Spor") (as he states directly) he too
uses both:

Разли́чные пе́сенки,
сиро́пом обли́тые,
одни́
  пи́шут
    ле́сенкой,
други́е –
ли́фтами.
О цвета́х,
   о ча́йках,
облака́х над ручьём.
А ещё
  ча́ще –
почти́ ни о чём.
   [< 1966]

The functions of the *stolbik* and *lesenka* as well as of the mixed form
are similar. Primarily, they highlight the individual syntagms or speech
units and thus place greater emphasis on individual words in the poem.[49]
If the segmentation occurs regularly at the borders of syntagms, as is the
case in Maiakovsky's *lesenka* poems, then the effect of placing a divi-
sion elsewhere will be similar to that of enjambment.[50] The breaks
may also draw attention to regular or occasional internal rhymes (*O
tsvetakh*/*oblakakh* in the Rozhdestvensky poem) and syntactic parallel-
ism (cf. especially the analogous third and fourth lines of Maiakovsky's
stepladder poem). Varying the number of segments may alter the tempo
of a poem. For instance, in the first stanza of Maiakovsky's column
poem the first and third lines are divided into three units, the fourth into
two, and the second remains whole. In the second stanza the pattern is
3-2-3-1. Presumably a line with three segments would be read more
slowly than an undivided line.

While the layout no doubt has some effect on the eye, a person who hears rather than reads a poem could receive a different impression. Stepladders or columns may influence a performer's recitation, but poets themselves do not always adhere to their own divisions when reading poems out loud.[51] The few available recordings of poems whose layouts exist in both conventional and column or stepladder forms indicate that a radical breaking up of the line may indeed affect the way a poem is read, but that the more usual creation of breaks at the borders of syntagmatic units only reinforces the already existing rhythm.[52] In any case, layout does not replace meter; the *stolbik* and *lesenka* play only a supporting role. Poems in these formats continue strict observance of iambic, trochaic, or *dol'nik* meters—a clear indication that meter remains the main organizing feature, while segmentalization has only a secondary effect on the rhythm. In purely accentual verse, where the number of unstressed syllables between stresses varies freely and thus no interplay occurs between rhythm and meter, the division into syntagms may assume slightly greater significance. Maiakovsky, for instance, tended to place each main stress into a unit of its own, thereby underscoring the organizing function of the accents.[53]

Although both the column and the stepladder possess similar functions, the column form is likely to have a more extreme effect on the reader. When a poem is written in columns, especially if it employs modern approximate rhyme, the line ends may be very difficult to determine. (As an experiment, go back to Maiakovsky's column poem, cover the rhyme scheme, and try reading it.) The *lesenka*, on the other hand, carefully preserves both the beginning and ending of each line, making the structure and the rhyme scheme clear.[54] The combination poems may also require careful reading. Note the following segment from the work by Rozhdestvensky already quoted above:

Начина́ются
       жа́рко.
Начина́ются
       с кри́ка
Голоса́ их
мужа́ют
оперя́ются
кры́лья.

The division is simple: two lines in *lesenka* form followed by four typographical lines in a column, which comprise two more lines of verse. Thus there are four verse lines in all. However, the alternating approximate rhymes may not be all that perceptible at first; until a pattern for the poem has been established, it requires a sensitive ear to tell just where the rhyme words are located.

Special punctuation and typographical effects are more the whim of the individual poet; they have been less likely to form traditions. Still, experiments with both are found among modern poets and are occasionally important for particular poems. Voznesensky has long been aware of the possibilities offered by typography; as in *Izopy* he sometimes seems as interested in the appearance as in the sound of a poem. In particular, long poems like *Oza* often employ several different typefaces to signal changes in topic or meter, offer an aside, or provide emphasis. Occasionally Voznesensky is equally unconventional in his punctuation:

К нам забреда́л Була́т
под не́бо на́ших хи́жин
костля́вый как бурла́к
он мо́лод был и хи́щен

и о́гненной насту́рцией
робе́я и нагле́я
гита́ра как нату́рщица
лежа́ла на коле́нях

она́ была́ смирне́й
чем в та́инстве дика́рь
и тёмный го́род в не́й
гуде́л и затиха́л

                              1960

Here the lack of punctuation may prove disconcerting (though there is an exclamation mark at the end of the next stanza in the poem). While this experiment is an extreme example, highly unusual punctuation may have a secondary effect on the rhythm. Many of Tsvetaeva's poems are noteworthy in this regard.[55] In the poem quoted above in the section on enjambment, she made heavy use of both hyphens (to set off the key prefix and to underline its meaning of apartness) and dashes (to set off whole words or syntactic units).

DISRUPTIONS OF RHYTHM

In one sense nearly all the features discussed in this study can be divided into two categories. For the most part the emphasis has been on regularly recurring elements that serve to establish a pattern: the sequence of stressed and unstressed syllables (meter and rhythm), the caesura, rhyme, stanzaic form, parallelism, and sound repetitions. But also important for verse are deviations from or changes in a pattern—what one scholar has grouped together as disruptions of rhythm (*pereboi ritma*).[56] These disruptions include changes in meter or rhythm, the appearance of heterostanzaic forms, and variations in the rhyme scheme. Enjambment by definition is a kind of disruption since the expected syntactic break at the end of the verse line does not occur. The main formal devices of closure are also in some way "disruptive"; all involve a change in the expected pattern. Even the repetition of an earlier line goes against the norm and thus disappoints the reader's expectations. Disruptions may be mild, such as a change in the rhyme scheme, or they may be sharp—the shift from one meter to the next in polymetrical compositions. The first would hardly be noticed by the average reader, while the second would be difficult to miss.

Breaks in a poem's patterns are important because they often underscore key moments in the thematic development. The more noticeable disruptions such as turning from stanzaic to nonstanzaic poetry or from one meter to another in polymetrical compositions often accompany a shift in topic. Very often the more subtle changes—the extended use of a particular rhythmic variation, a sudden emphasis on hypermetrical stressing, a series of syntactic breaks within a line—will help focus attention on lines that are central to a poem's meaning. Thus when analyzing a given poem, once the description of versification features has been completed it is always important to seek the lines that seem unusual. More often than not, whether consciously or intuitively, a poet will use disruptions of rhythm to highlight particular segments of a poem that are especially significant.

THE SEMANTICS OF VERSE FORMS

Many of the secondary rhythmic features discussed in this chapter often help emphasize aspects of a poem's meaning. Intonation refers to the use of a manner or tone that frequently underscores a poem's subject matter. Even a seemingly mechanical feature such as a poem's layout on the page may single out key phrases or words. And of course enjambment as well as all the other disruptions of rhythm are more often than not motivated by the effort to accentuate certain moments.

Few would disagree that the formal, essentially nonsemantic elements in a work can, at the very least, serve as auxiliary instruments for conveying a poem's meaning.[57] For instance, a poem that follows the form of a classical sonnet belongs to or is perhaps reflecting a specific tradition. A poet's use of free verse places him, in the context of Russian poetry, within a relatively limited circle of writers and indicates a definite break with the predominant norms. Even without considering their content, the highly unusual rhythmic structures of Tsvetaeva's poems are sufficient to indicate the work of a writer for whom the emotional power of verse is a main concern.

Much more complex and controversial is the question of whether formal elements can be said to have any inherent meaning. In one sense the answer is probably negative. There do not seem to be sufficiently definable distinctions between, say, iambic pentameter and iambic tetrameter or between the sound t and the sound f to cause each of them to have an invariant meaning for all people at all times. But the building blocks of a poem do not exist in the abstract. They are found in some context, be it a language (or conceivably even a group of languages), a literary movement, a writer's oeuvre, a cycle of poems, or the individual work.[58] And within one or the other of these contexts an element may impart a consistent meaning on its own.

Claims for the semantic import of seemingly nonsemantic features should be made cautiously; the meaning is rarely if ever universal but depends on the particular context, even if that context is sometimes as broad as an entire literary tradition. Of the various formal elements that may bring particular associations to a poem, the three most widely investigated—at least within the Russian tradition—are the sound texture of Russian verse, the role of grammar in poetry, and the connection between meter and meaning.

SOUND TEXTURE

The sounds that make up words play an important role in poetry; indeed, some would say that the greater attention paid to the sound texture of verse is a, if not the, distinguishing feature between poetry and nonpoetic writing—that poetic meaning is conveyed not so much through sounds as in the very sounds themselves.[59] Obvious instances include onomatopoeia and certain experiments with neologisms. More subtle and widespread are repetitions and plays on particular sounds: consonants, vowels, or some combination of the two. Both types of sound may be involved, although many studies have emphasized one at the expense of the other.

In rhymed poems, of course, repetitions occur at the ends of lines, but internal repetitions (as well as repetitions involving both rhyme words and those within lines) can establish links between words, creating series that at times are elaborate. As noted earlier, within the context of a given work such repetitions may assume a semantic function, especially when certain sounds become associated with a given theme while others accompany a different (often opposed) concept.[60] Sound repetitions may, however, assume an "extracontextual" meaning as well.[61] Words may become regularly connected with others in the popular imagination, whether or not an etymological relationship actually exists. Therefore the use of a particular word may bring to mind others that do not appear within the poem in question.[62]

Around the beginning of the twentieth century, when many poets became more concerned with the sound texture of verse, several—such as Balmont, Belyi, and Khlebnikov—made conscious efforts to find inherent meanings for Russian sounds, paying particular attention to consonants.[63] Recently, scholars have explored this topic as well. Meanings are associated not just with the sounds but with the phonemic distinctive features that comprise each sound. The efforts to discuss consonants from this viewpoint have led so far to conclusions that are best regarded as still tentative.[64] The most successful study to date has been Kiril Taranovsky's examination of the phonemic distinctive features in vowels.[65] He found, for instance, that all the "narrow" vowels (u, y, i) share the distinctive feature of diffuseness, which may express "incompleteness, loss of inner balance, weakness even distress." The vowels i and e, both acute, are opposed to u and o, both grave; the difference may be summarized as brightness versus darkness. A particularly "dark" passage cited by Taranovsky occurs at the beginning of Pushkin's poem "The Demons" ("Besy"), where five of the thirteen stressed vowels are u, and all four of the rhyme words contain u either in the stressed syllable or in the one preceding:

> Мча́тся ту́чи, вью́тся ту́чи;
> Невиди́мкою луна́
> Освеща́ет сне́г лету́чий;
> Му́тно не́бо, но́чь мутна́.
>
> 1830

The distinctive feature of compactness (found most notably in a, but also in o and e) is often associated with the notions of majesty, vastness, power, and completeness. Taranovsky pointed out that stressed a is prominent in Blok's early poetry, where it appears along with the key theme of the Beautiful Lady (Prekrásnaia Dáma).[66] Similarly, compact-

ness also helps emphasize the theme in the opening stanza of this sonnet
by Matveeva:

> Поэ́т и сла́ва – не́т опа́сней спла́ва.
> Не в по́льзу лба́м назва́ние чела́.
> И ча́сто, ча́сто – чуть прихо́дит сла́ва –
> Ухо́дит то́, за что́ она́ пришла́.
>
> 1962-64

Over half the stressed vowels (eleven out of eighteen) are *a*, while all
but one of the rest are the compact *o* and *e*. The concentration of com-
pact vowels, to say nothing of the unusually heavy stressing (only two of
the twenty ictuses are unstressed), is well suited to the stanza's weighty
topic.

While the phonemic distinctive features of sounds may contribute to
the effect of a passage, two caveats are in order. First, it makes little
sense to pick out two or three stressed vowels and make assertions about
their semantic import. If so subtle a component as phonemic distinctive
features is to have an effect, it must occur over at least several lines and
involve a reasonable number of stressed vowels. Second, mere counting
is not always enough; it is necessary to keep in mind the average fre-
quency of a sound in the language. Thus if 33 percent of all the stressed
vowels in a sample were *a*, it might be tempting to draw conclusions
about that sound's importance for the passage; however, on the average
stressed *a* appears just about that often in Russian. For the record, a
little more than 20 percent of the stressed vowels used in Russian are *o*,
about 20 percent are *e*, just under 10 percent are *u*, and around 5 percent
are *y*. The surveys currently available disagree on the frequency of *i*,
but it seems to fall in the range of 10 to 15 percent.[67] Finally, unstressed
vowels as well as consonants may also be significant. (Note the un-
stressed *u*s in the above excerpt from Pushkin's "The Demons" as well
as the play on the consonants *m*, *t*, and especially *ch*.) While poets
themselves are not always fully aware of how they create the sound tex-
ture of a poem, they certainly make use of other sounds in addition to
the stressed vowels.

THE GRAMMAR OF POETRY

Just as the sound texture of verse depends to a degree on repetitions,
so too are parallelisms important for the effect achieved by a poem's
"grammar." But recurrences of individual grammatical forms in the po-

etic text account for only one aspect of the topic. Certain grammatical oppositions inherent to the broader context of the language itself (such as impersonal as opposed to personal sentences or passive as opposed to active constructions) may be of semantic significance for a poetic work. Furthermore, the choice to use one grammatical form instead of another may affect the way in which a poem is perceived. Roman Jakobson, who has done much to elucidate this quality of poetry, stated the matter succinctly:

> Any noticeable reiteration of the same grammatical concept becomes an effective poetic device. Any unbiased, attentive, exhaustive, total description of the selection, distribution and interrelation of diverse morphological classes and syntactic constructions in a given poem surprises the examiner himself by unexpected, striking symmetries and antisymmetries, balanced structures, efficient accumulation of equivalent forms and salient contrasts, finally by rigid restrictions in the repertory of morphological and syntactic constituents used in the poem, eliminations which, on the other hand, permit us to follow the masterly interplay of the actualized constituents. Let us insist on the strikingness of these devices; any sensitive reader, as Sapir would say, feels instinctively the poetic effect and semantic load of these grammatical devices, "without the slightest attempt at conscious analysis," and in many cases the poet himself in this respect is similar to such a reader.[68]

Two points in this passage should be emphasized. First, the effect may come about in any number of ways: virtually any of the grammatical categories in a language may play a role, and the repetitions may involve symmetry, antisymmetry, and even "mirror antisymmetry,"[69] or they may be of a less regular sort. In other words, neither the grammatical category nor the manner in which it recurs need be salient or unusual. And this leads to the second point. The effect is often subtle. While a careful analysis can bring it out, most readers, and for that matter the poet too, will sense the result without being directly aware of its exact nature or how it was created.

Grammatical devices are no more able to insure that a poem will be good than is a poet's ability to write correct iambic pentameter verse. However, a talented poet will often make use of grammatical constructions to enhance the organization as well as the cogency of a work. In his seminal essay on this topic, Jakobson pointed out how Pushkin was able to use the interaction of grammatical forms—what Jakobson, following Gerard Manley Hopkins, came to term "figures of grammar"—to make up for the relative lack of the usual poetic figures in "I loved you" ("Ia vas liubil").[70] Perhaps Jakobson's most extensive analysis of

a single poem from this viewpoint is his exegesis of Blok's "A girl was
singing in the church choir" ("Devushka pela v tserkovnom khore"),
where he combines his remarks on the grammatical patterning of the
poem with a thorough examination of the rhythmic, sound, and se-
mantic correspondences that are complemented by the grammatical
features.[71]

METER AND MEANING

So far the discussion of semantics has dealt with two topics—pho-
nemics and grammar—that are as much aspects of linguistics as poet-
ics. The notion of meter, on the other hand, is inseparable from the
study of verse. Perhaps for this reason efforts to assign synaesthetic
value to particular meters predate the discussions of the meanings that
can be assigned to sounds or grammatical forms in poetry. From the
very start, theoreticians of syllabo-tonic poetry claimed that certain me-
ters were more suitable for given types of verse. Thus Sumarokov, in his
essay "On Versification" ("O stoposlozhenii") written in the 1770s, said:

> The trochee is a delicate foot and is best suited for the most delicate works,
> but lacking the liveliness of the iamb it should, in my opinion, be used more
> in the works that resemble it. . . . The iamb is a proud, lively, and majestic
> foot, but I do not know whether it makes sense for us to use it almost exclu-
> sively when we write odes—although I have also written trochaic odes—for
> the iamb is dedicated to conversation and belongs more to the epic, to trag-
> edy, comedy, and satire, than to the ode.[72]

Sumarokov then went on to describe the ternary meters: the dactyl is
chameleonlike, the amphibrach can be both lively and tender, the ana-
pest—proud and lively—is suitable for odes.

Writing a century and a half later, the acmeist poet Gumilev reached
conclusions of his own:

> Each meter has its own soul, its own peculiarities and tasks: the iamb, which
> seems to be going downstairs (the stressed syllable is a tone lower than the
> unstressed), is free, clear, firm and transmits human speech wonderfully, as
> well as the intensity of the human will. The trochee—rising, inspired—is
> always excited; sometimes it is touched, sometimes amused: its field is
> singing.[73]

He too said a few words about the ternary meters: the dactyl is powerful
and majestic, the anapest swift and impetuous, the amphibrach lulling
and limpid.

The two quotations, at first glance, seem to have little in common; interestingly though, both poets were largely in agreement about the iamb, which struck them as best suited for conveying speech and seemed broadest in its applicability. While their specific remarks about the trochee differ, each found it more limited than the iamb in the types of verse for which it should be used. To Sumarokov it was delicate and should be used only in that type of verse; to Gumilev it was excited (or agitated—*vzvolnovan*) and thus inclined toward emotionally heightened verse and singing. Their remarks about ternary meters have still less in common, though ternaries did not come into broad use until well after Sumarokov's time (and, it may be recalled, his article was the first in Russian even to describe the amphibrach). Further, the very differences between the two quotations in this regard help make them all the more typical of analogous utterances by poets over the years. Relatively little agreement was reached about the ternary meters, while iambic and trochaic verse gave rise to definite and for the most part similar impressions.

Recent scholarship has attempted to provide explanations for the attitudes toward the binary meters. Researchers have noted that an iambic rhythm is smoother than its trochaic counterpart. When people are asked to produce a trochaic rhythm, they tend to prolong the interval after the two-beat unit and the interval after the ictus. In the two-beat iambic unit the ictus and the end of the unit appear at the same beat, therefore only that one interval is prolonged. As a result it becomes more difficult to "automatize" trochaic than iambic verse.[74] Thus it is possible to explain why, as Gumilev noted, trochaic verse is commonly used in songs (and for that matter in children's rhymes and other verse with a strong beat). Both singing and shouting out of children's rhymes provide sharp distinctions between the ictuses and the other syllables. These distinctions are strengthened by the relatively rough trochaic rhythm, while in iambic verse the rhythm is more regular and closer to the tone of ordinary speech.[75] Such differences, it should be remembered, represent only tendencies; they are not absolute (for instance, there are many iambic songs). Nevertheless, the song genres of Russian folk poetry favor trochaic over iambic verse, while a disproportionate number of literary poems that have become well-known songs are trochaic (e.g., Pushkin's "The storm covers the sky with darkness," ["Buria mgloiu nebo kroet"] and Lermontov's "Sleep, my beautiful baby" ["Spi, mladenets moi prekrasnyi"]).

More extensive claims for the relationship between meter and genre remain tentative. For the most part, the clear relationships that can be found (such as the use of unrhymed iambic pentameter in drama or iambic hexameter in early "heroic" poetry) seem primarily a result of literary influence rather than of any quality inherent to the meter.[76] Indeed, the relationship between some of the traditional stanzaic forms (for example, the *terzina* and the ten-line stanza used in odes) and specific genres is somewhat stronger.[77] Efforts have also been made to find a connection between the frequency of tropes and individual meters. The results so far are limited, though they seem to indicate that within the oeuvre of certain poets such a link may well exist. Whether the relationship holds up on a larger scale remains to be seen.[78]

Greater evidence exists for an affinity between individual meters and themes. The pioneering effort in this regard is Kiril Taranovsky's study of the trochaic pentameter.[79] The meter was extremely rare in Russian poetry until Lermontov wrote "Vykhozhu odin ia na dorogu," which was soon set to music and also gained renown as a song. Taranovsky noted that the trochaic pentameter, in reflecting the two basic laws that he himself defined for Russian syllabo-tonic poetry, tends to stress the second, third, and fifth ictuses most strongly, thereby creating an asymmetrical rhythmic pattern. The synaesthetic quality of the rhythm makes it particularly suitable for poetry dealing with a journey, a theme already hinted at in the first line of the poem. Taranovsky went on to detail an entire "Lermontov cycle," which was to achieve its fullest development only in the twentieth century, especially in poems by Blok and Esenin. The subsequent works present one or more variations on the main themes of the original piece in the tradition: the dynamic motif of a journey is opposed to the static motif of life, and there are ruminations on life and death as a lone individual comes into contact with indifferent nature.[80] Besides this lyric cycle, the trochaic pentameter is also linked to an epic tradition that arose primarily from translated works in the middle of the nineteenth century and affected Maiakovsky as well as many other poets of the Soviet period. The more general significance of Taranovsky's article is twofold: first, he showed that verse rhythm, even though it lacks any totally independent meaning, nevertheless may come to be of synaesthetic significance within a broad context; second, he pointed out how a single work may influence the themes associated with the meter in which that work was composed, especially if the meter is an uncommon one.[81]

Taranovsky's work on this topic has been continued by M. L. Gasparov, who concentrates on meters and rhyme schemes without paying as much attention to rhythmic patterns. In the first (and still most convincing) of his studies, Gasparov examined poems written in the trochaic tetrameter with $A'bA'b$ rhyme (that is, alternating dactylic and masculine rhyme).[82] He found two specific traditions. One dated back to Zhukovsky's original use of this meter for translating works by Byron and Schiller; the poems in this series offer a contrast between a bright depiction of the past and a dark depiction of the present. In the other tradition, which started with Nekrasov, the meter is used to describe peasant life and for humorous verse. Examining a less rare form—the trochaic trimeter with $AbAb$ rhyme—Gasparov found a thematic "trilogy" of death, nature, and everyday life that accounts for over half the poems in the meter, and he cited Lermontov's "Mountain Peaks" ("Gornye vershiny") as a pivotal work in the tradition.[83] However, with more common meters it becomes increasingly difficult to pin down individual themes. Hence in studies of the iambic and amphibrachic trimeters he discussed the "semantic aureole"—the entire group of predominant motifs—associated with each meter and established the series of "subtraditions" that have appeared as well in poems of the meter.[84] His goal was to suggest the main thematic ties exhibited by meters rather than to define just one or two all-inclusive cycles.[85] Such investigations, besides specifying the semantic connections that arise for metrical forms, can show the significance of individual poems or foreign models for subsequent use of a meter as well as the dynamics behind the development and intermingling of themes in particular traditions.[86]

Sound, grammar, and meter are not, of course, the only features that may assume semantic value. The type of rhymes, stanzaic forms, even the arrangement of the text on the page also may be important for the system of structures in a poem and have an effect on its meaning.[87] To be sure, the relationship between form and meaning is often complex and difficult to specify; to venture into this area of analysis requires familiarity with the critical literature, a knowledge of the poetic text, and sensitivity to the poem itself. Especially it requires a thorough awareness and understanding of the metrical, rhythmic, rhyme, and other elements that have been the subject of this book. Once that ability has been achieved it is possible to explore the tantalizing if not yet completely understood correlation between the organization of a poem and its meaning.

APPENDIX

Some Practical Guides

ALL TOO OFTEN examinations of lyrics, even by established scholars, contain only casual references to matters such as meter and rhyme scheme.[1] Among the essays that do concentrate on rhythm, sound patterning, and the like, several are instructive. Jakobson's studies of poetic parallelism, while not easy reading, provide a useful guide for treating sound and rhythm as well as grammar. Lawrence Feinberg's discussion of Pasternak's "Hamlet" provides an extensive application of the same technique.[2] The analysis of Voloshin's "Northeast" ("Severovostok") by Kiril Taranovsky combines the approach of his article on the trochaic pentameter with that of his article on phonemic distinctive features, albeit now of consonants more than vowels. One theme of the poem—the journey—is reinforced by the rhythm, which ties the poem to the "Lermontov cycle" of works in trochaic pentameter. A second important motif—the wind—is conveyed in part by the frequent repetition of strident consonants, while at the end of the poem a quieter tone is introduced by the use of labials.[3] The history of the trochaic pentameter also figures in L. L. Belskaia's analysis of Esenin's "I don't regret or shout or cry" ("Ne zhaleiu, ne zovu, ne plachu").[4] She details the influence of other poetry written in this meter—especially by Blok—on Esenin's poem and then proves that the third stanza is singled out by a distinctive and varied rhythm that creates both a culmination and a turning point in the middle of the poem.

In a detailed analysis of Vladimir Lugovskoi's "How a Man Sailed with Odysseus" ("Kak chelovek plyl s Odisseem"), S. I. Gindin attempts to show how the rhythm and intonation of this unrhymed poem (in which all but 2 of the 275 lines are in iambic pentameter) correspond to developments in the work's content.[5] Gindin divides his investigation into three parts. First, he provides extensive information about the poem's rhythmic make-up, comparing his data with both theoretical models and use of this meter by other poets. Second, he points out variations in the rhythmic qualities of the poem from section to section, paying special attention to the distribution of masculine and feminine clausulae. Finally, in the third section Gindin attempts to link rhythmic and intonational features to the story being told. His step-by-step approach to the investigation can serve as a guide for similar studies of long poetic works.

Perhaps the clearest outline of a method for dealing with shorter poems has been provided by P. A. Rudnev over the course of several articles. In a fine study of the way in which meter can be related to meaning, he examines, first of all, the last poem in Blok's cycle *On Kulikovo Field*—"Again above Kulikovo Field" ("Opiat' nad polem Kulikovym")—and offers both structural and semantic reasons for Blok's shift from trochaic tetrameter in a draft version to the iambic tetrameter of the published text. The second part of the article is devoted to Blok's use of the iambic trimeter, in particular the themes that became associated with Blok's application of the meter; the results are used to question the usual dating of a lyric rewritten long after it was first composed.[6] Elsewhere, employing Lermontov's "The Sail" ("Parus") as an example, he delineates a method for describing each line in a poem (by indicating rhythmic structure, stressed vowels, word boundaries, rhyme pattern, and syntax).[7] While this article offers the most thorough explanation of his method, a study published several years earlier contains a particularly impressive application of the same approach to Blok's "All is calm on the bright face":

> Всё ти́хо на све́тлом лице́.
> И роси́стая по́лночь тиха́.
> С немы́м торжество́м на лице́
> Открыва́ю гра́ни стиха́.
>
> Шепчу́ и звеню́, как струна́.
> То́ – ночны́е цветы́ – не слова́.
> Их росу́ убели́ла луна́
> У подно́жья Её торжества́.

1903

While a quick reading of the poem yields few obvious unusual qualities, Rudnev notes that the fourth line is singled out in several ways. The pair of feminine word boundaries within the line contrast the line with its neighbors, both of which exhibit a pair of masculine word boundaries; the stressed vowels in the line are all *a* (and once established this vowel appears in the rhyme syllable throughout the second stanza). It is the only line in the poem not written in amphibrachic or anapestic trimeter, but instead is written in three-stress *dol'niki*. As Rudnev notes, there are three spheres in the poem: the highest belongs to an unspecified "She" and appears at both the beginning and end of the work, the middle is that of nature, while the lowest (and innermost within the poem) belongs to the lyric *I*. The entire poem turns on the key fourth line, which introduces the *I* and marks a transition: until that point the emotional intensity grows, but immediately afterward a catharsis occurs that carries through until the end.[8]

Formal devices do not always point so clearly to a particular line; nevertheless, an examination of their role usually brings out ways in which they enhance the poem's message and points to aspects of the poet's technique that otherwise remain hidden. For the following three analyses I have purposely selected poems that lack highly unusual or salient structural features, yet some of the formal elements are important for each work's overall effect.

The earliest of the poems is a sixteen-line lyric by Tiutchev:

От жи́зни то́й, что бушева́ла зде́сь,
От кро́ви то́й, что зде́сь реко́й лила́сь,
Что́ уцеле́ло, что́ дошло́ до на́с?
Два-три́ курга́на, ви́димых подне́сь...

Да два́-три́ ду́ба вы́росли на ни́х,
Раски́нувшись и широко́ и сме́ло.
Красу́ются, шумя́т, — и не́т им де́ла,
Чей пра́х, чью па́мять ро́ют ко́рни и́х.

Приро́да зна́ть не зна́ет о было́м,
Ей чу́жды на́ши при́зрачные го́ды,
И пе́ред не́й мы сму́тно сознаём
Себя́ сами́х — лишь грёзою приро́ды.

Поочерёдно все́х свои́х дете́й,
Сверша́ющих сво́й по́двиг беспол́езный,
Она́ равно́ приве́тствует свое́й
Всепоглоща́ющей и миротво́рной бе́здной.

                          1871

The poem contains four four-line stanzas and is basically written in iambic pentameter. However, the poem's last line is in iambic hexameter. Tiutchev was not adverse to disrupting the meters of his poems; recall, for example, the *dol'niki* lines in "Last Love" or Turgenev's efforts to "correct" what he viewed as Tiutchev's departures from sound poetic practice. Here the odd line appears at the very end of the poem, and the extra length, which breaks the established pattern, serves as an element of closure. Although the lyric is too short for statistical analysis to be very meaningful, a few qualities are still worth noting. In the first fifteen lines of the poem the stressing follows the alternation of strong (first, third, fifth) and weak ictuses that is typical for the iambic pentameter, while the actual percentages of stressing on each ictus are fairly close to those for Tiutchev's poetry as a whole.[9] The most common rhythmic variation for the iambic pentameter is the fifth (where stress is omitted on the fourth ictus), which usually accounts for about 25 to 33 percent of the lines in a poem. Here it appears in seven of the fifteen iambic pentameter lines, and what is more, six of those lines occur in groups: lines 4 and 5, and then all the lines of the third stanza.

The rhyme pattern of the poem is noteworthy. The first two stanzas are *abba* (actually the second stanza is *aBBa* with an inner feminine rhyme pair), and the last two stanzas are *aBaB*. The change suggests a 2+2 structure for the poem as a whole, or at least a break of sorts after the second stanza. Similarly, the two halves of the poem exhibit differences in their grammatical features. The first half is marked by various types of parallelisms and repetitions: the analogous syntactic structures of the first and second lines, the repetitions of structures within the third and eighth lines, the paired words within lines 6 (two adverbs) and 7 (two verbs), and the repetition of *dva-tri* in lines 4 and 5. The second half lacks this sense of balance and order; further, whereas in the first half a syntactic break occurs at the end of each line, in the second half breaks are missing at the ends of lines 11 and 15. The poem's adjectives are concentrated in the second half, especially in the last stanza, while the first half contains many more verbs—there are four finite verbs in each of the first two stanzas and only one in the last.

Each of the four stanzas focuses on a distinct topic. In the first, the distant past is recalled and the poet wonders what aspects of it have come down to the present. The second stanza focuses on the oak trees, which are indifferent to that life and to the poet's concerns as well. The third makes a more general point about nature's disinterest in humanity; but in the fourth nature becomes more menacing, seeming to devour people in its abyss. The first two stanzas, therefore, are the more specific, presenting the concrete imagery of the burial mounds and the oak trees. The finite verbs keep the description moving along, while repetitions and parallels impart unity to the entire section. Particularly important are the links between lines 4 and 5—the repetition of *dva-tri*, the reference to the two specific objects (the burial mounds and then the oak

trees) that give the impetus to the poet's subsequent musings, and the
repetition of the same rhythmic variation. The climax of the poem,
however, occurs in the third stanza. The break with the previous stanzas
is emphasized by the change in rhyme scheme as well as by the shift to a
more abstract level with the influx of adjectives. The focus is not on
definite oak trees but on nature. And indeed the word *priroda* both
opens and closes the third stanza, which is further tied together by the
use of the same rhythmic variation in each of its lines. The key point
that we are only a fancy of nature appears in the last two lines of the
stanza. Our attention is drawn not only by the enjambment that links the
two lines but also by the alliteration over the last two words of line 11
and the first two of line 12. The fourth stanza deepens the idea of the
third, with the final dark note—the reference to the abyss—emphasized
by the lack of a break between the last two lines as well as by the extra
ictus at the very end of the poem, the same ictus that contains the word
bezdnoi.

The second example is a 1914 poem by Akhmatova, "He was jeal-
ous, worried, and tender":

Был он ревнивым, тревожным и нежным,	í ᵕ 1 ᵕ 2 ᵕ 2 ᵕ 1
Как божье солнце, меня любил,	1 ᵕ 1 ᵕ 2 ᵕ 1 ᵕ 0
А чтобы она не запела о прежнем,	1 ᵕ 2 ᵕ 2 ᵕ 2 ᵕ 1
Он белую птицу мою убил.	1 ᵕ 2 ᵕ 2 ᵕ 1 ᵕ 0
Промолвил, войдя на закате в светлицу:	1 ᵕ 2 ᵕ 2 ᵕ 2 ᵕ 1
"Люби меня, смейся, пиши стихи!"	1 ᵕ 2 ᵕ 2 ᵕ 1 ᵕ 0
И я закопала весёлую птицу	1 ᵕ 2 ᵕ 2 ᵕ 2 ᵕ 1
За круглым колодцем у старой ольхи.	1 ᵕ 2 ᵕ 2 ᵕ 2 ᵕ 0
Ему обещала, что плакать не буду,	1 ᵕ 2 ᵕ 2 ᵕ 2 ᵕ 1
Но каменным сделалось сердце моё,	1 ᵕ 2 ᵕ 2 ᵕ 2 ᵕ 0
И кажется мне, что всегда и повсюду	1 ᵕ 2 ᵕ 2 ᵕ 2 ᵕ 1
Услышу я сладостный голос её.	1 ᵕ 2 ᵕ 2 ᵕ 2 ᵕ 0

The three four-line stanzas adhere to the most common of the Russian
rhyme patterns, *AbAb*. The meter is four-stress *dol'niki* with a constant
one-syllable anacrusis and full stressing throughout the poem. Full
stressing is unusual in modern *dol'niki*. By the date of this work it was
more common to omit stresses occasionally, particularly on the first and
third ictuses, thereby creating a rhythm not unlike that of the iambic
tetrameter. However, in the early 1900s omitted stresses were still rare,
and the rhythm did not come to express fully the effect of regressive
accentual dissimilation until the 1920s.[10] As a relatively early example
of four-stress *dol'niki*, this poem bears definite traces of the *dol'niki*'s

ternary origins in both the fully stressed lines and the preponderance of two-syllable intervals between the ictuses. Even today four-stress *dol'niki*—unlike the three-stress—tend to maintain more of a resemblance to ternaries by continuing to favor the two-syllable interval. In this case the poem closely resembles amphibrachic tetrameters, both because the one-syllable anacrusis is a constant and because eight of the twelve lines are written within the norms of that meter. Only the first, second, fourth, and sixth lines contain *dol'niki* rhythmic variations. Thus the final six lines of the poem maintain perfectly regular amphibrachs without any hypermetrical stressing (unless one counts the weak stress on *ia* in the last line) to break the almost monotonous rhythm. The first stanza, on the other hand, is much less regular: each of the first four lines contains a different rhythmic variation, and each contains a different number of syllables—ranging from nine to twelve. The first line could even give a reader the wrong impression about the poem's dominant rhythm. Since *byl* and *on* are both normally weakly stressed, it would be reasonable to consider the first ictus as coinciding with the first syllable, thereby creating a line in dactylic tetrameter. Only in retrospect, once the one-syllable anacrusis has become fully established, does the proper reading for the first line become evident. In the second stanza, line 5 of the poem provides the second instance of an amphibrachic rhythmic variation, but then, as if in direct contrast, the next line contains the sharpest rhythmic disruption of the entire work. The hypermetrical stressing on *menia* gives the line five stresses, and falling as it does on a two-syllable word the extra stress can noticeably affect the rhythm. Also, the series of three imperatives, separated from each other by the natural syntactic pauses in such a series and by their incommensurable meanings, helps make the line's rhythm almost prosaic. Immediately afterward the amphibrachic tetrameter becomes established and continues until the end.

One or two aspects of the sound pattern are worth mentioning. The end of the first stanza contains many labial stops (*b/p*): eight over the last three lines, six in just the last two. The abruptness of these stops builds up to the climax at the end of that stanza, when the "he" kills the white bird. A contrast is provided by the poem's final line, where the combination of the fricative *s* and liquid *l* appears twice before stressed vowels and a third time in inverted form. The alliteration of the *k* sound in line 8 picks up on the same sound in the previous line and is echoed by its appearance in individual words over the next three lines as well;

several (*zakopala*, *kolodtsem*, *plakat'*, *kamennym*: bury, well, cry, stone) form a sequence that underscores the topic of these lines.

The use of grammatical categories is significant. There are three figures in the poem: *on*, *ia* (the narrator), and *ona* (the bird). Since both the *she* and the *I* are feminine, they are linked grammatically; they are further tied together as objects of "his" violence—one directly, the other by implication. During the first six lines *on* is the subject. First he is described, then he kills the white bird, and finally he barks his series of orders to the narrator. Thus the more "irregular" rhythm of the first six lines is connected with the *he*; the most irregular rhythm, in the sixth line, contains his only words in the poem, and it is significant that they comprise a series of imperatives. As the subject changes to *I*, the rhythm becomes more regular and the tone calmer. Note especially the eighth line, where the only series of feminine word boundaries in the poem causes all the rhythmic and word units to share the same boundaries: Ză krúglўm | kŏlódtsĕm | ŭ stárŏi | ŏl'khí. Yet the regular rhythm contrasts with the harsh *k* sounds: the narrator's own tension and the inner turmoil as she remains externally calm become palpable. Then at the end the atmosphere eases; the dominant sound repetition is that of *sl*. Except for the mention of her promise to him, "he" disappears. The final reference is to "her" voice, that of the bird; but in light of the similarity in gender between the *ona* and the *ia*, the narrator could be referring to her own voice as well: she too will sing (write poems) again.

Arseny Tarkovsky's "The Manuscript" ("Rukopis'"), which is dedicated to Anna Akhmatova, provides the final example:

Я ко́нчил кни́гу и поста́вил то́чку
И ру́копись перечита́ть не мо́г.
Судьба́ моя́ сгоре́ла ме́жду стро́к,
Пока́ душа́ меня́ла оболо́чку.

Так блу́дный сы́н срыва́ет с пле́ч соро́чку,
Так со́ль море́й и пы́ль земны́х доро́г
Благословля́ет и кляне́т проро́к,
На а́нгелов ходи́вший в одино́чку.

Я то́т, кто жи́л во времена́ мои́,
Но не́ был мно́й. Я мла́дший из семьи́
Люде́й и пти́ц, я пе́л со все́ми вме́сте

И не поки́ну пи́ршества живы́х –
Прямо́й гербо́вник и́х семе́йной че́сти,
Прямо́й слова́рь их свя́зей корневы́х.

[<1962]

In certain ways this most recent of the three poems is also the most "classical" in form. It contains a traditional stanzaic form, the Petrarchan sonnet, with an octet (*AbbA AbbA*) based on two rhymes followed by a sextet (in this case *ccDeDe*) that avoids a closing couplet. The rhymes do not exhibit any of the approximations that have become common in the twentieth century. Tarkovsky in general is fairly conservative in his rhyme practice, and the poem contains rhymes that, say, Lermontov would have regarded as exact. As is typical for the sonnet, the poem is written in iambic pentameter. While few twentieth-century poems observe a caesura, this work exhibits what Taranovsky has called a movable caesura.[11] Ten of the fourteen lines observe a word break after the fourth syllable, and the remainder have a break after the fifth. This regularity, while not affecting the rhythm in the way that a constant caesura would, is nonetheless sufficient to create a tendency toward a bipartite line structure with slight breaks between the two parts of each line. The rhythmic pattern for the poem as a whole is interesting in that the third ictus, which would usually be the second most strongly stressed in an iambic pentameter poem, is less frequently stressed than either of the first two ictuses as well as, of course, the fifth. In fact, this so-called falling rhythm for the iambic pentameter is not uncommon in the twentieth century, though it is atypical for poems written earlier. On the other hand, stressing throughout is somewhat heavier than expected for a modern work. In the twentieth century poems in iambic pentameter usually contain stresses on about 75 percent of their ictuses; here, more like nineteenth-century poems, just over 80 percent are stressed. The reason for the higher figure is evident from glancing at the rhythmic variations for each line. Even though Tarkovsky omitted two stresses on no fewer than four lines, he also used five lines that are fully stressed— an unusually high number for a poem of this length.

Word boundaries, which affect the way stressing patterns are perceived, play a small but noteworthy role in the poem. All three of the internal word boundaries in the first line are feminine, but elsewhere masculine word boundaries are more prominent. The four masculine word boundaries in line 6 mean that the boundaries for both the word and rhythmic units coincide throughout. Masculine word boundaries are also predominant in the first half of the sextet: all the word boundaries in line 9 are masculine, as are all but the last internal word boundary in the next two lines.

There are at least two significant aspects to the sound patterning. The first concerns the stressed vowels. In the first stanza the vowel *a* appears often (seven times), especially toward the end; afterward, stressed *a* becomes much less frequent and, except for the first stanza, occurs considerably less often than the norm predicts. Compact vowels (*a*, *o*, *e*) as a group account for fourteen of the sixteen stressed vowels in the first stanza. A sharp increase occurs in the number of acute vowels toward the middle of the concluding sextet. Note especially the assonance based on *e* (four of the five stressed vowels) in line 11 and on *i* (two out of three) in line 12. Both *i* and *e* can be described as "bright" vowels, which contrast with the dark *o* and *u*.[12] Indeed, the frequency of *i* and *e* vowels marks a shift from the second quatrain (lines 5 through 8), where the vowel *o* is more prominent. The second important instance is the play on sounds that occurs over the last several lines of the poem. Two words both in lines 11 and 12 begin with *p*, and in the following two lines the anaphora likewise consists of a word beginning with *p*. Furthermore, perhaps by chance the two consonants in *pel* represent the initial letters of the previous two nouns in the line, and it is precisely the people and the birds who unite in the singing with the *ia*, the poem's narrator. Finally, the most noticeable consonant sounds in the final line of the poem are those that begin the four main words—*p*, *s* (twice), and *k*—as well as *r*, which appears no fewer than three times. Taken together, they form an anagram of the consonant sounds in the poem's title, *rukopis'*.

Once again the sound texture, rhythmic variations, and grammatical structure lend support to the poem's thematic development. In line 1 the exclusively feminine word boundaries, which tend to read more smoothly than masculine ones, exhibit a calm, regular rhythm, while the omission of stress on the middle ictus in each of the first two lines helps create the bipartite line structure that dominates throughout. The syntax of these lines is also important since the word *i* creates a clear division between the two halves of line 1, while the inversion in line 2 singles out the first two words (which include the poem's title) and provides a break between the first four syllables and the next six. The predominance of compact stressed vowels, with their associated notions of completeness and majesty, reinforce the sense of solemnity that pervades the first stanza.

An abrupt change occurs at the beginning of the second stanza, where lines 5 and 6 of the poem are linked both by anaphora and by the full stressing in each. The sixth line with its exclusively masculine word boundaries also has a particularly distinctive rhythm. The last three lines of the quatrain contain an entire series of inversions: the first of these lines should really be the last; the second should be the first and is itself inverted (with *prorok*, the sentence's subject, receiving special emphasis by its appearance in the rhyme position); while the third line should be second and also contains an internal inversion of its own. The complicated syntax and distinct rhythmic changes contrast with the first quatrain. And of course there is a thematic contrast as well with the movement away from the *I* of the first stanza to the two comparisons (prodigal son, prophet) that take up the second. Further, the heavy stressing of lines 5 and 6 slows down the reading, and the weighty tone is in keeping with the biblical imagery that is introduced.

Over the last six lines the focus again shifts back to the *I*—lines 9 through 11 all contain the word *ia*—but now it is no longer the *I* of the first stanza. The narrator has come to embody the features mentioned in the second quatrain as well. The poem's key lines occur at the center of the sextet, beginning midway through line 10 and continuing to the end of line 12. Frequent alliteration and assonance (line 11: "ptits, ia pel so vsemi vmeste"; line 12: "pokinu pirshestva") call attention to the lines, as does the enjambment, while the predominance of "bright" stressed vowels lends a positive note to the role the poet sees for himself. The final two lines offer an elaboration of that role, and the anagram of *rukopis'* as well as the anaphora and near-exact grammatical parallelism of the final two lines all impart a sense of closure to the entire poem.

These analyses are meant to be more suggestive than exhaustive. They do not elaborate every rhythmic quality or sound repetition that plays a role in the poems, and certainly another reader could find yet other features worthy of emphasis. The remarks are offered with the hope that they are sufficiently provocative to inspire the practical use of the information provided in the body of this study, for familiarity with the meters, rhythms, rhymes, and other organizational elements of Russian verse is the initial step toward knowledgeable reading of the poetry.

Notes

PREFACE

1. M. L. Gasparov has pointed to connections between Briusov's theory and his practice in the article "Briusov-stikhoved i Briusov stikhotvorets (1910–1920-e gody)." Briusov's experimental verse appears in the collection *Opyty*, which has been reprinted in *Sobranie sochinenii*. His writings on verse theory appeared in *Kratkii kurs nauki o stikhe*; a revised version of this book was published in 1924 as *Osnovy stikhovedeniia*. For contemporary opinions of Briusov's theories, see Roman Jakobson, "Briusovskaia stikhologiia i nauka o stikhe," and B. V. Tomashevskii, "Valerii Briusov kak stikhoved." More recently, S. I. Gindin has brought out several previously unpublished items on versification by Briusov and has also written extensively and sympathetically about Briusov's theories. See, for instance, "V. Ia. Briusov o rechevoi prirode stikha i stikhotvornogo ritma i o russkikh ekvivalentakh antichnykh stikhotvornykh razmerov"; "Transformatsionnyi analiz i metrika (iz istorii problemy)"; "Vzgliady V. Ia. Briusova na iazykovuiu priemlemost' stikhovykh sistem i sud'by russkoi sillabiki (po rukopisiam 90-kh godov)"; and "Briusovskoe opisanie metriki russkogo stikha s tochki zreniia sovremennoi tipologii lingvisticheskikh opisanii."

2. Belyi presented his essential ideas in a series of articles that were included in *Simvolizm: Kniga statei*. The essays include "Lirika i eksperiment," "Opyt kharakteristiki russkogo chetyrekhstopnogo iamba," "Sravnitel'naia morfologiia ritma russkikh lirikov v iambicheskom dimetre," and "'Ne poi, krasavitsa, pri mne . . .' A. S. Pushkina (Opyt opisaniia)." On the reaction of one contemporary to Belyi's theories, see Thomas Beyer, "The Bely-Zhirmunsky Polemic."

3. See the bibliography for references to the most important works by Tomashevskii, Zhirmunskii, and Jakobson in the field of verse theory. Some of Tomashevskii's pioneering work has only recently been published; see L. S. Fleishman, "Tomashevskii i Moskovskii lingvisticheskii kruzhok" for an early article as well as documents concerning the early reception of his theories.

4. B. V. Tomashevskii, "Stikh i ritm," p. 62.

INTRODUCTION

1. For a more detailed comparison of Russian and English based on some of the material presented here see Barry P. Scherr, "Russian and English Versification: Similarities, Differences, Analysis."

2. B. V. Tomashevskii, "Ritmika chetyrekhstopnogo iamba po nabliudeniiam nad stikhom *Evgeniia Onegina*," pp. 105–6.

3. Gustav Herdan, *The Advanced Theory of Language as Choice and Chance*, table 97, p. 287. These figures are based on surveys by Herdan of Pushkin's verse, Turgenev's *Rudin*, Tolstoy's *Childhood, Boyhood, and Youth*, and Tolstoy's *War and Peace*.

4. Cf. V. A. Nikonov, "Mesto udaren'ia v russkom slove," p. 3. Nikonov counts proclitics and enclitics as separate words, but his findings regarding stress placement largely support Shengeli's data.

5. Georgii Shengeli, *Traktat o russkom stikhe*, pp. 20–21, 25; Tomashevskii, "Ritmika," pp. 104–5.

6. Vladimir Nabokov, *Speak, Memory: An Autobiography Revisited*, p. 220.

7. For succinct comparisons of Russian and English prosody, see M. L. Gasparov, "Russkii iamb i angliiskii iamb," pp. 408–9, and Vladimir Nabokov, *Notes on Prosody*, pp. 50–51. The subject is covered in more detail by V. M. Zhirmunskii in *Vvedenie v metriku*, pp. 71–79; and by Robin Kemball in *Alexander Blok: A Study in Rhythm and Metre*, pp. 53–156.

8. For a review of some problems posed by English stress see James Bailey, *Toward a Statistical Analysis of English Verse*, pp. 16–21.

9. Brief comparisons between English and Russian rhyme can be found in Nabokov, *Notes*, pp. 85–95; and Kemball, *Alexander Blok*, pp. 55–64.

10. More recent developments in English verse theory include applying the principles of transformational generative linguistics to poetry; the new specialization is often referred to as "generative metrics." The pioneering work in the field is an article by Morris Halle and Samuel Jay Keyser, "Chaucer and the Study of Prosody."

11. The exceptions include Bailey, *Toward a Statistical Analysis*; idem, "Linguistic Givens and Their Metrical Realization in a Poem by Yeats"; and Marina Tarlinskaja's massive study, *English Verse: Theory and History*.

1 DEFINITIONS AND BACKGROUND

1. Vladimir Nabokov, in fact, uses the term *false pyrrhic* because in his view the so-called Russian pyrrhic is not at all equivalent to the classical pyrrhic foot (*Notes*, pp. 8, 12–13).

2. Exceptions to this rule are extremely rare and limited primarily, though not exclusively, to lines written in unrhymed iambic pentameter. For examples, see Kiril Taranovsky, *Ruski dvodelni ritmovi*, pp. 8–12.

3. Rudnev discusses polymetrical compositions in a number of articles. He summarizes their use by Blok in "O sootnoshenii monometricheskikh i polimetricheskikh konstruktsii v sisteme stikhotvornykh razmerov A. Bloka," and by Nekrasov in "Polimetricheskie kompozitsii Nekrasova."

4. Taranovsky, *Ruski dvodelni ritmovi*, pp. 13–45.

5. James Bailey, "Some Recent Developments in the Study of Russian Versification," p. 156.

6. S. M. Bondi claims that some metrists during the first quarter of the twentieth century distorted the true nature of rhythm by seeing it as a deviation from

meter rather than as a major determinant of a poem's effect in its own right. Elsewhere in the same article Bondi has some thoughtful remarks on the essential nature of rhythm. See Bondi, "O ritme."

7. George Saintsbury, *Historical Manual of English Prosody*, pp. 33, 274, 289.

8. Taranovsky finds evidence for what might be termed a "movable caesura" that oscillates between the third and fourth syllables in the trochaic pentameter (*Ruski dvodelni ritmovi*, pp. 276–77); James Bailey discusses a similar phenomenon for the iambic pentameter in "The Evolution and Structure of the Russian Iambic Pentameter from 1880 to 1922." Tomashevskii (*O stikhe*, pp. 240–43) is skeptical about the concept of a movable caesura. However, metrists who deal with Russian poetry limit the term *movable caesura* to cases when every or nearly every line in a poem contains a word boundary on one of two neighboring syllables. This is still a stricter definition of the caesura than is common in English poetry.

9. Taranovsky, *Ruski dvodelni ritmovi*, pp. 146–57. This chapter contains a history of iambic pentameter throughout the eighteenth and nineteenth centuries, paying special attention to those poems in which the caesura occurs frequently enough to be a rhythmical feature (that is, at least 75 percent of the lines have a caesura) but not frequently enough to be called a constant. Taranovsky calls this transitional feature a "free caesura" (*slobodan medijan*). For our purposes the word *caesura*, when used without a modifier, will imply a constant caesura.

10. Tables 9 and 10 appended to Taranovsky's *Ruski dvodelni ritmovi* show that these tendencies hold not just for the brief examples quoted here but also for the iambic pentameter used by all poets in the nineteenth century. On the average, poems with a caesura stress the third ictus 95 percent of the time and the fourth ictus 40 percent; the corresponding figures for the iambic pentameter without caesura are 85 percent and 54 percent.

11. Cf. Bailey, *Toward a Statistical Analysis*, pp. 12–13.

12. Kiril Taranovsky, "O ritmicheskoi strukture russkikh dvuslozhnykh razmerov," p. 421.

13. M. L. Gasparov, "Iamb i khorei sovetskikh poetov," p. 103.

14. Taranovsky, "O ritmicheskoi strukture," pp. 421–22.

15. Roman Jakobson, "Ob odnoslozhnykh slovakh v russkom stikhe," pp. 239, 241–42.

16. Exceptions to this rule are extremely rare; Jakobson cites several in "Ob odnoslozhnykh slovakh," p. 242. It is interesting to note the similarities between this prohibition and the comments by Halle and Keyser regarding the "stress maximum" ("Chaucer," p. 197). Halle and Keyser also prefer to speak of strong and weak positions instead of feet, as do many Russian metrists. Since Halle is familiar with Russian verse theory, it is possible that certain concepts first applied to Russian poetry lie at the base of generative metrics.

17. Jakobson, "Ob odnoslozhnykh slovakh," p. 244. M. L. Gasparov has provided further evidence for the proclivity of weakly stressed words to appear on the weaker ictuses and in places where there is hypermetrical stressing. See Gasparov, "Legkii stikh i tiazhelyi stikh."

18. For a concise survey of work done on the verse forms of the *byliny*, see A. M. Astakhova, *Byliny: Itogi i problemy izucheniia*, pp. 143–62. A broader and more detailed survey covering all aspects of folk verse is M. P. Shtokmar, *Issledovaniia v oblasti russkogo narodnogo stikhoslozheniia*, pp. 17–135.

19. A. F. Gil'ferding, *Onezhskie byliny*, I, 66.

20. James Bailey, "The Epic Meters of T. G. Rjabinin as Collected by A. F. Gil'ferding," pp. 9–10.

21. Much of the information in the following paragraphs is based on the article by Bailey cited in the previous footnote and on "The Metrical Typology of Russian Narrative Folk Meters." Also useful was M. L. Gasparov's "Russkii bylinnyi stikh." Both researchers use Gil'ferding's first edition (1873), which contains many more stress marks and elisions than the fourth edition. In preparing the more recent editions the editors have gone back to Gil'ferding's manuscripts; however, Gil'ferding himself proofread the first part of the 1873 edition just before his death in 1872, thus that edition may well reflect his own corrections (see Bailey, "Epic Meters," pp. 10–11). I follow the terminology of Bailey's "Metrical Typology," which discusses four types of narrative folk verse: trochaic, accentual, and two other kinds of folk meters. Gasparov talks of three separate meters. In addition to trochaic poetry, he distinguishes between what he calls the *taktovik* (or strict accentual verse) and a looser type of accentual verse. (For a discussion of these terms as they apply to literary poetry, see chapter 3.) He claims that the *taktovik* is the basic meter of the *bylina*, although in fact the original meter appears to have been trochaic. In some cases his arguments are open to question as well. For instance, he examines six of Riabinin's songs, but the six he chooses include all three in which Riabinin employed accentual lines. Therefore Gasparov's tables make it appear that Riabinin used trochaic and accentual meters more or less equally, whereas in fact only 17 percent of the eighteen songs he performed for Gil'ferding were in accentual verse.

22. Bailey, "Epic Meters," pp. 11–15.

23. Ibid., pp. 12, 14; cf. Bailey, "The Trochaic Song Meters of Kol'cov and Kašin," pp. 15–18.

24. On stress shifts in folk verse see Shtokmar, *Issledovaniia*, pp. 347–77.

25. The use of embryonic rhyme in the *bylina* is discussed by V. M. Zhirmunskii in *Rifma: Ee istoriia i teoriia*, pp. 402–24.

26. Roman Jakobson, "Studies in Comparative Slavic Metrics," pp. 35–39.

27. K. V. Chistov and B. E. Chistova, comps., *Prichitaniia*, p. 83.

28. A. V. Pozdneev, "Evoliutsiia stikhoslozheniia v narodnoi lirike XVI–XVIII vekov," pp. 42–43.

29. Bailey, "Kol'cov and Kašin," p. 16.

30. In fact, Russian poets were sometimes influenced not by folk songs but by the *pesenniki*, or song books, which contained literary poems and Western songs along with works of Russian folk origin. Cf. Bailey, "Kol'cov and Kašin," pp. 6–8.

31. James Bailey, "Literary Usage of a Russian Folk Song Meter," and A. N. Bezzubov, "Piatislozhnik." The term *piatislozhnik* or *penton* is frequently used by Soviet scholars to imply a "foot" containing five syllables. Thus they con-

sider the 5+5 meter to be based on a five-syllable foot with stress on the middle syllable. My preference is to follow Bailey's terminology; on the question of pentons, see the final section of chapter 2.

32. Kiril Taranovsky, "Formy obshcheslavianskogo i tserkovnoslavianskogo stikha v drevnerusskoi literature XI–XIII vv.," p. 382.

33. V. I. Dal', *Poslovitsy russkogo naroda*, p. 66.

34. S. G. Lazutin, "Nekotorye voprosy stikhotvornoi formy russkikh poslovits," pp. 141–42.

35. M. P. Shtokmar, "Stikhotvornaia forma russkikh poslovits, pogovorok, zagadok, pribautok," p. 151.

36. Much of what has been said here about proverbs also applies to riddles; cf. V. V. Mitrofanova, "Ritmicheskoe stroenie russkikh narodnykh zagadok."

37. Perhaps the most thorough study of this form to date is Brigitte Stephan's *Studien zur russischen Častuška und ihrer Entwicklung*. See also S. G. Lazutin, *Poetika russkogo fol'klora*, pp. 181–202.

38. These examples are from V. S. Bakhtin, comp., *Chastushka*, pp. 188, 187 respectively.

39. N. S. Trubetzkoy, "O metrike chastushki," pp. 10–13.

40. For a detailed discussion of literary poems based on folk verse, see M. L. Gasparov, "Russkii narodnyi stikh v literaturnykh imitatsiiakh."

41. For a treatment of this topic see Roman Jakobson, "The Slavic Response to Byzantine Poetry."

42. Antonina Gove, "Literalism and Poetic Equivalence in the Old Church Slavonic Translation of the Akathistos Hymn," "Slavic Liturgical Hymns as a Repository of Byzantine Poetics," and "The Evidence for Metrical Adaptation in Early Slavic Translated Hymns."

43. A. M. Panchenko, *Russkaia stikhotvornaia kul'tura XVII veka*, p. 14.

44. L. I. Timofeev, "Ritmika 'Slova o polku Igoreve.'"

45. Riccardo Picchio, "On the Prosodic Structure of the *Igor Tale*."

46. V. I. Stelletskii, "K voprosu o ritmicheskom stroe 'Slova o polku Igoreve.'"

47. A. V. Pozdneev, "Stikhoslozhenie drevnei russkoi poezii."

48. Ibid., pp. 12–13.

49. Taranovsky, "Formy obshcheslavianskogo," pp. 377–78.

50. Ibid., p. 380.

51. L. I. Sazonova, "Printsip ritmicheskoi organizatsii v proizvedeniiakh torzhestvennogo krasnorechiia starshei pory ('Slovo o zakone i blagodati' Ilariona, 'Pokhvala sv. Simeonu i sv. Savve' Domentiana)," p. 44.

52. Panchenko, *Russkaia stikhotvornaia*, p. 14.

53. Ibid., pp. 5–16.

54. For an extensive survey of theories regarding possible verse traditions in Old Russian literature see Světla Mathauserová, *Drevnerusskie teorii iskusstva slova*, pp. 57–105.

55. Panchenko, *Russkaia stikhotvornaia*, pp. 22–26. L. I. Ibraev in "Rifmovnik (K probleme proiskhozhdeniia russkogo rechevogo stikha)" has interpreted events during this period quite differently. He considers the *rifmovnik*— by which he means virtually all types of rhymed lines in the seventeenth century

(rhymed verse, rhymed prose, the *raeshnik*)—to be the progenitor of Russian verse. Apparently he wishes to deny the importance of foreign influences (and of syllabic verse in general) for the development of Russian poetry, but his theory fails to account for the actual changes in subsequent Russian verse practice.

56. Panchenko, *Russkaia stikhotvornaia*, pp. 66–77.

57. Ibid., p. 34.

58. V. E. Kholshevnikov, "Russkaia i pol'skaia sillabika i sillabo-tonika," pp. 31–39.

59. Rimvydas Silbajoris, *Russian Versification: The Theories of Trediakovskij, Lomonosov, and Kantemir*, p. 6.

60. The extent of nonfeminine rhyme and the problem of accounting for it have been the subject of sharp disagreements among Russian scholars. Two articles that appeared in the same collection as Kholshevnikov's "Russkaia i pol'skaia sillabika" address this topic: P. N. Berkov, "K sporam o printsipakh chteniia sillabicheskikh stikhov XVII–nachala XVIII v."; and A. M. Panchenko, "O rifme i deklamatsionnykh normakh sillabicheskoi poezii XVII v."

61. M. L. Gasparov, "Russkii sillabicheskii trinadtsatislozhnik," pp. 48–49.

62. Ibid.

63. Ibid., pp. 49–52. Gasparov's figures call into question L. I. Timofeev's assertion (in "Sillabicheskii stikh," pp. 48–49) that the masculine caesura gradually became more frequent throughout the entire period when syllabic verse was being written.

64. See, for example, A. P. Kviatkovskii, *Poeticheskii slovar'*, p. 308.

65. S. M. Bondi, "Trediakovskii, Lomonosov, Sumarokov," p. 94; Gasparov, "Russkii trinadtsatislozhnik," p. 59. On the other hand, Timofeev felt that there was a tonic basis to syllabic verse and that the syllabo-tonic system evolved directly from it ("Sillabicheskii stikh," p. 58). The notion that such an evolution took place has been around since the nineteenth century. For a discussion of the topic that complements Gasparov's views, see James Bailey, "The Versification of the Russian *Kant* from the End of the Seventeenth to the Middle of the Eighteenth Century."

66. V. E. Kholshevnikov, *Osnovy stikhovedeniia*, p. 17.

67. Gasparov, "Russkii trinadtsatislozhnik," pp. 59–63.

68. G. A. Gukovskii, *Russkaia literatura XVIII veka*, p. 63. Gasparov asserts that the syllabo-tonic system triumphed precisely because it made the distinction between prose and poetry more sharp than it had been in the syllabic system. See Gasparov, "Oppozitsiia 'stikh—proza' i stanovlenie russkogo literaturnogo stikha," p. 329. On pp. 324–26 Gasparov also claims that the lack of any true distinction between prose and poetry in Old Russian literature means that there was no developed verse tradition at the time.

69. Gasparov, "Russkii trinadtsatislozhnik," p. 39.

2 THE CLASSICAL METERS

1. On the introduction of syllabo-tonic verse in Russia see John Bucsela, "The Birth of Russian Syllabo-Tonic Versification"; B. P. Goncharov, "O reforme russkogo stikhoslozheniia v XVIII veke (K probleme ee natsional'nykh

istokov)"; C. L. Drage, "The Introduction of Russian Syllabo-Tonic Prosody"; and G. S. Smith, "The Reform of Russian Versification: What More Is There to Say?"

2. V. K. Trediakovskii, *Izbrannye proizvedeniia*, pp. 370–76.

3. Silbajoris, *Russian Versification*, pp. 21–23.

4. M. V. Lomonosov, *Izbrannye proizvedeniia*, p. 489.

5. Gukovskii, *Russkaia literatura*, pp. 88–89.

6. For a detailed discussion of Lomonosov's increasing use of "pyrrhic" feet see Kiril Taranovsky, "Rannie russkie iamby i ikh nemetskie obraztsy."

7. On the hexameter see Richard Burgi, *A History of the Russian Hexameter*.

8. Antiokh Kantemir, *Sobranie stikhotvorenii*, pp. 408–11, 414.

9. Ibid., p. 413.

10. Trediakovskii, *Sochineniia*, pp. 121–78. The full title of the essay is "Sposob k slozheniiu Rossiiskikh Stikhov protiv vydannogo v 1735 gode ispravlennyi i dopolnennyi."

11. Sumarokov, "O stoposlozhenii," pp. 384–86.

12. M. L. Gasparov, "Metricheskii repertuar russkoi liriki XVIII–XX vv.," p. 45. Rudnev refers to imitations of the Greek and Latin hexameter as "six-stressed *dol'niki*." See Rudnev, "Iz istorii metricheskogo repertuara russkikh poetov XIX–nachala XX v.," p. 136.

13. Cf. James Bailey, "Russian Binary Meters with Strong Caesura from 1890 to 1920," p. 119. See n. 31, chap. 1, for references to articles discussing this meter.

14. For examples see the section "Lines," chap. 1.

15. Kholshevnikov, *Osnovy stikhovedeniia*, pp. 50–51; James Bailey, "The Metrical and Rhythmical Typology of K. K. Slučevskij's Poetry," p. 109.

16. Bailey, "Epic Meters," p. 12. Kholshevnikov (*Osnovy stikhovedeniia*, p. 49) overstates the similarity between the iamb and the trochee when he claims that the only difference between them is in the anacrusis. Tomashevskii notes that as a result of the difference at the beginning of the line iambs and trochees are sharply opposed to one another. Ternary meters, on the other hand, sound more or less alike and therefore can be mixed within the same poem. See Tomashevskii, *Stikh i iazyk*, pp. 59–60.

17. It is not difficult to derive a formula for finding the number of possible rhythmic variants. Since the last ictus must be stressed, and there are two choices for each of the other ictuses (stressed or unstressed), the formula for a line without caesura is 2^{n-1}, where n is the number of ictuses in the line. If the line contains a caesura, the formula becomes $2^{n-1} - 2^{c-1}$, where c is the number of ictuses after the caesura. For example, in an iambic pentameter line with a caesura after the second foot, $n = 5$ and $c = 3$. The number of possible variants is therefore $2^4 - 2^2$ or twelve.

18. Taranovsky, *Ruski dvodelni ritmovi*, p. 85. Rhythmic variations for the iambic pentameter are shown on pp. 196 and 239, for the iambic hexameter on p. 126, and for the iambic trimeter on p. 96. Trochaic trimeter is described on p. 303, tetrameter on p. 64, pentameter on p. 293, and hexameter on p. 317.

19. Ibid., p. 86.

20. Belyi, *Simvolizm*, p. 295.

21. For a detailed discussion of various "weakly stressed" words see Zhirmunskii, *Vvedenie v metriku*, pp. 85–107.

22. Taranovsky, *Ruski dvodelni ritmovi*, pp. 68–70.

23. Gasparov, "Iamb i khorei," p. 92.

24. James Bailey, "The Basic Structural Characteristics of Russian Literary Meters," p. 18.

25. Kiril Taranovsky, "Chetyrekhstopnyi iamb Andreia Belogo," pp. 130–32, 134–36. The figures are based on the table on p. 136. A similar rhythmic form appears in Marina Tsvetaeva's poetry of the early 1920s; see G. S. Smith, "The Versification of Marina Tsvetayeva's Lyric Poetry, 1922–1923," p. 29.

26. Gasparov, "Iamb i khorei," pp. 89–91.

27. Taranovsky, "Chetyrekhstopnyi iamb Belogo," pp. 137–45.

28. M. M. Girshman and O. A. Orlova, "Chetyrekhstopnyi iamb Nekrasova i Polonskogo i problema tipologii iambicheskogo ritma v russkoi poezii 50–kh godov XIX veka"; L. L. Bel'skaia, "Chetyrekhstopnyi iamb S. Esenina"; Kiril Taranovsky, "Stikhoslozhenie Osipa Mandel'shtama (s 1908 po 1925 god)"; and James Bailey, "The Verse of Andrej Voznesenskij as an Example of Present-Day Russian Versification."

29. K. D. Vishnevskii, "Russkaia metrika XVIII veka," p. 236.

30. M. V. Lomonosov, "Kratkoe rukovodstvo k krasnorechiiu," p. 407.

31. Taranovsky, *Ruski dvodelni ritmovi*, p. 148.

32. For a list of longer works employing the unrhymed iambic pentameter during this period see Bailey, "Evolution and Structure," pp. 143–46.

33. Gasparov, "Metricheskii repertuar," pp. 54, 57; Bailey, "Evolution and Structure," p. 121.

34. Bailey, "Evolution and Structure," p. 131.

35. See nn. 8 and 9, chap. 1, for discussions of the terms *free* and *movable* caesura. Essentially, a free caesura is absent from a significant number of lines (up to 20 or 25 percent of the total), while a movable caesura may oscillate between two neighboring syllables.

36. Gasparov, "Iamb i khorei," p. 104.

37. A similar leveling of stress throughout the line when the caesura is absent occurs in Russian poetry around the turn of the century. See Bailey, "Evolution and Structure," p. 122.

38. On the French decasyllable see B. V. Tomashevskii, "Piatistopnyi iamb Pushkina," pp. 226–27. The Russian version has heightened stressing on the second ictus, while in the French decasyllable stress on the second ictus is a constant.

39. Bailey, "Evolution and Structure," pp. 122–23; Taranovsky, *Ruski dvodelni ritmovi*, pp. 169–72, 341.

40. Bailey, "Evolution and Structure," p. 123.

41. On Mandel'shtam's usage of the iambic pentameter see Taranovsky, "Stikhoslozhenie Mandel'shtama," pp. 102–4.

42. Ibid., p. 111.

43. Taranovsky, *Ruski dvodelni ritmovi*, pp. 224–31.

44. Bailey, "Evolution and Structure," p. 123.

45. On the similarities and differences between the French Alexandrine and its Russian equivalent in the eighteenth and at the beginning of the nineteenth centuries see W. N. Vickery, "Russkii shestistopnyi iamb i ego otnoshenie k frantsuzskomu aleksandriiskomu stikhu." Other remarks on the usage of this meter in the eighteenth century can be found in Vishnevskii, "Metrika XVIII veka," pp. 168–69; and Taranovsky, *Ruski dvodelni ritmovi*, pp. 98–99.

46. Gasparov, "Iamb i khorei," pp. 55–56.

47. Cf. table 7 appended to Taranovsky's *Ruski dvodelni ritmovi*.

48. Taranovsky, *Ruski dvodelni ritmovi*, p. 106.

49. M. I. Kievskii, "Shestistopnyi iamb N. Zabolotskogo," p. 40.

50. Gasparov, "Iamb i khorei," pp. 118–21.

51. Taranovsky, "Stikhoslozhenie Mandel'shtama," pp. 105–8.

52. Ibid., p. 106, for the figures on Mandel'shtam.

53. Vishnevskii, "Metrika XVIII veka," pp. 162–64.

54. K. D. Vishnevskii, "Metrika Nekrasova i ee zhanrovo-ekspressivnaia kharakteristika," p. 250.

55. Gasparov, "Metricheskii repertuar," pp. 46–47, 57.

56. Taranovsky, *Ruski dvodelni ritmovi*, table 5.

57. Vishnevskii, "Metrika XVIII veka," table 3, p. 236. For general remarks on the usage of the trochaic tetrameter in the eighteenth century see pp. 189–98. On this period see also C. L. Drage, "Trochaic Metres in Early Russian Syllabo-Tonic Poetry."

58. N. V. Lapshina, I. K. Romanovich, and B. I. Iarkho, *Metricheskii spravochnik k stikhotvoreniiam A. S. Pushkina*, p. 130; idem, "Iz materialov Metricheskogo spravochnika k stikhotvoreniiam M. Iu. Lermontova," p. 136.

59. Anthony D. Briggs, "The Metrical Virtuosity of Afanasy Fet," p. 361; Vishnevskii, "Metrika Nekrasova," p. 243.

60. Gasparov, "Metricheskii repertuar," pp. 48–49.

61. Vishnevskii, "Metrika XVIII veka," p. 198.

62. M. L. Gasparov, "K semantike daktilicheskoi rifmy v russkom khoree," p. 144. On this type of line see also Vishnevskii, "Metrika XVIII veka," pp. 193–94; and Drage, "Trochaic Metres," pp. 373–74.

63. L. L. Bel'skaia, "Iz nabliudenii nad ritmami S. Esenina," p. 102.

64. Gasparov, "Iamb i khorei," p. 99.

65. Smith, "Tsvetayeva's Lyric Poetry," p. 31; Bailey, "Basic Characteristics," p. 27.

66. V. V. Ivanov, "Metr i ritm v 'Poeme kontsa' M. Tsvetaevoi," pp. 196–200.

67. Vishnevskii, "Metrika XVIII veka," pp. 199–200.

68. For a detailed discussion of the trochaic pentameter and its thematic associations as well as of the role played by Lermontov's "Vykhozhu odin ja na dorogu" in that meter's usage see Kiril Taranovsky, "O vzaimootnoshenii stikhotvornogo ritma i tematiki."

69. Gasparov, "Metricheskii repertuar," p. 61.

70. Ibid., pp. 54, 59.

71. Taranovsky, *Ruski dvodelni ritmovi*, pp. 276–77.

72. Gasparov, "Metricheskii repertuar," pp. 46–47.

73. Vishnevskii, "Metrika XVIII veka," pp. 200–201.

74. Taranovsky, *Ruski dvodelni ritmovi*, pp. 304–6, 325–29.

75. In the third line of this example the word *prokliatyi* is normally stressed on the second syllable; however, according to Vladimir Dahl's dictionary of Russian, in some dialects the stress is on the first syllable. I am presuming that Kliuev had in mind the less common stress, which would be in keeping with the meter.

76. Bailey, "Verse of Voznesenskij," p. 158.

77. I have analyzed the version of this poem published in *Dubovyi list violonchel'nyi*. In at least one earlier publication there were several more short lines among the thirty-two in the poem; see Voznesenskii, *Ten' zvuka*, pp. 89–90.

78. Gasparov, "Metricheskii repertuar," p. 59.

79. Vishnevskii, "Metrika XVIII veka," p. 189.

80. Bailey, "Basic Characteristics," p. 24.

81. Zhirmunskii, *Vvedenie v metriku*, p. 47.

82. V. E. Kholshevnikov, "Russkie trekhslozhnye razmery (v sopostavlenii s pol'skimi)," pp. 308–9. Cf. M. L. Gasparov's "Trekhstopnyi amfibrakhii i trekhstopnyi anapest v XIX i XX v.," p. 126.

83. For a tentative analysis of this problem in ternary meters see Gasparov, "Trekhstopnyi," pp. 156–69.

84. Ibid., pp. 178–79.

85. A. K. Lojkine, "Nekrasov's Anapaests," p. 58.

86. Gasparov, "Trekhstopnyi," pp. 182, 187.

87. Ibid., p. 190.

88. Poets occasionally omitted the initial stress in dactylic lines, and at least one poet active during the second half of the nineteenth century also left some ictuses *within* dactylic lines unstressed. See Bailey "Metrical and Rhythmical Typology of Slučevskij," pp. 107–8.

89. A detailed listing of the lines in which Pasternak omitted stresses can be found in the thorough treatment of this topic by Gleb Struve, "Some Observations on Pasternak's Ternary Meters."

90. Bailey, "Basic Characteristics," p. 31.

91. Taranovsky, *Ruski dvodelni ritmovi*, table 2.

92. On the early use of the ternary meters see K. D. Vishnevskii, "Stanovlenie trekhslozhnykh razmerov v russkoi poezii."

93. Gasparov, "Metricheskii repertuar," p. 51; Vishnevskii, "Metrika XVIII veka," pp. 254–55.

94. Gasparov, "Metricheskii repertuar," pp. 62–65.

95. T. S. Gvozdikovskaia, "Sud'by trekhslozhnykh razmerov v sovremennoi poezii."

96. Gasparov, "Metricheskii repertuar," p. 47; Vishnevskii, "Metrika XVIII veka," p. 257; Gvozdikovskaia, "Sud'by," p. 122.

97. Although he does not consider dactylic lines in which stress is omitted on the first syllable, G. A. Shengeli offers similar reasons for the relative unpopularity of the dactyl in *Tekhnika stikha*, p. 67.

98. Gvozdikovskaia, "Sud'by," p. 122.

99. See, for example, Saintsbury, *Historical Manual of English Prosody*,

p. 268. Saintsbury believes that the amphibrach can generally "be better arranged as anapests . . . and that the amphibrach is unnecessary, or, at any rate, very very rare in English."

100. Vishnevskii, "Metrika XVIII veka," p. 254.

101. Cf. Lermontov's poem "Borodino" written in seven-line iambic stanzas according to the scheme 4434443 or his trochaic poem "Ty idësh' na pole bitvy" which employs the same stanza. For a list of Lermontov's mixed meters see Lapshina, Romanovich, and Iarkho, "Iz materialov," p. 137.

102. P. A. Rudnev, "Metricheskii repertuar A. Bloka," p. 227. The figure of 25 percent is arbitrary, but somewhere around this level the "main" meter no longer predominates and it becomes necessary to describe the poem by a term that will embrace all the types of lines within it.

103. S. A. Shakhverdov, "Metrika i strofika E. A. Baratynskogo," p. 319.

104. Thus Tomashevskii, for instance, discusses mixed and variable meters as related phenomena in his *Kratkii kurs poetiki*, pp. 75–76.

105. L. I. Timofeev, "Vol'nyi stikh XVIII veka," p. 103.

106. M. L. Gasparov, "Vol'nyi khorei i vol'nyi iamb Maiakovskogo," pp. 394–96.

107. Vishnevskii, "Metrika XVIII veka," pp. 180–86, 236; Timofeev, "Vol'nyi stikh," pp. 100–102.

108. On the nineteenth-century usage of this meter, see M. P. Shtokmar, "Vol'nyi stikh XIX veka."

109. Gasparov, "Metricheskii repertuar," p. 55.

110. Shtokmar, "Vol'nyi stikh," pp. 118, 139 (table of line lengths used by various poets), 148.

111. G. O. Vinokur, "Vol'nye iamby Pushkina," pp. 24–27.

112. S. A. Matiash, "Russkii i nemetskii vol'nyi iamb XVIII–nachala XIX veka i vol'nye iamby Zhukovskogo," p. 92.

113. B. V. Tomashevskii, "Stikh *Goria ot uma*," p. 137.

114. Matiash, "Russkii i nemetskii," pp. 97–98.

115. Tomashevskii, "Stikh *Goria ot uma*," pp. 142–43; Timofeev, "Vol'nyi stikh," pp. 85–86, 107.

116. Timofeev, "Vol'nyi stikh," p. 78.

117. Gasparov, "Vol'nyi khorei," pp. 372–73.

118. Ibid., pp. 379 (table), 381, 397.

119. Ibid., p. 396.

120. Zhirmunskii, *Rifma*, pp. 272–73; Bailey, "Russian Binary Meters," pp. 114–15.

121. L. E. Liapina, "Sverkhdlinnye razmery v poezii Bal'monta," p. 122.

122. Bailey, "Russian Binary Meters," pp. 124–25.

123. Shengeli, *Tekhnika stikha*, p. 59.

124. The term is from Zhirmunskii, *Rifma*, p. 272, who discusses the phenomenon on pp. 271–81. Several other scholars have touched upon the topic, primarily in passing, but by far the most detailed treatment is in Bailey's "Russian Binary Meters."

125. Bailey, "Russian Binary Meters," p. 112.

126. For stressing in the iambic tetrameter with strong caesura see Bailey,

"Russian Binary Meters," p. 117. For the regular iambic tetrameter see the table appended to Kiril Taranovsky, "Ruski četvorostopni jamb u prvim dvema decenijama XX veka."

127. The most thorough discussion of this form can be found in Bailey, "Literary Usage"; cf. Bezzubov, "Piatislozhnik."

128. Bailey, "Literary Usage," pp. 440–41.

129. Bailey, "Russian Binary Meters," pp. 124–25.

130. Ibid., p. 126.

131. Liapina, "Sverkhdlinnye razmery," p. 122, quotes "Kaplia." According to her count, Bal'mont truncated or expanded the caesura in some 207 works (p. 124).

132. For a detailed analysis of the strong caesura in the works of Igor' Severianin see Nikolaj Chardžiev, "Maiakovskii i Igor' Severianin," pp. 317–25.

133. On paeons see Kholshevnikov, *Osnovy stikhovedeniia*, pp. 37–39.

134. B. Ia. Bukhshtab, "O strukture russkogo klassicheskogo stikha," p. 399. However, Briusov omits quite a few stresses in the poem "Buria s berega"; cf. the following two lines:

Perekídyvaemye, oprokídyvaemye   ∪∪⏐́∪∪∪−∪∪∪⏐́∪∪∪∪∪
. . . .
S neudérzhavaemost'iu perebrásyvaemye   ∪∪⏐́∪∪∪−∪∪∪⏐́∪∪∪∪∪

135. Boris Tomashevskii, *Russkoe stikhoslozhenie*, pp. 15–16; idem, *Stilistika i stikhoslozhenie*, pp. 403–4.

136. Bukhshtab, "O strukture," pp. 399–403; Kholshevnikov, *Osnovy stikhovedeniia*, p. 38.

137. Bukhshtab, "O strukture," pp. 402–4.

138. Bukhshtab also points out ("O strukture," p. 403) that the absence of a caesura after the sixth syllable makes the poem unusual for one written in iambic hexameter. His statement is true enough, though as noted in the section on the iambic hexameter a form of that meter without the caesura and with very strong (albeit not quite constant) stressing on the fourth and eighth syllables of the line was pioneered by Mandel'shtam well before Kushner wrote his poem.

139. Bailey, "Russian Binary Meters," p. 125.

140. For instance, the trochaic hexameter without caesura has constant stressing on the second and fourth ictuses along with decreased stressing on the odd ictuses from the beginning toward the end of the line (cf. table 16, lines 6 and 7); yet the meter clearly is regarded by poets as trochaic, not as a type of paeon.

141. The term *penton* was apparently first used by Vladimir Piast in *Sovremennoe stikhovedenie*, p. 274; the term is also found in Shengeli, *Tekhnika stikha*, pp. 143–45. I have elected to use *penton* as well since that word seems the most felicitous in English. Tomashevskii simply talks of "five-syllable meters" (*piatistopnye razmery*) in *Teoriia literatury*, pp. 122–23; cf. idem, *Stilistika i stikhoslozhenie*, pp. 404–5. Several Russian metrists now prefer the term *piatislozhnik*; see for instance Bezzubov's article "Piatislozhnik," and Kholshevnikov, *Osnovy*, pp. 39–40. Kviatkovskii, in *Poeticheskii slovar'*, pp. 230–33, uses *piatidol'nik*.

142. Zhirmunskii, *Vvedenie v metriku*, p. 221, calls it a "basic trochaic meter with the introduction of a strong caesura and dactylic ending." Tomashevskii, *Russkoe stikhoslozhenie*, p. 53, simply points to the similarity of this line to trochaic verse.

143. Thus Tomashevskii's example of what he calls a direct attempt to write a penton (as opposed to a penton that arises from the imitation of folk meters) is, whatever the author's intent, still a regular 5 + 5 meter (*Stilistika i stikhoslozhenie*, p. 405; the poem is A. K. Tolstoi's "If I knew" ["Kaby znala ia, kaby vedala"]). Earlier, in *Teoriia literatury*, p. 123, he had described Gumilev's "The Dragon" ("Drakon") as an example of a "pure" five-syllable meter without a constant caesura albeit with a large amount of hypermetrical stressing; below are the opening lines of that poem:

Из-за све́жих во́лн океа́на   ∪∪—∪∪∪∪—∪
Кра́сный бы́к припо́днял рога́,   ∪∪—∪∪∪∪—
И бежа́ли ла́ни тума́на   ∪∪—∪∪∪∪—∪
Под скали́стые берега́.   ∪∪—∪∪∪∪—

                              1918-19

The schema given here would be for a penton; however, the presence of one stress between the constantly stressed third and eighth syllables in the great majority of the lines points to a typical pattern for the three-stress *dol'nik* (discussed in the next chapter). Thus there is no more need for the term *penton* to describe these lines than there is for the term *paeon* to describe the poems treated earlier in this section.

144. Shengeli, *Teoriia stikha*, p. 146.

3 NONCLASSICAL VERSE

1. On the history and structure of the *dol'nik* see M. L. Gasparov, "Russkii trekhudarnyi dol'nik XX v.," and idem, "Chetyrekhiktnyi dol'nik."

2. Gasparov, "Metricheskii repertuar," pp. 47, 71–72.

3. As Zhirmunskii has pointed out (*Vvedenie v metriku*, pp. 200–201), such meters differ from purely Russian forms only in that they originated from other sources.

4. On Trediakovskii's translation and the reaction to it see Burgi, *Russian Hexameter*, chaps. 3, 4.

5. Ibid., pp. 71–72.

6. Vishnevskii, "Metrika XVIII veka," pp. 217–18.

7. M. Iu. Lotman, "Geksametr (Obshchaia teoriia i nekotorye aspekty funktsionirovaniia v novykh evropeiskikh literaturakh)," pp. 31–32.

8. S. M. Bondi, "Pushkin i russkii gekzametr," p. 347.

9. M. L. Gasparov, "Prodrom, Tsets, i natsional'nye formy geksametra," p. 377.

10. For the history of the hexameter in Russia after 1850 see Burgi, *Russian Hexameter*, chap. 8.

11. For a description of the Greek and Latin hexameter see Gasparov, "Prodrom, Tsets," pp. 365–69.

12. Burgi, *Russian Hexameter*, pp. 59–60, notes that only fourteen of the first one hundred lines in *Tilemakhida* are purely dactylic; forty-seven lines omit a syllable after one ictus, twenty-nine after two ictuses, and ten after three.

13. Bondi, "Pushkin i gekzametr," pp. 322–23.

14. Burgi, *Russian Hexameter*, pp. 79–82, 112–17.

15. On the polemics concerning Gnedich's choice of the hexameter see especially Bondi, "Pushkin i gekzametr," pp. 325–28; and Burgi, *Russian Hexameter*, chap. 5.

16. Bondi, "Pushkin i gekzametr," p. 327.

17. S. I. Ponomarev, "K izdaniiu *Iliady* v perevode Gnedicha," pp. 36–37.

18. Bondi, "Pushkin i gekzametr," pp. 327–28.

19. Gasparov, "Prodrom, Tsets," pp. 377–79.

20. Ibid., p. 376.

21. Vishnevskii, "Metrika XVIII veka," p. 258, found 115 works in elegiac distich during the first half of the nineteenth century; for the use of this meter by Pushkin and his contemporaries, see Burgi, *Russian Hexameter*, chap. 7. Bondi, "Pushkin i gekzametr," pp. 347–67, offers a detailed analysis of the elegiac distich in Pushkin's poetry.

22. For these examples and for much of the following discussion I am indebted to G. S. Smith's fine article, "Logaoedic Metres in the Lyric Poetry of Marina Tsvetayeva."

23. Ibid., pp. 330–32. Smith also points to some of the problems involved in classifying borderline cases in which one or two of the lines do not adhere to the regular pattern.

24. Gasparov, "Russkii trekhudarnyi dol'nik," pp. 90–97, 104–5. In fact his examples of the *dol'nik* in Smeliakov (p. 96) and Tsvetayeva (p. 102) could be interpreted as logaoedic verse with the stress occasionally omitted on the middle ictus. Here is part of the excerpt he takes from Tsvetaeva's "Poem of the End" ("Poema kontsa"):

– За́втра с за́паду вста́нет со́лнце!   ◡◡⏤◡◡⏤◡⏤◡
– С Иего́вой порвёт Дави́д!   ◡◡⏤◡◡⏤◡⏤
– Что́ мы де́лаем? – Расстаёмся.   ◡◡⏤◡◡–◡⏤◡
– Ничего́ мне не говори́т   ◡◡⏤◡◡–◡⏤

Сверхбессмы́сленнейшее сло́во: ◡◡⏤◡◡–◡⏤◡
Рас-стаёмся. – Одна́ из ста́?   ◡◡⏤◡◡⏤◡⏤
Про́сто сло́во в четы́ре сло́га,   ◡◡⏤◡◡⏤◡⏤◡
За кото́рыми пустота́.   ◡◡⏤◡◡–◡⏤

1924

Gasparov himself points to the hazy border between the *dol'nik* and logaoedic verse in Tsvetaeva. Since this entire section of "Poema kontsa" includes a few lines that fall outside the regular pattern of the excerpt quoted by Gasparov, V. V. Ivanov interprets the meter of the section as being intermediate between the *dol'nik* and logaoedic verse; see Ivanov, "Metr i ritm," pp. 174–75.

25. Taranovskii, "Stikhoslozhenie Osipa Mandel'shtama," p. 118, n. 46; Bailey, "Some Recent Developments," p. 188.

26. Smith, "Logaoedic Metres," p. 339, lists no fewer than nine different variations for the logaoedic trimeter in Tsvetaeva's poetry.

27. The formula for the number of possible rhythmic variations in the stem (assuming that all the intervals between ictuses consist of one or two syllables) is $2^{n-1} - 2$, where n is the number of ictuses in the line. Since the anacrusis may have zero, one, or two syllables, this figure is multiplied by three to find the number of variations for the given line type.

28. Zhirmunskii, *Vvedenie v metriku*, pp. 211–12.

29. For a description of the various Greek and Latin logaoedic stanzas that have appeared in Russian verse see V. E. Kholshevnikov, "Logaedicheskie razmery v russkoi poezii," pp. 430–32.

30. Ibid., pp. 432–33.

31. For a description of the different lengths and variations in eighteenth-century logaoedic lines, see Vishnevskii, "Metrika XVIII veka," pp. 212–16.

32. Smith, "Logaoedic Metres," p. 332.

33. This has been pointed out by Zhirmunskii, *Vvedenie v metriku*, p. 213.

34. Kholshevnikov, "Logaedicheskie razmery," p. 434.

35. Ibid., p. 436.

36. On Zhukovskii's use of *dol'niki* see S. A. Matiash, "K voprosu o genezise russkogo dol'nika: Dol'niki V. A. Zhukovskogo."

37. James Bailey, "Blok and Heine: An Episode from the History of Russian *dol'niki*, pp. 13–14; 21, n. 40.

38. N. V. Sushkov, Tiutchev's brother-in-law, and Turgenev both appear to have had a hand in changing several of the poems (including "Silentium!") for the first (1854) collection of Tiutchev's poetry; on the history of this volume see K. V. Pigarev, *Zhizn' i tvorchestvo Tiutcheva*, pp. 137–44.

39. Gasparov, "Russkii trekhudarnyi dol'nik," pp. 87–90; Bailey, "Blok and Heine," pp. 1–6.

40. A counterexample is provided by Blok's translations of Heine which were completed after Blok had written most of his original *dol'nik* poems. In his translations Blok makes a conscious attempt to adhere as closely as possible to the binary rhythm of the original, and therefore the translations display a markedly different rhythm than his original *dol'niki*, which have a ternary basis. See Bailey, "Blok and Heine," pp. 6–13.

41. Gasparov, "Russkii trekhudarnyi dol'nik, p. 89.

42. For (slightly different) lists of the specific poems see Bailey, "Blok and Heine," p. 20, n. 27; and P. A. Rudnev, "Metricheskii repertuar A. Bloka," pp. 264–65.

43. On Esenin's use of the *dol'nik* see L. L. Bel'skaia, "Esenin i Maiakovskii (K probleme stikhotvornogo novatorstva)," pp. 34–37.

44. A survey of fifty-nine poets active during the 1960s shows that fifty-one used the *dol'nik* systematically; of these, twenty-one employed the *dol'nik* between 15 and 47 percent of the time. See E. K. Ozmitel' and T. S. Gvozdikovskaia, "Materialy k metricheskomu repertuaru russkoi liricheskoi poezii (1957–1968 gg.)," p. 119.

45. James Bailey has generalized Jakobson's law about hypermetrical stressing, which was originally formulated for binary meters, to make it apply to ter-

nary meters and the *dol'nik* as well. Bailey's formulation reads: "If any syllable of a polysyllabic word in binary meters, ternary meters, or *dol'niki* corresponds to an ictus, then the stress of this word must coincide to *some* ictus within the line" (James Bailey, "The Three-Stress *Dol'niki* of George Ivask as an Example of Rhythmic Change," p. 156).

46. The first full description of the rhythmical features and possible structures in the three-stress *dol'nik* is to be found in Taranovsky, "Stikhoslozhenie Osipa Mandel'shtama," pp. 114–20.

47. Gasparov, "Russkii trekhudarnyi dol'nik," pp. 75–79.

48. Ibid., p. 71.

49. James Bailey proposes a slightly different border: "poems in which at least one-fifth of the intervals diverge from the *dol'nik* norm and/or in which at least one-third of the lines are unlike the *dol'nik* will be considered to be written in strict accentual verse." See Bailey, "The Development of Strict Accentual Verse in Russian Literary Poetry," p. 89.

50. On the problems associated with analyzing both three-stress and four-stress *dol'niki* see Gasparov, "Russkii trekhudarnyi dol'nik," p. 70; and idem, "Chetyrekhiktnyi dol'nik," pp. 250–54.

51. Bailey, "Blok and Heine," p. 11.

52. On the characteristics of the period see Gasparov, "Russkii trekhudarnyi dol'nik," pp. 69–71, 76–77.

53. Ibid., pp. 91–94.

54. Ibid., p. 95.

55. Bailey, "Three-Stress *Dol'niki* of Ivask," pp. 166–67.

56. These conclusions are based on the data provided in Gasparov, "Russkii trekhudarnyi dol'nik," p. 69.

57. On Gumilev's use of three-stress *dol'niki* see Earl D. Sampson, "*Dol'niks* in Gumilev's Poetry," pp. 24–31.

58. Bailey, "Some Recent Developments," p. 187.

59. Thus G. S. Smith classifies this poem as logaoedic; see "Logaoedic Metres," p. 348.

60. Extreme adherents of the "Tsvetaeva" type (including Tsvetaeva herself) use variations III or VI in 95 percent or more of all lines. Examples of such poems can be found in Bagritskii (though not in all his *dol'nik* works) and in the later poetry of Smeliakov, among others. Many more poets favor variations III and VI but still use other variations in 20 or 30 percent of their lines. See Gasparov, "Russkii trekhudarnyi dol'nik," pp. 98–99.

61. Bailey treats this point thoroughly in "Three-Stress *Dol'niki* of Ivask."

62. James Bailey has provided a detailed analysis of the three-stress line in Voznesenskii's poetry with separate statistics for each kind of anacrusis: zero-syllable, one-syllable, two-syllable, and variable. Voznesenskii, at least through the early 1970s, used the three-stress *dol'nik* more often than any other single meter. Bailey, "Verse of Voznesenskij," pp. 165–67.

63. Joseph Brodsky, *A Part of Speech*, p. 151. The Spanish romance (or ballad) is based on an eight-syllable line with a final stress on the next-to-last syllable and rhyme between the final two vowels (but not necessarily any consonants that may be present) of the even lines. The same two vowels are normally

used throughout the poem. See David W. Foster, *The Early Spanish Ballad*, pp. 184–88. A modern group of ballads, García Lorca's *Romancero Gitano* could well have served as an inspiration for this work by Brodsky. The *Gypsy Ballads* have been translated into Russian as *Tsyganskii romansero* in a collection of García Lorca's poems called *Lirika*, pp. 73–112. Most of the translations are by A. M. Geleskul and use three-stress *dol'niki* to render the syllabic lines of the original. However, the special rhythm of Brodsky's poem differs from these translations. Most of Brodsky's lines contain seven syllables rather than the eight that are the rule for the Spanish ballad. At the same time Brodsky's feminine endings (rhymed *ABAB* or *AABB*) imitate the ballad through their constant stress on the penultimate syllable of the line.

64. Gasparov, "Chetyrekhiktnyi dol'nik."

65. Ibid., pp. 256–57. My percentages are extrapolated from Gasparov's survey and are based on the 41,876 lines that are "correct" for the four-stress *dol'nik*.

66. Ibid., pp. 286–89. My own terminology and classification differ somewhat from Gasparov's.

67. For a detailed analysis of "Liubliu" see A. N. Kolmogorov and A. M. Kondratov, "Ritmika poem Maiakovskogo," pp. 62–67.

68. A. N. Kolmogorov and A. V. Prokhorov, "O dol'nike sovremennoi russkoi poezii" (1964), p. 85.

69. Bailey, "Basic Structural Characteristics," p. 38, n. 41. Bailey's statistics differ slightly from those presented by Kolmogorov and Prokhorov, "O dol'nike" (1964), pp. 85, 87. In "O dol'nike" (1963), p. 85, the latter note that this is the first long Russian poem to employ the *dol'nik*.

70. These figures are extrapolated from the data provided by Kolmogorov and Prokhorov, "O dol'nike," (1964), pp. 85–86.

71. I am indebted to G. S. Smith for pointing out the importance of this meter.

72. For general remarks on strict accentual verse see James Bailey, "The Accentual Verse of Majakovskij's 'Razgovor s fininspektorom o poèzii'," p. 25; idem, "Development of Strict Accentual Verse," pp. 87–88; and M. L. Gasparov, "Taktovik v poezii XX veka," pp. 299–308.

73. On the history of this term see Gasparov, "Taktovik v poezii," pp. 295–99.

74. See Gasparov, "Russkii narodnyi stikh v literaturnykh imitatsiiakh."

75. Much has been written in recent years on Pushkin's imitations of folk verse. For instance, on "Skazka o rybake i rybke" see V. M. Zhirmunskii, "Russkii narodnyi stikh v 'Skazke o rybake i rybke.'" S. P. Bobrov devoted two articles to the verse of the "Pesni zapadnykh slavian" (see the bibliography for listings of both), while A. N. Kolmogorov provided a commentary on Bobrov's findings in "O metre pushkinskikh 'Pesen zapadnykh slavian.'" Still of some interest are the remarks on the "Pesni" in a 1945 article by S. M. Bondi, "Narodnyi stikh u Pushkina," pp. 407–20.

76. For a detailed analysis of the line types found in the "Pesni" see Gasparov, "Russkii narodnyi stikh," pp. 89, 93–96. In the last line *kladbishche* has a now-archaic stress on the second syllable.

77. For lists of works in strict accentual verse see M. L. Gasparov, "Taktovik v russkom stikhoslozhenii XX v.," pp. 82–83; and Bailey, "Development of Strict Accentual Verse," pp. 107–8.

78. Gasparov, "Metricheskii repertuar," p. 47.

79. Gasparov, "Taktovik v poezii," p. 302.

80. Bailey, "Development of Strict Accentual Verse," pp. 97, table 1; and 101, table 5.

81. Ibid., p. 103.

82. See especially the data in Gasparov, "Taktovik v poezii," pp. 301–5, 322–40; and in Bailey, "Development of Strict Accentual Verse," pp. 90–109.

83. Bailey, "Development of Strict Accentual Verse," p. 100.

84. Ibid., pp. 107–9, for a list of poems by Kuzmin in strict accentual verse and for statistical data on his works as well as on those by other poets.

85. The main qualities of these verse types are discussed by Taranovsky, *Ruski dvodelni ritmovi*, pp. 6–7; Gasparov, "Taktovik v poezii," pp. 340–44; and Bailey, "Development of Strict Accentual Verse," p. 107.

86. Gasparov, "Metricheskii repertuar," pp. 71–72.

87. M. L. Gasparov, "Aktsentnyi stikh Maiakovskogo," pp. 454–66.

88. A. L. Zhovtis, "Ot chego ne svoboden svobodnyi stikh?" pp. 45–46, 49.

89. M. L. Gasparov, "Osnovnye poniatiia russkoi metriki," p. 17.

90. V. S. Baevskii, *Stikh russkoi sovetskoi poezii*, p. 66.

91. O. A. Ovcharenko, "K voprosu o tipologii svobodnogo stikha," pp. 237–38; and Jaak Põldmäe, "Tipologiia svobodnogo stikha," pp. 86–87.

92. Bailey, "Verse of Voznesenskij," pp. 169–70; Põldmäe, "Tipologiia," p. 87.

93. V. M. Zhirmunskii, "Stikhoslozhenie Maiakovskogo," pp. 539–46.

94. Gasparov, "Aktsentnyi stikh," pp. 404–6.

95. Ibid., pp. 456–57, for a chart comparing the early and late work.

96. Ibid., p. 411.

97. Ibid., p. 448.

98. Ibid., pp. 456–57.

99. Khlebnikov's "Zhuravl'" is analyzed as a form of accentual verse by Gasparov, "Aktsentnyi stikh," pp. 454, 456, 459–60; the Martynov poem is cited by Zhovtis, "Ot chego," p. 46, as an example of a work that is not in free verse precisely because it contains rhyme.

100. Baevskii, *Stikh*, p. 66.

101. G. K. Sidorenko, "Svobodnyi stikh v ego otnoshenii k sistemam stikhoslozheniia," pp. 114–15; A. L. Zhovtis, "O kriteriiakh tipologicheskoi kharakteristiki svobodnogo stikha (Obzor problemy)," pp. 74–76. Also, the meaning of the term may evolve along with poetic traditions and changing perspectives on poetic practice. Thus at the beginning of the twentieth century in Russia *free verse* could refer to the other types of nonclassical poetry as well.

102. Rudnev, "Metricheskii repertuar Bloka," p. 226.

103. O. A. Ovcharenko, "Svobodnyi stikh i verlibr."

104. This point has been made by several scholars; see for instance Iu. N. Tynianov, *Problema stikhotvornogo iazyka*, p. 55.

105. Zhovtis, "Ot chego," p. 36. There the essences are said to change regularly (*periodicheski*); I have changed this to *irregularly* (*neperiodicheski*) in keeping with the later formulation adopted by Zhovtis; see "Problema svobodnogo stikha i evoliutsiia stikhovykh form," abstract of doctoral dissertation, Kiev State University, 1975, p. 15.

106. Arvo Mets, "O svobodnom stikhe," pp. 73–74.

107. V. S. Baevskii et al., "K istorii russkogo svobodnogo stikha," p. 89. Much of the information given here on the usage of free verse is based on this extensive article.

108. See, for instance, A. L. Zhovtis, "U istokov russkogo verlibra (Stikh 'Severnogo moria' Geine v perevodakh M. L. Mikhailova)," pp. 397–99. Zhovtis calls these translations examples of vers libre, though he notes that all the intervals between stresses have either one or two syllables. Bailey, "Blok and Heine," p. 17, n. 11, refers to them as *vol'nye dol'niki*.

109. For a list, see Rudnev, "Metricheskii repertuar Bloka," pp. 250–51. Several of the poems are analyzed by A. L. Zhovtis in "Verlibry Bloka." The poems in free verse include "Na perekrestke," "K vecheru vyshlo tikhoe solntse," "Kogda vy stoite na moem puti," and "Ona prishla s moroza." This last poem is discussed below.

110. The entire cycle is examined by G. S. Vasiutochkin in "Ritmika 'Aleksandriiskikh pesen.'"

111. For instance, in Mandel'shtam's "Nashedshii podkovu," analyzed by Herbert Eagle in "On the Free Verse Rhythm of Mandelstam's 'Horseshoe Finder.'"

112. See the range of views in the discussion by Arvo Mets et al., "Ot chego ne svoboden svobodnyi stikh?"

113. For a discussion of the first two approaches given below and an attempt to use both to analyze Esenin's free verse see L. L. Bel'skaia, "K voprosu o dvukh kontseptsiiakh svobodnogo stikha v sovetskom stikhovedenii."

114. Baevskii's analysis of Vinokurov's free verse includes a detailed application of this method; see Baevskii, *Stikh*, pp. 69–91.

115. Zhovtis prefers this approach. For examples see "Ot chego," pp. 26–35, and "Verlibry Bloka," pp. 131–45.

116. Põldmäe, "Tipologiia," pp. 92–98; Zhovtis, "Ot chego," pp. 46–50.

117. Baevskii et al., "K istorii," p. 98.

118. The entire poem is analyzed in some detail by Ovcharenko, "K voprosu," pp. 235–37.

119. Baevskii, *Stikh*, pp. 84–86.

120. Ibid., pp. 69–91.

121. Rudnev, "Metricheskii repertuar Bloka," pp. 227–28, 242–53; P. A. Rudnev, "Metricheskii repertuar V. Briusova," pp. 334–35, 337, 343–45.

122. This applies to the works by Blok that Rudnev lists as transitional metrical forms between the three-stress *dol'nik* and the three-stress *taktovik* (i.e., strict accentual verse), and to those that are transitional between the four-stress *dol'nik* and the four-stress *taktovik*. See Rudnev, "Metricheskii repertuar Bloka," p. 265.

123. Rudnev, "Metricheskii repertuar Briusova," p. 337.

124. The only extensive treatment of this phenomenon and the source for the information in this section is G. S. Smith, "Compound Meters in the Poetry of Marina Cvetaeva."

125. Ibid., p. 119.

126. Rudnev, "Metricheskii repertuar Bloka," pp. 228–35; idem, "O stikhe dramy A. Bloka 'Roza i Krest'"; idem, "Opyt opisaniia i semanticheskoi interpretatsii polimetricheskoi struktury poemy A. Bloka 'Dvenadtsat'"; idem, "Metricheskii repertuar Briusova," pp. 318–27; idem, "Polimetricheskie kompozitsii Nekrasova."

127. Rudnev, "Iz istorii," p. 113.

128. Rudnev, "Polimetricheskie kompozitsii Nekrasova," pp. 160–62.

129. Ibid., p. 175.

130. V. A. Sapogov has devoted special attention to the polymetrical works of Karolina Pavlova; synopses of his studies can be found in "O polimetricheskikh kompozitsiiakh Karoliny Pavlovoi" and "K probleme tipologii polimetricheskikh kompozitsii (O polimetrii u N. A. Nekrasova i K. K. Pavlovoi)."

131. Individual works by Blok have been analyzed in detail by Rudnev (cf. n. 126); for descriptions of polymetrical compositions by Tsvetaeva see Ivanov, "Metr i ritm"; G. S. Smith, "Versification and Composition in Marina Cvetaeva's *Pereuločki*"; and idem, "Marina Cvetaeva's *Poèma gory*: An Analysis." On Maiakovskii see V. V. Ivanov, "Ritm poemy Maiakovskogo 'Chelovek.'"

132. On the frequency of polymetrical compositions in children's poetry see V. P. Rudnev, "Metricheskii repertuar detskoi poezii (Chukovskii, Marshak, Mikhalkov, Barto)."

133. Bailey, "Verse of Voznesenskij," pp. 168–69.

134. According to figures given by Rudnev, only two of Briusov's thirty-one polymetrical compositions and none of those by Blok are written entirely in nonclassical meters. "Metricheskii repertuar Briusova," p. 323.

135. M. Iu. Lotman, "Metricheskii repertuar I. Annenskogo," p. 127.

136. Rudnev, "Metricheskii repertuar Briusova," pp. 318–19.

4 RHYME AND STANZAIC FORMS

1. Some define rhyme as occurring only at the end of the line and thus reject use of the term *internal rhyme*. L. I. Timofeev, *Osnovy teorii literatury*, p. 304.

2. B. V. Tomashevskii, "K istorii russkoi rifmy," p. 234.

3. Kholshevnikov, *Osnovy stikhovedeniia*, p. 79. Exceptions to this rule are noted below in the section "Exact Rhyme and Approximate Rhyme."

4. D. S. Samoilov, *Kniga o russkoi rifme* (1973), p. 21; as mentioned in the text, I have amended Samoilov's definition slightly to make it more flexible. In the second edition (1982) Samoilov replaces his own definition with a quotation from a more general formulation by O. A. Fedotov (p. 18). Subsequent references are to the 1982 edition of Samoilov's book.

5. V. V. Maiakovskii, *Polnoe sobranie sochinenii v trinadtsati tomakh*, pp. 100–106.

6. Samoilov, *Kniga*, p. 12.

7. Dwight L. Bolinger, "Rime, Assonance, and Morpheme Analysis." For groups of words related by both sound and meaning, see esp. pp. 130–33.

8. Zhirmunskii, *Rifma*, pp. 247–48.

9. Ibid., p. 246, where Zhirmunskii emphasizes this effect of rhyme, claiming that it has an "organizing function in the metrical composition of a poem."

10. For more on these three main functions of rhyme see Thomas Eekman, *The Realm of Rime: A Study of Rime in the Poetry of the Slavs*, pp. 16–22.

11. William C. Rickert, "Rhyme Terms," p. 37. This article offers a useful compendium of the terms that have commonly been used by English critics to describe other types of rhyme as well.

12. Three such dictionaries have been compiled by J. Thomas Shaw: *Pushkin's Rhymes: A Dictionary*; *Baratynskii: A Dictionary of the Rhymes and a Concordance to the Poetry*; and *Batiushkov: A Dictionary of the Rhymes and a Concordance to the Poetry*. The only such Soviet publication (others apparently exist in manuscript) to date is the "Slovar' rifm M. Iu. Lermontova," compiled by V. V. Borodin and A. Ia. Shaikevich.

13. For a summary of rhyme notation see the chart at the end of the editorial note in Gasparov, ed., *Russkoe stikhoslozhenie XIX v.*, p. 13. Note that quatrains in which only the even lines rhyme have often been described as *abcb*; in this system such a quatrain would be assigned the notation *xaxa*.

14. See Rickert, "Rhyme Terms," pp. 39–40, for a list and the terminology used to describe other types of internal rhyme. Examples of this phenomenon in Russian poetry are discussed by Zhirmunskii, *Rifma*, pp. 271–81.

15. For examples of internal rhyme among contemporary poets see A. L. Zhovtis, "Russkaia rifma 1960–1970-x godov (zametki i razmyshleniia)."

16. These types of rhyme are described and their development is traced in the third chapter of Zhirmunskii's *Rifma* (pp. 304–76). In several ways his classification differs from that of more recent scholars whose work is described below in the text.

17. M. L. Gasparov, "Rifma Bloka," p. 35.

18. Samoilov, *Kniga*, p. 184.

19. Much of the information in this and the following paragraphs is based on Zhirmunskii, *Rifma*, pp. 308–34.

20. Although poets do not seem to have regarded such rhymes as discordant, Lermontov and Griboedov reduced their numbers while revising their drafts for publication. See V. V. Danilin and E. F. Danilina, "Slovo v rifme M. Iu. Lermontova," p. 85.

21. See Shaw, *Baratynskii*, p. xxi.

22. Zhirmunskii, *Rifma*, pp. 332–33. As Roman Jakobson pointed out, this kind of rhyme is closely related to the truncated rhymes described above. See Jakobson, "K lingvisticheskomu analizu russkoi rifmy," pp. 10–11.

23. Lermontov's frequent recourse to this last category is discussed by G. A. Levinton in "Kak naprimer na IU." Jakobson, "K lingvisticheskomu analizu," pp. 11–12, points out that such rhymes are by no means irregular because the phoneme *j* rhymes with the element of softness in the soft consonant at the end of the other word (in the example here [tvojá / dit'á]).

24. T. Walter Herbert, "Near Rimes and Paraphones," p. 447.

25. V. Ia. Briusov, "Levizna Pushkina v rifmakh."

26. Briusov made this point in a review of Zhirmunskii's book on rhyme. See Briusov, "O rifme," esp. pp. 548–50.

27. On this change in modern rhyme, see A. V. Isachenko, "Iz nabliudenii nad 'novoi rifmoi.'"

28. Shaw, *Baratynskii*, p. xiii.

29. A. K. Tolstoi, *Sobranie sochinenii v chetyrekh tomakh*, pp. 107–9.

30. On the significance of Tolstoi's rhyme practice, see Samoilov, *Kniga*, pp. 180–82.

31. The following classification is based loosely on Zhirmunskii, *Rifma*, pp. 286–90; and on the modifications suggested by Samoilov, *Kniga*, pp. 34–54.

32. Samoilov, *Kniga*, pp. 71–73.

33. For other examples of such combinations see Zhirmunskii, *Rifma*, p. 289; and Samoilov, *Kniga*, pp. 48–49. A still more extreme form of modern rhyme, called pretonic rhyme by Iu. I. Mineralov, occurs when all the main correspondences *precede* the stressed vowel (as in korónnyi / koróva). See Mineralov, "Fonologicheskoe tozhdestvo v russkom iazyke i tipologiia russkoi rifmy," esp. pp. 63–64, 67–76.

34. These examples are from M. P. Shtokmar, *Rifma Maiakovskogo*, p. 73.

35. Ibid., p. 75.

36. The only major study to date on heteroaccentual rhymes and the source for the examples given here is V. F. Markov, "V zashchitu raznoudarnoi rifmy (informativnyi obzor)." Markov offers both a history of this type of rhyming as well as numerous examples and a breakdown into various categories.

37. As James Bailey has pointed out, such rhymes might be better termed "archaic rhymes," since at one time these words formed exact phonetic rhymes in English. See "Parallelism or Antiparallelism?" p. 256.

38. These examples are from Zhirmunskii, *Rifma*, p. 289.

39. Kholshevnikov, *Osnovy stikhovedeniia*, p. 79, employs the term *nedostatochnaia rifma* for this phenomenon, reserving *bednaia* to describe any rhyme in which the consonants are not the same. However, since identity of supporting consonants is not required for any rhymes other than open masculine, his use of *bednaia* in that sense does not seem quite justified.

40. Zhirmunskii, *Rifma*, pp. 350–54, argues that all such rhymes should be regarded as approximate since the independent word is stressed more strongly and hence pronounced a little differently than the corresponding unstressed vowel in the other word of the rhyme pair. Samoilov, *Kniga*, pp. 182–84, prefers to regard rhymes such as these examples from Lermontov as exact within the literary tradition; I find his position the more convincing.

41. Samoilov, *Kniga*, pp. 234–35.

42. On this phenomenon see Baevskii, *Stikh*, pp. 92–101. The term *shadow rhyme* is his.

43. For still fuller discussions of this topic see Zhirmunskii, *Rifma*, pp. 304–76; Samoilov, *Kniga*, chaps. 3–5, 7–10; and Eekman, *Realm*, pp. 97–146.

44. Gasparov, "Rifma Bloka," pp. 41–42.

45. Zhirmunskii, *Rifma*, p. 239, 305. He sees this process as actually beginning in the eighteenth century. Briusov objected to this term, believing that a new kind of rhyming was coming into existence that was no less demanding than the old; see "O rifme," pp. 547–48.

46. Jakobson, "K lingvisticheskomu analizu," p. 5; Samoilov, *Kniga*, pp. 13–15, uses the term *degrammatization*. W. K. Wimsatt thinks that the movement away from grammatical rhyme is crucial for the distinction between poetry and prose: "It would be only an exaggeration, not a distortion, of principle to say that the difference between prose and verse is the difference between homoeoteleuton [pairing of words with the same endings] and rhyme" (*The Verbal Icon: Studies in the Meaning of Poetry*, pp. 153–54).

47. Eekman, *Realm*, pp. 30–32.

48. For one effort to find the ultimate source of rhyme see John W. Draper, "The Origin of Rhyme."

49. Zhirmunskii, *Rifma*, pp. 402–24.

50. On approximate rhyme in the minor genres see Samoilov, *Kniga*, pp. 66–75. In chap. 6 he discusses rhyme in the *chastushka*.

51. On early Russian rhyme see Eekman, *Realm*, pp. 87–97.

52. Smith, "The Reform of Russian Versification," pp. 41–42:

53. Kantemir, *Sobranie*, pp. 412–13.

54. Ibid., pp. 410–13. Note that Kantemir rhymes voiced and voiceless consonants not just at the ends of words and before voiceless consonants (the two places in which they are phonetically identical), but also before the letter *n*, where they are pronounced differently. That is, he rhymes not just vódka / glótka but also udóbnyi / stópnyi.

55. On Lomonosov's rhyming practice see Samoilov, *Kniga*, pp. 99–102.

56. On enrichment in Sumarokov see Dean S. Worth, "On Eighteenth-Century Russian Rhyme," pp. 59–71.

57. Samoilov, *Kniga*, pp. 102–13.

58. Zhirmunskii, *Rifma*, pp. 337–38.

59. Ibid., pp. 339–40.

60. Zhirmunskii, *Rifma*, p. 337; Tomashevskii, "K istorii," pp. 236–60; Jakobson, "K lingvisticheskomu analizu," pp. 1–6; V. A. Zapadov, "'Sposob proiznosheniia stikhov' i russkaia rifma XVIII veka"; idem, "Derzhavin i russkaia rifma XVIII veka." Eventually Zhirmunskii largely accepted Jakobson's view while continuing to reject Tomashevskii's; see Zhirmunskii, "O russkoi rifme XVIII v." For a useful survey of the arguments in the above works see Worth, "On Eighteenth-Century Rhyme," pp. 49–54. Recent contributions to the controversy have been made by Gasparov, ("Rifma Bloka," pp. 37–38), who suggests that foreign influences may have been responsible for the requirement of identity in post-tonic vowels, and by Michael Shapiro, who detects a different hierarchy of phonological values that held sway in the eighteenth century and continued for some time thereafter in the poetic tradition. See Shapiro, *Asymmetry: An Inquiry into the Linguistic Structure of Poetry*, pp. 180–94.

61. Samoilov, *Kniga*, p. 119.

62. Ibid., p. 153.

63. See Danilin and Danilina, "Slovo," p. 82.

64. Cf. n. 23.

65. Samoilov, *Kniga*, p. 165.

66. M. L. Gasparov, "Nekrasov v istorii russkoi rifmy," pp. 84–85.

67. Gasparov, "Rifma Bloka," p. 43.

68. Samoilov, *Kniga*, p. 16.

69. Ibid., pp. 226–39.

70. Ibid., pp. 239–45.

71. On truncation and heterosyllabic rhyming in Maiakovskii see Shtokmar, *Rifma*, pp. 37–42, 72–80, respectively.

72. Zhovtis, "Russkaia rifma," p. 77.

73. Of course Pushkin did use some enrichment in his poetry, even if it is not as pervasive as Briusov implies. See Samoilov, *Kniga*, pp. 132–35.

74. See for instance the article on blank verse by Sverre Lyngstad in the *Princeton Encyclopedia of Poetry and Poetics*, pp. 78–81.

75. On the probable etymology of the term *belyi stikh*, see Tomashevskii, *Stilistika*, p. 365.

76. The first three of these categories follow those suggested by B. O. Unbegaun, *Russian Versification*, p. 152.

77. On the topic of borrowings see Tomashevskii, *Russkoe stikhoslozhenie*, pp. 88–89.

78. Note should also be made of a 1799 play by V. T. Narezhnyi, *Krovavaia noch', ili padenie domu Kadmova*. Strictly speaking, the work is written in variable iambs, but most of the lines are pentameters. The preference for pentameter lines at such an early date as well as the frequency of unstressed final ictuses (nearly 17 percent of the pentameters) are among the unique features of this work. See James Bailey, "An Early Example of Russian Dramatic Blank Verse: Narezhnyi's Tragedy *Krovavaia noch'*."

79. V. A. Nikonov, "Strofika," pp. 99–100.

80. B. V. Tomashevskii, "Strofika Pushkina," pp. 52–53.

81. Ernst Häublein, *The Stanza*, pp. 53–71.

82. For a discussion of structural features in the stanza see G. M. Pechorov, "Tipologiia strof V. V. Maiakovskogo."

83. Shengeli, *Traktat o russkom stikhe*, pp. 111–21; G. S. Smith, "Stanza Rhythm and Stress Load in the Iambic Tetrameter of V. F. Xodasevič"; and idem, "Stanza Rhythm in the Iambic Tetrameter of Three Modern Russian Poets." In his more recent article Smith notes that this tendency is more pronounced in quatrains with the rhyme scheme *AbAb* than those with *aBaB*.

84. Ian K. Lilly, "On Adjacent and Nonadjacent Russian Rhyme Pairs."

85. Gasparov, ed., *Russkoe stikhoslozhenie XIX v.* Unfortunately, the treatment of stanzaic forms is not always consistent from one handbook to the next. Some of the most thoughtful comments on the classification of stanzas are included in L. P. Novinskaia's handbook on Tiutchev, "Metrika i strofika F. I. Tiutcheva"; see esp. pp. 377–83.

86. Thus Novinskaia's classification of Tiutchev's stanzas (see previous note) includes a detailed breakdown of heterostanzaic poems, which are not common in the work of many other poets. Conversely, in some of the other handbooks the

grouping together of all single-stanza poems, with no breakdown according to length or rhyme scheme, provides inadequate information.

87. Tomashevskii, "Strofika Pushkina," p. 135.

88. A different approach to the problem of classification has been suggested by K. D. Vishnevskii in "Arkhitektonika russkogo stikha XVIII–pervoi poloviny XIX veka." He places traditional forms and single-stanza poems (up to eight lines) together in one major grouping. He then lists the various "regulated forms," which include but are not limited to the regular types of stanzas. These are distinguished from the "unregulated forms" on the one hand and from "compound forms" on the other. The latter concept is particularly useful for dealing with poems that are partly stanzaic and partly not, as well as with poems that contain inserts in a totally different form. On the whole, though, the more conventional classification is simpler to apply for ordinary purposes.

89. Many examples of the most common forms in use during the eighteenth century can be found in the extensive study by Reinhard Lauer, *Gedichtform zwischen Schema und Verfall: Sonett, Rondeau, Madrigal, Ballade, Stanze, und Triolett in der russischen Literatur des 18. Jahrhunderts.*

90. V. S. Baevskii, "Strofika sovremennoi liriki v otnoshenii k strofike narodnoi poezii," p. 52.

91. G. S. Smith, "The Stanza Typology of Russian Poetry, 1735–1816: A General Survey," pp. 193–99. His research supersedes that of K. D. Vishnevskii in "K voprosu ob ispol'zovanii kolichestvenniykh metodov v stikhovedenii," pp. 140–41.

92. Baevskii, "Strofika sovremennoi liriki," p. 53.

93. On this phenomenon see M. L. Gasparov, "Tsepnye strofy v russkoi poezii nachala XX veka."

94. Baevskii, "Strofika sovremennoi liriki," p. 53. For figures on somewhat more recent poetry see S. Shuniaeva, "Strofika sovremennogo russkogo stikha (Na statisticheskom urovne)."

95. Russian renditions of ghazals by a major figure in fifteenth-century Uzbek literature are discussed in A. Klimenko, "Gazeli Alishera Navoi v russkikh poeticheskikh perevodakh."

96. The triolet and rondeau are discussed by Lauer, *Gedichtform*, pp. 62–66, 231–33. Interestingly, the more complicated form, the rondeau, was known already to Trediakovsky at the very beginning of the syllabo-tonic tradition in Russia, while the triolet appeared only in 1778, and then in an anonymous translation. The triolet remained little used until the 1790s.

97. Häublein, *Stanza*, p. 39.

98. Ibid., pp. 40–41.

99. For more on the early history of this stanza in Russian, especially with reference to Katenin's theories about the form the octave should take, see N. V. Izmailov, "Iz istorii russkoi oktavy." The most detailed account of the Russian ottava rima and the controversies surrounding its use can be found in E. G. Etkind, *Russkie poety-perevodchiki ot Trediakovskogo do Pushkina*, pp. 155–201.

100. V. S. Sovalin, ed., *Russkii sonet: XVIII–nachala XX veka* (557 pp.);

and Boris Romanov, ed., *Russkii sonet: Sonety russkikh poetov XVIII–nachala XX veka* (512 pp.). Both collections appeared in 1983, and, not surprisingly, there is much overlap in the selections.

101. The classical studies of this form are L. P. Grossman, "Oneginskaia strofa"; G. O. Vinokur, "Slovo i stikh v *Evgenii Onegine*"; and Tomashevskii, "Strofika Pushkina," pp. 111–33.

102. Tomashevskii, "Strofika Pushkina," p. 112.

103. A. A. Iliushin, "K istorii Oneginskoi strofy," pp. 94–96.

104. For a thorough discussion of Lermontov's poems in the Onegin stanza, see M. A. Peisakhovich, "Oneginskaia strofa v poemakh Lermontova."

105. Iliushin, "K istorii," p. 97.

106. Trediakovskii was the first to employ the ballade schema, in a poem that he composed in French. Later, Derzhavin imitated the French ballade, and several poets influenced by him used the form. However, the main ballad tradition in Russia, which received its impetus from Zhukovskii's translations, followed English and German models. Thus the French ballade stanza never became well established in Russian. Lauer, *Gedichtform*, pp. 21, 49–51, 370–72, 386–87.

107. Häublein, *Stanza*, p. 31.

108. On Lermontov's nine-line stanzas see M. A. Peisakhovich, "Strofika Lermontova," pp. 479–81.

109. On the structure of this stanzaic form see Kiril Taranovsky, "Iz istorii russkogo stikha XVIII v. (Odicheskaia strofa AbAb‖CCdEEd v poezii Lomonosova)."

110. The poem is "Poslanie Lide" (1816); J. Thomas Shaw, "Large Rhyme Sets and Puškin's Poetry," p. 236.

111. Although she does not discuss changes in meter, the best introduction to classifying heterostanzaic poems is by Novinskaia (see n. 85).

112. The late M. A. Peisakhovich wrote a series of articles on the nonstanzaic poetry of several nineteenth-century Russian writers; his general findings on the topic are summarized in "Astroficheskii stikh i ego formy."

113. Ibid., pp. 98, 102–4.

114. M. A. Peisakhovich, "Astroficheskii stikh Nekrasova," p. 88, table.

115. Peisakhovich also distinguishes a relatively small group of nonstanzaic poems in which couplets and quatrains play roughly equal roles; Pushkin's "Graf Nulin" is one example. However, sometimes other rhyme combinations occur as well, so the distinction between this category and freely rhymed verse is not totally clear. "Astroficheskii stikh i ego formy," pp. 105–6.

116. Vishnevskii gives equal prominence to unrhymed and rhymed stanzas in his classification. "Arkhitektonika," passim, esp. table on p. 66.

5 SECONDARY RHYTHMIC FEATURES

1. Shengeli, *Traktat o russkom stikhe*, sec. 1, pp. 37–88, employs the term *modulation* to describe various arrangements of word boundaries over entire lines.

2. Tomashevskii, "Piatistopnyi iamb Pushkina," pp. 204–9. The extensive

footnote on these pages provides formulas for binary lines with and without caesura.

3. Shengeli, *Traktat o russkom stikhe*, pp. 74–75, gives totals for the trimeter and tetrameter. On the ternary pentameters see I. N. Golenishchev-Kutuzov, "Slovorazdel v russkom stikhoslozhenii," pp. 32–33.

4. Tomashevskii, "Piatistopnyi iamb Pushkina," pp. 209–10, notes that the enormous number of possible modulations for the iambic pentameter makes it difficult to obtain meaningful statistics; even examining several thousand lines would not be sufficient to guarantee against chance fluctuations in the frequencies of one modulation or another.   •

5. In the 1920s Tomashevskii also dealt at length with word boundaries in another extensive article, "Ritmika chetyrekhstopnogo iamba po nabliudeniiam nad stikhom *Evgeniia Onegina*." Jakobson treated the topic in "Bolgarskii piatistopnyi iamb—v sopostavlenii s russkim" (originally published in 1932), while Taranovsky analyzed word boundaries for all the poems examined in *Ruski dvodelni ritmovi*.

6. A. N. Kolmogorov and A. V. Prokhorov, "K osnovam russkoi klassicheskoi metriki," esp. pp. 409–13. For a study that touches on word boundaries in a nonclassical poem see A. N. Kolmogorov, "Primer izucheniia metra i ego ritmicheskikh variantov." The examples in this latter item are from Tsvetaeva's poetry; an article that appeared in the same collection as Kolmogorov's also pays some attention to Tsvetaeva's use of word boundaries: Ivanov, "Metr i ritm v 'Poeme kontsa' M. Tsvetaevoi."

7. Tomashevskii, "Ritmika," pp. 111–12.

8. Tomashevskii, *Stikh i iazyk*, p. 25.

9. B. V. Tomashevskii, "Ritm prozy ('Pikovaia dama')," pp. 308–14.

10. I. I. Kovtunova, "Poriadok slov v stikhe i proze," p. 58.

11. See G. N. Akimova, "O nekotorykh osobennostiakh poeticheskogo sintaksisa," which compares sentence lengths in odes by Lomonosov and Sumarokov with the sentence lengths in their scholarly and rhetorical prose.

12. The manner in which syntagms appear in lines of poetry is discussed by Zh. A. Dozorets, "Sintaksicheskaia struktura stroki i ee chlenenie na sintagmy."

13. Much of the following paragraph is based on remarks by Tomashevskii in *Stilistika*, pp. 269–82.

14. Fiona Björling, "On the Question of Inversion in Russian Poetry," p. 13. Her study focuses on adjective-noun inversions in Pushkin's iambic tetrameter poetry.

15. Kovtunova, "Poriadok slov," pp. 44–45.

16. On semantic implications of word order see Kees Verheul, "Poetry and Syntax." He notes that enjambment and meter are other aspects of verse that do not have inherent meaning but may acquire a specific function within a given text or group of texts.

17. Tomashevskii, *Stilistika*, pp. 274–75.

18. Roman Jakobson, "Grammatical Parallelism and Its Russian Facet," pp. 98–108.

19. Antonina Filonov Gove, "Parallelism in the Poetry of Marina Cvetaeva," pp. 172–73. Gove borrows her working definition of parallelism from Robert Austerlitz, "Parallelismus."

20. The seminal article on grammatical parallelism in poetry is Roman Jakobson's "Poeziia grammatiki i grammatika poezii."

21. Gove, "Parallelism," p. 172. As she points out, such parallelism is a distinctive feature of Tsvetaeva's poetry.

22. V. M. Zhirmunskii, *Kompozitsiia liricheskikh stikhotvorenii*, p. 451. I have modified somewhat his categorization of parallel structures. For an extensive discussion of the topic, see pp. 450–527.

23. M. S. Lobanova, "K voprosu o stikhovom perenose [Fr. enjambement]," p. 68. Here and on pp. 69–70 she provides a history of the term's usage in Russian.

24. Tomashevskii, *Stilistika*, pp. 442–43.

25. This list is from Kiril Taranovsky, "Some Problems of Enjambement in Slavic and Western European Verse," pp. 83–84.

26. Zhirmunskii, *Vvedenie*, pp. 154–55. Zhirmunskii, though, had not worked out the criteria for distinguishing situations where the inner syntactic break on one of the lines is required (types 4 and 5) from those where enjambment occurs in any case (types 1–3).

27. Barbara Herrnstein Smith, *Poetic Closure: A Study of How Poems End*, p. 36.

28. Mark E. Suino, "Poetic Closure," pp. 271–73.

29. On the use of repetition in closure see Zhirmunskii, *Kompozitsiia*, pp. 483–92; pp. 502–18 contain a detailed discussion of ring structures and their variants.

30. B. Smith, *Closure*, pp. 59–63.

31. For a discussion of alliteration from this standpoint see Jess B. Bessinger, Jr., "Alliteration."

32. On some of the more common consonant clusters that enter into the sound texture of poems and on the words most frequently associated with them see N. A. Kozhevnikova, "Iz nabliudenii nad zvukovoi organizatsiei stikhotvornogo teksta."

33. Osip Brik, "Zvukovye povtory (Analiz zvukovoi struktury stikha)."

34. For a critique of Brik's approach see Wladimir Weidlé, *Embriologiia poezii: Vvedenie v fonosemantiku poeticheskoi rechi*, pp. 123–24.

35. Anagrams in Russian poetry are the subject of several papers by V. S. Baevskii and A. D. Koshelev; for one of their fuller expositions see "Poetika Bloka: Anagrammy."

36. The name for this phenomenon and the first attempt to explore it in Russian literature are by V. P. Grigor'ev, "Paronimicheskaia attraktsiia v russkoi poezii XX v."

37. Bolinger, "Rime."

38. Gigor'ev, "Paronimicheskaia," pp. 137–39.

39. B. M. Eikhenbaum, *Melodika russkogo liricheskogo stikha*, pp. 330–31.

40. The characteristics of conversational and melodic verse presented here

are based largely on the exposition by Kholshevnikov, *Osnovy stikhovedeniia*, chap. 4, pp. 136–63.

41. V. M. Zhirmunskii, "Melodika stikha (Po povodu knigi B. M. Eikhenbauma *Melodika stikha*, Pb., 1922)," pp. 89–90.

42. In recent years some scholars have attempted to view intonation, rather than meter, as the basic organizing principle behind much modern poetry, most notably that of Maiakovskii. So far, however, metrical analysis continues to yield more concrete results (on this point see the reference in n. 47 below). Both B. P. Goncharov (for instance, in "Maiakovskii: Novator stikha") and S. V. Kalacheva (e.g., "Liricheskii geroi rannego Maiakovskogo i evoliutsiia stikha") have pursued the study of intonational patterns extensively. On some difficulties of this approach see A. M. Moldovan, "Melodika stikha (Voprosy terminologii)."

43. A. L. Zhovtis, "V boevom poriadke . . . (O graficheskoi kompozitsii stikhotvornogo proizvedeniia)," pp. 128–31.

44. The best account of the various experiments with layout and typography occurs in Vladimir Markov, *Russian Futurism: A History.*

45. Voznesenskii, *Ten' zvuka*, pp. 155–66; Voznesenskii's explanatory introduction is on pp. 155–60.

46. On Belyi's use of unusual layouts see Herbert Eagle, "Typographical Devices in the Poetry of Andrey Bely," and Gerald Janecek, "Intonation and Layout in Belyj's Poetry." Belyi set forth his own views in prefaces to the collections *Posle razluki* and *Zovy vremen* (this second collection was never actually published); the two prefaces may be found in *Stikhotvoreniia i poemy*, pp. 546–50, 560–68. The latter also appears in *Novyi zhurnal*, no. 102 (1971), pp. 91–99, where it is mistakenly presented as a previously unpublished work.

47. Gasparov, "Aktsentnyi stikh," pp. 434–37.

48. On Voznesenskii's column and stepladder forms see V. P. Grigor'ev, "Grafika i orfografiia u A. Voznesenskogo."

49. For a discussion of how these forms may influence a poem's meaning see Herbert Eagle, "The Semantic Significance of Step-Ladder and Column Forms in the Poetry of Belyj, Majakovskij, Voznesenskij, and Roždestvenskij."

50. M. L. Gasparov, "Ritm i sintaksis: Proiskhozhdenie 'lesenki' Maiakovskogo," pp. 162–63.

51. Bailey, "Verse of Voznesenskij, p. 171, n. 6; cf. Eagle, "Semantic Significance," p. 19, n. 20.

52. Belyi intentionally obliterated the usual line endings with his column forms (actually adding part of a line to the preceding line so that the boundary is lost); the one recording reflects the new rhythm that results (Janecek, "Intonation, pp. 84–87). Maiakovskii, however, retains a division based on individual syntagms; although the only evidence is a single poem written out in two different ways, it seems clear that the intonational breaks occur in largely the same places both times.

53. Gasparov, "Aktsentnyi stikh," pp. 439–41.

54. Zhovtis, "V boevom poriadke," p. 146.

55. On Tsvetaeva's punctuation see N. S. Valgina, "Stilisticheskaia rol' znakov prepinaniia v poezii M. Tsvetaevoi." Belyi, in putting so much emphasis

on the layout of his verses, believed that punctuation was relatively ineffectual in conveying the intonation. However, he thought that Tsvetaeva's beloved dash was better than the other punctuation marks. Klavdiia Bugaeva, "Stikhi: Ob Andree Belom," pp. 106–7.

56. V. E. Kholshevnikov, "Pereboi ritma." Note Annenskii's sonnet, "Pereboi ritma" (with *pereboi* in the singular), which includes some extreme instances of enjambment.

57. For a concise discussion of how a poem's form may convey meaning see V. A. Zaretskii, "Ritm i smysl v khudozhestvennykh tekstakh."

58. This delineation of different contextual levels is based on Efim Etkind's discussion of ways in which individual words may be perceived; see Etkind, *Materiia stikha*, chap. 3, pp. 185–249.

59. Weidlé, *Embriologiia poezii*, pp. 133–34.

60. For an analysis of the manner in which vocalic sounds may achieve this effect see G. I. Sedykh, "Zvuk i smysl: O funktsii fonem v poeticheskom tekste (na primere analiza stikhotvoreniia M. Tsvetaevoi 'Psikheia')." An essay concentrating on consonantal sounds is Johanna Renate Döring, "Semantizatsiia zvukovykh struktur v poeme Pasternaka 'Vysokaia bolezn'.'"

61. E. V. Nevzgliadova, "O zvukosmyslovykh sviaziakh v poezii," p. 26.

62. See n. 36, 37 above. For a detailed discussion of the lexicon associated with a single word in Russian see O. V. Shul'skaia, "Funktsii paronimii v khudozhestvennoi rechi (paronimicheskie sviazi slova *dym* v russkoi poezii)."

63. For instance one scholar (A. G. Kostetskii, "Lingvisticheskaia teoriia V. Khlebnikova"), by combing through nine of Khlebnikov's articles, has constructed an "alphabet of the mind," which shows the meanings that Khlebnikov assigned to Russian consonants.

64. See Lawrence G. Jones, "Consonantal Tonalities in Russian Verse." Cf. A. P. Zhuravlev, "Soderzhatel'nost' foneticheskoi formy poeticheskogo teksta"; a more detailed explication of Zhuravlev's efforts to establish inherent meanings for both consonants and vowels can be found in *Foneticheskoe znachenie*. He makes many valuable points; however, some of his claims for the synaesthetic values of sounds seem too general, and he tends to base his analyses on spelling rather than pronunciation.

65. Kiril Taranovsky, "The Sound Texture of Russian Verse in the Light of Phonemic Distinctive Features."

66. Ibid., p. 117.

67. Ibid., p. 120.

68. Roman Jakobson, "Poetry of Grammar and Grammar of Poetry," pp. 92–93. The original Russian version of this quotation can be found in "Poeziia grammatiki i grammatika poezii," on pp. 70–71 of the same volume.

69. Lawrence E. Feinberg, "The Grammatical Structure of Boris Pasternak's *Gamlet*," p. 101. The entire essay provides a detailed application of the techniques suggested by Jakobson.

70. Jakobson, "Poeziia grammatiki," pp. 72–75.

71. This essay, originally published in 1966, is reprinted in Jakobson's *Selected Writings*, vol. 3, where it is followed by a more recent analysis of Blok's "Golos iz khora." The same volume also contains analyses of poems in lan-

guages other than Russian; several of these, such as the study (coauthored with Lawrence Jones) of Shakespeare's Sonnet 129 and the article (coauthored with Claude Lévi-Strauss) on "Les Chats" by Baudelaire, have received much attention from Western scholars.

72. A. P. Sumarokov, "O stoposlozhenii," pp. 390–91.

73. N. S. Gumilev, *Sobranie sochinenii v chetyrekh tomakh*, p. 195.

74. Daniel Laferrière, "Iambic versus Trochaic: The Case of Russian," pp. 85–94.

75. Ibid., pp. 127–29.

76. On this topic see R. A. Papaian, "Nekotorye voprosy sootnosheniia metra i zhanra." Cf. his more cautious treatment of meter and genre in *Sravnitel'naia tipologiia natsional'nogo stikha: Russkii i armianskii stikh*, pp. 91–136. Papaian also discusses the affinity of trochaic meters for songs, though many of the other relations he discovers could be explained more as instances of influence.

77. For brief remarks on the relationship between stanzaic forms and genre see Iu. I. Levin, "Semanticheskii oreol metra s semioticheskoi tochki zreniia," p. 152.

78. R. A. Papaian's original article on this topic deals with Blok's poetry: "K voprosu o sootnoshenii stikhotvornykh razmerov i intensivnosti tropov v lirike A. Bloka." On pp. 137–79 of *Sravnitel'naia tipologiia* he supplements his earlier study by analyzing the poetry of Vaan Ter'ian from this standpoint.

79. Taranovsky, "O vzaimootnoshenii stikhotvornogo ritma i tematiki."

80. Ibid., p. 297.

81. Weidlé, *Embriologiia poezii*, pp. 214–25, objects to some of Taranovsky's claims. While admitting that Lermontov's poem influenced the use of this meter in the second half of the nineteenth century, Weidlé believes that Blok's and Esenin's poetry in the meter bears little relationship to Lermontov's. He also questions Taranovsky's remarks regarding the rhythm of the trochaic pentameter in Russian. While some of Weidlé's specific points about isolated passages are a matter of interpretation and seem to be a question of personal preference, his general objections are based on a totally different view of what constitutes rhythm and on rather narrow thematic interpretations.

82. Gasparov, "K semantike daktilicheskoi rifmy v russkom khoree."

83. M. L. Gasparov, "Metr i smysl: K semantike russkogo trekhstopnogo khoreia."

84. M. L. Gasparov, "Semanticheskii oreol metra (K semantike russkogo trekhstopnogo iamba)," and idem, "Semanticheskii oreol trekhstopnogo amfibrakhiia."

85. Gasparov's approach, as well as Taranovsky's, is questioned by L. I. Timofeev in *Slovo v stikhe*, pp. 144–59. In many ways Timofeev's approach to poetry is similar to Weidlé's; thus he too finds individual counterexamples to support the view that broad statistical data may conceal the specific nature of a given poem or line. In general, Timofeev plays down the role of rhythmic and metrical features; he tries to show, for instance, that in revising their own works, poets choose words more for their semantic than for their rhythmic qualities. While no one would argue that the connotations of the words a poet chooses are

important for a poem, it does not necessarily follow that the poem's overall rhythmic qualities are not.

86. Levin, "Semanticheskii oreol," p. 153.

87. On the way in which various kinds of "rhythmic series" may play a role in a poem's structure see E. G. Etkind, "Ritm poeticheskogo proizvedeniia kak faktor soderzhaniia."

APPENDIX

1. For instance, in one Soviet collection devoted to two dozen separate analyses of poems by as many poets, few of the scholars pay more than passing attention to the subtle effects of meter, rhythm, and other formal aspects of organization. G. M. Fridlender, ed., *Poeticheskii stroi russkoi liriki*.

2. See especially Jakobson, "Poeziia grammatiki," as well as other studies in *Selected Writings*, vol. 3, and Feinberg, "Grammatical Structure."

3. Kiril Taranovsky, "Zvukopis' v 'Severovostoke' M. Voloshina."

4. L. L. Bel'skaia, "Opyt vnetekstovogo i tekstovogo analiza poeticheskogo proizvedeniia."

5. S. I. Gindin, "Ritmika, intonatsiia i smyslovaia kompozitsiia v poeme Vl. Lugovskogo 'Kak chelovek plyl s Odisseem.'"

6. P. A. Rudnev, "Metr i smysl."

7. P. A. Rudnev, "O printsipakh opisaniia i semanticheskogo analiza stikhotvornogo teksta na metricheskom urovne."

8. P. A. Rudnev, "Stikhotvorenie A. Bloka 'Vse tikho na svetlom litse . . .' (Opyt semanticheskoi interpretatsii metra i ritma)."

9. Taranovsky, *Ruski dvodelni ritmovi*, table 12.

10. Gasparov, "Chetyrekhiktnyi dol'nik," pp. 276–78; note esp. table 6, p. 277.

11. Taranovsky, *Ruski dvodelni ritmovi*, pp. 146–47, makes 75 percent the lower limit for the frequency of lines with word boundaries after the fourth syllable in iambic pentameter poems with movable caesura. However, given the brief length of the poem (which allows just four lines without a break after the fourth syllable to bring the figure down to slightly under 75 percent) and the consistent presence of a word boundary after the fifth syllable for the four lines in question, it seems reasonable to claim the presence of a movable caesura.

12. Taranovsky, "Sound Texture," p. 121.

Bibliography

The following list includes all works mentioned in the foot-notes as well as other items consulted while researching this book. For easy reference from the footnotes, multiple articles by a single author are listed alphabetically by title. When the author is a compiler or editor, the work(s) in question will be found at the end of the entries for that person. The names of three journals have been abbreviated:

IJSLP   *International Journal of Slavic Linguistics and Poetics*
RusL   *Russian Literature*
SEEJ   *Slavic and East European Journal*

Collections of articles have their own entries as do individual studies within those collections that are mentioned in the notes. The titles of several such collections have also been abbreviated in the entries for articles:

ITS   V. E. Kholshevnikov, ed., *Issledovaniia po teorii stikha*
O stikhe   B. V. Tomashevskii, *O stikhe: Stat'i*
RP   Thomas Eekman and Dean S. Worth, eds., *Russian Poetics: Proceedings of the International Colloquium at UCLA, September 22–26, 1975*
SP   Roman Jakobson, C. H. van Schooneveld, and Dean S. Worth, eds., *Slavic Poetics: Essays in Honor of Kiril Taranovsky*
SRS   M. L. Gasparov, *Sovremennyi russkii stikh: Metrika i ritmika*
TS   V. E. Kholshevnikov, D. S. Likhachev, and V. M. Zhirmunskii, eds., *Teoriia stikha*

Akimova, G. N. "O nekotorykh osobennostiakh poeticheskogo sintaksisa." *Voprosy iazykoznaniia* 26 (1977), no. 1, 96–108.
Astakhova, A. M. *Byliny: Itogi i problemy izucheniia.* Moscow and Leningrad: Nauka, 1966. See pp. 143–62 for a concise survey of work done until that time on the verse forms of the *byliny.*
Attridge, Derek. *The Rhythms of English Poetry.* English Language Series, no. 14. Longman: London and New York, 1982. Includes a discussion of the generative approach to date (pp. 34–55); part 3 offers his own effort to formulate a set of metrical rules.

Austerlitz, Robert. "Parallelismus." In *Poetics, Poetyka, Poetika*, ed. Donald Davie et al., vol. 1, pp. 439–43. Warsaw: Państwowe Wydawnictwo Naukowe, 1961.

Baevskii, V. S. *Stikh russkoi sovetskoi poezii: Posobie dlia slushatelei spetskursa*. Smolensk: Smolenskii pedagogicheskii institut, 1972. Includes sections on free verse (pp. 57–91) and shadow rhyme (pp. 92–101).

——. "Strofika sovremennoi liriki v otnoshenii k strofike narodnoi poezii." In *Problemy stikhovedeniia*, ed. M. L. Gasparov et al., pp. 51–67.

Baevskii, V. S.; Ibraev, L. I.; Kormilov, S. I.; and Sapogov, V. A. "K istorii russkogo svobodnogo stikha." *Russkaia literatura* 18 (1975), no. 3, 89–102.

Baevskii, V. S., and Koshelev, A. D. "Poetika Bloka: Anagrammy." *Uchenye zapiski Tartuskogo gosudarstvennogo universiteta* 459: *Tvorchestvo A. A. Bloka i russkaia kul'tura XX veka* (*Blokovskii sbornik*) 3 (1979), 50–75. The longest of several articles by these authors on the subject of anagrams in Russian poetry.

Bailey, James. "The Accentual Verse of Majakovskij's 'Razgovor s fininspektorom o poèzii.'" In *SP*, pp. 25–31.

——. "The Basic Structural Characteristics of Russian Literary Meters." In *Studies Presented to Professor Roman Jakobson by His Students*, ed. Charles E. Gribble, pp. 17–38. Cambridge, Mass.: Slavica, 1968. A brief survey of all the main meters in Russian; good starting point for a serious study of Russian verse theory.

——. "Blok and Heine: An Episode from the History of Russian *Dol'niki*." *SEEJ* 13 (1969), no. 1, 1–22.

——. "The Development of Strict Accentual Verse in Russian Literary Poetry." *RusL*, no. 9 (1975), 87–109. Here and in "The Accentual Verse of Majakovskij's 'Razgovor s fininspektorom o poèzii'" Bailey analyzes what he calls "strict accentual verse" and what Gasparov terms the *taktovik*. This item provides the best introduction to the topic.

——. "An Early Example of Russian Dramatic Blank Verse: Narezhnyi's Tragedy *Krovavaia noch'*." *Study Group on Eighteenth-Century Russia, Newsletter* (Leeds, England), no. 11 (1983), 34–39.

——. "The Epic Meters of T. G. Rjabinin as Collected by A. F. Gil'ferding." In *American Contributions to the Seventh International Congress of Slavists*, vol. 1, *Linguistics and Poetics*, ed. Ladislav Matejka, pp. 9–32. Slavistic Printings and Reprintings, no. 295. The Hague: Mouton, 1973.

——. "The Evolution and Structure of the Russian Iambic Pentameter from 1880 to 1922." *IJSLP* 16 (1973), 119–46.

——. "Linguistic Givens and Their Metrical Realization in a Poem by Yeats." *Language and Style* 8 (1975), no. 1, 21–33. Shows that Yeats's "Cap and Bells" could be considered an example of what Russian scholars call three-stress *dol'niki*.

——. "Literary Usage of a Russian Folk Song Meter." *SEEJ* 14 (1970), no. 4, 436–52. On the so-called 5+5 trochaic meter, used most notably in the poetry of Kol'tsov.

——. "The Metrical and Rhythmical Typology of K. K. Slučevskij's Poetry." *IJSLP* 18 (1975), 93–117.

————. "The Metrical Typology of Russian Narrative Folk Meters." In *American Contributions to the Eighth International Congress of Slavists*, vol. 1, *Linguistics and Poetics*, ed. Henrik Birnbaum, pp. 82–103. Columbus, Ohio: Slavica, 1978. Bailey is currently working on an extensive monograph devoted to folk versification; in the meantime, this remains the best single treatment of the topic.

————. "Parallelism or Antiparallelism?" Review of Michael Shapiro, *Asymmetry: An Inquiry into the Linguistic Structure of Poetry. Folia Slavica* 1 (1977), no. 2, 244–64.

————. "Russian Binary Meters with Strong Caesura from 1890 to 1920." *IJSLP* 14 (1971), 111–33.

————. "The Russian Three-Stress *Dol'nik* with Zero Anacrusis." *IJSLP* 23 (1981), 113–31.

————. "Some Recent Developments in the Study of Russian Versification." *Language and Style* 5 (1972), no. 3, 155–91. An extensive review of *TS*.

————. "The Three-Stress *Dol'niki* of George Ivask as an Example of Rhythmic Change." *IJSLP* 13 (1970), 155–67.

————. *Toward a Statistical Analysis of English Verse: The Iambic Tetrameter of Ten Poets*. Lisse, The Netherlands: Peter de Ridder Press, 1975. Applies the Russian linguistic-statistical method to English verse. Good to read before attempting Tarlinskaja's study *English Verse: Theory and History*.

————. "The Trochaic Song Meters of Kol'cov and Kašin." *RusL*, no. 12 (1975), 5–27. A study of folk influence on literature; cf. Bailey's earlier study "Literary Usage of a Russian Folk Song Meter."

————. "The Verse of Andrej Voznesenskij as an Example of Present-Day Russian Versification." *SEEJ* 17 (1973), no. 2, 155–73.

————. "The Versification of the Russian *Kant* from the End of the Seventeenth to the Middle of the Eighteenth Century." *RusL* 13 (1983), no. 2, 123–73.

Bakhtin, V. S., comp. *Chastushka*. Biblioteka poeta, Bol'shaia seriia, 2d ed. Moscow and Leningrad: Sovetskii pisatel', 1966.

Beaver, Joseph C. "The Rules of Stress in English Verse." *Language* 47 (1971), no. 3, 586–614. Modifies the Halle-Keyser approach by offering a different set of stress rules, which do much to improve the original theory. Beaver, who was the first to use the term *generative metrics*, set forth his views in a series of articles (of which this is the single most complete statement) during the late 1960s and early 1970s.

Belousov, A. "O metricheskom repertuare poezii I. A. Bunina." In *Russkaia filologiia: Tretii sbornik nauchnykh studencheskikh rabot*, ed. P. A. Rudnev et al., pp. 48–61. Tartu: Tartuskii gosudarstvennyi universitet, 1971.

Bel'skaia, L. L. "Chetyrekhstopnyi iamb S. Esenina." In *Voprosy statisticheskoi stilistiki*, ed. B. N. Golovin et al., pp. 228–37. Kiev: Naukova dumka, 1974.

————. "Esenin i Maiakovskii (K probleme stikhotvornogo novatorstva)." *Trudy Kirgizskogo gosudarstvennogo universiteta: Filologicheskie nauki* 19: *Seriia Voprosy poetiki* 2 (1975), 33–41.

————. "Iz nabliudenii nad ritmami S. Esenina." *Filologicheskii sbornik* (Alma-Ata), 4 (1965), 102–10.

332   Bibliography

————. "K voprosu o dvukh kontseptsiiakh svobodnogo stikha v sovetskom stikhovedenii." *Russkaia literatura* (Alma-Ata), 6 (1976), 90–98.

————. "Opyt vnetekstovogo i tekstovogo analiza poeticheskogo proizvedeniia." *Russkaia literatura* (Alma-Ata), 5 (1975), 60–68.

Belyi, A. *Simvolizm: Kniga statei.* Moscow: Musaget, 1910. See the articles "Lirika i eksperiment" (pp. 231–85), "Opyt kharakteristiki russkogo chetyrekhstopnogo iamba" (pp. 286–330), "Sravnitel'naia morfologiia ritma russkikh lirikov v iambicheskom dimetre" (pp. 331–95), and "'Ne poi, krasavitsa, pri mne . . .' A. S. Pushkina (Opyt opisaniia)" (pp. 396–428). Includes the first published use of a statistical approach to the study of Russian verse, though Belyi's theoretical conclusions have been largely rejected by subsequent scholars.

————. *Stikhotvoreniia i poemy.* Biblioteka poeta, Bol'shaia seriia, 2d ed. Moscow and Leningrad: Sovetskii pisatel', 1966.

Berkov, P. N. "K sporam o printsipakh chteniia sillabicheskikh stikhov XVII–nachala XVIII v." In *TS*, pp. 294–316.

————. *Lomonosov i literaturnaia polemika ego vremeni, 1750–1765.* Moscow and Leningrad: Akademiia nauk SSSR, 1936.

Bessinger, Jess B., Jr. "Alliteration." In *Princeton Encyclopedia of Poetry and Poetics*, ed. Alex Preminger, pp. 15–16. Princeton: Princeton University Press, 1965.

Beyer, Thomas R., Jr. "The Bely-Zhirmunsky Polemic." In *Andrey Bely: A Critical Review*, ed. Gerald Janecek, pp. 205–13. Lexington, Ky.: University Press of Kentucky, 1978.

Bezzubov, A. N. "Piatislozhnik." In *ITS*, pp. 104–17.

Björling, Fiona. "On the Question of Inversion in Russian Poetry." *Slavica Lundensia* 5 (1977), *Litteraria*, 7–84.

Bobrov, S. P. "K voprosu o podlinnom stikhotvornom razmere pushkinskikh 'Pesen zapadnykh slavian.'" *Russkaia literatura* 7 (1964), no. 3, 119–37.

————. "Opyt izucheniia vol'nogo stikha pushkinskikh 'Pesen zapadnykh slavian.'" *Teoriia veroiatnostei i ee primeneniia* 9 (1964), no. 2, 262–72.

Bolinger, Dwight L. "Rime, Assonance, and Morpheme Analysis." *Word* 6 (1950), no. 2, 117–36. A discussion based on English examples of the phenomenon explored in Russian verse by V. P. Grigor'ev, "Paronimicheskaia attraktsiia v russkoi poezii XX v."

Bondi, S. M. "Narodnyi stikh u Pushkina." In *O Pushkine: Stat'i i issledovaniia*, pp. 372–441. Moscow: Khudozhestvennaia literatura, 1978.

————. "O ritme." In *Kontekst 1976: Literaturno-teoreticheskie issledovaniia*, ed. A. S. Miasnikov, et al., pp. 100–129. Moscow: Nauka, 1977.

————. "Pushkin i russkii gekzametr." In *O Pushkine: Stat'i i issledovaniia*, pp. 310–71. Moscow: Khudozhestvennaia literatura, 1978.

————. "Trediakovskii, Lomonosov, Sumarokov." Introduction to V. Trediakovskii, *Stikhotvoreniia*, Biblioteka poeta, pp. 7–113. Leningrad: Sovetskii pisatel', 1935.

Borodin, V. V., and Shaikevich, A. Ia., comps. "Slovar' rifm M. Iu. Lermontova." In *Lermontovskaia entsiklopediia*, ed. V. A. Manuilov, pp. 666–716. Moscow: Sovetskaia entsiklopediia, 1981.

Briggs, Anthony D. "The Metrical Virtuosity of Afanasy Fet." *Slavonic and East European Review* 52 (1974), no. 128, 355–65.

Brik, O. M. "Zvukovye povtory (Analiz zvukovoi struktury stikha)." In *Poetika*, vols. 1–2, pp. 58–98. Petrograd, 1919.

Briusov, V. Ia. *Kratkii kurs nauki o stikhe: Chast' I, Chastnaia metrika i ritmika russkogo stikha.* Moscow: Al'tsiona, 1919. An earlier version of *Osnovy stikhovedeniia.*

———. "Levizna Pushkina v rifmakh." In *Sobranie sochinenii v semi tomakh*, vol. 7, pp. 148–63. Moscow: Khudozhestvennaia literatura, 1975. Originally published in 1928.

———. "O rifme." In *Sobranie sochinenii v semi tomakh*, vol. 6, pp. 544–56. Moscow: Khudozhestvennaia literatura, 1975. Originally published in 1924.

———. *Opyty.* In *Sobranie sochinenii v semi tomakh*, vol. 3, pp. 455–544. Moscow: Khudozhestvennaia literatura, 1974. Originally published in 1918.

———. *Osnovy stikhovedeniia: Kurs V.U.Z., Chasti I i II, Obshchee vvedenie, Metrika i ritmika.* 2d ed. Moscow: Giz, 1924. Knowledgeable, but idiosyncratic in its terminology and theory. See n. 1 to the preface for various articles on Briusov's versification work.

Brodsky, Joseph. *A Part of Speech.* New York: Farrar, Straus, and Giroux, 1980.

Brogan, T. V. F. *English Versification, 1570–1980: A Reference Guide with a Global Appendix.* Baltimore: Johns Hopkins University Press, 1981. A comprehensive, annotated listing of works on English versification; the appendix includes about 250 (nonannotated) items under the heading "Slavic."

Bucsela, John. "The Birth of Russian Syllabo-Tonic Versification." *SEEJ* 9 (1965), no. 3, 281–94.

Bugaeva, Klavdiia. "Stikhi. Ob Andree Belom." *Novyi zhurnal*, no. 102 (1971), pp. 103–9.

Bukhshtab, B. Ia. "O strukture russkogo klassicheskogo stikha." *Uchenye zapiski Tartuskogo gosudarstvennogo universiteta* 236: *Trudy po znakovym sistemam* 4 (1969), 386–408. The most detailed of several articles in which Bukhshtab offers some provocative challenges to the usual view of the relationship between meter and rhythm.

Burgi, Richard. *A History of the Russian Hexameter.* Hamden, Conn.: Shoe String Press, 1954.

Cable, Thomas. "Recent Developments in Metrics." *Style* 10 (1976), no. 3, 313–28. The most accessible critique of the early generative theories; questions the value of the entire methodology.

Chardžiev, Nikolaj. "Maiakovskii i Igor' Severianin." *RusL* 6 (1978), no. 4, 307–46.

Chatman, Seymour. *A Theory of Meter.* The Hague: Mouton, 1965. A carefully constructed theory based on structural principles, but difficult to apply in practice. In this approach, metrical analysis ultimately rests on a composite of possible readings.

Chisholm, David. "Generative Prosody and English Verse." *Poetics* 6 (1977), no. 2, 111–53. Criticizes the first version of Kiparsky's theory and suggests instead a revised version of Magnuson-Ryder.

Chistov, K. V., and Chistova, B. E., comps. *Prichitaniia*. Biblioteka poeta, Bol'shaia seriia, 2d ed. Leningrad: Sovetskii pisatel', 1960.

Dal', V. I. *Poslovitsy russkogo naroda: Sbornik.* Moscow: GIKhL, 1957.

Danilin, V. V., and Danilina, E. F. "Slovo v rifme M. Iu. Lermontova (Stikhotvoreniia: Statisticheskii analiz)." In *Leksika russkogo iazyka: Respublikanskii sbornik*, ed. V. D. Bondaletov, pp. 80–88. Riazan': Riazanskii gosudarstvennyi pedagogicheskii institut, 1979.

Döring, Johanna Renate. "Semantizatsiia zvukovykh struktur v poeme Pasternaka 'Vysokaia bolezn'.'" In *Boris Pasternak, 1890–1960: Colloque de Cerisy-la-Salle (11–14 septembre 1975)*, pp. 143–54. Bibliothèque russe de l'Institut d'études slaves 47. Paris: Institut d'études slaves, 1979.

Dozorets, Zh. A. "Sintaksicheskaia struktura stroki i ee chlenenie na sintagmy." In *Aktual'nye voprosy grammatiki i leksiki russkogo iazyka: Sbornik trudov*, ed. L. Iu. Maksimov, pp. 79–96. Moscow: Moskovskii gosudarstvennyi pedagogicheskii institut, 1978.

Drage, C. L. "The Introduction of Russian Syllabo-Tonic Prosody." *Slavonic and East European Review* 54 (1976), no. 4, 481–503.

———. "Trochaic Metres in Early Russian Syllabo-Tonic Poetry." *Slavonic and East European Review* 38 (1960), no. 91, 361–79.

Draper, John W. "The Origin of Rhyme." *Revue de littérature comparée* 31 (1957), no. 1, 74–85.

Eagle, Herbert. "On the Free Verse Rhythm of Mandelstam's 'Horseshoe Finder.'" *Russian Literature Triquarterly*, no. 4 (1972), pp. 331–46.

———. "The Semantic Significance of Step-Ladder and Column Forms in the Poetry of Belyj, Majakovskij, Voznesenskij, and Roždestvenskij." *Forum at Iowa on Russian Literature* 1 (1976), 1–19.

———. "Typographical Devices in the Poetry of Andrey Bely." In *Andrey Bely: A Critical Review*, ed. Gerald Janecek, pp. 71–85. Lexington, Ky.: University Press of Kentucky, 1978.

Eekman, Thomas. *The Realm of Rime: A Study of Rime in the Poetry of the Slavs.* Bibliotheca slavonica, no. 15. Amsterdam: Adolf M. Hakkert, 1974. A broader study than those on rhyme by Samoilov and Zhirmunskii; consequently pays less attention to Russian rhyme itself. Good on the early history and useful for comparative studies.

Eekman, Thomas, and Worth, Dean S., eds. *Russian Poetics: Proceedings of the International Colloquium at UCLA, September 22–26, 1975.* Columbus, Ohio: Slavica, 1982. Includes over a dozen papers on Russian verse theory by American, English, Polish, and Russian scholars. Abbreviated throughout the bibliography as *RP*.

Eikhenbaum, B. M. *Melodika russkogo liricheskogo stikha*, 1922. Reprinted in *O poezii*, pp. 327–511. Leningrad: Sovetskii pisatel', 1969. Cf. the review of this work by V. M. Zhirmunskii which is reprinted in *Teoriia literatury, Poetika, Stilistika* (Leningrad: Nauka, 1977), pp. 56–93.

Epstein, Edmund L., and Hawkes, Terence. *Linguistics and English Poetry.* Studies in Linguistics: Occasional Papers, no. 7. Buffalo: Department of Anthropology and Linguistics, University of Buffalo, 1959. Application of

Trager-Smith to English poetry. Good on the variety of English lines, but, like most structural approaches, ends up with an overly complex system (e.g., finds 6,236 types of English iambic feet).

Etkind, E. G. *Materiia stikha*. Bibliothèque russe de l'Institut d'études slaves 48. Paris: Institut d'études slaves, 1978. A broad study that contains many useful observations about formal aspects of Russian verse; particularly strong on some of the secondary rhythmic features.

―――. "Ritm poeticheskogo proizvedeniia kak faktor soderzhaniia." In *Ritm, prostranstvo i vremia v literature i iskusstve*, ed. B. F. Egorov, pp. 104–21. Leningrad: Nauka, 1974.

―――. *Russkie poety-perevodchiki ot Trediakovskogo do Pushkina*. Leningrad: Nauka, 1973.

Feinberg, Lawrence E. "The Grammatical Structure of Boris Pasternak's *Gamlet*." In *SP*, pp. 99–124.

[Fleishman, L. S.] "Tomashevskii i Moskovskii lingvisticheskii kruzhok." *Uchenye zapiski Tartuskogo gosudarstvennogo universiteta* 422: *Trudy po znakovym sistemam* 9 (1977), 113–32.

Foster, David W. *The Early Spanish Ballad*. New York: Twayne, 1971.

Fridlender, G. M., ed. *Poeticheskii stroi russkoi liriki*. Leningrad: Nauka, 1973.

García Lorca, Federico. *Lirika*. Moscow: Khudozhestvennaia literatura, 1966.

Gasparov, M. L. "Aktsentnyi stikh Maiakovskogo." In *SRS*, pp. 398–468.

―――. "Briusov-stikhoved i Briusov-stikhotvorets (1910–1920-e gody)." In *Briusovskie chteniia 1973 goda*, ed. K. V. Aivazian, pp. 11–43. Erevan: Sovetakan grokh, 1976.

―――. "Chetyrekhiktnyi dol'nik." In *SRS*, pp. 245–93.

―――. "Iamb i khorei sovetskikh poetov." In *SRS*, pp. 76–125.

―――. "K analizu russkoi netochnoi rifmy." In *RP*, pp. 103–15.

―――. "K semantike daktilicheskoi rifmy v russkom khoree." In *SP*, pp. 143–50.

―――. "Legkii stikh i tiazhelyi stikh." *Uchenye zapiski Tartuskogo gosudarstvennogo universiteta* 420: *Studia metrica et poetica* 2 (1977), 3–20. Like Jakobson's "Ob odnoslozhnykh slovakh," considers the effect of lightly stressed as opposed to fully stressed words on creating the rhythm of the verse line. Translated in G. S. Smith, ed. and trans., *Metre, Rhythm, Stanza, Rhyme*.

―――. "Materialy o ritmike russkogo 4-stopnogo iamba XVIII veka." *RusL* 12 (1982), no. 2, 195–216.

―――. "Metr i smysl: K semantike russkogo trekhstopnogo khoreia." *Izvestiia Akademiia nauk*, Seriia literatury i iazyka, 35 (1976), no. 4, 357–66.

―――. "Metricheskii repertuar russkoi liriki XVIII–XX vv." In *SRS*, pp. 39–75.

―――. "Nekrasov v istorii russkoi rifmy." In *N. A. Nekrasov i russkaia literatura: Sbornik nauchnykh trudov* 43 (3), ed. N. N. Skatov, pp. 77–89. Iaroslavl': Iaroslavskii gosudarstvennyi pedagogicheskii institut, 1976.

―――. "Oppozitsiia 'stikh—proza' i stanovlenie russkogo literaturnogo stikha." In *Semiotyka i struktura tekstu: Studia poświęcone VII Międzyna-*

rodowemu Kongresowi Slawistóv, ed. Maria Renata Mayenowa, pp. 325–
35. Wrocław: Zakład Narodowy im. Ossolińskich, 1973.

———. "Osnovnye poniatiia russkoi metriki." In *SRS*, pp. 11–17.

———. "Prodrom, Tsets, i natsional'nye formy geksametra." In *Antichnost' i Vizantiia*, ed. L. A. Freiberg, pp. 362–85. Moscow: Nauka, 1975.

———. "Rifma Bloka." *Uchenye zapiski Tartuskogo gosudarstvennogo universiteta* 459: *Tvorchestvo A. A. Bloka i russkaia kul'tura XX veka (Blokovskii sbornik)*, 3 (1979), 34–49.

———. "Ritm i sintaksis: Proiskhozhdenie 'lesenki' Maiakovskogo." In *Problemy strukturnoi lingvistiki, 1979*, ed. V. P. Grigor'ev, pp. 148–68. Moscow: Nauka, 1981.

———. "Russkii bylinnyi stikh." In *ITS*, pp. 3–47. A shorter version appears in *SRS*.

———. "Russkii iamb i angliiskii iamb." In *Philologica: Issledovaniia po iazyku i literature. Pamiati akademika Viktora Maksimovicha Zhirmunskogo*, ed. V. N. Iartseva, pp. 408–15. Leningrad: Nauka, 1973.

———. "Russkii narodnyi stikh v literaturnykh imitatsiiakh." *IJSLP* 19 (1975), 77–107. A broad survey of the topic; contains much useful information.

———. "Russkii sillabicheskii trinadtsatislozhnik." In *Metryka słowiańska*, ed. Zdzisława Kopczyńska and Lucylla Pszczołowska, pp. 39–63. Wrocław: Zakład Narodowy im. Ossolińskich, 1971.

———. "Russkii trekhudarnyi dol'nik XX v." In *TS*, pp. 59–106. With this article, research on Russian nonclassical verse came of age. A detailed analysis of the development and rhythmic variations exhibited by this meter, which has remained popular throughout the twentieth century. A shorter form of the article appears in *SRS*, pp. 220–44.

———. "Semanticheskii oreol metra (K semantike russkogo trekhstopnogo iamba)." In *Lingvistika i poetika*, ed. V. P. Grigor'ev, pp. 282–308. Moscow: Nauka, 1979.

———. "Semanticheskii oreol trekhstopnogo amphibrakhiia." In *Problemy strukturnoi lingvistiki, 1980*, ed. V. P. Grigor'ev, pp. 174–92. Moscow: Nauka, 1982.

———. *Sovremennyi russkii stikh: Metrika i ritmika*. Moscow: Nauka, 1974. Broad surveys on the use of Russian meters as well as investigations of iambic and trochaic verse in the twentieth century and pioneering studies of modern verse forms (*dol'niki* and the *taktovik*). The introduction is translated in G. S. Smith, ed. and trans., *Metre, Rhythm, Stanza, Rhyme*. Abbreviated throughout the bibliography as *SRS*.

———. "Taktovik v poezii XX veka." In *SRS*, pp. 294–351.

———. "Taktovik v russkom stikhoslozhenii XX v." *Voprosy iazykoznaniia* 17 (1968), no. 5, 79–90.

———. "Trekhstopnyi amfibrakhii i trekhstopnyi anapest v XIX i XX v." In *SRS*, pp. 126–219. The first study to probe in detail the rhythmic characteristics of the Russian ternary meters.

———. "Tsepnye strofy v russkoi poezii nachala XX veka." In *Russkaia sovetskaia poeziia i stikhovedenie*, ed. K. G. Petrosov et al., pp. 251–57. Moscow: Moskovskii oblastnoi pedagogicheskii institut, 1969.

————. "Vol'nyi khorei i vol'nyi iamb Maiakovskogo." In *SRS*, pp. 372–97.

————, ed. *Russkoe stikhoslozhenie XIX v.: Materialy po metrike i strofike russkikh poetov*. Moscow: Nauka, 1979. The collection contains metrical and stanzaic handbooks compiled by different scholars for nine Russian poets: Zhukovskii, Batiushkov, Vostokov, Pushkin, Del'vig, Baratynskii, Kol'tsov, Tiutchev, and Polonskii. Much useful data, though the commentaries and to some extent the tables vary in quality from handbook to handbook.

Gasparov, M. L.; Dzhrbashian, E. M.; and Papaian, R. A.; eds. *Problemy stikhovedeniia*. Erevan: Erevanskii gosudarstvennyi universitet, 1976. Deals with both Russian and Armenian poetry; the articles devoted to the former concentrate on stanzaic forms and on free verse.

Gil'ferding, A. F. *Onezhskie byliny*. 3 vols. 4th ed. Moscow and Leningrad: Akademiia nauk SSSR, 1949–51. The introduction by Gil'ferding, originally published in 1872, the year of his death, contains perceptive remarks on folk versification. For other nineteenth-century views see the items in this bibliography by Golokhvastov, Korsh, and Vostokov. While the fourth edition is cited here because it is more readily available, both Bailey and Gasparov prefer to use the texts of the first edition (St. Petersburg, 1873) for their metrical analyses.

Gindin, S. I. "Briusovskoe opisanie metriki russkogo stikha s tochki zreniia sovremennoi tipologii lingvisticheskikh opisanii." In *SP*, pp. 151–60.

————. "Obshchee i russkoe stikhovedenie. Sistematicheskii ukazatel' literatury, izdannoi v SSSR na russkom iazyke s 1958 po 1974 gg." In *ITS*, pp. 152–222. Virtually complete coverage of Russian-language items published in the Soviet Union during the period.

————. "Ritmika, intonatsiia, i smyslovaia kompozitsiia v poeme Vl. Lugovskogo 'Kak chelovek plyl s Odisseem.'" In *Problemy strukturnoi lingvistiki, 1978*, ed. V. P. Grigor'ev, pp. 230–65. Moscow: Nauka, 1981.

————. *Struktura stikhotvornoi rechi: Sistematicheskii ukazatel' literatury po obshchemu i russkomu stikhovedeniiu, izdannoi v SSSR na russkom iazyke s 1958 g: Chast' II, 1974–1980*. Nos. 4–6. Institute of Russian AN SSSR. Study Group on Experimental and Applied Linguistics. Preliminary Publications, vols. 146–48. Moscow, 1982. A continuation of Gindin's "Obshchee i russkoe stikhovedenie" through 1980; "Obshchee" also appeared in its original form as vols. 94–96 of this same series in 1976.

————. "Transformatsionnyi analiz i metrika (iz istorii problemy). *Mashinnyi perevod i prikladnaia lingvistika*, no. 13 (1970), 177–200.

————. "V. Ia. Briusov o rechevoi prirode stikha i stikhotvornogo ritma i o russkikh ekvivalentakh antichnykh stikhotvornykh razmerov." *Voprosy iazykoznaniia* 17 (1968), no. 6, 124–29.

————. "Vzgliady V. Ia. Briusova na iazykovuiu priemlemost' stikhovykh sistem i sud'by russkoi sillabiki (po rukopisiam 90-kh godov)." *Voprosy iazykoznaniia* 19 (1970), no. 2, 99–109.

Girshman, M. M., and Orlova, O. A. "Chetyrekhstopnyi iamb Nekrasova i Polonskogo i problema tipologii iambicheskogo ritma v russkoi poezii 50–kh godov XIX veka." *Uchenye zapiski Permskogo gosudarstvennogo universiteta* 304: *Problemy tipologii i istorii russkoi literatury*, 1976, 178–92.

Golenishchev-Kutuzov, I. N. "Slovorazdel v russkom stikhoslozhenii." *Voprosy iazykoznaniia* 8 (1959), no. 4, 20–34. On the topic of word boundaries see also Tomashevskii, *O stikhe*, pp. 94–137, 138–253, and Shengeli, *Traktat o russkom stikhe*, passim.

Golokhvastov, P. D. *Zakony stikha russkogo narodnogo i nashego literaturnogo: Opyt izuchenii.* St. Petersburg: Tipografiia Dobrodeeva, 1883. Contains unfavorable (and often highly questionable) comments on literary verse, but is the first to discuss the distinction between word stress and sense stress, which is important for the system of folk versification.

Goncharov, B. P. "Maiakovskii: Novator stikha." In *Maiakovskii i sovremennost'*, comp. A. M. Ushakov, pp. 191–217. Moscow: Sovremennik, 1977.

————. "O reforme russkogo stikhoslozheniia v XVIII veke (K probleme ee natsional'nykh istokov)." *Russkaia literatura* 18 (1975), no. 2, 51–69.

Gove, Antonina Filonov. "The Evidence for Metrical Adaptation in Early Slavic Translated Hymns." *Monumenta Musicae Byzantinae, Subsidia* 6: *Fundamental Problems of Early Slavic Music and Poetry*, 1978, 211–46.

————. "Literalism and Poetic Equivalence in the Old Church Slavonic Translation of the Akathistos Hymn." *IJSLP* 22 (1976), 61–73.

————. "Parallelism in the Poetry of Marina Cvetaeva." In *SP*, pp. 171–92.

————. "Slavic Liturgical Hymns as a Repository of Byzantine Poetics: The Case of the Akathistos Hymn." *Folia Slavica* 2 (1978), nos. 1–3, 130–40.

Grigor'ev, V. P. "Grafika i orfografiia u A. Voznesenskogo." In *Nereshennye voprosy russkogo pravopisaniia*, ed. L. P. Kalakutskaia, pp. 162–71. Moscow: Nauka, 1974.

————. "Paronimicheskaia attraktsiia v russkoi poezii XX v." *Sbornik dokladov i soobshchenii Lingvisticheskogo obshchestva Kalininskogo gosudarstvennogo universiteta* 5 (1975), 131–64.

Grossman, L. P. "Oneginskaia strofa." In *Pushkin: Sbornik pervyi*, ed. N. K. Piksanov, pp. 117–61. Moscow: Giz, 1924.

Gukovskii, G. A. *Russkaia literatura XVIII veka.* Moscow: Uchpedgiz, 1939.

Gumilev, N. S. *Sobranie sochinenii v chetyrekh tomakh.* Ed. G. P. Struve and B. A. Filippov. Vol. 4. Washington, D.C.: Victor Kamkin, Inc., 1968.

Gvozdikovskaia, T. S. "Sud'by trekhslozhnykh razmerov v sovremennoi poezii." *Trudy Kirgizskogo gosudarstvennogo universiteta: Filologicheskie nauki* 19: *Seriia Voprosy poetiki* 2 (1975), 121–26.

Halle, Morris, and Keyser, Samuel J. "Chaucer and the Study of Prosody." *College English* 28 (1966), no. 3, 187–219. The paper that started the interest in generative metrics. Attempts to establish a set of rules for determining whether or not a given line is metrical.

————. *English Stress: Its Form, Its Growth, and Its Role in Verse.* New York: Harper and Row, 1971. Offers a revised and improved version of their 1966 theory; however, the changes were not sufficient to satisfy many of their critics.

Halpern, Martin. "On the Two Chief Metrical Modes in English." *PMLA* 77 (1962), no. 3, 177–86. Another "traditional" paper; distinguishes between iambic verse, on the one hand, and all other types of syllabo-tonic poetry on the other.

Häublein, Ernst. *The Stanza*. The Critical Idiom, no. 38. London: Methuen, 1978.

Herbert, T. Walter. "Near Rimes and Paraphones." *Sewanee Review* 45 (1937), no. 4, 433–52.

Herdan, Gustav. *The Advanced Theory of Language as Choice and Chance*. Berlin and New York: Springer-Verlag, 1966.

Ibraev, L. I. "Rifmovnik (K probleme proiskhozhdeniia russkogo rechevogo stikha)." *Filologicheskie nauki* 17 (1975), no. 4 (88), 24–34.

Iliushin, A. A. "K istorii Oneginskoi strofy." In *Zamysel, trud, voploshchenie* . . . , ed. V. I. Kuleshov, pp. 92–100. Moscow: Moskovskii gosudarstvennyi universitet, 1977.

Isachenko, A. V. "Iz nabliudenii nad 'novoi rifmoi.'" In *SP*, pp. 203–29.

Ivanov, V. V. "Metr i ritm v 'Poeme kontsa' M. Tsvetaevoi." In *TS*, pp. 168–201.

———. "Ritm poemy Maiakovskogo 'Chelovek.'" In *Poetics, Poetyka, Poetika*, vol. 2, pp. 243–76. Warsaw: Państwowe Wydawnictwo Naukowe, 1966.

Izmailov, N. V. "Iz istorii russkoi oktavy." In *Poetika i stilistika russkoi literatury: Pamiati akademika Viktora Vladimirovicha Vinogradova*, ed. M. P. Alekseev et al., pp. 102–10. Leningrad: Nauka, 1971.

Jakobson, Roman. "Bolgarskii piatistopnyi iamb: V sopostavlenii s russkim." In *Selected Writings*, vol. 5, pp. 135–46. Originally published in 1932.

———. "Briusovskaia stikhologiia i nauka o stikhe." In *Nauchnye izvestiia* (Akademicheskogo tsentra Narkomprosa), vol. 2, pp. 222–40. Moscow: Giz, 1922.

———. "'Devushka pela': Nabliudeniia nad iazykovym stroem stansov Aleksandra Bloka." In *Selected Writings*, vol. 3, pp. 544–61.

———. "Grammatical Parallelism and Its Russian Facet." In *Selected Writings*, vol. 3, pp. 98–135.

———. "K lingvisticheskomu analizu russkoi rifmy." In *Studies in Russian Philology*, pp. 1–13. Michigan Slavic Materials, no. 1. Ann Arbor, Mich.: Department of Slavic Languages and Literatures, University of Michigan, 1962. Reprinted in *Selected Writings*, vol. 5, pp. 170–77.

———. "Ob odnoslozhnykh slovakh v russkom stikhe." In *SP*, pp. 239–52; reprinted in *Selected Writings*, vol. 5, pp. 201–14.

———. "Poetry of Grammar and Grammar of Poetry." In *Selected Writings*, vol. 3, pp. 87–97. An abbreviated variant of "Poeziia grammatiki i grammatika poezii."

———. "Poeziia grammatiki i grammatika poezii." In *Selected Writings*, vol. 3, pp. 63–86.

———. "Pokhvala Konstantina Filosofa Grigoriiu Bogoslovu." *Slavia* (Prague), 39 (1970), no. 3, 334–61.

———. *Selected Writings*. Vol. 3, *Poetry of Grammar and Grammar of Poetry*, ed. Stephen Rudy. The Hague: Mouton, 1981. As the title indicates, the volume is primarily devoted to the topic of grammar and poetry and includes analyses of poems written in several languages other than Russian.

———. *Selected Writings*. Vol. 5, *On Verse, Its Masters and Explorers*, ed.

Stephen Rudy and Martha Taylor. The Hague: Mouton, 1979. Includes *O cheshskom stikhe: Preimushchestvenno v sopostavlenii s russkim, Noveishaia russkaia poeziia*, many articles and reviews from various years, and a new "Retrospect" (pp. 569–601) that summarizes Jakobson's views on versification.

———. "Skorb' pobivaemykh u drov." In *Selected Writings*, vol. 3, pp. 304–10.

———. "The Slavic Response to Byzantine Poetry." In *Actes du XII° Congrès international d'Etudes byzantines*, ed. Georges Ostrogorsky et al., vol. 1, pp. 249–67. Belgrade, 1963.

———. "Stikhotvornye tsitaty v velikomoravskoi agiografii." *Slavistična revija* (Ljubljana), 10 (1957), 111–18.

———. "Studies in Comparative Slavic Metrics." *Oxford Slavonic Papers* 3 (1952), 21–66. Also appeared in *Selected Writings*, vol. 4, *Slavic Epic Studies* (The Hague: Mouton, 1966), pp. 414–63, under the title "Slavic Epic Verse: Studies in Comparative Metrics."

———. "'Tainaia sluzhba' Konstantina Filosofa i dal'neishee razvitie staroslavianskoi poezii." *Zbornik radova Vizantološkog instituta* 8 (*Mélanges Georges Ostrogorsky*), 1963, 153–66.

———. "Zametka o drevne-bolgarskom stikhoslozhenii." Rossiiskaia Akademiia nauk: *Izvestiia Otdeleniia russkogo iazyka i slovesnosti* 24 (1919 [publ. 1923]), no. 2, 351–58. Important for suggesting that early Slavic translations of Byzantine poetry were poetic as well. Jakobson returned to this problem many times in subsequent decades; see for instance "Stikhotvornye tsitaty v velikomoravskoi agiografii," "The Slavic Response to Byzantine Poetry," "'Tainaia sluzhba' Konstantina Filosofa i dal'neishee razvitie staroslavianskoi poezii," and "Pokhvala Konstantin Filosofa Grigoriiu Bogoslovu." For more complete references see the articles by Antonina Gove, "Literalism and Poetic Equivalence," "Slavic Liturgical Hymns," and "The Evidence for Metrical Adaptation." Or see F. V. Mareš, "Roman Jakobson and (Old) Church Slavonic Studies," in *Roman Jakobson: Echoes of His Scholarship*, ed. Daniel Armstrong and C. H. van Schooneveld (Lisse, The Netherlands: Peter de Ridder Press, 1977), pp. 253–57.

Jakobson, Roman; van Schooneveld, C. H.; and Worth, Dean S.; eds. *Slavic Poetics: Essays in Honor of Kiril Taranovsky*. Slavistic Printings and Reprintings, no. 267. The Hague: Mouton, 1973. About a third of the more than fifty articles by both Western and Soviet scholars deal with aspects of Russian versification. Bibliography of Taranovsky's works. Abbreviated throughout the bibliography as *SP*.

Janecek, Gerald. "Intonation and Layout in Belyj's Poetry." In *Andrey Bely: Centenary Papers*, ed. Boris Christa, pp. 81–90. Bibliotheca slavonica, no. 21. Amsterdam: Adolf M. Hakkert, 1980.

Jones, Lawrence Gaylord. "Consonantal Tonalities in Russian Verse." In *American Contributions to the Eighth International Congress of Slavists*, vol. 1, *Linguistics and Poetics*, ed. Henrik Birnbaum, pp. 408–31. Columbus, Ohio: Slavica, 1978.

———. "Tonality Structure in Russian Verse." *IJSLP* 9 (1965), 125–51.

Jones, Roy G. *Language and Prosody of the Russian Folk Epic.* Slavistic Print-
ings and Reprintings, no. 275. The Hague: Mouton, 1975.
Kalacheva, S. V. "Liricheskii geroi rannego Maiakovskogo i evoliutsiia stikha."
In *Aktual'nye problemy sotsialisticheskogo realizma*, ed. I. F. Volkov et al.,
pp. 198–225. Moscow: Moskovskii universitet, 1981.
Kantemir, Antiokh. *Sobranie stikhotvorenii.* Biblioteka poeta, Bol'shaia seriia,
2d ed. Leningrad: Sovetskii pisatel', 1956.
Kemball, Robin. *Alexander Blok: A Study in Rhythm and Metre.* Slavistic Print-
ings and Reprintings, no. 33. The Hague: Mouton, 1965.
Kholshevnikov, V. E. "Logaedicheskie razmery v russkoi poezii." In *Poetika i
stilistika russkoi literatury: Pamiati akademika Viktora Vladimirovicha Vi-
nogradova*, ed. M. P. Alekseev et al., pp. 429–36. Leningrad: Nauka, 1971.
————. *Osnovy stikhovedeniia: Russkoe stikhoslozhenie.* 2d ed. Leningrad:
Leningradskii gosudarstvennyi universitet, 1972. The most reliable and best
informed of all the textbooks written since the revival of interest in Russian
verse studies began in the early 1960s.
————. "Pereboi ritma." In *Russkaia sovetskaia poeziia i stikhovedenie*, ed.
K. G. Petrosov et al., pp. 173–84. Moscow: Moskovskii oblastnoi peda-
gogicheskii institut, 1969.
————. "Russkaia i pol'skaia sillabika i sillabo-tonika." In *TS*, pp. 24–58.
————. "Russkie trekhslozhnye razmery (v sopostavlenii s pol'skimi)." In
*Semiotyka i struktura tekstu: Studia poświęcone VII Międzynarodowemu
Kongresowi Slawistów*, ed. Maria Renata Mayenowa, pp. 305–13. Wrocław:
Zakład Narodowy im. Ossolińskich, 1973.
————. "Russkii sillabicheskii vos'mislozhnik." In *Metryka słowiańska*, ed.
Zdzisława Kopczyńska and Lucylla Pszczołowska, pp. 21–24. Wrocław:
Zakład Narodowy im. Ossolińskich, 1971.
————, comp. *Mysl', vooruzhennaia rifmami: Poeticheskaia antologiia po
istorii russkogo stikha.* Leningrad: Leningradskii universitet, 1983. An an-
thology of poems that illustrates both the history and range of Russian verse
forms.
————, ed. *Issledovaniia po teorii stikha.* Leningrad: Nauka, 1978. A sequel to
TS; includes bibliographies of recent work (cf. Gindin, "Obshchee i russkoe
stikhovedenie," and Lilly and Scherr, "Zarubezhnaia literatura.") Abbrevi-
ated throughout the bibliography as *ITS*.
Kholshevnikov, V. E.; Likhachev, D. S.; and Zhirmunskii, V. M.; eds. *Teoriia
stikha.* Leningrad: Nauka, 1968. An important collection of articles, pri-
marily devoted to meter and rhythm. Abbreviated throughout the bibliogra-
phy as *TS*.
Kievskii, M. I. "Shestistopnyi iamb N. Zabolotskogo." *Visnyk Kyjivs'koho uni-
versytetu, Serija filolohiji*, no. 14 (1972), pp. 39–43.
Kiparsky, Paul. "The Rhythmic Structure of English Verse." *Linguistic Inquiry*
8 (1977), no. 2, 189–247. The third of the generative approaches (after
Halle-Keyser and Magnuson-Ryder), based on the phonological theory of
Mark Liberman and Alan Prince (published in the same issue, pp. 249–
336). Kiparsky's method compares the phonological structure of the line
with its metrical structure. An earlier and quite different version of this the-

ory appeared as "Stress, Syntax, and Meter," *Language* 51 (1975), no. 3, 576–616.

Klimenko, A. "Gazeli Alishera Navoi v russkikh poeticheskikh perevodakh." *Masterstvo perevoda* 11 (1976), pp. 283–95.

Kolmogorov, A. N. "O metre pushkinskikh 'Pesen zapadnykh slavian.'" *Russkaia literatura* 9 (1966), no. 1, 98–111.

———. "Primer izucheniia metra i ego ritmicheskikh variantov." In *TS*, pp. 145–67. Detailed analysis of a "regularized three-stress *dol'nik*" line (what G. S. Smith would prefer to call a "logaoedic meter") in Tsvetaeva's poetry.

Kolmogorov, A. N., and Kondratov, A. M. "Ritmika poem Maiakovskogo." *Voprosy iazykoznaniia* 11 (1962), no. 3, 62–74.

Kolmogorov, A. N., and Prokhorov, A. V. "K osnovam russkoi klassicheskoi metriki." In *Sodruzhestvo nauk i tainy tvorchestva*, ed. B. S. Meilakh, pp. 397–432. Moscow: Iskusstvo, 1968.

———. "O dol'nike sovremennoi russkoi poezii." In *Voprosy iazykoznaniia* 12 (1963), no. 6, 84–95; 13 (1964), no. 1, 75–94. A pioneering study of Russian *dol'niki* and their rhythmic variants.

Korsh, F. E. *O russkom narodnom stikhoslozhenii.* Akademiia nauk: *Sbornik otdeleniia russkogo iazyka i slovesnosti* 67 (1901), no. 8. Contains interesting observations about folk accentuation, though the more theoretical passages are generally less satisfactory.

Kostetskii, A. G. "Lingvisticheskaia teoriia V. Khlebnikova." *Strukturnaia i matematicheskaia lingvistika*, no. 3 (1975), pp. 34–39.

Kovtunova, I. I. "Poriadok slov v stikhe i proze." In *Sintaksis i stilistika*, ed. G. A. Zolotova, pp. 43–64. Moscow: Nauka, 1976.

Kozhevnikova, N. A. "Iz nabliudenii nad zvukovoi organizatsiei stikhotvornogo teksta." In *Problemy strukturnoi lingvistiki, 1979*, ed. V. P. Grigor'ev, pp. 181–94. Moscow: Nauka, 1981.

Kviatkovskii, A. P. *Poeticheskii slovar'.* Moscow: Sovetskaia entsiklopediia, 1966.

Laferrière, Daniel. "Iambic versus Trochaic: The Case of Russian." *International Review of Slavic Linguistics* 4 (1979), nos. 1–2, 81–136. Employs findings from experimental psychology as part of an effort to account for differences in how the two types of meters are perceived.

Lapshina, N. V.; Romanovich, I. K.; and Iarkho, B. I. "Iz materialov *Metricheskogo spravochnika k stikhotvoreniiam M. Iu. Lermontova.*" *Voprosy iazykoznaniia* 15 (1966), no. 2, 125–37.

———. *Metricheskii spravochnik k stikhotvoreniiam A. S. Pushkina.* Moscow and Leningrad: Academia, 1934. This project, under the supervision of Iarkho, provided the impetus for subsequent compilation of metrical (or metrical and stanzaic) handbooks. The same authors also worked on the study of Lermontov's meters that was published, in part, many years later in "Iz materialov *Metricheskogo spravochnika k stikhotvoerniiam M. Iu. Lermontova.*" Their book on Pushkin's meters has largely been superseded by a metrical and stanzaic handbook on Pushkin compiled by M. Iu. Lotman and

S. A. Shakhverdov in Gasparov, ed., *Russkoe stikhoslozhenie XIX v.: Materialy po metrike i strofike russkikh poetov.*

Lauer, Reinhard. *Gedichtform zwischen Schema und Verfall: Sonett, Rondeau, Madrigal, Ballade, Stanze, und Triolett in der russischen Literatur des 18. Jahrhunderts.* Munich: Wilhelm Fink Verlag, 1975.

Lazutin, S. G. "Nekotorye voprosy stikhotvornoi formy russkikh poslovits." *Russkii fol'klor* 12 (1971): *Iz istorii russkoi narodnoi poezii*, 135–46.

————. *Poetika russkogo fol'klora.* Moscow: Vysshaia shkola, 1981. "Ritm, metrika, rifma" (chap. 3, pp. 148–202), discusses versification in proverbs and in the *chastushka* as well as elements of rhyme in fairy tales.

Levin, Iu. I. "Semanticheskii oreol metra s semioticheskoi tochki zreniia." In *Finitis duodecim lustris: Sbornik statei k 60-letiiu prof. Iu. M. Lotmana*, ed. S. G. Isakov, pp. 151–54. Tallin: Eesti raamat, 1982.

Levinton, G. A. "Kak naprimer na IU." *Russian Linguistics* 6 (1981), no. 1, 81–102.

Liapina, L. E. "Sverkhdlinnye razmery v poezii Bal'monta." In *ITS*, pp. 118–25.

Lilly, Ian K. "On Adjacent and Nonadjacent Russian Rhyme Pairs." *SEEJ* 24 (1980), no. 3, 245–55. Examines the two kinds of rhyme within the *AbAbCCdEEd* stanza as used by eighteenth-century poets.

————. "On the Rhymes of Bely's First Three Books of Verse." *Slavonic and East European Review* 60 (1982), no. 3, 381–89.

Lilly, Ian K., and Scherr, Barry P. "Russian Verse Theory Since 1974: A Commentary and Bibliography." *IJSLP* 27 (1983), 127–74. A less comprehensive but more accessible listing than Gindin's *Struktura stikhotvornoi rechi*. Unlike Gindin, includes coverage of studies published outside the USSR.

————. "Zarubezhnaia literatura po russkomu stikhovedeniiu, izdannaia s 1960 g.: Materialy k bibliografii." In *ITS*, pp. 223–31. Complements Gindin's "Obshchee i russkoe stikhovedenie" by listing materials published outside the Soviet Union.

Lobanova, M. S. "K voprosu o stikhovom perenose [Fr. enjambement]." *Vestnik Leningradskogo universiteta* 36 (1981), no. 2, 67–73.

Lojkine, A. K. "Nekrasov's Anapaests." *Melbourne Slavonic Studies*, nos. 9–10 (1975), pp. 54–63.

Lomonosov, M. V. *Izbrannye proizvedeniia.* Biblioteka poeta, Bol'shaia seriia, 2d ed. Leningrad: Sovetskii pisatel', 1965.

————. "Kratkoe rukovodstvo k krasnorechiiu." In *Sochineniia*, pp. 275–439. Moscow and Leningrad: GIKhL, 1961.

Lotman, M. Iu. "Geksametr (Obshchaia teoriia i nekotorye aspekty funktsionirovaniia v novykh evropeiskikh literaturakh)." *Uchenye zapiski Tartuskogo gosudarstvennogo universiteta* 396: *Studia metrica et poetica* 1 (1976), 31–54.

————. "Metricheskii repertuar I. Annenskogo (Materialy k metricheskomu spravochniku)." *Uchenye zapiski Tartuskogo gosudarstvennogo universiteta* 358: *Trudy po russkoi i slavianskoi filologii* 24 (1975), 122–47.

Lyngstad, Sverre. "Blank Verse." In *Princeton Encyclopedia of Poetry and*

Poetics, ed. Alex Preminger, pp. 78–81. Princeton: Princeton University Press, 1965.

Magnuson, Karl, and Ryder, Frank G. "The Study of English Prosody: An Alternative Proposal." *College English* 31 (1970), no. 8, 789–820. Criticizes Halle-Keyser and offers a different generative theory. Modified by the authors in *College English* 33 (1971), no. 2, 198–216.

Maiakovskii, V. V. *Polnoe sobranie sochinenii v trinadtsati tomakh.* Vol. 12. Moscow: GIKhL, 1959.

Markov, V. F. *Russian Futurism: A History.* Berkeley and Los Angeles: University of California Press, 1968.

———. "V zashchitu raznoudarnoi rifmy (informativnyi obzor)." In *RP*, pp. 235–61.

Mathauserová, Světla. *Drevnerusskie teorii iskusstva slova.* Acta Universitatis Carolinae Philologica, Monographia 63. Prague: Univerzita Karlova, 1976 [1979]. "Teoriia stikha" (chap. 3, pp. 57–105) discusses the work of earlier scholars on the question of verse forms in Old Russian literature.

Matiash, S. A. "K voprosu o genezise russkogo dol'nika: Dol'niki V. A. Zhukovskogo." *Filologicheskii sbornik* 11 (1972), 82–92.

———. "Russkii i nemetskii vol'nyi iamb XVIII–nachala XIX veka i vol'nye iamby Zhukovskogo." In *ITS*, pp. 92–103.

Merlin, V. V. "Chetyrekhstopnyi khorei detskogo fol'klora." *Fol'klor i literatura Urala* (Perm'), 4 (1977), pp. 59–72.

Mets, Arvo. "O svobodnom stikhe." In *Pisatel' i zhizn'* [vypusk 9], ed. S. D. Artamanov et al., pp. 64–77. Moscow: Moskovskii universitet, 1978.

Mets, Arvo et al. "Ot chego ne svoboden svobodnyi stikh?" *Voprosy literatury* 16 (1972), no. 2, 124–60. A discussion of this topic by nine poets, including—besides Mets—Samoilov, Slutskii, and Tarkovskii.

Mineralov, Iu. I. "Fonologicheskoe tozhdestvo v russkom iazyke i tipologiia russkoi rifmy." *Uchenye zapiski Tartuskogo gosudarstvennogo universiteta* 396: *Studia metrica et poetica* 1 (1976), 55–77. Includes a section dealing with "pretonic rhyme," a modern phenomenon in which all the main sound correspondences are to the left of the stressed vowels.

Mitrofanova, V. V. "Ritmicheskoe stroenie russkikh narodnykh zagadok." *Russkii fol'klor* 12 (1971): *Iz istorii russkoi narodnoi poezii*, 147–61.

Moldovan, A. M. "Melodika stikha (Voprosy terminologii)." *Voprosy russkoi literatury*, 1976, no. 1 (27), 117–24.

Nabokov, Vladimir. *Notes on Prosody.* Bollingen Series 72 A. New York: Pantheon, 1964.

———. *Speak, Memory: An Autobiography Revisited.* New York: G. P. Putnam's Sons, 1966.

Nevzgliadova, E. V. "O zvukosmyslovykh sviaziakh v poezii." *Filologicheskie nauki* 12 (1968), no. 4 (46), 23–34.

Nikonov, V. A. "Mesto udaren'ia v russkom slove." *IJSLP* 6 (1963), 1–8.

———. "Strofika." In *Izuchenie stikhoslozheniia v shkole*, ed. L. I. Timofeev, pp. 96–149. Moscow: Uchpedgiz, 1960. A basic introduction to the topic.

Novinskaia, L. P. "Metrika i strofika F. I. Tiutcheva." In *Russkoe stikhoslo-*

zhenie XIX v.: Materialy po metrike i strofike russkikh poetov, ed. M. L. Gasparov, pp. 355–413. Moscow: Nauka, 1979.

Ostolopov, N. F. *Slovar' drevnei i novoi poezii*. 3 vols. St. Petersburg: Rossiis-kaia akademiia, 1821. An early dictionary of poetic terms with long articles on the more important items. Not an original work but a useful compendium of the then-current ideas on verse.

Ovcharenko, O. A. "K voprosu o tipologii svobodnogo stikha." *Voprosy literatury* 23 (1979), no. 2, 223–38.

———. "Svobodnyi stikh i verlibr." *Russkaia rech'* 12 (1978), no. 4, 84–87.

Ozmitel', E. K., and Gvozdikovskaia, T. S. "Materialy k metricheskomu repertuaru russkoi liricheskoi poezii (1957–1968 gg.)." Kirgizskii gosudarstvennyi universitet. *Nauchnye trudy filologicheskogo fakul'teta* 16 (1970), 113–21.

Panchenko, A. M. "O rifme i deklamatsionnykh normakh sillabicheskoi poezii XVII v." In *TS*, pp. 280–93.

———. *Russkaia stikhotvornaia kul'tura XVII veka*. Leningrad: Nauka, 1973. Incorporates most of Panchenko's previous writings on versification in pre-eighteenth-century Russian literature.

Papaian, R. A. "K voprosu o sootnoshenii stikhotvornykh razmerov i intensivnosti tropov v lirike A. Bloka." In *Blokovskii sbornik*, ed. Z. G. Mints et al., vol. 2, pp. 268–90. Tartu: Tartuskii gosudarstvennyi universitet, 1972.

———. "Nekotorye voprosy sootnosheniia metra i zhanra." *Uchenye zapiski Tartuskogo gosudarstvennogo universiteta* 306: *Trudy po russkoi i slavianskoi filologii* 21 (1973), 46–64.

———. *Sravnitel'naia tipologiia natsional'nogo stikha: Russkii i armianskii stikh*. Erevan: Erevanskii gosudarstvennyi universitet, 1980.

Pechorov, G. M. "Tipologiia strof V. V. Maiakovskogo." In *Problemy tipologii sotsialisticheskogo realizma: Sbornik nauchnykh trudov*, ed. V. P. Druzin et al., pp. 96–109. Moscow: Moskovskii gosudarstvennyi pedagogicheskii institut, 1979.

Peisakhovich, M. A. "Astroficheskii stikh i ego formy." *Voprosy iazykoznaniia* 25 (1976), no. 1, 93–106. General presentation of the author's findings on this topic. Peisakhovich also devoted separate articles to the nonstanzaic poetry of Pushkin, Lermontov, and Nekrasov (see the next entry).

———. "Astroficheskii stikh Nekrasova." In *N. A. Nekrasov i ego vremia*, ed. A. M. Garkavi, vol. 3, pp. 74–93. Kaliningrad: Kaliningradskii gosudarstvennyi universitet, 1977.

———. "Oneginskaia strofa v poemakh Lermontova." *Filologicheskie nauki* 12 (1969), no. 1 (49), pp. 25–38.

———. "Strofika Lermontova." In *Tvorchestvo M. Iu. Lermontova: 150 let so dnia rozhdeniia, 1814–1964*, ed. U. R. Fokht, pp. 417–91. Moscow: Nauka, 1964.

———. "Strofika Nekrasova." *Nekrasovskii sbornik* 5 (1973), 202–32.

Piast, Vladimir. *Sovremennoe stikhovedenie: Ritmika*. Leningrad: Izdatel'stvo pisatelei v Leningrade, 1931.

Picchio, Riccardo. "The isocolic principle in Old Russian prose." In *SP*, pp. 299–331. The longest of several papers in which Picchio sets out to establish the prosodic principle behind certain writings in Old Russia.1 literature.

———. "On the Prosodic Structure of the *Igor Tale*." *SEEJ* 16 (1972), no. 2, 147–62.

Pigarev, K. V. *Zhizn' i tvorchestvo Tiutcheva*. Moscow: ANSSSR, 1962.

Põldmäe, Jaak. "Tipologiia svobodnogo stikha." *Uchenye zapiski Tartuskogo gosudarstvennogo universiteta* 422: *Trudy po znakovym sistemam* 9 (1977), 85–98.

Ponomarev, S. I. "K izdaniiu *Iliady* v perevode Gnedicha." *Sbornik Otdeleniia russkogo iazyka i slovesnosti Imperatorskoi Akademii nauk* 38 (1886), no. 7, p. 144.

Pozdneev, A. V. "Evoliutsiia stikhoslozheniia v narodnoi lirike XVI–XVIII vekov." *Russkii fol'klor* 12 (1971): *Iz istorii russkoi narodnoi poezii*, 37–46.

———. "Stikhoslozhenie drevnei russkoi poezii." *Scando-Slavica* 11 (1965), 5–24. A representative article by a scholar who devoted much research to the topic.

Rickert, William C. "Rhyme Terms." *Style* 12 (1978), no. 1, 35–46.

Romanov, Boris, ed. *Russkii sonet: Sonety russkikh poetov XVIII–nachala XX veka*. Moscow: Sovetskaia Rossiia, 1983.

Rudnev, P. A. "Iz istorii metricheskogo repertuara russkikh poetov XIX–nachala XX v." In *TS*, pp. 107–44.

———. "Metr i smysl." In *Metryka słowiańska*, ed. Zdzisława Kopczyńska and Lucylla Pszczołowska, pp. 77–88. Wrocław: Zakład Narodowy im. Ossolińskich, 1971.

———. "Metricheskii repertuar A. Bloka." In *Blokovskii sbornik*, ed. Z. G. Mints et al., vol. 2, pp. 218–67. Tartu: Tartuskii gosudarstvennyi universitet, 1972.

———. "Metricheskii repertuar Nekrasova: Vvedenie." *Uchenye zapiski Tartuskogo gosudarstvennogo universiteta*, vol. 358: *Trudy po russkoi i slavianskoi filologii* 24 (1975), 93–121.

———. "Metricheskii repertuar V. Briusova." In *Briusovskie chteniia 1971 goda*, ed. and comp. K. V. Aivazian, pp. 309–49. Erevan: Aiastan, 1973.

———. "O nekotorykh problemakh sovremennogo sovetskogo stikhovedeniia." In *Uchenye zapiski Kolomenskogo gosudarstvennogo pedagogicheskogo instituta: Voprosy romano-germanskogo iazykoznaniia* (1966), pp. 83–102. Includes coverage of the period between Shtokmar's work and the beginning dates for Gindin in *ITS*, pp. 152–222, and Lilly and Scherr, also in *ITS*, pp. 223–31.

———. "O printsipakh opisaniia i semanticheskogo analiza stikhotvornogo teksta na metricheskom urovne." *Voprosy istorizma i khudozhestvennogo masterstva* (Leningrad), 1 (1976), pp. 170–90.

———. "O sootnoshenii monometricheskikh i polimetricheskikh konstruktsii v sisteme stikhotvornykh razmerov A. Bloka." In *Russkaia sovetskaia poeziia i stikhovedenie*, ed. K. G. Petrosov et al., pp. 227–36. Moscow: Moskovskii oblastnoi pedagogicheskii institut, 1969.

———. "O stikhe dramy A. Bloka 'Roza i Krest.'" *Uchenye zapiski Tar-*

tuskogo gosudarstvennogo universiteta 251: *Trudy po russkoi i slavianskoi filologii* 15 (1970), 294–334.

———. "Opyt opisaniia i semanticheskoi interpretatsii polimetricheskoi struktury poemy A. Bloka 'Dvenadtsat'.'" *Uchenye zapiski Tartuskogo gosudarstvennogo universiteta* 266: *Trudy po russkoi i slavianskoi filologii* 18 (1971), 195–221.

———. "Opyt semanticheskogo analiza monometricheskoi i polimetricheskoi stikhovykh struktur na metricheskom urovne." *Uchenye zapiski Tartuskogo gosudarstvennogo universiteta* 306: *Trudy po russkoi i slavianskoi filologii* 21 (1973), 297–311.

———. "Polimetricheskie kompozitsii Nekrasova." In *N. A. Nekrasov i russkaia literatura: Vtoroi mezhvuzovskii sbornik*, ed. N. N. Skatov, vol. 40, pp. 159–77. Iaroslavl': Iaroslavskii gosudarstvennyi pedagogicheskii institut, 1975.

———. "Stikhotvorenie A. Bloka 'Vse tikho na svetlom litse . . .' (Opyt semanticheskoi interpretatsii metra i ritma)." In *Poetika i stilistika russkoi literatury: Pamiati akademika Viktora Vladimirovicha Vinogradova*, ed. M. P. Alekseev et al., pp. 450–55. Leningrad: Nauka, 1971.

Rudnev, V. P. "Metricheskii repertuar detskoi poezii (Chukovskii, Marshak, Mikhalkov, Barto)." In *Problemy iazyka i stilia v literature*, ed. D. N. Medrish, pp. 102–10. Volgograd: Volgogradskii pedagogicheskii institut, 1978.

Safronova, E. G. "Intonatsiia i stil' stikha (Na osnove eksperimental'nykh dannykh)." In *ITS*, pp. 85–91.

Saintsbury, George. *Historical Manual of English Prosody*. London: Macmillan, 1930.

Samoilov, D. S. *Kniga o russkoi rifme*. 2d ed. enl. Moscow: Khudozhestvennaia literatura, 1982. The first edition (1973) immediately became the best single source for information about the history of Russian rhyme. The second edition includes a new first chapter with an improved introduction to the main features of Russian rhyme as well as three new chapters at the end that carry the history of Russian rhyme from the 1920s (the first edition stopped with the 1910s) to the 1970s.

Sampson, Earl D. "*Dol'niks* in Gumilev's Poetry." *Russian Language Journal*, Supplementary Issue: *Toward A Definition of Acmeism* (1975), pp. 21–41.

Sapogov, V. A. "K probleme tipologii polimetricheskikh kompozitsii (O polimetrii u N. A. Nekrasova i K. K. Pavlovoi)." In *N. A. Nekrasov i russkaia literatura*, ed. V. A. Sapogov, pp. 97–100. Kostroma: Kostromskii gosudarstvennyi pedagogicheskii institut, 1971.

———. "O polimetricheskikh kompozitsiiakh Karoliny Pavlovoi." In *XXIII Gertsenovskie chteniia (Mezhvuzovskaia konferentsiia): Filologicheskie nauki*, ed. A. L. Grigor'ev et al., pp. 60–61. Leningrad: Leningradskii gosudarstvennyi pedagogicheskii institut, 1970.

Sazonova, L. I. "Printsip ritmicheskoi organizatsii v proizvedeniiakh torzhestvennogo krasnorechiia starshei pory ('Slovo o zakone i blagodati' Ilariona, 'Pokhvala sv. Simeonu i sv. Savve' Domentiana)." *Trudy Otdela drevnerusskoi literatury* 28 (1974), 30–46.

Scherr, Barry P. "Russian and English Versification: Similarities, Differences, Analysis." *Style* 14 (1980), no. 4, 353–78.

Sedykh, G. I. "Zvuk i smysl: O funktsii fonem v poeticheskom tekste (na primere analiza stikhotvoreniia M. Tsvetaevoi 'Psikheia')." *Filologicheskie nauki* 16 (1973), no. 1 (73), 41–50.

Shakhverdov, S. A. "Metrika i strofika E. A. Baratynskogo." In *Russkoe stikhoslozhenie XIX v.*, ed. M. L. Gasparov, pp. 278–328.

Shapiro, Michael. *Asymmetry: An Inquiry into the Linguistic Structure of Poetry*. Amsterdam: North-Holland Publishing Company, 1976.

Shaw, J. Thomas. "Large Rhyme Sets and Puškin's Poetry." *SEEJ* 18 (1974), no. 3, 231–51.

―――. *Pushkin's Rhymes: A Dictionary*. Madison: University of Wisconsin Press, 1974. Establishes the standard for rhyme dictionaries of Russian poetry. Two "by-products" of Shaw's investigation were published by the University of Wisconsin Press in 1975 and are also useful (in a sense more so since they also include concordances): *Baratynskii: A Dictionary of the Rhymes and a Concordance to the Poetry*, and *Batiushkov: A Dictionary of the Rhymes and a Concordance to the Poetry*.

Shengeli, G. A. *Tekhnika stikha*. Moscow: GIKhL, 1960. Valuable observations on individual topics, but the approach to the nonclassical Russian meters differs from the now generally accepted principles.

―――. *Traktat o russkom stikhe: Chast' pervaia, Organicheskaia metrika*. 2d ed. rev. Moscow and Petrograd: Giz, 1923. Contains numerous charts and tables that often complement the findings of Tomashevskii as collected in the latter's *O stikhe*, but lacks the theoretical soundness of the latter's studies. Deals in part with nonclassical verse as well.

Shtokmar, M. P. *Bibliografiia rabot po stikhoslozheniiu*. Moscow and Leningrad: GIKhL, 1933. The most complete source for articles on Russian verse theory up to 1933. Was later updated and supplemented by Shtokmar in *Literaturnyi kritik*, no. 8 (1936), pp. 194–205; no. 9, pp. 235–53. Cf. Jakobson's review in *Slavia* 13 (1934–35), nos. 2–3, 416–31.

―――. *Issledovaniia v oblasti russkogo narodnogo stikhoslozheniia*. Moscow: Akademiia nauk SSSR, 1952. While his own views on folk versification are questionable, on pp. 17–135 he gives a detailed account of previous theories.

―――. *Rifma Maiakovskogo*. Moscow: Sovetskii pisatel', 1958.

―――. "Stikhotvornaia forma russkikh poslovits, pogovorok, zagadok, pribautok." *Zvezda Vostoka* (Tashkent), 33 (1965), no. 11, 149–63.

―――. "Vol'nyi stikh XIX veka." In *Ars Poetica*, vol. 2, *Stikh i proza, Sbornik statei*, ed. M. A. Petrovskii and B. I. Iarkho, pp. 117–67. Moscow: GAKhN, 1928.

Shul'skaia, O. V. "Funktsii paronimii v khudozhestvennoi rechi (paronimicheskie sviazi slova *dym* v russkoi poezii)." In *Problemy strukturnoi lingvistiki 1980*, ed. V. P. Grigor'ev, pp. 222–31. Moscow: Nauka, 1982.

Shuniaeva, S. "Strofika sovremennogo russkogo stikha (Na statisticheskom urovne)." *Trudy Kirgizskogo gosudarstvennogo universiteta: Filologicheskie nauki* XVII (Seriia "Voprosy poetiki"). 1972. Pp. 132–34.

Sidorenko, G. K. "Svobodnyi stikh v ego otnoshenii k sistemam stikhoslo-
zheniia." In *Problemy stikhovedeniia*, ed. Gasparov et al., pp. 114–24.
Silbajoris, Rimvydas. *Russian Versification: The Theories of Trediakovskij,
Lomonosov, and Kantemir*. New York: Columbia University Press, 1968. Of-
fers translations into English of the major works on verse theory by the three
poets. Accompanied by an introductory essay and extensive notes.
Smith, Barbara Herrnstein. *Poetic Closure: A Study of How Poems End*. Chi-
cago: University of Chicago Press, 1968. Excellent discussion of the topic
based on English poetry; brief remarks on closure in Russian poetry can be
found in Zhirmunskii's *Kompozitsiia liricheskikh stikhotvorenii*, passim.
Smith, G. S. "Compound Meters in the Poetry of Marina Cvetaeva." *RusL* 8
(1980), no. 2, 103–23. Incisive analysis of a phenomenon known to have
appeared regularly only in Tsvetaeva's poetry.
———. "Logaoedic Metres in the Lyric Poetry of Marina Tsvetayeva." *Sla-
vonic and East European Review* 53 (1975), no. 132, 330–54.
———. "Marina Cvetaeva's *Poèma gory*: An Analysis." *RusL* 6 (1978), no. 4,
365–88. Concise and authoritative review of recent work on the topic.
———. "The Reform of Russian Versification: What More Is There to Say?"
Study Group on Eighteenth-Century Russia, Newsletter (Norwich, En-
gland), no. 5 (1977), pp. 39–44.
———. "Stanza Rhythm and Stress Load in the Iambic Tetrameter of V. F.
Xodasevič." *SEEJ* 24 (1980), no. 1, 25–36.
———. "Stanza Rhythm in the Iambic Tetrameter of Three Modern Russian
Poets." *IJSLP* 24 (1981), 135–52.
———. "The Stanza Typology of Russian Poetry, 1735–1816: A General Sur-
vey." *RusL* 13 (1983), no. 2, 175–204. Excellent both for the data and the
analyses. Eighteenth-century stanzaic forms are also treated in Vishnevskii's
long article "Russkaia metrika XVIII veka."
———. "Versification and Composition in Marina Cvetaeva's *Pereuločki*."
IJSLP 20 (1975), 61–92.
———. "The Versification of Marina Tsvetayeva's Lyric Poetry, 1922–1923."
Essays in Poetics 1 (1976), no. 2, 21–50.
———. "The Versification of V. F. Xodasevič, 1915–39." In *RP*, pp. 373–91.
———, ed. and trans. *Metre, Rhythm, Stanza, Rhyme*. Russian Poetics in
Translation, no. 7. Oxford: Holdan Books, 1980. Contains translations of
seven articles originally published in Russian, including the introduction to
SRS; Taranovsky, "O ritmicheskoi strukture russkikh dvuslozhnykh raz-
merov"; and Gasparov, "Legkii stikh i tiazhelyi stikh."
Sovalin, V. S., ed. *Russkii sonet: XVIII–nachalo XX veka*. Moscow: Moskov-
skii rabochii, 1983.
Stelletskii, V. I. "K voprosu o ritmicheskom stroe 'Slova o polku Igoreve.'"
Russkaia literatura 7 (1964), no. 4, 27–40.
Stephan, Brigitte. *Studien zur russischen Častuška und ihrer Entwicklung*.
Slavistische Beiträge, no. 38. Munich: Otto Sagner, 1969. Thoroughly ana-
lyzes both the history and characteristics of this modern folk form; her views
on meter differ from those expressed in Jakobson, "Studies in Comparative

Slavic Metrics"; Taranovsky, "The Identity of the Prosodic Bases of Russian Folk and Literary Verse"; and Trubetzkoy, "O metrike chastushki."

Struve, Gleb. "Some Observations on Pasternak's Ternary Meters." *Studies in Slavic Linguistics and Poetics in Honor of Boris O. Unbegaun*, ed. Robert Magidoff et al., pp. 227–44. New York: New York University Press, 1968.

Suino, Mark E. "Poetic Closure." In *Papers in Slavic Philology*, vol. 1, *In Honor of James Ferrell*, ed. Benjamin A. Stolz, pp. 271–75. Ann Arbor: Department of Slavic Languages and Literatures, University of Michigan, 1977.

Sumarokov, A. P. "O stoposlozhenii." In *Stikhotvoreniia*, ed. A. S. Orlov, pp. 383–402. Leningrad: Sovetskii pisatel', 1935. Originally written in the 1770s; the first essay to note the existence of amphibrachs in Russian.

Taranovsky, Kiril. "Chetyrekhstopnyi iamb Andreia Belogo." *IJSLP* 10 (1966), 127–47.

———. "Formy obshcheslavianskogo i tserkovnoslavianskogo stikha v drev-nerusskoi literature XI–XIII vv." In *American Contributions to the Sixth International Congress of Slavists*, vol. 1, *Linguistic Contributions*, ed. Henry Kučera, pp. 377–94. Slavistic Printings and Reprintings, no. 80. The Hague: Mouton, 1968. An important contribution to the search for verselike elements in Old Russian literature.

———. "The Identity of the Prosodic Bases of Russian Folk and Literary Verse." In *For Roman Jakobson: Essays on the Occasion of His Sixtieth Birthday, 11 October 1956*, comp. Morris Halle et al., pp. 553–58. The Hague: Mouton, 1956.

———. "Iz istorii russkogo stikha XVIII v. (Odicheskaia strofa AbAb‖ CCdEEd v poezii Lomonosova)." *XVIII vek*, no. 7 (1966), pp. 106–15.

———. "O ritmicheskoi strukture russkikh dvuslozhnykh razmerov." In *Poetika i stilistika russkoi literatury: Pamiati akademika Viktora Vladimirovicha Vinogradova*, ed. M. P. Alekseev et al., pp. 420–29. Leningrad: Nauka, 1971. Contains Taranovsky's final formulations of his basic laws for the rhythm of Russian verse and provides a concise summary of his main positions. Translated in G. S. Smith, ed. and trans., *Metre, Rhythm, Stanza, Rhyme*.

———. "O vzaimootnoshenii stikhotvornogo ritma i tematiki." In *American Contributions to the Fifth International Congress of Slavists*, vol. 1, *Linguistic Contributions*, pp. 287–322. Slavistic Printings and Reprintings, no. 46. The Hague: Mouton, 1963.

———. "Rannie russkie iamby i ikh nemetskie obraztsy." *XVIII vek*, no. 10 (1975): *Russkaia literatura XVIII veka i ee mezhdunarodnye sviazi*, pp. 31–38.

———. "Ruski četvorostopni jamb u prvim dvema decenijama XX veka." *Južnoslovenski Filolog* 21 (1955–56), 15–43.

———. *Ruski dvodelni ritmovi, I–II*. Monograph Series, Serbian Academy of Sciences, no. 217: Language and Literature Section, vol. 5. Belgrade: Naučna knjiga, 1953. *The* study of Russian binary meters. Offers some key theoretical formulations, while the massive collection of data has proven of use to many subsequent investigators.

———. "Some Problems of Enjambement in Slavic and Western European Verse." *IJSLP* 7 (1963), 80–87.

———. "The Sound Texture of Russian Verse in the Light of Phonemic Distinctive Features." *IJSLP* 9 (1965), 114–24.

———. "Stikhoslozhenie Osipa Mandel'shtama (s 1908 po 1925 god)." *IJSLP* 5 (1962), 97–125.

———. "Zvukopis' v 'Severovostoke' M. Voloshina." In *Orbis Scriptus: Dmitrij Tschižewskij zum 70. Geburtstag*, ed. Dietrich Gerhardt et al., pp. 835–40. Munich: Wilhelm Fink, 1966.

Taranovsky, Kiril, and Prokhorov, A. V. "K kharakteristike russkogo chetyrekhstopnogo iamba XVIII veka: Lomonosov, Trediakovskii, Sumarokov." *RusL* 12 (1982), no. 2, 145–94.

Tarlinskaja, Marina. *English Verse: Theory and History*. The Hague: Mouton, 1976. Termed by Brogan "the most extensive and most important study of English verse-structure produced in this century." Like Bailey, adapts the Russian linguistic-statistical approach to English, but is much wider in scope: based on an analysis of more than a hundred thousand lines of poetry written from the thirteenth through the nineteenth centuries. To date has had little influence on English metrists, though Attridge (in *The Rhymes of English Poetry*) uses the data in Tarlinskaja's (and Bailey's) studies while rejecting their overall metrical theory as too "traditional."

Timofeev, L. I. *Osnovy teorii literatury*. 3d ed. rev. Moscow: Prosveshchenie, 1966.

———. "Ritmika 'Slova o polku Igoreve'." *Russkaia literatura* 6 (1963), no. 1, 88–104.

———. "Sillabicheskii stikh." In *Ars poetica*, vol. 2, *Stikh i proza, Sbornik statei*, ed. M. A. Petrovskii and B. I. Iarkho, pp. 37–72. Moscow: GAKhN, 1928.

———. *Slovo v stikhe*. Moscow: Sovetskii pisatel', 1982.

———. "Vol'nyi stikh XVIII veka." In *Ars Poetica*, vol. 2, *Stikh i proza, Sbornik statei*, ed. M. A. Petrovskii and B. I. Iarkho, pp. 73–115. Moscow: GAKhN, 1928.

Tolstoi, A. K. *Sobranie sochinenii v chetyrekh tomakh*. Vol. 4. Moscow: Khudozhestvennaia literatura, 1964.

Tomashevskii, B. V. "K istorii russkoi rifmy." In *Trudy Otdela novoi russkoi literatury*, ed. B. S. Meilakh, vol. 1, pp. 233–80. Moscow and Leningrad: Akademiia nauk, SSSR, 1948. Not so much a full history as a close examination of several problems—most notably, disagrees with Zhirmunskii about the bases for the norms of eighteenth-century rhyme. Reprinted in Tomashevskii, *Stikh i iazyk: Filologicheskie ocherki*.

———. *Kratkii kurs poetiki*. Moscow and Leningrad: Gosudarstvennoe izdatel'stvo, 1928.

———. *O stikhe: Stat'i*. Leningrad: Priboi, 1929. An outstanding series of articles that came to serve as the basis for the modern linguistic-statistical approach to the study of Russian verse. Mostly uses Pushkin's work as examples, but the findings are of broad applicability. Abbreviated throughout the bibliography as *O stikhe*.

―――. "Piatistopnyi iamb Pushkina." In *O stikhe*, pp. 138–253.

―――. "Problema stikhotvornogo ritma." In *O stikhe*, pp. 3–36.

―――. "Ritm prozy ('Pikovaia dama')." In *O stikhe*, pp. 254–318.

―――. "Ritmika chetyrekhstopnogo iamba po nabliudeniiam nad stikhom *Evgeniia Onegina*." In *O stikhe*, pp. 94–137. Despite the specific titles, both this item and "Piatistopnyi iamb Pushkina" contain much of value for the general study of syllabo-tonic rhythm. Highly influential works that have not lost their significance.

―――. *Russkoe stikhoslozhenie: Metrika*. Petersburg: Academia, 1923.

―――. "Stikh *Goria ot uma*." In *Stikh i iazyk: Filologicheskie ocherki*, pp. 132–201.

―――. *Stikh i iazyk: Filologicheskie ocherki*. Moscow and Leningrad: GIKhL, 1959. Brings together several late studies on versification (including "K istorii russkoi rifmy," "Stikh *Goria ot uma*," and "Strofika Pushkina"; has bibliography of Tomashevskii's work on versification.

―――. "Stikh i ritm." In *O stikhe*, pp. 37–62.

―――. *Stilistika i stikhoslozhenie: Kurs lektsii*. Leningrad: Uchpedgiz, 1959. As the subtitle indicates, the book is based on a course and was not written as a textbook. Still, part 2 offers a sound introduction to Russian versification. Cf. his earlier *Russkoe stikhoslozhenie: Metrika*.

―――. "Strofika Pushkina." *Pushkin: Issledovaniia i materialy* 2 (1958), 49–184. A seminal article for modern studies of stanzaic forms. Tomashevskii's classification (see the appendix, pp. 134–84, for a catalogue of Pushkin's stanzaic forms) has, with minor modifications, become the model for subsequent scholars—cf. the nine handbooks in the collection *Russkoe stikhoslozhenie XIX v.*, edited by M. L. Gasparov. Reprinted without the appendix in Tomashevskii, *Stikh i iazyk: Filologicheskie ocherki*.

―――. *Teoriia literatury: Poetika*. 4th ed. Moscow and Leningrad: Gosudarstvennoe izdatel'stvo, 1928.

―――. "Valerii Briusov kak stikhoved." In *O stikhe*, pp. 319–25.

Trager, George L., and Smith, Henry Lee, Jr. *An Outline of English Structure*. Studies in Linguistics: Occasional Papers, no. 3. Norman, Okla.: Battenburg Press, 1951. A linguistic rather than a metrical study, but the description of English phonology, with four levels of stress, pitch, and juncture, was to serve as the basis for "structural" metrics.

Trediakovskii, V. K. *Izbrannye proizvedeniia*. Biblioteka poeta, Bol'shaia seriia, 2d ed. Leningrad: Sovetskii pisatel', 1963.

―――. *Sochineniia*. Vol. 1. St. Petersburg: A. Smirdin, 1849.

―――. *Stikhotvoreniia*. Biblioteka poeta. Leningrad: Sovetskii pisatel', 1935.

Trubetzkoy, N. S. "O metrike chastushki" (1927). Reprinted in *Three Phonological Studies*, pp. 1–22. Michigan Slavic Materials, no. 3. Ann Arbor: Department of Slavic Languages and Literatures, University of Michigan, 1963.

Tsar'kova, T. S. "Metricheskii repertuar N. A. Zabolotskogo." In *ITS*, pp. 126–51.

Tynianov, Iu. N. *Problema stikhotvornogo iazyka: Stat'i*. Moscow: Sovetskii pisatel', 1965.

Unbegaun, B. O. *Russian Versification*. Oxford: Oxford University Press, 1956. Concise and clear exposition of the basic principles, although written too early to take advantage of the important work in the field since the early 1960s.

Valgina, N. S. "Stilisticheskaia rol' znakov prepinaniia v poezii M. Tsvetaevoi." *Russkaia rech'* 12 (1978), no. 6, 58–66.

Vasiutochkin, G. S. "Ritmika 'Aleksandriiskikh pesen.'" *Lingvisticheskie problemy funktsional'nogo modelirovaniia rechevoi deiatel'nosti* (Leningrad), 3 (1976), pp. 158–67.

Velimirović, Miloš. "The Influence of the Byzantine Chant on the Music of the Slavic Countries." In *Proceedings of the XIIIth International Congress of Byzantine Studies, Oxford, 5–10 September 1966*, ed. J. M. Hussey, D. Obolensky, and S. Runciman, pp. 119–40. London: Oxford University Press, 1967.

Verheul, Kees. "Poetry and Syntax." In *Dutch Contributions to the Sixth International Congress of Slavicists*, ed. A. G. F. van Holk, pp. 153–64. The Hague: Mouton, 1968.

Vickery, W. N. "Russkii shestistopnyi iamb i ego otnoshenie k frantsuzskomu aleksandriiskomu stikhu." In *American Contributions to the Seventh International Congress of Slavists*, vol. 2, *Literature and Folklore*, ed. Viktor Terras, pp. 505–27. Slavistic Printings and Reprintings, no. 296. The Hague: Mouton, 1973.

———. " 'Vospominaniia v Tsarskom Sele' (1814) i 'Pamiatnik': K voprosu o strofike." In *SP*, pp. 485–97.

Vinokur, G. O. "Slovo i stikh v *Evgenii Onegine*." In *Pushkin: Sbornik statei*, ed. A. M. Egolin, pp. 155–213. Moscow: Goslitizdat, 1941. Provides a detailed discussion of the Onegin stanza.

———. "Vol'nye iamby Pushkina." In *Pushkin i ego sovremenniki: Materialy i issledovaniia*, ed. P. N. Sakulin, vol. 38/39, pp. 23–36., Leningrad: Akademiia nauk SSSR, 1930.

Vishnevskii, K. D. "Arkhitektonika russkogo stikha XVIII–pervoi poloviny XIX veka." In *ITS*, pp. 48–66. Suggests a new approach to the problem of classifying stanzaic forms in Russian poetry.

———. "K voprosu ob ispol'zovanii kolichestvennykh metodov v stikhovedenii." In *Kontekst 1976: Literaturno-teoreticheskie issledovaniia*, ed. A. S. Miasnikov, pp. 130–59. Moscow: Nauka, 1977.

———. "Metrika Nekrasova i ee zhanrovo-ekspressivnaia kharakteristika." In *Problemy zhanrovogo razvitiia v russkoi literature XIX veka*, ed. V. V. Shakhov, pp. 242–54. Riazan': Riazanskii gosudarstvennyi universitet, 1972.

———. "Russkaia metrika XVIII veka." *Uchenye zapiski Penzenskogo gosudarstvennogo pedagogicheskogo instituta*, no. 123: *Voprosy literatury XVIII veka* (1972), pp. 129–258. An extensive catalog of and commentary on the usage of verse forms during the early years of the syllabo-tonic tradition.

———. "Stanovlenie trekhslozhnykh razmerov v russkoi poezii." In *Russkaia sovetskaia poeziia i stikhovedenie*, ed. K. G. Petrosov et al., pp. 207–17. Moscow: Moskovskii gosudarstvennyi universitet, 1969.

———. "Strofika Lermontova." *Uchenye zapiski Penzenskogo gosudarstven-*

nogo pedagogicheskogo instituta, Seriia filologicheskaia 14 (1965), 3–131.

Vostokov, A. Kh. *Opyt o russkom stikhoslozhenii.* 2d ed. St. Petersburg: Morskaia tipografiia, 1817. Probably the most important work on verse theory of the nineteenth century. Includes a survey of the literary meters as well as the first scholarly effort to understand Russian folk versification.

Voznesenskii, Andrei. *Dubovyi list violonchel'nyi.* Moscow: Khudozhestvennaia literatura, 1975.

———. *Ten' zvuka.* Moscow: Molodaia gvardiia, 1970.

Weidlé, Wladimir. *Embriologiia poezii: Vvedenie v fonosemantiku poeticheskoi rechi.* Bibliothèque russe de l'Institut d'études slaves 55. Paris: Institut d'études slaves, 1980.

Wimsatt, W. K., Jr. "The Rule and the Norm: Halle and Keyser on Chaucer's Meter." *College English* 31 (1970), no. 8, 774–88. One of the many attacks on the Halle-Keyser theory; questions their concept of a "stress maximum" and affirms that it is necessary to distinguish between "rules" (absolute limits) and "norms."

———. *The Verbal Icon: Studies in the Meaning of Poetry.* Lexington, Ky.: University of Kentucky Press, 1964.

Wimsatt, W. K., Jr., and Beardsley, Monroe C. "The Concept of Meter: An Exercise in Abstraction." *PMLA* 74 (1959), no. 5, 585–98. A defense of "traditional" metrics against two approaches then coming into vogue. A generally solid paper that provoked much controversy (and subsequent interest in verse studies).

Worth, Dean S. "On Eighteenth-Century Russian Rhyme." *RusL* no. 3 (1972), 47–74. Includes a fine summary of the various positions taken by earlier scholars on the reasons for the peculiarities of eighteenth-century rhyme.

Zapadov, V. A. "Derzhavin i russkaia rifma XVIII veka." *XVIII vek*, no. 8: *Derzhavin i Karamzin v literaturnom dvizhenii XVIII–nachala XIX veka*, pp. 54–91.

———. "'Sposob proiznosheniia stikhov' i russkaia rifma XVIII veka." *Uchenye zapiski Leningradskogo gosudarstvennogo pedagogicheskogo instituta*, no. 320: *Problemy zhanra v istorii russkoi literatury* (1969), pp. 21–38.

Zaretskii, V. A. "Ritm i smysl v khudozhestvennykh tekstakh." *Uchenye zapiski Tartuskogo gosudarstvennogo universiteta* 181: *Trudy po znakovym sitemam* 2 (1965), 64–75.

Zhirmunskii, V. M. *Kompozitsiia liricheskikh stikhotvorenii.* In *Teoriia stikha*, pp. 431–536. Originally published in 1921; a useful discussion of parallelism and other forms of poetic structure.

———. "Melodika stikha (Po povodu knigi B. M. Eikhenbauma *Melodika stikha*, Pb., 1922)"; 1922. Reprinted in *Teoriia literatury, Poetika, Stilistika*, pp. 56–93. Leningrad: Nauka, 1977.

———. "O natsional'nykh formakh iambicheskogo stikha." In *TS*, pp. 7–23.

———. "O russkoi rifme XVIII." *XVIII vek*, no. 7 (1966), pp. 419–27.

———. *Rifma: Ee istoriia i teoriia.* In *Teoriia stikha*, pp. 233–430. Six decades after its first appearance, this remains a valuable study.

———. "Russkii narodnyi stikh v 'Skazke o rybake i rybke.'" In *Problemy sovremennoi filologii: Sbornik statei k semidesiatiletiiu akademika V. V. Vino-gradova*, ed. M. B. Khrapchenko et al., pp. 129–35. Moscow: Nauka, 1965.

———. "Stikhoslozhenie Maiakovskogo." In *Teoriia stikha*, pp. 539–68. Originally published in 1964.

———. *Teoriia stikha*. Leningrad: Sovetskii pisatel', 1975. Contains three important monographs from the 1920s (*Kompozitsiia liricheskikh stikhotvorenii*; *Rifma, ee istoriia i teoriia*; *Vvedenie v metriku: Teoriia stikha*), two articles from the 1960s, a bibliography of his verse studies, and an article on his work by V. E. Kholshevnikov.

———. *Vvedenie v metriku: Teoriia stikha*. In *Teoriia stikha*, pp. 5–232. Though originally published in 1925, still a reliable and useful source of information. The book has been translated—not entirely successfully—into English: *Introduction to Metrics: The Theory of Verse* (The Hague: Mouton, 1966).

Zhovtis, A. L. "O kriteriiakh tipologicheskoi kharakteristiki svobodnogo stikha (Obzor problemy)." *Voprosy iazykoznaniia* 19 (1970), no. 2, 63–77.

———. "O sposobakh rifmovaniia v russkoi poezii (K probleme strukturnykh sviazei v sovremennom stikhe). *Voprosy iazykoznaniia* 18 (1969), no. 2, 64–75. Cf. "On the problem of rhyme in the structure of modern Russian verse," in *SP*, pp. 559–67.

———. "Ot chego ne svoboden svobodnyi stikh?" In *Stikhi nuzhny . . . : Stat'i*, pp. 5–53.

———. "Russkaia rifma 1960–1970-x godov (zametki i razmyshleniia)." *Russkaia literatura* 24 (1981), no. 3, 76–85.

———. *Stikhi nuzhny . . . : Stat'i*. Alma-Ata: Zhazushy, 1968. Articles on free verse, typographical devices, comparative metrics, and individual poets.

———. "U istokov russkogo verlibra (Stikh 'Severnogo moria' Geine v perevodakh M. L. Mikhailova)." *Masterstvo perevoda* 7 (1970), 386–404.

———. "V boevom poriadke . . . (O graficheskoi kompozitsii stikhotvornogo proizvedeniia)." In *Stikhi nuzhny . . . : Stat'i*, pp. 128–63.

———. "Verlibry Bloka." In *Problemy stikhovedeniia*, ed. Gasparov et al., pp. 125–47.

Zhuravlev, A. P. *Foneticheskoe znachenie*. Leningrad: Leningradskii universitet, 1974.

———. "Soderzhatel'nost' foneticheskoi formy poeticheskogo teksta." *Voprosy stilistiki* (Saratov), 8 (1974), pp. 41–60.

Zlatoustova, L. V. "O edinitse ritma stikha i prozy." In *Aktual'nye voprosy strukturnoi i prikladnoi lingvistiki*, ed. E. I. Rodicheva and T. A. Zolotova, pp. 61–75. Publikatsii Otdeleniia strukturnoi i prikladnoi lingvistiki 9. Moscow: Moskovskii gosudarstvennyi universitet, 1980.

Zubova, L. V. "Semantika khudozhestvennogo obraza i zvuka v stikhotvorenii M. Tsvetaevoi iz tsikla 'Stikhi k Bloku'." *Vestnik Leningradskogo universiteta* 25 (1980), no. 2, 55–61.

Index of Poets

This index is confined to Russian poets whose work is mentioned in the text, notes, and tables. Numbers in italics indicate quotations: for writers popularly known by pseudonyms, real names are given in square brackets.

357

Subject Index

Designer: Mark Ong
Compositor: G & S Typesetters, Inc.
Compositor of Russian poetry: Hermitage
Text: 10/12 Times Roman
Display: Trump Mediaeval
Printer: Braun-Brumfield, Inc.
Binder: Braun-Brumfield, Inc.